ENCYCLOPEDIA
OF
ETHICS

ENCYCLOPEDIA
OF
ETHICS

Susan Neiburg Terkel

Executive Director

Institute for Ethics in Education

CONSULTING EDITOR

R. Shannon Duval

Department of Philosophy

Science, Technology, and Society Program

Pennsylvania State University

EDITOR

☑®

Facts On File, Inc.

Facts On File, Inc.
11 Penn Plaza
New York, NY 10001

Library of Congress Cataloging-in-Publication Data

Encyclopedia of ethics / Susan Neiburg Terkel, consulting editor ; R. Shannon
  Duval, editor.
     p.   cm.
  Includes bibliographical references and index.
  ISBN 0-8160-3311-0
  1. Ethics—Encyclopedias. I. Terkel, Susan Neiburg. II. Duval,
R. Shannon.
BJ63.E46 1999
170'.3—dc21   98-39932

Facts On File books are available at special discounts when purchased in bulk quantities for businesses, associations, institutions, or sales promotions. Please call our Special Sales Department in New York at 212/967-8800 or 800-322-8755.

You can find Facts On File on the World Wide Web at http://www.factsonfile.com.

Text design by Grace Ferrara
Cover design by Samadar Megged

Printed in the United States of America

MP FOF 10 9 8 7 6 5 4 3 2 1

This book is printed on acid-free paper.

For Jim

———————————⚬———————————

This book was developed and written by Book Builders Incorporated.

Consulting Editor:
Susan Neiburg Terkel
Executive Director
Institute for Ethics in Education

Editor:
R. Shannon Duval, Ph.D.
Department of Philosophy
Science, Technology, and Society Program
Pennsylvania State University

Advisers and Consultants:
Joshua Halberstam, Ph.D.
Center for Educational Innovation and Outreach
Teachers College, Columbia University

Matthew Lipman, Ph.D.
Institute for the Advancement for the Philosophy of Children
Montclair State University

Mary Mahowald, Ph.D.
Center for Clinical Medical Ethics
University of Chicago

Young Jay Mulkey, Ph.D.
President, Character Education Institute

Lisa Newton, Ph.D.
Progressive and Applied Ethics
Fairfield University

Other Contributors

Joseph DeMarco, Ph.D.
Department of Philosophy
Cleveland State University

Richard Fox, Ph.D.
Department of Philosophy
Cleveland State University

Robbie D. Hamilton
Science, Technology, and Society Program
Pennsylvania State University

James Royster, Ph.D.
Department of Philosophy
Cleveland State University

CONTENTS

PREFACE

Ethical inquiry requires an understanding of highly abstract ideas and terms, as well as a familiarity with certain works, people, events, and philosophical movements. To serve students and general readers, the editors decided to create a reference work that would provide a working vocabulary for the study of ethics. In addition to clarifying the terms and movements common to the field, we wanted to acquaint users with certain works, people, and events essential to understanding other works or to researching a topic on ethics. In addition to our ensuring that this volume would fill an essential reference need, we also sought to make *Encyclopedia of Ethics* a basic introduction to the subject, one, moreover, that would draw on both the classical line of ethical inquiry as well as issues drawn from contemporary culture.

Deciding exactly what to include and how comprehensive to make each entry was limited not only by space but by the consideration that the readers—especially high school and undergraduate students using the reference to compile research for papers, speeches, and debates—would probably have a strong interest in contemporary ethical issues. Thus, consensus was easy to reach for terms such as *utilitarianism* and *teleology,* which are standard in all ethical discourse, but decisions were more subjective when considering contemporary ethical issues. Again, considering our users, we chose to include *animal rights, capital punishment,* and *business ethics,* for example, over less commonly researched, albeit no less provocative, topics.

Determining which noteworthy people should be included in the encyclopedia was probably the most difficult content decision. The *Encyclopedia of Ethics* makes no attempt to be a who's who in ethics but rather it seeks to offer a balance of entries between those who have made erudite contributions and those who have contributed little academic discourse but much to the intense public dialogue about ethics. For example, Mohandas Gandi is as important to a discussion of euthanasia as, say, John Rawls is to a discussion of justice. Besides the decision to use gender-neutral language in the text, a few of the women selected for inclusion may appear to be somewhat obscure and unknown, a choice that may hint to some of political correctness and revisionism. Although we concede that men do indeed tip the scale with regard to historical contributions to ethics, we have tried to include those women who did make seminal contributions to the field, even if those contributions are not as widely known outside the field of ethics as the contributions of John Locke or Aristotle, for example.

To help readers access the information that is available in the encyclopedia, all entries have been cross-referenced, and for those who desire a more comprehensive or extensive treatment, a select but extensive bibliography has been provided. Any compendium dealing with extremely contemporary issues, as the *Encyclopedia of Ethics* does, is bound to exclude terms, people, and events that enter the general lexicon as swiftly as our modern media spins them into the public arena. Despite the seemingly extraordinary interest of the moment, many events occurred too late for inclusion. This shortcoming cannot be avoided, given that the study of ethics relies on the human heed to pursue the truth, a pursuit that has no deadlines, only the constancy of life itself.

—Susan Neiburg Terkel
Consulting Editor

ACKNOWLEDGMENTS

Any project of this scope is the result of the hard work of many people. I am grateful for the enthusiasm, good will, and energy of everyone who has been involved with this book. In particular, I would like to acknowledge the contributions of the reviewers of this manuscript whose suggestions improved our work immeasurably. I would also like to thank Rob Hamilton for his dogged research and careful writing and editing. Much of what is excellent about this work is a result of his extensive contributions. Stefan Berndes contributed the excellent essays on discourse ethics and ethics of science. Philip Lynn Clark, a Hall of Fame college athlete and Hall of Fame high school football coach, contributed the article on sportsmanship. It is fitting that another generation of young people should benefit from his many years of showing through action what it means to compete both successfully and ethically. Dr. Daniel W. Conway, Director of the Center for Ethics and Value Inquiry at the Pennsylvania State University, contributed the essay on existentialism. With warmth and appreciation I acknowledge this contribution as well as his friendship and keen professional advice. I gratefully acknowledge the contribution of Rev. David B. Dragseth who contributed the expert article on Martin Luther. Special thanks and gratitude to colleague and friend Dr. Jennifer Hockenbery, who stepped in enthusiastically to write the articles on Peter Abelard and Hildegard of Bingen. Most deeply I am grateful to Dr. James E. Meade, M.D., who contributed the articles on brain death, malpractice, medical ethics, organ donation, organ transplants, pain management, physician-patient relationship, and standards of care. In addition, Dr. Meade consulted on a number of other essays that touched on issues of medical or professional ethics. His generosity in sharing his time and expertise has made this a far better volume than it would otherwise have been. The final stages of the project could not have been completed without the expert assistance of Karen Snare of Pennsylvania State University who, along with Tracey Topper and Elizabeth Dooher of Book Builders, coordinated the logistics of a writing staff and editorial staff that spanned three continents. I am deeply grateful to colleagues Carl Mitcham and John Stuhr for their support and encouragement in all my activities. A good portion of this work occurred while I was a J. William Fulbright Fellow at the Center for Philosophy and Technology at Brandenburg Technical University in Cottbus, Germany. I am grateful to the Fulbright Commission for their support of my work in the ethical dimensions of the philosophy of technology. The completion of this project would not have been possible without the support and resources offered by Prof. Dr. Klaus Kornwachs and my colleagues Stefan Berndes, Kaethe Friedrich, and Michaela Hammer. For your collegiality, generosity, and friendship, I thank you. Finally, I happily and lovingly give my deepest thanks to my husband Jim. The consistency of your support, goodwill, interest, involvement, and encouragement sustains and inspires me in all that I do. Thank you so very much for everything.

—R. Shannon Duval
Editor

INTRODUCTION

All of us are engaged in ethical activity, even if we do not always think of our activities as ethical or unethical. What we eat, what we wear, how we treat those around us, and how we treat ourselves are all ethical activities. In fact, nearly all of our daily interactions have an ethical dimension. Ethics is not an abstract idea but rather a daily, lived activity. Because our ethical activities are tied closely to our many life activities as well as to the diverse activities of others, we are often confronted with competing courses of action. "Doing the right thing" is often easier said than done. Many of us would be happy to do the right thing, if only we could figure out what it is!

Thinking about ethics is complicated. It has both a personal dimension and a public dimension. Some ethical issues, like whether or not to eat meat, seem to be a matter of choice. Others, like whether or not to kill someone, seem to apply to all people. Now, you may have quickly thought of exceptions to those generalizations. If so, you can understand how quickly it becomes complicated to think about ethics. So, too, when we try to talk to others about ethical issues, we introduce further difficulties as we encounter other points of view. Yet, we cannot, and would not want to, avoid the fact that some amount of ethical reflection and conversation is a necessary part of human society.

The complexity of ethical action gives rise to the study of ethics. Reflecting on ethics is another way of thinking about what it means to be a good person or what it means to do the right thing. More particularly, the study of ethics is supposed to help us do the right thing at the right time, and in the right way, as well as to understand *what* we have done. Although ethics is not the special domain of philosophers or ethical theorists, such people have attempted to give us some tools and guidance as we cultivate our ethical lives. These are people who have cared deeply about ethical issues and who have realized that we need to establish a common language or vocabulary in order to talk about ethics. Ethicists and philosophers offer us a way to converse about questions that are important to us and to our communities. They are resources to help us become the kind of people we want to be and to build the types of communities in which we want to live. While philosophers have not agreed on exactly what the language of ethics should be or upon what those communities should look like, they have put forth alternatives from which we can both learn and choose. Moreover, they may establish the groundwork for our own creative and original ethical thought. The writers and editors of the *Encyclopedia of Ethics* have attempted to provide a starting point for learning about these alternatives.

It is not possible to detail all of the important ethical questions. In one sense, these questions are the ones that are real and immediate in your life. In another sense, pressing ethical questions are ones that affect us all, whether we pay attention to them or not. What we can do, however, is try to understand some basic questions in ethics, questions that lay the foundation for the many ethical issues that will arise in our lives. With these thoughts in mind, we have organized the compilation of entries around some basic terms and ideas relating to questions such as:

- What is goodness, and how do we know what is good?
- Is there one moral standard for everyone, or is goodness established by individuals or communities?
- To what extent are we free in our choices, and to what extent does our environment determine our choices?
- How do we balance the needs of individuals against the needs of groups?

We have included current ethical issues that are important not only in and of themselves but that serve as examples of the types of ethical demands we face in the late twentieth and early twenty-first centuries. You will find, for example, discussions on issues in medical ethics, legal ethics, business ethics, animal rights, and the women's movement. We also have introduced the leading historical figures in the study of ethics, as well as many contemporary theorists and activists who have shaped the modern approach to ethics. The encyclopedia is meant to be a starting point for your investigations and you are encouraged to build from what you find here to learn more about the topics we address, as well as those that the constraints of time and space forced us to omit in this volume. In order to help with continued investigations, we have included a bibliography that suggests excellent resources for further reading.

Within the encyclopedia itself, you will find that there are deep disagreements among ethical thinkers about both approaches and answers to ethical questions, as well as about ethical language and ethical issues. You will discover that just as you may have strong ethical disagreements with friends, coworkers, schoolmates, or family members, those who have spent many years studying ethical issues do find that they have strong disagreements. This should not be discouraging to you, for within this text, you also will find many of the words, ideas, and role models necessary to express and refine your ethical views and your ability to share them with others. Further, with research and understanding, your ability to listen to and understand others when they attempt to express their ethical ideas to you also should be refined. In fact, conversation itself has an ethical dimension, and the ways in which we treat both those who agree with our views and those who disagree with us is an expression of our ethical outlook.

Finally, while we ethicists continue to investigate whether or not there are any ethical absolutes in thinking, studying, and writing about ethics, we would like to offer some strategies for your ethical inquiries:

- There are usually more than two sides to any ethical issue—try to consider multiple positions and don't become trapped in "either/or" reasoning.
- Try to look for who is advantaged and who is disadvantaged by any ethical position or decision. Are these divisions ethically acceptable to you?
- Try to listen and to reflect when you are reading or when another person is talking, rather than formulating what you will say in defense of your own position. After you have given the best possible interpretation of what you have read or heard, formulate your own response.
- Conversations do not have to be competitions. There does not have to be a moral winner and a moral loser in every ethical debate or dilemma. Consider whether it is ethical to use words as "weapons." Consider seeking greater understanding rather than "victory." At the same time, remember that you do not have to subject yourself to an ethical debate that is not goodwilled or honest. These are issues that are important to you and should be treated with care.

On behalf of the writers and editors who have worked diligently and carefully on this project, we hope the resources in *Encyclopedia of Ethics* will serve to promote ever more rich and rewarding investigations of questions that matter to you.

—R. Shannon Duval

Ethics in Our Daily Lives

I am often asked: "How can you teach ethics? No one's opinion is better than anyone else's. Morality is a matter of taste, and everyone is entitled to his and her beliefs—one person likes vanilla, the other likes chocolate."

I'm no longer surprised when, twenty minutes later, I see the same staunch advocate of the philosophy that "ethics is just a matter of personal likes and dislikes" engaged in a furious moral dispute. For example, the topic may be the ethics of assisted suicide. But if our moral judgments are only expressions of personal tastes, why the heated debate? Why is this fellow complaining about his opponent's "convoluted moral reasoning" and shouting about how "she's missing the crucial moral difference between killing and letting die"? No one argues for hours about the relative merits of ice cream flavors.

We do, of course, take moral arguments seriously, accepting some as persuasive and dismissing others as flawed. These arguments matter, for they sometimes can even persuade us to kill or allow ourselves to be killed. But we should also emphasize that ethics is not just about momentous decisions such as the justification for war, capital punishment, or abortion, nor only about such "weighty" personal questions as "How should I live my life?" We also regularly confront ethical consideration in the course of our daily lives: in our friendships (should you lie to help your buddy?), in dealing with our families (are you obligated to care for your siblings?), in our careers (is it immoral to work for a cigarette company?), and with regard to our emotions (is anger sometimes justifiable? Is courage still a virtue if used in service of evil?).

Deliberating about ethics is, after all, the distinctive attribute of our species. In the biblical tradition of the Western world, for example, human history begins when the first couple eats the forbidden fruit of knowledge. The awareness they gain is not about physics or monetary policy, or artistic techniques, but the ability to distinguish "good" from "evil." Thereafter, humans will always have to make choices. They will henceforth determine how to live and how to die and will be responsible for their decisions. Those who think we ought not make value judgments are of course themselves making a value judgment (as the words "ought not" suggest) and, in general, making a mistaken judgment at that. Certainly, we need to distinguish between adopting a moral stand and imposing it on others. But as the biblical story suggests, to be human is to evaluate, to consider alternative actions, and to choose.

So where do we go for answers?

One place to begin is right here, in this superb, pioneering, and comprehensive *Encyclopedia of Ethics*. No, you won't find solutions to moral dilemmas—no one volume, no thousand volumes, can do that. On the contrary, even a casual perusal of this book illuminates why the subject matter of ethics is as varied and complex as the human condition itself. The reader will come away with a richer understanding of the different ethical theories and practices that have been part of our human heritage the world over and appreciate the need for informed and tempered moral views rather than the rote formulations that are all too commonplace.

This encyclopedia covers the spectrum of ethics. The term "ethics," we should point out, is ambiguous. Sometimes it refers to the moral beliefs of a particular group or creed, for example, "the ethics of Sparta" or "Buddhist ethics." Sometimes it refers to the academic discipline, as when one takes a course in ethics. Some writers try to differentiate between morality and ethics, but these days, most freely substitute one term for the other. There are, however, several major categories or fields that make up the much broader topic known as ethics. The most relevant of these are encompassed in this single volume.

Descriptive ethics. This branch of ethical studies examines the actual ethical rules and practices of a designated group. As such, this branch of ethics is of special interest to anthropologists, sociologists and historians, and other social scientists. Questions that fall within purview would include: What do the Inuit people believe about suicide? What is appropriate sexual behavior among the Samoans? What do American Catholics believe about birth control?

Metaethics. The philosophical concerns of this aspect of ethics are not targeted to establishing what is morally right or wrong but the nature of language in general. Are ethical statements true or false concerns in the same way that statements in science are true or false? When our friend above insisted that all ethical views were purely matters of taste he was engaging in metaethics (in fact, his view has had its supporters but few contemporary philosophers would espouse his crude formulation of this viewpoint).

Normative ethics. What makes one's life a good life? Which virtues make for good character? What, in fact, are the grounds for deeming one behavior right and another wrong? What justifies morality? Rationality? Human happiness? God? Biology? Self-interest? These and other frameworks have been proposed, developed, as well as criticized, by philosophers and religious leaders throughout the centuries. Subjects in this branch of ethics include Greek ethics, Christian ethics, Utilitarianism, Kantian ethics, and sociobiology.

Applied ethics. Is cloning immoral? Do we have obligations to future generations? Do you owe loyalty to your company? Is corporeal punishment justified? Is affirmative action equitable? Applied ethics addresses the day-to-day moral dilemmas that we routinely face both as a society and as individuals. Some problems in applied ethics, such as the morality of gossip, or killing the innocent in war, have been around from the beginning of human enterprise, while other dilemmas, such as surrogate motherhood or the right to privacy on the internet, are recent issues arising from modern technology. This encyclopedia includes helpful reviews of the most pressing and significant problems in applied ethics.

One of my favorite observations about philosophy comes from the twentieth century thinker Ludwig Wittgenstein, who said, "In philosophy, the winner of the race is the one who gets there last." The aim is the journey, not the destiny. When it comes to ethics, of course, we don't always appreciate the luxury of leisurely reflection because we often must make immediate decisions. But as users of this encyclopedia will find, ethical issues are rarely simple, and diverse approaches are plausible. Often the best people can do is make as honest and informed a decision as they can, also recognizing the plausibility of other conclusions.

So enter this encyclopedia and the world of ethics. Go to the topic you want to research and find the basic information you need. Don't be surprised when you also find yourself eager to continue your search, to join others in exploring how to live a life more decent, more noble, more involving, and more enjoyable.

—Joshua Halberstam

ENCYCLOPEDIA
OF
ETHICS

A

ABELARD, PETER (1079–1142) French philosopher and theologian responsible for the defeat of ultra-realism. Abelard, trained first as a dialectician and then as a theologian, made great strides in the debate concerning the nature of universals. The prevailing view of his time, ultra-realism, claimed that all individuals in a class or species shared one substance, differing from one another only accidentally. Abelard, claiming that such a view led to pantheism and absurdity, stated that individuals linked by a universal did not share the same substance but only the same name. However, Abelard qualified this theory, stating that the universal was not a subjective construct but an objective logical unity. Thus, individuals do share an actual species or class, although they do not share a single substance. Abelard's theory, which escaped the difficulties of ultra-realism while still insisting upon the objectivity of universals, quickly became the preferred position. In the field of ethics, Abelard is known for his understanding of the role of the conscience in making ethical decisions. He also believed that knowledge and intention were important in establishing moral guilt or innocence.

However, Abelard's attempt to use dialectic in certain theological discussions was met with hostility from his contemporaries, who believed that he was trying to reason away the mystery implicit in certain church doctrines. In 1121, he was condemned for his book *On the Unity and the Trinity of the Divine*. He was later denounced by Bernard de Clairveaux for trying to reason away the mystery of the Trinity. In 1141 he was convicted of heresy and condemned by Pope Innocent II. The same ideas that caused him to be condemned in his own lifetime caused him to be hailed by church reformers and rationalist philosophers. Both praised Abelard's courage to stand against church authority, the rationalists praising his use of reason and dialectic in theological matters.

Abelard is, perhaps, most remembered today for his famous love affair with HELOÏSE, a young women he was asked to tutor. The pair's love resulted in a child and a secret marriage. But their passion was ended when Heloïse's uncle, fearing Heloïse's placement in a convent signaled Abelard's termination of their bond, had Abelard castrated. Heloïse, in guilt and grief, took the veil and joined a convent, while Abelard fled to an abbey. The two continued to write loving letters to each other. Their relationship is still remembered and poetized as a great paradigm of passionate love.

ABORTION The spontaneous expulsion of an embryo or fetus during pregnancy (a miscarriage), or the deliberate termination of the life of an embryo or fetus.

The deliberate termination of life is the subject of moral controversy in which "pro-life" proponents argue that abortion is morally wrong and "pro-choice" proponents maintain either that abortion is morally permitted or that pregnant women have a right to abortions. According to the Supreme Court's decision in *Roe v. Wade* (1973), the legality of abortion in the United States today depends on the fetus's stage of development, that is, whether an abortion is performed during the first, second, or third trimester of pregnancy. Some moral traditions have made a distinction between the times before and after *quickening,* the first time fetal movement is felt by the pregnant woman, or between the times before and after *viability,* when a fetus is able to survive outside the womb. Many people think that the morality of abortion depends on other factors, believing, for example, that abortion is justified in cases of rape or incest.

Because the choice to have an abortion is usually a choice to terminate a fetus, pro-life groups argue that the fetus has a right to life and that abortion is therefore murder. Pro-choice groups justify deliberate abortion in various ways, as acts of self-defense, as EUTHANASIA, or because in their view the fetus is not a person (*see* PERSONHOOD). They sometimes argue that only persons have a RIGHT TO LIFE; if fetuses are not persons, fetuses do not have this right. Discussions of this issue often focus on what it means to have legal or moral personhood and whether, or at what stage of development, a fetus satisfies the definition of personhood. The pro-life position is that human life, or personhood, begins at conception.

Depending on how they are interpreted, the pro-life and pro-choice positions may or may not be opposed to one another. For example, if the pro-life position is interpreted to mean that abortions are always wrong and the pro-choice to mean that abortions are never wrong, then they are opposed. However, if the pro-life position allows that abortions are sometimes permitted, even if only in rare cases, and the pro-choice position allows that abortions are sometimes wrong, they are not necessarily opposed—unless, of course, they cannot agree on when or in which cases abortions are or are not justified. Indeed people in the pro-choice group sometimes claim that they are not really arguing about the morality of abortion; rather, they are mainly concerned about who has the right to make the choice of having or not having an abortion. They believe that pregnant women have the right to make this choice and that the government does not have the right to make this choice for them. Thus, a distinction may be made between the authority to make a decision and the correctness of that decision. However, pro-life advocates find it difficult to understand how a person can have a right to do something that—in their opinion—is morally wrong and why the government does not prevent what they consider to be an immoral act.

ABSOLUTES   Ideas or entities that are not subject to restriction or qualification.

God is often said to be *the* absolute, for God is not supposed to be dependent on anything; indeed, everything is supposed to be dependent on God. Monarchs are sometimes said to be absolute, meaning that their authority is not subject to any higher authority, even the law. Ideas or judgments may also be said to be absolute if they are thought to be true without qualification or if their truth is not dependent on any other truth. Absolutist theories hold that the rightness or wrongness of an act is not relative to individuals or society: what is right or wrong is universally so, without exception. Moral principles are often held to be absolute for this reason: they apply to all persons at all places and times. Absolutes are opposed to things that are relative (*see* RELATIVISM), or dependent on a particular context or perspective. In ethics, some theories are classified as relative because they hold that the morality of acts or the correctness of judgments about acts are subject to the customs of society or to the opinions of individuals.

ABSOLUTION   Official statement of forgiveness of sins by religious authority, often given in the Catholic Church.

Absolution requires sinners to express regret for their behavior and a desire to repent. The statement of absolution is often accompanied by the prescription of some kind of penance. In the past, penance may have required payment of money to the church, an act of public contrition, or even some form of pilgrimage, but today penance is usually limited to forms of devotion such as prayer.

ABSTINENCE   Voluntary restraint from acting on a physical or psychological desire.

Abstinence is a form of self-discipline used by many religions as a method of attaining purity or a spiritual ideal (*see* IDEALS). Practitioners of BUDDHIST ETHICS and YOGA, for example, use abstinence as an aid to achieving the state of nirvana through meditation and the extinction of consciousness. Many religious traditions promote the ideal of abstinence from premarital sex, and the Roman Catholic Church requires its priests to remain celibate on the assumption that sexual abstinence makes them less likely to be distracted from their devotions. Other common examples of abstinence include oaths of poverty and fasting. *See also* ASCETICISM.

ACCOUNTABILITY   The responsibility of moral agents (*see* MORAL AGENCY) for their actions.

In moral theory, persons are thought to be responsible for fulfilling their moral obligations. Persons are not thought to be responsible and therefore should not be held accountable, for actions (*see* ACT) that they are forced to perform or are not free to avoid. For example, people are not usually held responsible for failing to do things that they are not physically or psychologically capable of doing.

Philosophers vary in their attitudes toward accountability. Some hold that we are almost always in control of our destiny and should therefore be accountable for most of what we do. Others believe that far less of the world is under our control, and thus our accountability for our actions is lessened. Still other philosophers believe that humans act solely in response to upbringing, social pressure, social conditioning, or from deep and difficult-to-understand subconscious motivation (*see* MOTIVE) and therefore should not be considered accountable for most of the things they do, no matter what those acts may be. *See also* RESPONSIBILITY.

ACT   Something a person does.

In ETHICS, a morally significant act is usually assumed to be something a person does by choice (*see* FREEDOM). Not all behavior, therefore, would count as morally significant action, for example, things that are done without INTENTION or by accident. According to some theories, such as those of Thomas AQUINAS, the nature of an act, morally speaking, is determined by what a person chooses to do or intends, not by what actually happens. If a person chooses to commit murder but fails, that person would be guilty of choosing an immoral act (*see* IMMORALITY), even though nobody is actually killed.

A moral agent (*see* MORAL AGENCY) is a person capable of moral action or of making choices between RIGHT and WRONG acts. (Persons or other conscious beings, such as animals, who are affected by those actions are called moral patients.) In ethics, agents deliberate (*see* DELIBERATION) about which acts they should choose or which course of action they should follow. Theories that hold that the object of moral reasoning is to judge moral actions are sometimes called act-oriented theories, and those that focus on the moral CHARACTER of agents are called agent-oriented theories.

Acts are sometimes divided into *acts of commission* and *acts of omission* in order to distinguish an act, like cheating, from a failure to act, such as refusing to help a person in need. Passive euthanasia, for example, means allowing persons to die by *not* doing things to keep them alive, and this is sometimes called an act of omission. Choosing to do something to kill a person, such as poisoning them, would be considered an act of commission.

ACT UTILITARIANISM   *see* UTILITARIANISM.

ADDAMS, JANE (1860–1935)   American social and political philosopher, best known as the founder of the Hull House settlement in Chicago. Hull House functioned as a short-term shelter for homeless immigrants (*see* IMMIGRA-TION) who came to Chicago in the late nineteenth century seeking jobs. Addams's social work included finding housing, employment, education, and health care for unskilled immigrants who spoke no English.

Many pragmatist philosophers (*see* PRAGMATISM), including John DEWEY and George Herbert Mead, studied and worked with Addams. Among Addams's extensive writings are books and articles on ethical issues (*see* ETHICS) that affected women, children, and immigrants. An early article, "Ethical Survivals in Municipal Corruption" (*International Journal of Ethics,* 1898) analyzed whether people have a duty to obey the law when they are exploited and oppressed by a corrupt government (*see* CORRUPTION). In *Democracy and Social Ethics* (1902) Addams argued that it was possible to form a society based on the MORAL PRINCIPLES of EQUALITY, JUSTICE, and self-determination without destroying the social and moral VALUES held by immigrants from different societies. She lectured widely on the IMMORALITY of EXPLOITATION, child labor, and the subjection of immigrants to poor living and working conditions.

Addams wrote many books and pamphlets on the moral duty of government to provide free public education, women's right to higher education, and women's right to vote (*see* WOMEN'S RIGHTS).

In addition to being a strong advocate for social causes, she was a well-known pacifist (*see* PACIFISM). Her books *Newer Ideals of Peace* (1907) and *The Overthrow of the War System* (1915) argued that war was immoral and that individuals had a moral obligation to oppose war.

ADULTERY Voluntary sexual relations between a married person and someone other than his or her spouse.

Adultery is seen as WRONG in almost all cultures, although the actual level of TOLERANCE varies. In some ancient cultures, adultery was punishable by death, and in Western Europe and North America today it is still seen as an offense serious enough to justify DIVORCE.

There are many reasons why people commit adultery today; however, its incidence seems to be increasing, partially because MARRIAGE is no longer seen as a practical, economic union but as a purely emotional one based on LOVE. When the initial euphoria that often accompanies the start of a relationship eventually wears off, there may no longer be a strong incentive to stay faithful to a spouse, particularly if one or both partners feel that emotional needs are not being met.

AESARA OF LUCANIA (*c.* 350 B.C.) Greek female philosopher from Lucania, author of *On Human Nature.*

Little is known about this author other than that she may have been a contemporary of PLATO. *On Human Nature* is the only portion of her work that survives.

In this fragment, Aesara maintains that the human soul has three parts: the mind, spiritedness, and DESIRE. The mind analyzes ideas and reaches decisions. Spiritedness is the part of the soul that gives a person the ability to carry out decisions. Desire contains moral emotions such as LOVE.

Aesara believed that the human soul is the model for society, and that if we understand the nature of the soul we can understand how society ought to be. She argued that it is wrong for philosophers to exclude principles of love, CARE, and concern from theories about JUSTICE. LAW and justice should be thoughtful, taking into account all relevant ideas and PRINCIPLES. They should also be judgmental, reflecting the society's shared social judgments (*see* JUDGMENT) about people's obligations and duties (*see* OBLIGATION). The legal system should contain laws that deter crime and serve as standards or guidelines of good behavior, just as a strong moral CHARACTER should resist the temptations created by WRONG or excessive desires.

In the administration of justice, judges should take into account special circumstances under which people might be excused for not following the law.

On Human Nature is an interesting early example of what contemporary FEMINIST ETHICS calls "the ethic of care."

AESOP'S FABLES Simple animal tales from ancient Greece, written to illustrate a moral lesson or principle (*see* PRINCIPLES).

Some scholars believe that Aesop was a freed slave who rose to high office during the sixth century B.C. because of his learning and insight. Others argue that Aesop is simply a name invented to identify several stories written by various authors on a similar theme.

Aesop's fables are simple, unambiguous, and rarely more than a paragraph long. They are concerned with such themes as the value of friendship, the need to recognize one's limitations, and the consequences of evil or stupidity.

AFFIRMATIVE ACTION A social policy used to ensure that women and minorities are adequately represented in occupations, sports, and education.

Affirmative action policies were formulated in response to certain prevalent and harmful types of DISCRIMINATION. In the past, many women and minorities were consistently discouraged from jobs, participating in athletic endeavors, and from applying for various educational positions. Those who have supported affirmative action have developed various techniques to rectify such unfair practices. Strategies range from actively encouraging applications from minorities to using quotas or strict numerical goals in hiring policies. Proponents of affirmative action typically insist that the people who gain under such policies must meet all legitimate qualifications.

Affirmative action policies are controversial because they treat people differently based on group traits. For example, an employer who sup-ports affirmative action may give a job to one qualified person rather than to another equally qualified candidate primarily because the candidate is female, Hispanic, or African American. Some have objected that such hiring practices are immoral because they are not based primarily on the applicant's ability to do the job. For this reason, opponents sometimes refer to affirmative action as "reverse discrimination." Supporters of affirmative action counter that such apparently biased (*see* BIAS) policies are justified considering the degree of discrimination to which women and minorities have been subject over the centuries and that, in some cases, the benefits of affirmative action outweigh its inherent bias.

AGAPE *See* LOVE.

AGEISM A form of DISCRIMINATION based on the view that age is an indicator of a person's physical, intellectual, and sometimes moral COMPETENCY.

Ageism can lead to the denial of RIGHTS and liberties to people because they are either "too young" or "too old." For example, the belief that elderly people have impaired reflexes is thought to justify prohibiting them from doing such things as driving a car, working, or controlling their own assets. Because these activities significantly affect a person's quality of life and ability to exercise AUTONOMY, such limitations on FREEDOM constitute discrimination based on age rather than on a person's actual capacity. At most, statistical findings may indicate the need to test the capacities of elderly people in order to verify that, for example, their eyesight and reflexes are adequate for operating a car safety.

Ageism is not only discrimination against the elderly. With young people, ageism determines when they may be granted rights. While denying liberties requires a special JUSTIFICATION, granting liberties to anyone who reaches a certain age (such as giving sixteen-year-olds the right to be employed or to drive a car) may be justified either by common sense or by statistical data that confirms common sense. In almost all cases, society has determined that the LAW may set age requirements for the exercising of certain CIVIL RIGHTS. In special cases, however, such as with mentally disabled adults, civil rights may be denied.

Ageism also contributes to the denial of a young person's right to live alone or to marry because of the belief that people under age 18 are not mature enough to make competent choices. Although such a belief is often justified, in individual cases it may not be. In such cases, ageism is kept in check by legal systems that permit a child to petition for exemption from the restrictive law.

The law, however, does not always protect young people involved in criminal activity (*see* CRIME) from prosecution as adults. For example, the perceived need to stem the crimes resulting from drug trafficking has led to the finding that some children are competent and do know right from wrong. A new crime bill states that a 13-year-old who is heavily involved in drug trafficking, for example, can be tried as an adult and receive a life sentence with no parole. In such cases, the legal protection from criminal prosecution that other minors enjoy is removed.

This new proposal reflects an inconsistency in social policy because the same child who is considered an adult with respect to her or his RESPONSIBILITY for committing a crime is simultaneously considered a child with respect to exercising liberties such as the right to marry or to vote.

AGENCY   *See* MORAL AGENCY.

AGENT   *See* ACT.

AHIMSA   *See* NONVIOLENCE.

AIDS (Acquired Immunodeficiency Syndrome   Often fatal cluster of immune system disorders including mouth fungus, pneumonia, tuberculosis, cancer, and dementia.

The AIDS syndrome is a collection of conditions or complications that result from immune deficiency brought on by infection with HIV, the virus that causes AIDS. Immune deficiency indicates that the immune system has been weakened, and syndrome indicates a collection of symptoms.

AIDS is often used incorrectly as a catch-all term for infection with HIV. HIV is the human immunodeficiency virus, so called because it infects the immune system and weakens it. People with HIV infection do not necessarily have AIDS. AIDS is one stage of a series of stages in HIV infection. When people are first infected with HIV, they may show no obvious symptoms for a long time. When they begin to show symptoms of a weakened immune system, they are said to have AIDS-related complex, or ARC. When the immune system is weakened severely, people exhibit specific infections and tumors. It is at this stage that people have AIDS.

HIV infection is primarily a sexually transmitted disease. It is transmitted by both homosexual and heterosexual activity. The AIDS virus is present in many body fluids, including blood, semen, vaginal secretion, menstrual blood, and in saliva in small amounts. It is also transmitted by intravenous drug use, by blood and blood products, and from mother to infant during pregnancy, at the time of delivery, or shortly after birth. The most common known methods of spreading AIDS are through anal sex, sexual intercourse, birth, and blood transfusion. HIV is not transmitted by household or casual contact, by body fluids other than blood or semen, or by insects.

DISCRIMINATION against those who are perceived to have AIDS or who are HIV positive has been widespread throughout the course of the epidemic. The consequences of knowledge of one's HIV status can be loss of employment, loss of income, uninsurability, unavailability of professional services, loss of housing, and so on. The Americans with Disabilities Act (1990) has ameliorated this situation by stipulating uniform, enforceable antidiscrimination protection without the need for federal involvement or funding or special state laws (*see* LAW).

Many believe that people with HIV infection have an ethical (*see* ETHICS), and in some places, a legal RESPONSIBILITY to notify people that they may have been exposed to HIV; this means anyone with whom they have had sex involving exchange of body fluids or with whom they have shared needles, and it applies to past as well as current and future relationships. For practical purposes most authorities recommend notifying all contacts for the past one or two years as an absolute minimum. *See also* DISABILITY RIGHTS; GAY RIGHTS.

AL-GHAZĀLĪ (1058–1111)   One of the most renowned theologians, philosophers, ethicists (*see* ETHICS), and mystics (*see* MYSTICISM) of Islam.

The objective in al-Ghazālī's ethical thought is a mystical HAPPINESS that comes from nearness to GOD. This deep, pervasive happiness is the result of developing ten VIRTUES, each subsequent virtue arising out of and founded on the one before: repentance, patience, gratitude, hope, fear, poverty, asceticism, divine unity, trust, and finally love.

Al-Ghazālī understood love to be that which inclines HUMAN NATURE toward pleasure or happiness. The supreme form of love comes from recognizing that the most profound and lasting pleasure lies only in nearness to God. According to al-Ghazālī, all other pleasures are temporary and only hint at the completely satisfying happiness that come from nearness to God.

ALIENATION   Estrangement of persons from one another.

People become alienated when they regard each other as foreign to themselves, treating them as different *kinds* of people and thinking of them as strange, peculiar, or even hostile. People who are alienated from one another see each other as *types* or objects, rather than as individual persons or subjects. People feel alienated when they feel they do not belong to a group or are excluded by others. Alienation often exists when people feel excluded from an "inside" group, as in high school cliques, where members of the clique treat nonmembers as different or weird. Judging (*see* JUDGMENT) individuals by their nationality, race, religion, sex, or social class is both an expression of, and may engender, alienation.

The concept of alienation receives special attention in existentialist philosophy (*see* EXISTENTIALISM) in which the experiential relationship between self and others is explored. In Jean-Paul SARTRE's philosophy, for example, people become alienated by trying to define themselves, marking off their differences from others, and treating others as essentially different. Indeed, they believe that some individuals ACT *because* they have a certain nature and not because they freely choose their actions. According to Sartre, when people fall into such thinking, they are in "bad FAITH" with one another and are deceiving themselves.

Alienation is also important in the political philosophy of Karl MARX. Marx considered alienation to be one of the pernicious side effects of a capitalist society (*see* CAPITALISM). Marx held that the division between the owners and the workers (or bourgeoisie and the proletariat) was so complete that alienation was the inevitable result of any capitalist economy.

ALLAH   *see* GOD.

ALLOPATHIC MEDICINE   A type of medical practice that treats a disease by producing a second, less serious medical condition that destroys the original disease. For example, allopathic medicine may treat cancer with surgery, radiation, or chemotherapy. Each of these treatments causes some HARM or injury to the patient's body. For example, cutting open the patient to remove a tumor surgically harms the patient because surgery causes pain. It also injures the patient's body and creates a risk of infection.

In contrast, homeopathic medicine treats or prevents disease by using small quantities of the same or a similar disease. For example, vaccination against polio is a homeopathic treatment that uses small quantities of the polio virus to help patients develop immunity to that disease.

Allopathic and homeopathic treatments both raise ethical (*see* ETHICS) issues because they seem to violate the moral principle (*see* PRINCIPLES) of NONMALEFICENCE, "do no harm." When physicians take the HIPPOCRATIC OATH, they swear to do no harm to the patient. If all available treatments can be expected to cause some harm to the patient, how can the physician cure the patient and also uphold the principle of nonmaleficence? The physician is morally justified (*see* JUSTIFICATION) in inflicting the harm or injury in part because the surgery cures or treats the original disease and in part because the harm created by this form of allopathic treatment is less serious than the harm that would be caused by the disease.

ALTRUISM
Action, or a disposition to act, in the interest or WELFARE of others.

Altruists are persons who try to do GOOD things for other people without expecting something in return. In ethical theory (*see* ETHICS) an altruist is one who believes that altruistic acts are possible and that altruistic acts, at least sometimes, ought to be performed. In this sense, altruism is opposed to EGOISM, the belief that people always act in their own SELF-INTEREST. Because many moralists have assumed that MORALITY requires altruistic acts, they have argued against egoists who believe that morality can be explained on the basis of self-interest alone. Thomas HOBBES, for example, tried to explain ethics on the assumption of egoism, and Joseph BUTLER tried to show that this assumption is false.

AMORALITY
Lack of regard for ideas of RIGHT conduct.

Amoral persons reject the applicability of MORALS to their own lives. Unlike an immoral person, who acts contrary to moral norms, an amoral person may simply reject the validity of moral standards. Some may do this consciously by proclaiming that moral standards are irrelevant or pernicious. In other cases, people may be called amoral when they act as though moral standards do not matter. Because those who are indifferent to morality may commit harmful (*see* HARM) or even vicious actions, the judgment of amorality often carries negative associations.

Sometimes animals as well as people are referred to as amoral. For example, we do not judge horses by moral standards. A horse may be agreeable or bad tempered but not selfless or EVIL. Some say that for this reason horses may be considered amoral. Other philosophers counter that the term *amoral* does not apply to animals precisely because they are incapable of either moral or immoral actions. Rather, we should say that we simply do not apply moral standards to such creatures; the term *amoral* should be reserved for human beings who either reject or disregard morality.

Another thorny issue concerns cases where people disagree over whether a certain action is amoral. For instance, most believe that the choice of whether to eat meat or abstain from it is not subject to moral evaluation but is merely a matter of preference. But many believe that eating meat is immoral. So whether or not an action is genuinely amoral is often a matter of debate. *See also* IMMORALITY; MORALITY.

ANARCHY
The complete absence of POWER structures, including legal, government, and corporate.

Anarchy may refer to a chaotic, lawless, and violent situation free from ethical and social constraints (*see* ETHICS). As an ethical and political belief, however, anarchy is a utopian (*see* UTOPIA) form of an egalitarian ideal (*see* EGALITARIANISM) that holds that all power structures involve EXPLOITATION and OPPRESSION and, therefore, should be eliminated.

Anarchists generally reject not only the AUTHORITY of government but also the authority of other social institutions. Therefore, an anarchist might also denounce the legitimacy of religion or structured social arrangements such as those found in a large company or in a school. They argue that people are basically GOOD and that free from the tyranny of exploitation they will be motivated to help and assist each other.

Anarchism as an ideal (*see* IDEALISM) was first proposed in France in 1840 by Pierre-Joseph Proudhon and achieved its greatest strength in Spain and Italy in the first half of the twentieth century. Anarchist movements were eventually crushed in these countries by fascist governments (*see* FASCISM) in the years preceding World War II.

Many modern anarchists now believe that true anarchy is impossible because people are primarily motivated by SELF-INTEREST. Therefore, they support limited government for the purpose of breaking up oppressive monopolies (*see* MONOPOLY) and other concentrations of power and to assist those who have been disadvantaged by the behavior of others. This form of anarchism is sometimes called social LIBERTARIANISM.

There are some extreme supporters of anarchy who do teach that LAW and order makes people weak. They argue that a strong or self-reliant person needs neither police protection nor the protection of a legal system. The chaos that results from this lack of law and order tests the strength and independence of people, naturally weeding out those who are not fit enough to survive.

In general, however, this type of SOCIAL DARWINISM is antithetical to most anarchists because it simply replaces one form of oppression with another. For example, instead of a capitalist government defending the property interests of the rich and powerful, a feudal system is created whereby the rich and powerful simply defend themselves and where there are no checks and balances at all on the ability of the elite (*see* ELITISM) to oppress others.

Most people today reject anarchism as unworkable and impractical and are not convinced that all government is necessarily oppressive. Although governments often represent the interests of influential majorities, they can also work in the interests of the less powerful and can protect citizens from foreign aggressors.

ANIMAL RESEARCH   *See* ANIMAL RIGHTS.

ANIMAL RIGHTS   The RIGHT of animals to be free (*see* FREEDOM) from cruel treatment or neglect.

Philosophers differ over whether animals have rights and about the sorts of rights they have. Ethical issues (*see* ETHICS), for example, arise over killing animals for sport, for food, or for medical research. Protests are often staged against those who hunt, eat meat, or wear fur coats, for example. Traditionally, philosophers have maintained that animals, unlike human beings, do not have rights because they are unable to REASON. Animal-rights theorists such as the philosopher Peter Singer criticize this view, calling it *specieism* because it attributes rights only to members of the human species.

Advocates of animal rights believe that animals share certain properties with humans that make animals bearers of rights. For example, animals, like humans, are living beings capable of feeling both physical and psychological pain. Therefore, animals are said to have the right to freedom from deliberate infliction of unnecessary pain. *Sentientism,* the ethical view that it is morally wrong to cause unnecessary pain to animals, provides the foundation for laws (*see* LAW) that prohibit cruelty to animals.

Among those who defend animal rights, three views can be distinguished: *narrow sentientism, broad sentientism,* and *inherentism.* Narrow sentientism (sometimes called animal husbandry) holds that the scope of animal rights is limited to prohibiting unnecessary physical pain, such as that caused by injury or neglect of domesticated animals. According to this restricted view of animal rights, some animals may be justifiably killed for use as food, clothing (leather, fur), jewelry (ivory, pearl), or recreation (hunting). Further, animals are permitted to be domesticated for use as companions (pets), for recreation (in circuses), for education (in zoos), for food (milk) and for clothing (wool). This philosophical view can be traced in Western cultures to the Bible's statement (Genesis 1: 26–30) that humans hold dominion over animals.

Broad sentientism is the theory that it is wrong to kill animals except in cases of self-defense. Many who hold this view are vegetarians (see VEGETARIANISM) who will not consume meat because doing so is the result of a moral harm (see MORALITY) done to an animal. A sentientist view of animal rights also holds that domestication of wild animals is morally wrong because it breaks up natural family groups and confines animals. Some broad sentientists refuse to use animal byproducts such as milk and wool that can only be obtained by unnaturally confining animals.

The broadest theory of animal rights is known as inherentism. Inherentism holds that not only do animals have rights not to be killed or to be domesticated but also that they have inherent rights not to be exploited (see EXPLOITATION) by having their natural habitats destroyed. This view is also part of some accounts of ENVIRONMENTAL ETHICS and is sometimes said to derive from biblical commands (Corinthians 2: 8, 9) that humans have STEWARDSHIP of, rather than dominion over, the planet, its environment, its natural resources, and its animals.

ANTISEMITISM PREJUDICE against or persecution of Jews.

The word *Semite* can refer to any of the people who populated southwestern Asia in ancient times but is now almost exclusively used to refer to a member of the Hebrew or Jewish ethnic group (see JEWISH ETHICS). Antisemitism has a long and grim history beginning with the Diaspora, which was the exile of the Jews from their home in ancient Palestine. The ancient Greeks and Romans persecuted the Jews on religious grounds (see RELIGION AND MORALITY). In medieval Europe, the Christian church (see CHRISTIAN ETHICS) denied them many CIVIL RIGHTS, including the possibility of occupying government office, owning land, and participating in guilds. The Jews had to resort to tax collecting, moneylending, and other stigmatized practices in order to survive economically.

In the late Middle Ages, most Jews lived in western Europe. Despotic kings, the bubonic plague, and the Spanish Inquisition helped to drive the Jewish people out of their newfound home. By the late 1500s, they had relocated to eastern Europe. The new intellectual climate fostered during the Enlightenment (see ENLIGHTENMENT ETHICS) helped to create some TOLERANCE for religious difference. The late 19th century, however, saw a rise in racial persecution (see RACISM), especially in Germany and Russia. After World War I, hatred of the Jews increased, reaching its peak in Adolf Hitler's campaign to eliminate them altogether in World War II (see GENOCIDE) when an estimated 6 million Jews were murdered in the HOLOCAUST.

In the United States, antisemitism has tended to take more subtle forms, such as denying Jews membership in private clubs and refusing to hire them for certain jobs. Prejudice against Jews is sustained by the stereotype of the clannish Jew who is rich and greedy. Many contemporary ethicists have been striving to reveal how antisemitic stereotypes influence moral attitudes (see MORAL OPINION).

A POSTERIORI Coming later or afterward in space, time or some other ordering.

In philosophy some ideas are said to be a posteriori, meaning that we are not born with them or that they come to us through experience. EMPIRICAL KNOWLEDGE, for example, is said to be a posteriori because it is derived from observation: it comes from outside the mind by way of the senses. A posteriori is opposed to *a priori,* or that which is prior. A priori ideas are innate and not derived from sense experience. A priori knowledge is knowledge "from within." This knowledge consists of ideas we have prior to experience.

In ETHICS, moral principles (*see* PRINCIPLE) are sometimes thought to be a priori, or innate, for they are supposed to be dictated by REASON and not by sense experience. According to other theories, however, our knowledge of GOOD and bad, RIGHT and WRONG, is a posteriori and comes, therefore, through experience.

APPLIED ETHICS   The use of moral RULES or PRINCIPLES in actual situations.

Applied ETHICS is sometimes called practical ethics, meaning any attempt to determine through REASON what is a RIGHT or WRONG thing to do in a particular case, or even in a certain type of case. BIOETHICS is considered to be a field of applied ethics wherein people try to resolve controversial issues that arise in the delivery of health care or in biological research. Just one of the problems in bioethics is the question of when or under what conditions health-care professionals are morally justified in withholding care or treatment, including cases in which people are allowed to die or to end their own lives. BUSINESS ETHICS is a field of applied ethics in which attempts are made to resolve such problems as insider trading and whistle-blowing.

Any moral issue may be the subject of applied ethics. The study of applied ethics goes beyond the assertion of beliefs or opinions or the citation of authorities and includes arguments for and against opposing positions. People who work in this field try to demonstrate that their opinions are supported by GOOD reasons or evidence or that there are flaws in the arguments of their opponents.

Applied ethics is usually contrasted with theoretical ethics. In theoretical ethics, philosophers often try to discover principles and rules; in applied ethics, writers very often apply the principles or rules advocated by one theory or another. Thus, in applied ethics, a writer may propose a utilitarian solution to a moral problem by applying the principles of utilitarianism to it. Another writer may cite another theory. As a consequence, the kind of answer obtained frequently depends upon the theoretical assumptions made, so a natural-law solution to a problem may look very different from a utilitarian one. For this reason, the solution to everyday practical problems often depends a great deal on the solution of theoretical issues or upon the kind of theoretical assumptions made.

People often engage in arguments over controversial moral issues without making any explicit assumptions about which, if any, moral theory is correct. They may simply cite a rule or a principle or appeal to convention or tradition to justify their position, without any attempt to find theoretical support. Popular arguments, as opposed to philosophical papers, articles, or books, are often little more than articulations of positions held by an institution or a group or of some individual's intuitions or feelings, without any serious attempt to find out who is right. Applied ethics, by contrast, is usually considered to be a field of inquiry wherein the participants are attempting to find the answers—not simply to assert or defend positions already held. In actual practice, of course, moral arguments may be a combination of both.

People usually start off by asserting a position and then trying to defend it but, in the course of conversation or investigation, may be led to discover reasons for changing their minds. Applied ethics is then an attempt to persuade others by offering them reasons for changing or continuing to hold their moral beliefs. It is also an attempt to influence public or institutional policy by bringing about changes in the law or in social rules.

A PRIORI   *See* A POSTERIORI.

AQUINAS, THOMAS (1225–1274) Scholastic philosopher widely regarded as the single most-influential ethical philosopher (*see* ETHICS) of the Middle Ages.

Aquinas was born near the end of the Middle Ages, when knowledge lost during the previous centuries began to reemerge. At that time scholars believed that only the spiritual realm, discovered through REVELATION and FAITH, was worthy of human contemplation. The rediscovered ideas, however, used REASON as a tool to explain the physical world, and many believed that the two could not coexist. Aquinas was instrumental in reconciling these two positions with the help of the work of ARISTOTLE, whom he greatly admired.

Aquinas believed that GOD designed all things with a specific purpose (*see* TELEOLOGY) in mind, and that this purpose could be learned by observing how something behaves. For example, because a rock falls when dropped, it can be deduced that one purpose of a rock is to head downwards. Human purposes can also be deduced through observation, and include such natural desires as eating and sleeping, as well as such intellectual desires, as learning and reasoning. Aquinas concluded that for human beings, a good act (*see* GOOD; ACT) is one that is intended to help as many people as possible fulfill their purposes.

This does not mean that everything should be permitted, however. Not all talents are equally important, and it is possible that humans can be mistaken about what is really good. Aquinas believed that human decisions needed to be supplemented by an understanding of God's divine LAW, which is given to humans through revelation. He also assumed that ultimately the best use of the intellect was to study and learn about God; therefore this overriding goal could also be used as an important tool in helping to guide moral decision making (*see* MORALITY).

Aquinas's synthesis of the ideas of faith and reason also extended to the idea that it was possible to prove God's existence through reason. In all he proposed five different logical proofs, the most important of which was the "first cause argument." This is related to what we now know as Newton's first law, that a body at rest tends to remain at rest unless acted on by an outside force. Aquinas argued that as nothing can move without some external force being applied to it, there must at some point have been an "unmoved mover" to start the whole thing going in the first place. This unmoved mover could not have come from the physical world and therefore must have been God. This argument can be criticized, however, by arguing either that it is not illogical to have a sequence continue to infinity or that the unmoved mover could have been some force other than God.

Aquinas was declared a saint (*see* MORAL SAINT) by the Roman Catholic Church in 1323, and his work became the foundation for an influential philosophical movement known as Thomism. Most important, however, his success at making reason and RATIONALITY palatable to an influential church previously hostile to these ideas greatly contributed to the development of western ethical philosophy.

ARISTOTLE (384–322 B.C.) An ancient Greek philosopher whose philosophy, including his ETHICS, continues to be a major influence in the history of ideas.

Aristotle was a student of PLATO. Aristotle's philosophy is generally thought to be in agreement with Plato's in many ways but also to be more naturalistic (*see* NATURALISTIC ETHICS) than Plato's. Aristotle's philosophy places more emphasis on the importance of the natural or observable world than Plato does. In contrast to Plato, for example, Aristotle argued that our ideas are derived from sense experience. Aristotle was a natural scientist and logician who founded and classified many of the sciences that still exist today.

Aristotle's moral philosophy (*see* MORALITY) is contained primarily in his *Nichomachean Ethics,* a treatise dedicated to his son. Like Plato, Aristotle was a teleologist (*see* TELEOLOGY) who maintained that all actions are aimed at ends that are perceived as GOOD. He was also a SELF-REALIZATION theorist because he held that persons should actualize their potentialities, becoming, according to their nature, what they are capable of being. His ethics focus on an analysis of the goods appropriate to human beings according to what he called their function and the means of achieving these goods. Because he defined humans as rational (*see* RATIONALITY) animals, he concluded that both rational and animal goods are appropriate to them. But he considered the life of REASON the highest good because rationality is humankind's defining characteristic and because the life of reason is itself divine.

In ethics, the function of reason is to order the goods of life and the means of attaining them so that persons can actualize their potentialities. Self-actualization and the satisfaction of accomplishment that it brings are what Aristotle meant by HAPPINESS, the ultimate goal of human life. People who do not order their lives are in conflict with themselves and are unhappy because they allow some of the things they do to interfere with other things they are capable of doing. They might find it difficult to study, for example, because they are constantly pulled away by running to the refrigerator or by watching television. If they had an ordered life and self-discipline, they would put aside a time for eating, a time for recreation, and a time for study so that these activities would not interfere with one another.

Aristotle, therefore, described VIRTUES as good HABITS and as means between extremes. He advocated the ancient Greek ideal of the GOLDEN MEAN, of not indulging too much or too little in any activity but rather leading a life of moderation. The virtue of TEMPERANCE, for example, lies at the mean between the extremes of eating or drinking too much or too little. The virtue of COURAGE lies between cowardice and foolhardiness. VICE, for Aristotle, was a habitual or an excessive dedication to one type of good to the exclusion of other goods needed to develop the whole person.

ART AND PUBLIC POLICY   *See* CENSORSHIP.

ASCETICISM   Rigorous self-discipline that often takes the form of self-denial, in its most extreme forms involving self-mortification, the purposeful infliction of discomfort or pain on oneself.

Asceticism is found in all religious traditions, though by no means are all religious practitioners ascetics. Asceticism normally takes such forms as fasting, sleep limitation, comfort restriction, and voluntary poverty. Extreme forms include lying on a bed of nails, pushing thin nails through the cheeks, whipping the body with chains, holding an arm up until it atrophies, and staring at the sun.

In these extreme forms, asceticism represents an attempt to triumph over the body, which may be seen either as inherently evil or as simply the seat of drives that are contrary to religious aspirations. In its moderate expressions, asceticism represents a practical attempt to avoid distraction, which then gives a person more time and energy for spiritual and moral pursuits. *See also* ABSTINENCE.

ATHEISM   The doctrine that GOD does not exist.

An atheist is a person who denies the existence of God. Atheists are distinguished from *agnostics,* who claim that God's existence cannot be known or proved but concede that God may exist. Thus, agnostics are likely to hold that proofs of the existence of God are inconclusive, whereas atheists are likely to offer reasons for thinking that God does not exist, or for thinking that religion is EVIL (*see* RELIGION AND MORALITY).

One argument that atheists often use to demonstrate that God does not exist is the problem of evil. The argument is as follows: If God did exist, there would be no evil in the world, but because there *is* evil in the world, God does not exist. Other arguments against religion are often based on the HARM that religion causes, for example, the persecution of one religion by another or the persecution of nonbelievers by believers.

At times atheism is not so much asserted as implied. In ETHICS, for instance, people often advocate the doctrine of RELATIVISM, or the belief that they are subject to no AUTHORITY but their own, a position that seems to imply atheism. In contrast, to believe in God is to believe that there is an absolute authority, higher than humans or human society. Moreover, the belief that there is only one God carries with it the ethical implication that there is one LAW for everyone. Thus, to hold that MORALITY is relative to humans is to deny the existence of an absolute moral authority. This is the objection many religions have against HUMANISM, which maintains that humans are the highest form of being, thereby denying the existence of God.

Some people who claim to be humanists also claim to be religious, and atheistic humanism has had philosophic proponents as well. One of the most famous atheistic humanists is Auguste Comte, who believed that in the EVOLUTION of human thought, people have outgrown religion. Comte held that in prescientific ages people were religious or superstitious but that the religious phase of history was followed by a period of metaphysics and, finally, by the age of science.

Some people believe that ethics would be impossible without religion, but many nonreligious people have moral beliefs. For example,

PLATO and ARISTOTLE, regarded as pagans by Christian (*see* CHRISTIAN ETHICS) and Jewish philosophers (*see* JEWISH ETHICS), developed influential ethical theories. Others, such as Thomas HOBBES and Jean-Paul SARTRE have built their philosophies on atheistic assumptions. Even Thomas AQUINAS argued that knowledge of the NATURAL LAW is available to everyone and does not need REVELATION or FAITH to support it, although he also believed faith reveals ethical truths (*see* TRUTH) not available without it. He thought that pagans could understand the concept of JUSTICE, but that they did not understand the doctrine of LOVE.

AUGUSTINE (354–430)   A bishop and saint of the Catholic Church who wrote voluminously on questions of philosophy and religion (*see* RELIGION AND MORALITY). His most famous works are *Confessions* and *The City of God*, in which he explains Christian doctrine (*see* CHRISTIAN ETHICS) according to his interpretation of PLATO and neo-Platonism. These writings have had enormous influence upon the subsequent history of Christian theology, both Protestant and Catholic. For instance, both Thomas AQUINAS and Martin LUTHER were influenced by his ideas.

Augustine saw ETHICS as essentially a choice between being and nonbeing, between the way to GOD, the source of all being and goodness, and the way to nothingness (the deprivation of being), represented as SIN or separation from God. For Augustine, everything is GOOD in that it exists or has being. What we call EVIL is a lack or absence of being. To be able to see is good, but to be blind is bad. Thus, evil, strictly speaking, does not exist or have being. By this kind of analysis, Augustine tried to solve the problem of evil: the problem of how an all good and all powerful God can create a world with evil in it. His answer was that everything created by God is good, for everything that exists is good in that it has being. Evil, the deprivation of goodness, is not created by God; it is not created by anything. God allows degrees of being or goodness, however; as a result, some things are not other things, or they lack the kinds of goodness other things have. Because, for example, nothing created by God *is* God, everything other than God must lack God's perfection and, therefore, be imperfect. But nothing is absolutely evil (*see* ABSOLUTES), for absolute evil would be complete nonexistence.

Augustine argued that although the concepts PREDESTINATION and FREEDOM may seem incompatible, Christians must believe in both: predestination because God is all-powerful and all-knowing, and freedom because ethics, or personal RESPONSIBILITY, requires it. He argued that God can have foreknowledge of free human acts (*see* ACT) because God's knowledge of what people will freely choose does not prevent them from freely choosing it. He also argued that, although God is the ultimate cause of everything that happens and so by his grace enables humans to perform good acts, God does not cause people to do evil. By distinguishing between choosing to use God's grace (the *efficient* will) and choosing not to use it (the *deficient* will), Augustine tried to show that doing good requires God's grace or causal POWER, but that evil, which is a lack of goodness, requires no cause or power at all.

AUTHENTICITY A state of being in which one fully and genuinely accepts the truth about one's condition and limitations and chooses to take responsibility for living wholly and completely as and for oneself as a totality.

The concept of authenticity initially appeared in the works of Martin Heidegger, an existentialist philosopher, and has been described by Jean-Paul SARTRE and others as the primary (some would say only) VIRTUE of EXISTENTIALISM.

Authenticity is to be contrasted with *bad faith,* which is inauthentic and involves trying to conform to how we believe others would like to see us, or otherwise trying to avoid full responsibility for, and ownership of, our own choices. To do so seems restrictive and self defeating to existentialists, who believe that because the world we experience is simply an extension of ourselves, it is impossible for anything "outside" to exert any control over us. Although limits can and do exist in the existentialist worldview, they believe that we are in no position to assume them in advance.

AUTHORITY A person or opinion cited to support a belief. In reasoning (*see* REASON) or in argumentation, an appeal to the source of an idea, where that source is regarded as having special knowledge or as being in a special position to know.

In religion (*see* RELIGION AND MORALITY), GOD is often appealed to as a source of belief, for God is supposed to know everything, and therefore what God says must be true (*see* TRUTH). Experts, such as scientists or professionals, may also be cited to support beliefs, for they are supposed to know more, at least about certain subjects, than other people do.

In ETHICS, people often like to think that they speak with authority or that their beliefs have some special sort of authorization. Thus they may cite, for example, the BIBLE or the U.S. Constitution to support their beliefs. In ethics, the challenge "Who says?" may be understood as a request for authorization, and the answer might be, "God says," or "Society says," or even, "I say," if one regards oneself as the source of one's own moral views (*see* MORAL OPINION).

In LOGIC, appeals to authority are said to be FALLACIES, or mistakes in reasoning. The mere fact that someone says or thinks that something is true does not make it true, no matter who that person may be. Even experts can make mistakes. Likewise, societies and governments can also advocate false ideas. For this reason scientific investigators do not believe things just because some authority says so but because they have evidence to support their claims. But, of course, some people are more likely than others to have knowledge because of their special training or experience, and their opinions may therefore be rightly regarded as more authoritative than the opinions of others.

People may also have authority in the sense that they occupy positions of authority and consequently are accorded the POWER to make a JUDGMENT or decision of a certain kind. For example, an umpire in a baseball game has the authority to call balls and strikes; according to the rules of the game the umpire's calls are accepted as authoritative, even if some of them are questionable or wrong. When Congress passes a bill and it is signed by the president, the bill becomes LAW according to powers granted by the Constitution. Such laws may or may not be good laws, but they are laws nonetheless. Therefore, it is sometimes the case that some things are true because certain people say or decide they are. Such truths are sometimes said to be societal facts as opposed to bare facts or natural facts because they depend on institutional rules. Having a diploma or a degree, for instance, is not a natural fact in the sense that being a man or a woman is: it is a property or characteristic that is conferred upon persons by authorities, according to the rules of educational institutions.

The rules of society, then, have authority because they *are* rules, even if sometimes they are not very good ones. Insofar as they are the rules or are generally accepted as rules, people will expect one another to obey them and will rely upon this OBEDIENCE. Such reliance should be taken into account in considering whether or not a rule should be broken, even if one happens to think the rule is wrong. Acceptance of a rule does not make it good, however, and there may be good reasons to change the rules.

AUTONOMY   The ability or right to be self-governing or self-ruling.

There is a sense in which practically all people are autonomous and can make their own decisions, and in general we do in fact assume that most people should be free from interference in the conduct of their personal lives. Hence we may say that everyone has a right to autonomy.

However, except for anarchists (*see* ANARCHY), most people believe that a person should not be entitled to exercise full autonomy if to do so is morally wrong or would otherwise interfere with another's rights. We nearly all agree that some things should not be permitted, such as murder, kidnapping, or rape. In other instances, what should be permitted is less clear, as in the case of secondhand cigarette smoke, where the right of someone to smoke may interfere with someone else's right to breathe fresh air.

Ethicists generally believe that a right to autonomy should not include the ability to do something morally wrong. According to Immanuel KANT, autonomy refers to an individual's ability to determine moral law by use of REASON. Kant thought that people should act only according to those rules than can be willed to be universal laws, or laws that apply in the same way to all people. He held that people are bound by moral law and have no right to do what is morally wrong.

More recently, some authors have used the word *autonomy* to refer to freedom of choice, or a person's ability to choose (*see* FREEDOM). Others have used the word to mean a person's right to choose (*see* RIGHTS). Still others have meant by it a person's competence to make decisions.

Individuals or groups with the ability to make decisions that others are not allowed to make may also be said to have autonomy—for example, someone in a position of AUTHORITY or a specialist with special COMPETENCY in a particular area. In these cases, it may be useful or necessary to draw an arbitrary line when deciding which individuals or groups should be allowed autonomy in a certain area. For example, it may be decided that people should not be allowed to drink alcohol before the age of 21, even though there are young people with responsible drinking habits and older people who drink irresponsibly.

Autonomy entails RESPONSIBILITY. If a person freely chooses to commit a crime, then he or she is normally thought to be responsible for that choice. From a legal standpoint, the only people who are not considered to be responsible for their own actions are those with a severe mental handicap, such as insanity.

Today, it is commonly accepted that competant adults have the right to make morally permissible choices without interference from others. People are generally allowed a wide range of discretion in the conduct of their personal lives, even when the choices they make are poor ones. For example, we will usually respect the right of someone to smoke even if it is bad for the health, as to do otherwise would be a form of PATERNALISM.

B

BEAUVOIR, SIMONE DE (1908–1986)
French existentialist (*see* EXISTENTIALISM) feminist philosopher (*see* FEMINIST ETHICS).

De Beauvoir's philosophy held that human existence should be characterized by overcoming the limitations of one's own situation in life. According to de Beauvoir, humans can be truly free only in a society in which they respect the FREEDOM of others. Society should guarantee freedom of expression and EQUALITY for all persons.

In *The Ethics of Ambiguity* (1947), de Beauvoir argued that society does not treat women as equal to men and does not respect what she called women's "projects" (the actions women choose to engage in) as of equal VALUE to men's. Women are identified as "other" by men. This identification has the effect of separating the two sexes and of labeling women as persons of less moral importance (*see* MORALITY) than men. Even when women are permitted to choose, neither motherhood nor "women's professions" are given equal respect by men when compared to men's "projects." Therefore, women's place in society, their moral status, and their RIGHTS are "ambiguous."

In *The Second Sex* (1949), de Beauvoir distinguished between biological femaleness (sex) and socialized femininity (gender). She argued that women can become free by "transcending" (overcoming male-imposed limitations) biological sexual identity and the imposed identity of motherhood. In order to transcend sex and gender, women should choose how they will live socially as female, for "one is not born, but rather becomes, a woman."

In addition to being a philosopher, de Beauvoir wrote many best-selling novels and was a political activist who protested the French war in Algeria, the war in Vietnam, and laws prohibiting abortion. She was also the lifelong companion of philosopher Jean-Paul SARTE. *See also* WOMEN'S RIGHTS.

BEECHER, CATHARINE WARD (1800–1878) Nineteenth-century American philosopher who showed how PURITANISM's view of women's moral status and its emphasis on the virtues (*see* VIRTUE) of piety, moral RESPONSIBILITY, simplicity, self-denial, and personal SACRIFICE, was consistent with UTILITARIANISM.

In *The Elements of Mental and Moral Philosophy Founded upon Experience, Reason, and the Bible* (1831), Beecher argued that we exist in a social system in which all are dependent on others for HAPPINESS. By promoting social virtue in others, each person contributes to the development of the greatest social happiness through submission to AUTHORITY, self-denial, and self-sacrifice for the good of all (*see* SELFLESSNESS).

Beecher also shared Puritanism's view of women's moral nature. In philosophy, this view is known as *sexual complementarity:* GOD created women and men differently so that their virtues would complement each other. Beecher considered women naturally more virtuous than men. Women have natural duties to be good wives and mothers who set examples for their husbands and for their children, whom they are preparing to become virtuous members of society. Virtue is instilled by teaching, persuasion, and example. Beecher believed that women should not be given the RIGHT to vote because it was the duty of men to run the state.

Many of Beecher's philosophical writings concern the ethical behavior of individuals and the ethical duties of women. She also held that ETHICS has a larger, social purpose. Social ethics should create social stability. Conflict and division destroy, rather than promote, the greatest GOOD for the greatest number of people.

Beecher was also an outspoken opponent of SLAVERY prior to the Civil War. In *An Essay on Slavery and Abolitionism with Reference to the Duty of American Females* (1837), Beecher supported women's exercise of moral leadership (*see* MORAL EXEMPLAR) through political activism to abolish slavery. She argued that FREEDOM for all is of the greatest social utility; therefore, slavery needed to be abolished.

According to Beecher, PRINCILPES of BENEVOLENCE (doing good for others) and utility were subject to the principle of *rectitude*: Personal sacrifice for the good of others must be motivated by the desire to right social wrongs and by a commitment to principles of SOCIAL JUSTICE. Beecher believed that not all methods for encouraging the greatest happiness were justified (*see* JUSTIFICATION), however, and that some methods, like slavery, should be opposed. In *An Appeal to the People on Behalf of their Rights as Authorized Interpreters of the Bible* (1860), Beecher argued that "one must not only choose to promote the greatest possible happiness, but must choose the right way of doing it."

BELIEF *See* FAITH.

BENEFICENCE Doing GOOD, especially for others.

The exhortation or command to do good is often thought to be a first principle of ETHICS and is called the principle of beneficence. Thomas AQUINAS, for example, saw that the first principles of ethics as "Do good" and "Avoid EVIL." Such a principle also seems to be assumed in other systems or theories. Utilitarians (*see* UTILITARIANISM) claim that persons have an OBLIGATION to do good or to produce pleasure to the extent that they can, and to avoid evil or pain (*see* HEDONISM) as much as possible.

Beneficence may be given a more restricted interpretation if taken to mean doing good for others, as opposed to oneself. In any case, it is distinguished from BENEVOLENCE, for a person might do good for others without wishing to do so or without being motivated by a desire to help them, just as one may wish to help others but fail to do so. In moral systems (*see* MORALITY) that judge actions by intentions or motives, however, the ideas of benevolence and beneficence are related, for a person could not choose to perform a beneficent act without intending to do so. *See also* ALTRUISM.

BENEVOLENCE Wishing or wanting what is GOOD for others.

Ethicists (*see* ETHICS) often make a distinction between benevolence, which is the desire to do good, and BENEFICENCE, which is the act of doing good, even though in everyday conversation, benevolence is often intended to imply both. Ethicists distinguish between the two concepts because someone could do good without realizing it or even when they intend to do harm. For example, a maliciously inclined vandal may destroy stored food that was later found to be contaminated with a deadly poison. Because this act has positive consequences, in preventing deaths from eating contaminated food, it might be described as beneficent, but not benevolent. This distinction is particularly important in an ethical system such as UTILITARIANISM, which argues that actions must always be judged (*see* JUDGMENT) on their consequences alone.

Benevolence is often said to be a MOTIVE for action, where the intention of the act is to do good for someone else, as opposed to doing good for oneself. Thus, benevolence is usually contrasted with SELF-INTEREST or self-love (*see*

NARCISSISM), as in Joseph BUTLER's philosophy. It appears that people sometimes perform acts in their own self-interest, acts that they also sometimes perform in the interest of others. Sometimes, indeed, they may have both motives, thinking that something will benefit themselves as well as others.

Philosophic arguments about benevolence tend to focus on the questions of whether the motive of benevolence is necessary for morally correct behavior (see MORALITY) and whether, indeed, it is even possible for people to be benevolent. The philosophic position of EGOISM denies that people can be motivated by a desire to help others, except as a means of helping themselves. Altruists (see ALTRUISM), by contrast, argue that helping others as a means to helping oneself is not true benevolence, that benevolence can be, and often is, an end in itself.

BENTHAM, JEREMY (1748–1832) English jurist and philosopher and founder of UTILITARIANISM.

Bentham's major work is entitled *Principles of Morals and Legislation,* in which he argued that the goal of MORALITY is to produce the greatest GOOD for the greatest number of people, often called "the greatest HAPPINESS principle." His philosophy is hedonistic (see HEDONISM) and rests upon the belief that happiness consists of pleasure. According to Bentham, actions (see ACT) that increase pleasure or happiness are good, and actions that increase pain are bad. He developed a hedonic calculus to determine the morality of an action. To use this calculus, one considers the consequences of a course of action in terms of the pleasure and pain of all the people concerned. Pain and pleasure are measured by such factors as intensity, duration, and extent and the good calculated based on these results. In Bentham's thought, some pleasures are "pure" while others are "fecund." Pure pleasures are not mixed with pain. Fecund pleasures are those which are not

only pleasurable in themselves but also lead to other pleasures. Bentham was concerned only with the amounts of pleasure or pain produced by an action, not the quality or kind of pleasure produced. He said, for example, that "pushpin is as good as poetry," meaning that no one kind of thing is superior to any other, except as it produces more pleasure.

Bentham developed his moral philosophy as a theoretical foundation for legislative change. He held that "the *Public Good* ought to be the object of the legislator: *General Utility* ought to be the foundation of his reasonings." Bentham has had considerable influence on subsequent philosophy and on legal (see LAW) and economic theory. For example, John Stuart MILL's work on utilitarianism has its foundations in Bentham's thought.

BHAGAVAD GITA The most widely read and influential Hindu scripture.

The Bhagavad Gita is made up of 18 short chapters excerpted from one of India's major epics, the *Mahabharata,* composed between 300 B.C. and A.D. 300. It involves a discussion between two characters: Arjuna, a member of the warrior CASTE and leader of an army about to engage in battle; and Krishna, Arjuna's charioteer, who is the incarnation of the GOD Vishnu. Because the army opposing Arjuna includes his own relatives and people he respects, Arjuna is reluctant to perform his duty and argues against going into battle against them. Krishna continually counters Arjuna's arguments and urges him to fulfill his duty (see DHARMA; OBLIGATION). Arjuna is finally convinced and decides to go into battle.

Although the Bhagavad Gita seems to endorse and even glorify warfare, it should be interpreted symbolically, not literally. Indeed, GANDHI, the 20th century's greatest pacifist (see PACIFISM), praised the Bhagavad Gita and found much guidance and solace in it. The real battle in the Bhagavad Gita is between Arjuna's lower, conditioned, fearful self and his higher, spiritual self. Indeed, in the course of their discussion, Arjuna and Krishna cover much that is highly abstract and spiritual or philosophical in nature.

One of the principal teachings of the Bhagavad Gita is "actionless action" (*see* ACT). Krishna declares: "He who sees inaction in action, he is wise." Here, the "inaction" Krishna is referring to is the need to eliminate selfish (*see* SELFISHNESS), self-centered goals (*see* EGOISM) when acting. An action is thus RIGHT if it is done without concern for any personal gain or loss that may ensure. For example, one should give money to the poor because it is the right thing to do, not because it feels good or because it will impress bystanders. *See also* HINDU ETHICS.

BHAKTI YOGA   A system of YOGA centering on LOVE and devotion.

One of the most widely practiced yogic systems in India, Bhakti Yoga calls for the practitioner to devote himself or herself resolutely, without reservation, in loving self-surrender to a deity, a GOD or Goddess, of personal choice. Typically, the devotee commits to the traditional deity of his or her family but is free to chose from any among the thousands that make up the Hindu pantheon. The particular deity chosen is not as important as the quality of the devotion and submission directed at the God or Goddess.

The surrender and devotion of a bhakta (one who follows Bhakti Yoga) is also typically directed to a personal guru, or spiritual teacher. This teacher not only instructs but exemplifies the spiritual and moral qualities (*see* MORALITY) that the devotee hopes to acquire.

Ideally, the loving self-surrender of the devotee to the deity and guru results in a reduction of self-centeredness, perhaps even a dissolving of the EGO insofar as it gives rise to self-assertion over the needs and rights of others. This new orientation is reflected both in religious purification and in ethical action. *See also* HINDU ETHICS.

BIAS   A subtle prejudice or tendency to favor one side over another.

A bias is not based on facts or rational analysis (*see* RATIONALITY) but is a special advantage given to one side without proper regard to circumstances. Bias is often unintentional. For example, a school teacher might call on boys more than girls to answer a question. The teacher may give preferential treatment to one group over another without even realizing it. Bias is different from PREJUDICE, which typically involves a JUDGMENT with little or no basis in fact.

People are biased when they only see one side of an issue. Frequently, we know and appreciate our own desires, needs, responsibilities, sacrifices, CUSTOMS, and personal HABITS. In conflicting circumstances, it is natural to see ourselves as RIGHT and others as WRONG. Because we usually know less about the characteristics and viewpoints of others than we know about our own, it often happens that people exhibit a bias in favor of their own interests even when they believe they have carefully and objectively (*see* OBJECTIVITY) considered all the facts. A biased person might make moral decisions (*see* MORALITY) without adequately appreciating the circumstances of others or by giving too much consideration to his or her own situation.

Eliminating bias is not easy because detecting bias is often difficult. For example, an employer may have a bias against hiring young people. Even if he or she regularly hires older candidates instead of those who are younger and more qualified, the employer may occasionally hire a young person if no one older applies for the job. In some cases, young people who are outstandingly well qualified may even end up with the job despite the employer's bias.

While we can sometimes see bias in others, bias is often most difficult to detect in ourselves. Indeed, those who are on the receiving end of others' biases are in fact often biased themselves. For example, someone who is considered unattractive by many in society may still prefer to be friends with people who are considered attractive.

Because bias is often thought to be morally wrong, people may be obliged to develop ways to detect it. This might be accomplished by looking for unexpected differences in achievement based on personal traits, comparing our preferences with the preferences of other cultures, and examining differences in judgments made by people from different groups.

BIBLE   Sacred scripture of Jews and Christians.

Although the Bible does not contain a systematic or developed ethical system (*see* ETHICS), scattered throughout are many warnings, arguments, and narratives that set forth the biblical moral ideal (*see* IDEALS). These have been worked into more or less systematic form by Jewish and Christian ethicists.

The Bible is considered by Jews and Christians to be the revealed word of GOD. However, great divergence exists within both communities on what this means. Fundamentalists (*see* FUNDAMENTALISM) believe that the Bible literally is the Word of God, and therefore they tend to interpret it literally. Others believe that the Bible contains interpretations of the word of God, and therefore they endeavor to separate the timeless TRUTH from its time-bound, cultural expression.

The exact form the Bible takes varies depending on the religion (*see* RELIGION AND MORALITY) in which it is used. The Jewish version of the Bible is often called the TORAH or Tanakh and is based upon the Old Testament divided into 24 books. The Christian Protestant version of the Bible divides the Old Testament into 39 books and includes the additional 27 books of the New Testament. Versions of the Bible used by Roman and Eastern Orthodox Catholics include additional books that are no longer used by either Judaism or Protestantism.

The central ethical directives in the Bible are summarized by the TEN COMMANDMENTS, although the exact number of commandments varies between religious traditions. In the Jewish tradition, the essence of the commandments is summarized in three points by Micah (6:8), who says "He has told you, O mortal, what is GOOD; and what does the Lord require of you but to do JUSTICE, and to love kindness, and to walk humbly with your God?"

In the Christian tradition, the MORALITY of the New Testament is also based on Old Testament morality. Matthew (22:37–39) quotes JESUS as saying " 'You shall LOVE the Lord your God with all your heart, with all your soul, and with all your mind.' This is the greatest and first commandment. And the second is like it: 'You shall love your neighbor as yourself.' On these two commandments hang all the LAW and the prophets." The linking of the first commandment, which is explicitly religious, with the second commandment, which is explicitly moral, demonstrates that Jesus saw religion and morality to be integral and essential to each other, and this interpretation is generally accepted by most commentators. *See also* CHRISTIAN ETHICS; JEWISH ETHICS.

BIGOTRY   *See* PREJUDICE.

BILL OF RIGHTS   The first ten amendments to the U.S. Constitution.

Officially adopted in 1791, the Bill of Rights is a collection of provisions that make it illegal for the government to prohibit certain types of individual behavior. It also prohibits the federal government from regulating things that are the RESPONSIBILITY of the states.

Important amendments include provisions that: (I) Guarantee FREEDOM of speech, (II) Support the RIGHT to bear arms, (IV) Prohibit unreasonable search and seizure, (V) Support DUE PROCESS and prohibit forced self-incrimination, (VI) Require speedy trials and adequate criminal (*see* CRIME) defense, (VII) Support trial by jury, (VIII) Prohibit "cruel and unusual PUNISHMENT," and (IX) Allow for other unspecified RIGHTS "retained by the people."

Interpretations of provisions in the Bill of Rights vary. One of the most controversial provisions is the Second Amendment. The Second Amendment states, "A well regulated Militia, being necessary to the security of a free State, the right of the people to keep and bear Arms, shall not be infringed." The Supreme Court in *United States v. Miller* (1939) held that this was only intended to apply to a "well-regulated Militia," like the police force or army reserve. It has also been pointed out that the founders would never have imagined "arms" could include such things as automatic weapons and nuclear bombs. Opponents of this position however argue that the provision exists so that citizens have the means to protect themselves against a tyrannical government (*see* OPPRESSION).

In practice, the Supreme Court has often limited the scope of provisions in the Bill of Rights. For example, the Supreme Court in *United States v. Schenck* (1919) held that not all speech was protected by the First Amendment and that "substantive evils" such as "shouting fire in a crowded theater," could be banned. The First Amendment is also limited in schools. In *Hazelwood School District v. Kuhlmeier* (1988), it was held that school administrators who fund student activities, such as newspapers or plays, could censor the content of the activity if they believed it to be "inappropriate" or "harmful." *See also* CIVIL RIGHTS; HUMAN RIGHTS.

BIOETHICS   A field of study within APPLIED ETHICS that focuses on ethical issues (*see* ETHICS) arising within the academic disciplines and professional practices of the life sciences.

Bioethics includes the study of ethical issues in fields such as medicine (*see* MEDICAL ETHICS), nursing, biology, zoology, and environmental science (*see* ENVIRONMENTAL ETHICS).

The term was first proposed in 1971 by Van Rensselaer Potter to refer to ethical issues regarding population and environment. But most of the published books and articles in bioethics concern the professional practice of medicine and nursing; medical research; dentistry; psychiatry and psychology and their related counseling fields; pharmacy; and PUBLIC HEALTH.

The advance of life-supporting technologies in the 1960s and 1970s ignited one of the most controversial bioethics issues in medicine, DEATH AND DYING. Traditionally, death was determined by a lack of pulse or the cessation of breathing. Once medical technologies such as the respirator and heart-lung machine made it possible to sustain LIFE indefinitely, a new definition of death became necessary. This definition is important morally (*see* MORALITY) so that those patients who are seriously ill could have the RIGHT to the treatment necessary to survive, while other patients who can be sustained artificially but have little or no hope of recovery would not be maintained on life-support machines. Discussion of this issue led to a revision in the medical determination of when death occurs. BRAIN DEATH, rather than lack of heartbeat, became the legal definition of death throughout the United States. More recently, this debate has involved the question of physician-assisted suicide (*see* EUTHANASIA). Proponents of physician-assisted suicide believe that a terminally ill patient has the right to a painless death under the care of a physician. Opponents believe that it is never appropriate for a physician to euthanize a patient actively.

Another area of bioethics pertains to research ethics, which involves issues such as the ethical use of human subjects in research. In order for research to be ethical, subjects must give INFORMED CONSENT. This means that subjects must be informed of both the nature of the experiment and the possible consequences of participation. They must also be fully informed and understand what alternative courses of treatments are possible, including the option of refusing treatment altogether.

The economic dimension of bioethics often concerns the distribution of scarce medical resources or the selection of patients for limited medical services. For example, PRINCIPLES of bioethics should assist in determining which patients will receive organ transplants (*see* ORGAN TRANSPLANTS) when donated organs are limited.

In the mid-1990s bioethics has come to be associated closely with issues of cloning, EUGENICS, and GENETIC ENGINEERING. As researchers continue to discover more and more information about human genetic makeup, society faces new ethical issues. For example, we have already identified specific genes that may lead to certain disease. While this may be valuable information to the patient or to prospective parents, it remains controversial whether or not other people have a right to that information. Should insurance companies also be notified? What about employers? In the future, it may be possible for parents to choose the genetic characteristics of their children. Those interested in bioethics will attempt to guide legislation and decision-making processes to help individuals and society determine the moral boundaries of the use of this new technology.

BIRTH CONTROL   *See* CONTRACEPTION.

BLASPHEMY   Behavior that is insulting to, or contemptuous of, a sacred person, deity (*see* GOD), or thing.

What actually constitutes blasphemy varies widely between religious traditions, but most have at least some PROHIBITION against the practice. In the Judeo-Christian tradition, blasphemy is prohibited in the TEN COMMANDMENTS, which states "You shall not take the name of the Lord your God in vain."

Blasphemy has also been prohibited by LAW in many countries throughout history and in many cases was punishable by death. In the United States, several states still have laws prohibiting blasphemy, although these are generally no longer enforced. In some other countries, however, blasphemy remains a serious CRIME. In 1989 Muslim leaders in Iran sentenced author Salman Rushdie to death in absentia for his novel *The Satanic Verses,* which they believed blasphemed Islam.

BRAIN DEATH   When the brain no longer functions although the rest of the body does.

With the advent of medical technology that can keep a person alive who would otherwise die (*see* DEATH AND DYING), brain death has become the standard for determining the point at which life-support machines can be turned off. An electroencelograph (EEG) is used to document brain death. Electrodes are placed on the patient's scalp in order to record brain activity; the absence of such activity constitutes brain death. At this point there is little or no debate as to the appropriateness of turning off life-sustaining machines such as a ventilator and even discontinuing life-sustaining fluids such as intravenous lines and antibiotics because the individual in question is considered dead. Although it is true that very simple brain activity is needed for even the most basic functions such as breathing and heartbeats, more-complex brain function is needed to qualify as LIFE. Very little controversy surrounds the use of brain death as the standard for cessation of treatment. Yet there remains a great deal of debate concerning appropriate treatment during the intervening time between health and the illnesses and infirmities that can precede brain death. *See also* BIOETHICS; MEDICAL ETHICS.

BUDDHIST ETHICS   A system and CODE of behavior based on the world view, social organization, and spiritual PRACTICE of Buddhism, the religion founded by Siddhartha Gautama.

Siddhartha, or Buddha, Gautama was a yogi born in the fifth or sixth century B.C. The name *the Buddha* is a title of honor meaning "enlightened one." Although there have been many Buddhas, the phrase "*the* Buddha" usually refers to Buddha Gautama.

The Buddha's teachings are founded on his belief that all human suffering and discontent are due to personal DESIRE, which causes people to want things to be different from what they actually are (*see* FOUR NOBLE TRUTHS). For Buddhists, spiritual realization and ethical action (*see* ETHICS) are inseparable. Each of the three major branches of Buddhism, *Theravada, Mahayana,* and *Vajrayana,* has a slightly different approach to ethics.

The first of these, *Theravada,* focuses on the EIGHTFOLD PATH as a way to avoid suffering and discontent. One part of this "Training in MORALITY" involves three principles: RIGHT speech, which is to speak the truth and not insult others; right livelihood, which is to choose an occupation in keeping with Buddhist principles (for example, bartending is a poor choice because alcohol disrupts mental clarity and may result in suffering); and right behavior.

Right behavior includes ten precepts, of which only the first five are relevant to all Buddhists. They specify that one should refrain from (1) killing (including animals), (2) stealing, (3) adultery, (4) lying and insults, and (5) drinking alcohol. The last five apply to monks and nuns only and prohibit (6) eating after noon, (7) music, dance, and plays, (8) perfume and jewelry, (9) luxurious beds, and (10) handling money. None of the last five precepts are seen as EVIL in themselves but are simply considered to be inappropriate worldly concerns for those seeking to lead an intensely spiritual life.

Mahayana Buddhists believe that the *Theravadan* moral system focuses too much on personal salvation and individual morality and not enough on the RESPONSIBILITY of one human being for another. *Mahayanans* have therefore created a more altruistic ethic (*see* ALTRUISM) that gives special elevated moral status to one who is close to achieving NIRVANA (a *bodhisattva*); yet it postpones this final step in order to help relieve suffering (*see* KARUNA) and help others toward their own enlightenment. Helping others can be achieved by spending numerous lifetimes cultivating six perfections: generosity, moral virtue, patience, vigor, meditation, and wisdom. Some

lists also include four additional perfections: skillful means of helping others, commitment to achieving enlightenment, the POWER to effect change, and knowledge of the mysteries of human existence.

The third branch of Buddhism, *Vajrayana,* sets forth the ideal (*see* IDEALS) of the *mahasiddha,* a magician or "being of great power," in the belief that the *Mahayanan bodhisattva* path to enlightenment is too slow (because it involves reincarnation through many rounds of existence). By mastering the techniques of meditation, *mahasiddhas* gain mastery over natural processes. For example, some are reputed to be able to fly, run impossibly fast, or touch distant objects with ease. Although they will be unable to achieve nirvana if they use their powers for personal gain, some do engage in activities that may seem wrong to conventional morality, such as sexual promiscuity. Nevertheless, like *bodhisattvas, mahasiddas* are believed to be empowered by a special wisdom and compassion that enables them to aid others altruistically.

For *bodhisattvas* and *mahasiddhas,* ethics is no longer simply a matter of following a code of behavior or even of applying moral PRINCIPLES, but it is a series of necessary steps toward an advanced state of being. *See also* DHARMA; KARMA.

BUSINESS ETHICS   A CODE of moral (*see* MORALITY) professional behavior, or the branch of APPLIED ETHICS that examines business practices.

Business ethics involves questions about the proper conduct in professional matters including relationships with employers, clients, and colleagues. LOYALTY is a key issue in business ethics. For example, a company that decides to move its plant to another country may wrestle with the question of how much RESPONSIBILITY it has to lifelong workers. On the other hand, employees must decide whether to stay with companies during difficult times or whether their services are always available to the highest bidder. Related to questions of loyalty is WHISTLE-BLOWING, which occurs when an employee divulges an illegal or immoral action (*see* IMMORALITY) taking place within a company or a government. While it may seem obvious that keeping harmful information from the public or from the government is immoral, the repercussions may cause HARM to the company, the workers in the company, the company's town or city, and the worker who is blowing the whistle.

Business ethics is also concerned with determining when special protection for workers is required or how much risk is acceptable for the workers. Ethical businesspeople also consider such questions as whether they should adopt AFFIRMATIVE ACTION requirements or whether firms have special obligations to other nations, especially, for example, to employees in underdeveloped nations who work for low wages but retain little local benefits from a company's profits. Client relationships are also an important part of business ethics. Ethical treatment (*see* ETHICS) of clients revolve around issues such as CONFIDENTIALITY, the disclosure of CONFLICTS OF INTEREST, TRUTH in advertising, and fair trading practices. The moral requirements of business in relation to the environment is also a subject of concern in business ethics. Moral professionals seek to work profitably while also preserving necessary resources.

In addition to describing the set of concerns faced by professional people, business ethics also refers to the study of the morality of business practices. There are many centers and journals devoted to business ethics. Classes in business ethics are taught in the philosophy departments and business schools of many universities and colleges.

Business ethics involves a moral evaluation of the social and human problems that occur in doing business. It also explores the moral implications of the variety of practices employed to achieve commercial success.

BUTLER,   JOSEPH (1692–1752)   An English clergyman who is best known in ETHICS for his analysis of human motivation (*see* MOTIVE) set forth in his *Fifteen Sermons Preached at the Rolls Chapel* and in particular for his arguments against EGOISM.

By distinguishing four motives of human action (*see* ACT)—CONSCIENCE, BENEVOLENCE, NARCISSISM, and passion (*see* PASSIONS AND EMOTIONS), he tried to show that there is not simply one motive, such as self-love or SELF-INTEREST, as egoists maintain. The four motives he mentions can be shown to be distinct because they can conflict with one another, although they do not necessarily conflict. For example, doing things for oneself in self-interest can conflict with doing things for another out of benevolence: keeping food and not sharing it, for example, as opposed to sharing it and not having it for oneself. Doing one thing conflicts with doing the other because it is not possible to do both at once. But some acts may be both self-interested and benevolent because they are meant to help both oneself and others.

In Butler's philosophy, motives are distinguished by their objects, as the motive of self-interest is to do GOOD for oneself, while the motive of benevolence is to do good for another. To act according to the dictates of conscience is the highest motive, that is, to perform an act not because it is in one's own interest or the interest of another but because it is RIGHT. Butler describes conscience as a rational faculty (*see* RATIONALITY) according to which we can discern what is morally right or WRONG.

C

CAPITAL PUNISHMENT Lawful (*see* LAW) execution of a criminal by the state, also known as the death penalty.

The question of when, if ever, it is permissible for the state to impose the death penalty is a matter of considerable debate. Opponents generally argue that capital punishment is uncivilized and barbaric. They point out that criminals often commit crimes (*see* CRIME) without considering the consequences and that the threat of life imprisonment is an effective deterrent to crime. Opponents also note that it is practically impossible to guarantee that an innocent person will never be executed.

Some arguments used by those who favor capital punishment include the necessity to exact REVENGE on criminals and that, in the case of MURDER, the PUNISHMENT should fit the crime (*see* LEX TALIONIS). In Western societies, however, neither of these PRINCIPLES is generally believed to be an appropriate JUSTIFICATION for punishment.

More successful arguments in favor of capital punishment are based on the principles of DETERRENCE and RETRIBUTION. In the case of deterrence, it is suggested that a harsh penalty will force criminals to consider their actions *before* committing a crime and that if they do commit crime, the death penalty will stop them from doing it again. In the case of retribution, it has been argued that society as a whole is justified in imposing capital punishment for the most heinous of crimes because this is the only way of collectively repudiating certain behavior which most people find repugnant. Opponents are unlikely to be convinced by either principle, however, because neither is clear on why capital punishment is better than life imprisonment.

Although still common in many parts of the world, by the mid-1990s the United States was the only western democracy where the death penalty was still being used.

CAPITALISM An economic and political system that relies on large-scale production, competition, private ownership of the means of production, and minimal political interference in the economy.

Capitalism is built on private investment in businesses. Whether or not a business survives depends on its ability to compete in the marketplace. The means of production—factories, machinery, office equipment, and so forth, all of which are called *capital*—are owned by those who in turn hire others to do the day-to-day work of the firm. In a purely capitalistic economy, economic FREEDOM dominates. The government is not expected to regulate the economy or to provide for any individual's economic security or hospital care. These services are to be obtained by individuals acting in their own economic SELF-INTEREST.

Many claim that a capitalistic economy is the only way to ensure efficiency and genuine freedom. Others argue that a capitalistic system is immoral (*see* IMMORALITY): It is unable to protect people from EXPLOITATION; it cannot protect the environment, and it does not ensure that all people have the basic goods needed to live a fulfilling life. Furthermore, an unregulated capitalistic system can suffer from economic depressions and recessions—involving serious unemployment and loss of production—that can only be effectively avoided, at least in the most severe cases, by public regulation of the economy.

There are few, if any, pure capitalistic systems in the world today. All advanced economies have a central government that exerts significant influence on the economy; public management of commerce thus coexists with private ownership and competition.

CARDINAL SINS   The sins of PRIDE, covetousness, LUST, ENVY, GLUTTONY, anger, and sloth; also known as the *seven deadly sins*.

The cardinal sins, and their opposites, the CARDINAL VIRTUES, were grouped together in the form we know today by Christian ethicists (*see* CHRISTIAN ETHICS) early in the Middle Ages and soon became important themes in religion (*see* RELIGION AND MORALITY) and the arts. The cardinal sins were not necessarily the most heinous or EVIL of transgressions. Rather, they were believed to be especially capable of leading one into further SIN.

CARDINAL VIRTUES   The virtues of PRUDENCE, JUSTICE, TEMPERANCE, and COURAGE (sometimes also known as *fortitude*).

In ancient and medieval philosophy, all "natural" virtues (*see* VIRTUE) were classified under these four groups. In medieval CHRISTIAN ETHICS, the cardinal virtues were complemented by the CARDINAL SINS and the three "religious" virtues of FAITH, CHARITY, and HOPE. Together, these 14 virtues and sins (*see* SIN) were thought to encompass the full range of human behavior. The cardinal virtues are supposed to be mutually supportive so that if a person has one of them, he or she is likely to have the others. Similarly, failure to display one can lead to failure to display the other virtues.

CARE   A VIRTUE that involves a selfless (*see* SELFLESSNESS) concern for others.

A caring person is typically kind and considerate. A standard example of care is the relationship between a husband and wife. In a caring relationship, both spouses are actively concerned with each other's WELFARE.

Some philosophers have seen care as the foundation of proper moral behavior (MORALITY). This position is called an ethic of care. An ethic of care may be understood as distinct from an ethic of JUSTICE, which is based on rules such as "Do not lie" and principles such as "Promote happiness." People who embrace an ethic of care feel that the view of morality as governed by rules and principles is too impersonal. They argue that morality can and should involve immediate responses based on concern and LOVE. Carol GILLIGAN, for example, describes an ethic of care based on attachment to others and the desire to preserve relationships with them. She contrasts the responsibilities (*see* RESPONSIBILITY) that arise from caring relationships with obligations (*see* OBLIGATION) based on individual RIGHTS and IMPARTIALITY toward others.

Those who oppose an ethic of care argue that an emphasis on care over rules can lead us to do immoral things (*see* IMMORALITY). For example, care for another might lead us to break a moral rule, as when a parent lies to help a child overcome an embarrassing moment. Proponents of an ethic of justice argue that the only kind of care that is morally proper occurs when moral rules and principles are also obeyed.

CASTE   A hereditary class within the fivefold system of social organization in India, particularly of the labor force.

The caste system relies on both tradition (*see* CUSTOMS) and religious AUTHORITY. While it is viewed as morally (*see* MORALITY) unfair by many people, it has enabled India to be surpassed only by China as the world's oldest continuous society. The caste system is rigid—it is no more possible to change one's caste in India than it is to change one's nationality or ethnicity. Belief (*see* FAITH) in reincarnation is essential to the working of the caste system. Caste can be changed only through rebirth; one moves up the scale by fulfilling caste duty (*see* DHARMA) and down by failing to do so.

The highest, most prestigious and privileged caste is that of the Brahmins. While the word *Brahmin* is related to both *Brahman*, the Ultimate in Hinduism, and *Brahma*, the creator GOD in Hinduism, it must not be confused with these similar terms. Traditionally, Brahmins have been responsible for both religion and education in Indian society. In fact, until modern times education in India was almost exclusively religious.

Kshatriyas form the second caste, which engages in government and defense. The third caste is the Vaishyas, who own land, create goods, and manage stores. They are viewed as equal in status to scientists, technicians, businesspeople, and merchants. Laborers compose the fourth caste, known as Shudras. They are similar in status to masons, carpenters, and electricians.

Until the twentieth century, there was a group falling outside the caste structure known as outcasts or untouchables. They were considered unclean and not to be touched, because physical contact was believed to pollute the traditionally pure higher caste Hindus. The only jobs available to the untouchables were those involving work with human waste, decaying matter, and dead animals. In short, they were expected to perform work that the higher castes regarded as too menial or unclean to do themselves. The untouchables were butchers, tanners, and sanitation workers. Mohandas Karamchand GANDHI championed the RIGHTS of the untouchables, renaming them Harihans, "Children of God." His efforts have helped to improve their position in Indian society.

During the latter half of the twentieth century, the Indian government has attempted to rectify some of the inequities inherent in the caste system. Other things being equal, lower-caste persons are given preference over higher-caste persons in matters of government employment and education. Although not identical in practice, this attempt to mitigate the effects of the caste system might be compared to AFFIRMATIVE ACTION in the United States.

While the rigidity and restriction of the caste system is repugnant from a Western moral perspective, the central principle that governs movement up or down the caste scale—fulfillment of duty—is universally acknowledged: one's position in life improves to the extent that one does the best one can within a given situation, whatever it may be, and that one's situation worsens when one fails to do so. *See also* HINDU ETHICS.

CASUISTRY   A moral theory (*see* MORAL SENSE THEORIES) outlining the resolution of moral problems (*see* DILEMMA) by the comparison of similar cases.

Casuists believe that we should resolve the ethical questions (*see* ETHICS) of a particular moral problem by considering different but related cases that involve greater complexity. The goal is to identify the relevant similarities and differences among cases in order to determine the proper moral rule (*see* RULES) to apply to a given problem. Casuists start with a simple MAXIM or rule, called, a dictum. A dictum might be a rule such as "Do not lie" or "Obey your parents." Next, they present a paradigm case, a clear example of a situation in which the maxim should be followed. Then the casuist changes the case little by little to consider whether the maxim still holds. In this way casuists can refine the rules or principles that best apply to the moral problem at hand. Casuistry has been traditionally associated with religious traditions (*see* RELIGION AND MORALITY). Today casuistry has been revived in the field of MEDICAL ETHICS where the consideration of relevantly similar cases may help determine, for example, when life support should and should not be continued.

Proponents of casuistry hold it to be a good way to approach moral problems because it actively seeks to account for the subtleties of moral issues. Those who are skeptical, however, challenge the validity of the maxims upon which casuistry rests. They ask: Where do we get the original maxims? Who is making the judgments (*see* JUDGMENT)? How do we know that the people who established the method of casuistry were morally wise (*see* MORAL EXEMPLAR)? Reasoning (*see* REASON) from one case to a similar one may also yield misleading results. For example, a lie to defend one's life may be thought to be proper. So, a lie to defend one's honor might seem proper to those who hold honor to be as dear as life. Little by little, many lies may begin to seem appropriate. This type of reasoning by small doses, sometimes called a SLIPPERY SLOPE, fuels skeptics' concerns.

CATEGORICAL IMPERATIVE   In the philosophy of Immanuel KANT, the moral LAW that is both an end in itself (*see* ENDS/MEANS) and a necessary action for each person.

A categorical imperative is a universal moral principle (*see* PRINCIPLES) that is dictated by REASON. To term it *categorical* means that the law is not subject to contingencies or exceptions, while to term it an *imperative* means that we must, by the very fact of being rational (*see* RATIONALITY), obey the directive. A categorical imperative directs us to ACT so that the MAXIM of our actions could be raised to a universal law. This means that one's actions should be able to be undertaken by everyone without resulting in any contradictions. For example, Kant argued that suicide is an immoral act because the integrity of moral life cannot be maintained if everyone chooses suicide. Categorical imperatives must also be ends in themselves. This claim means that a categorical imperative always directs us to act with ultimate respect for absolute VALUE (*see* ABSOLUTES). For example, Kant directs us to act in such a way that we never use ourselves or any other person as a means to an end; rather, we must always respect each person's inherent human DIGNITY and worth.

Those who subscribe to RELATIVISM oppose categorical imperatives, arguing that moral decisions (*see* JUDGMENT) should take into account the particulars of a given situation rather than attempting to provide absolute RULES for all situations. Those who adhere to CONSEQUENTIALISM argue that actions are moral to the extent that they produce moral outcomes, not to the extent that they can become universal.

CATHERINE OF SIENA (*c.* 1347–1380)   An Italian nun of the order of San Domenico, a mystic (*see* MYSTICISM), and one of the great philosophers of the fourteenth century.

It is not known at what age Catherine became a nun. She did not enter a convent but instead became a recluse, living in her parents' home. She left only to travel to cities throughout Italy and France to preach sermons that later were published as *Orazioni* (Sermons).

In *Orazioni,* Catherine taught religious HUMANISM and the importance of charitable acts (*see* ACT) as ways of reducing class differences and helping the poor. Central to her ETHICS was the view that individuals must recognize their moral RESPONSIBILITY to CARE for their neighbors. Wealth brought a special moral responsibility to provide for the poor (*see* POVERTY). She taught that everyone had a MORAL IMPERATIVE to LOVE their neighbors and give service to the COMMUNITY by renouncing worldly goods and donating personal assets for the care and support of those who lived in poverty. The poor could meet their duties (*see* OBLIGATION) toward the community by performing community service. In Catherine's view, CHARITY was the foundation for social JUSTICE, as well as for personal virtues (*see* VIRTUE) such as patience, COURAGE, and HUMILITY.

CENSORSHIP   Restricting access to material considered objectionable. Any form of communication may be subject to censorship, including public speech, conversation, books, art, music, and motion pictures.

Censorship is often considered acceptable when children are denied access to material that adults believe could HARM them, but differences of opinion arise about what material adults should be allowed to access. Which ideas are subject to censorship differs widely between countries.

Most governments censor material that many of their citizens consider obscene. Depending on the culture, OBSCENITY may include anything depicting nudity or sexual situations, ranging from CONTRACEPTION to PORNOGRAPHY; material that is libelous or blasphemous (*see* BLASPHEMY); and material that is deemed to advocate LIFESTYLES that many people consider objectionable, commonly including HOMOSEXUALITY. Other times, governments deem it necessary to ban the dissemination of material that it believes will compromise "national security," including anything from secret documents to material that is simply critical of a government or established religion.

In the United States, the use of profanity and sexually explicit material is prohibited (*see* PROHIBITION) in media accessible to the general public, like radio and television. However, these prohibitions are rarely enforced, primarily because media organizations are aware of what they can and cannot broadcast; they therefore censor themselves to avoid the possibility of a criminal penalty (*see* CRIME). On the other hand, media that is not as accessible to the general public, such as motion pictures, are allowed more latitude because it is easier to limit access to this material to those who specifically choose to access it.

Some philosophers have argued that censorship is morally WRONG because it creates an environment in which ideas cannot compete for attention. As a result, we may fail to discover the TRUTH because unpopular or offensive ideas are not necessarily false. For example, the sixteenth-century astronomer Galileo discovered that Earth was not at the center of the universe; instead, it revolves around the sun. He was persecuted and ordered to retract this claim because his work was thought to undermine the AUTHORITY of the church by proving that one of the church's teachings was false.

Some ethicists (*see* ETHICS) argue that censorship is justified (*see* JUSTIFICATION) when used to discourage DISCRIMINATION or PREJUDICE, even when the statements themselves are true. For example, the statement "African Americans commit crimes," is true because people of all ethnic groups commit crimes. Because only African Americans are mentioned, however, this could lead others to the false conclusion that *only* African Americans commit crimes, and this may in turn breed intolerance.

Although often banned in other countries, intolerant speech is generally protected in the United States because of the First Amendment to the Constitution (*see* BILL OF RIGHTS), which guarantees FREEDOM of speech. Many supporters of the First Amendment argue that freedom of speech is only worthwhile if unpopular speech is protected. This is because popular speech is unlikely to be censored and therefore, is unlikely to need constitutional protection. Another common justification for freedom of speech is that speech needs to be public so that others can point out the flaws in objectionable arguments.

CHARACTER   The totality of a person's disposition or personality.

Character is formed by relatively fixed HABITS of thought and action (*see* ACT), including beliefs (*see* FAITH), attitudes, preferences, VALUES, and behavior. For example, a person who regularly lies, cheats (*see* CHEATING), and swindles may be said to have a dishonest character. In contrast, someone who is basically honest (*see* HONESTY) but who occasionally tells a white lie will not typically be condemned as dishonest. Thus, the concept of character includes consistent habits of speech and action: a single bad action does not necessitate a wicked (*see* WICKEDNESS) character.

Ancient philosophy made character, rather than INTENTION or action, the focus of moral evaluation. According to ARISTOTLE, character was a disposition or set of habits that one acquired through training. Thus, a person with a virtuous character performs GOOD deeds, while a person with a vicious character performs EVIL deeds. This view was dominant until the modern era, when the focus of attention shifted from character to intention (*see* MENS REA) and action. Immanuel KANT believed, for instance, that a person's worth is measured by his or her intentions only. The twentieth century has seen a resurgence in Aristotelian ETHICS and a consequent rediscovery of the concept of character. *See also* VIRTUE ETHICS.

CHARITY An act done out of goodwill that unselfishly seeks to improve the welfare of others.

The term *charity* derives from *caritas,* the Latin word for Christian LOVE. Charitable acts are acts of ALTRUISM or BENEVOLENCE. Charity might also be thought of as a disposition that manifests itself in kindly social deeds. Charity may involve both giving aid or benefit to someone in need or refraining from harming an individual. A charitable attitude is one that holds human beings in high regard and seeks to view them in the best light. This attitude also entails being quick to forgive when injured.

Charity should be distinguished from friendliness or good nature. Charity is not simply being nice or sympathetic to people in need but also acting for their good. A charitable act is aimed not only at relieving suffering but, more important, at promoting the best interest of the individual. Therefore, a charitable act may actually seem unsympathetic. Charitable acts seek to achieve JUSTICE, and therefore do not show favoritism. An act of charity may be public, or it may be anonymous. Because the nature of charity is unselfishness and not a desire for recognition, some hold that an act of charity is more virtuous if the benefactor remains anonymous than if the benefactor is known.

Charity is sometimes thought to be an OBLIGATION and sometimes not. Sometimes acts of charity are distinguished from duties because they are said to be "above and beyond" the call of duty (*see* SUPEREROGATION). In traditional CHRISTIAN ETHICS, acts of charity are included in COUNSELS OF PERFECTIONS: things a person can do to become perfect, or more nearly perfect, but not required by duty. Where charity is regarded as a duty, it appears to be an imperfect duty (see PERFECT/IMPERFECT DUTIES), for it is not fully determinate in specifying exactly what it requires. If one has a duty to give to the poor, for example, there is no way of telling exactly when this duty has been satisfied, for it does not tell how much we should give, how often, or to whom.

CHEATING Gaining an unfair advantage as a result of deceitful or dishonest conduct.

Cheating is generally considered WRONG because a cheater gains her or his advantage from the HONESTY of the vast majority of people. If everyone cheated, then there would be less advantage associated with cheating. For example, a cheater may win a cross-country race because she or he takes a short cut that is not allowed. But if everyone takes the short cut, then the fastest runner will still win.

There are disadvantages to cheating as well. In the case of the runners, those who cheat are also cheating *themselves.* They are getting less exercise, failing to improve their abilities, and deceiving other people. Therefore, even if cheating does not provide a comparative advantage in relation to one's peers, it is still taking an easy route to success, and the result of this is that there is less incentive to do one's best. Those who come to rely on cheating to pass math tests, for example, are unlikely to see the point of studying and may soon find that they have no knowledge of the subject at all. On the other hand, those who struggle to learn the material and do their homework will almost certainly end up much more accomplished mathematicians, even if their final grades are not as good as the cheaters'. Honest people will be more likely to succeed on their own MERIT later on if cheating becomes more difficult, such as in a university entrance exam. Cheating, therefore, may simply provide an excuse to be lazy. Because most activities are designed to be done in a certain way for a specific reason, cheating often defeats the purpose of undertaking that activity in the first place. *See also* FAIRNESS.

CHILD ABUSE   Cruel and intentional (*see* INTENTION) mistreatment of a child by an adult.

Virtually no one disagrees with the principle (*see* PRINCIPLES) that children should be protected from abuse, but exactly what constitutes abuse and how children are best protected from it are matters of considerable debate.

Forms of child abuse generally fall into four categories: physical neglect (*see* NEGLIGENCE), which includes failure to provide adequate clothing, food, and medical treatment; physical abuse, which may include beatings and other infliction of pain; emotional mistreatment, which includes verbal abuse and the failure to support a child emotionally; and SEXUAL ABUSE, which is any form of sexual contact between an adult and a child.

Child abuse is rarely committed by strangers. Instead, people in positions of RESPONSIBILITY and trust (*see* TRUSTWORTHI- NESS), such as scoutmasters, babysitters, priests, or close relatives, and, in the majority of cases, the parents and primary caregivers themselves are often to blame. Child abusers are not usually people who hate children; rather, their actions (*see* ACT) are more often than not triggered by a range of personal problems and, in some cases, are themselves victims of child abuse.

Child abuse can occur because a caregiver is a heavy user of alcohol or other drugs, is mentally ill and fails to understand the needs of her or his children, or has little outside support and cannot cope with the responsibilities of child rearing. In some instances, people who are guilty of neglect may simply not have enough money to pay for an adequate level of care.

In such cases, making additional resources and assistance available to the parent and child can provide the support to overcome the problems they are facing. Such assistance might take the form of emotional support, financial assistance, employment, and child care or education in child-care skills.

Cases of sexual abuse do not necessarily follow the same pattern as other forms of abuse and tend to be distributed far more evenly across all groups and classes in society. Sexual abusers are often men who otherwise appear to be model citizens. Because child sexual abuse tends to be far less closely tied to identifiable disadvantage and mental illness than other forms of abuse, society sees sexual abuse as a serious and reprehensible problem that warrants harsh punishment.

What exactly constitutes abuse is the subject of much debate. For example, parents in many households use spanking and other forms of corporal punishment to discipline children; yet many people have begun to see this as a form of abuse. In this case and others, what is defined as abuse by some is also GOOD and proper according to the beliefs (*see* FAITH, MORALS) and religions (*see* RELIGION AND MORALITY) of others.

Another area of significant ethical (*see* ETHICS) debate is the question of what to do when it is suspected that child abuse may have occurred or is occurring. Parental RIGHTS advocates believe that a child should stay with his or her biological parents whenever possible, unless evidence of abuse is overwhelming. They believe that the biological family unit is the most healthy environment available for children. Because definitions of abuse vary, many believe parents are best qualified to decide what is best for their children. It has also been argued that removing children from families is a traumatic experience for everyone and may create more problems than it solves.

CHILDREN'S RIGHTS advocates counter that many children will suffer from unnecessary abuse if child protection agencies are too reluctant to act on behalf of children at RISK. Furthermore, they suggest that parents' rights are simply a way of protecting extreme and socially unacceptable child-rearing practices. Because children are often at the mercy of their parents, childrens' rights activists argue that governments have an OBLIGATION to set and enforce standards that specify what parental behavior is appropriate.

CHILDREN'S RIGHTS The minimum standards of treatment and respect to which all children are entitled.

Historically, the RIGHTS of children have not been significantly studied by ethicists (*see* ETHICS). Children were traditionally seen as family resources under the AUTHORITY of the leader of the household, whose RESPONSIBILITY it was to determine what rights and duties were appropriate. In general, what was best for the child was best for the family. Children pulled their own weight and contributed to the family profession in whatever way they could.

During the industrial revolution, however, people began to work separately from their families, and children often ended up working in factories, frequently in brutal and dangerous conditions. This lead eventually to a public outcry and resulted in various laws specifying the minimum age at which children could work. In the United States, the Fair Labor Standards Act, passed in 1938, specified a minimum working age of 14. Almost all countries now have some regulation in place stating the minimum age at which children can work, although the degree of enforcement varies.

During the twentieth century, the movement toward guaranteeing children certain rights and protections accelerated, and various laws were passed to guarantee children's right to an education, good health, and FREEDOM from abuse. In 1989, the United Nations passed the international Convention on the Rights of the Child. The convention specifies that all ratifying nations (nations that agree to be bound by it) agree that children and youths under 18 share many rights with adults, as well as rights unique to them. Broadly speaking the convention emphasizes that in all cases, any government action involving children must be in the child's best interests. It states that children are entitled to be free from DISCRIMINATION because of arbitrary characteristics such as their race, language, sex, national origin, disability, and the behavior and characteristics of their parents. It states that governments have the responsibility to provide children with "the highest attainable standard" of health and nutrition and with free elementary level education. Possibly most significantly, however, it specifies that children have a right to be heard and to be consulted in decisions that affect them.

By 1996, only two nations—the United States and Somalia—had not ratified the convention. The United States has refused to accept several provisions of the convention, including Article 37, which states in part that those under 18 "shall be subjected to . . . neither CAPITAL PUNISHMENT nor life imprisonment without possibility of release." There appears to be little likelihood that the United States will ratify the convention in the near future, and in the case of capital punishment, the United States continues to execute and sentence to death people who were younger than 18 at the time of their CRIME.

Questions regarding children's rights sometimes conflict with the common belief that parents should be the ones to determine what is best for their children. What one parent sees as CHILD ABUSE may simply be discipline to another. Disciplining children by spanking, for example, is an illegal form of child abuse in some European nations, but is considered entirely appropriate in many other parts of the world. This can lead to a conflict between advocates of children's rights and parent's rights advocates, who believe that parents are entitled to a high degree of discretion in the way they choose to raise their children, free from government interference. *See also* HUMAN RIGHTS.

CHOICE   *See* FREEDOM.

CHRISTIAN ETHICS   The moral PRINCIPLES and RULES espoused in the Christian religion (*see* RELIGION AND MORALITY).

Christian ETHICS begin with and repeatedly return to the MORALITY taught and exemplified by JESUS Christ. Because most Christians regard Jesus as the son of GOD, as God in human form, the morality he taught and lived is believed to derive from God.

This morality insists on a fundamental transformation of the inner person in the heart, rather than mere conformity to an objective standard of behavior. For example, simply to abstain from adultery is insufficient; one must not even lust after another person. Such a high standard of morality is only possible through an empowering that comes from God. At the same time, there must also be a resolute participation in a PSYCHOSPIRITUAL DISCIPLINE, which may extend throughout one's entire lifetime.

Because the apostle Paul gave theological and ethical shape to the spiritual experience exemplified in the teaching and actions of Jesus, he is sometimes regarded as the second founder of Christianity. He set forth the controlling objective of Christian ethics in his letter to the church at Rome: "Do not be conformed to this world, but be transformed by the renewing of your minds, so that you may discern what is the will of God—what is GOOD and acceptable and perfect" (Romans 12:2). Paul's understanding of Christian morality was influenced by three factors: (1) the high ideal (*see* IDEALS) of Jesus's exemplary life and moral teaching (*see* MORAL EXEMPLAR), (2) Paul's perception of the contrast between the Jewish law (*see* JEWISH ETHICS) and Jesus's moral demand, and (3) his own inability—despite great effort—to live this thoroughly moral life ("I do not do the good I want, but the EVIL I do not want is what I

do."—Romans 7:19). Because of Paul's inability to emulate the high standards he believed Jesus demanded, he came to believe that humans are born in a fallen state (akin to Adam and Eve after they sinned and were expelled from the Garden of Eden, theologically known as original SIN). He believed that this inherent tendency to sin can be countered only through a cleansing and empowering that is freely granted by God. Thus Paul and Christian ethical systems, generally, came to hold that a morally upright or sinless life is possible only through divine gift (grace) *and* personal effort (works).

All ethical systems of Christianity recognize the BIBLE as the primary literary source for moral reasoning. However, Christian ethicists generally concede that the Bible, while full of moral insights and warnings, does not contain a single, coherent ethical system. Consequently, Christian ethicists vary greatly in their views of how the Bible is actually to be used in forming a coherent ethical system. In addition to drawing from the Bible, the ethicists of the three major traditions (*see* CUSTOMS) of Christianity— Eastern Orthodoxy, Roman Catholicism, and Protestantism—typically draw from their respective church traditions and teachings in the course of their moral reasoning.

The most distinctive feature of Eastern Orthodox ethics lies in its emphasis on spirituality. The goal of both morality and spirituality is to become like God by means of ASCETICISM and prayer. This aspiration derives in part from Psalms 82:6—"You are gods, children of the Most High." This does not mean that humans have become equal (*see* EQUALITY) to God. A distinction is always maintained between humans who are created in the image and likeness of God on one hand, and the Uncreated God on the other. Because humans are created in the *image* of God, they possess the moral capacities that are essential to becoming like God, namely, free will (*see* FREEDOM), intellect, JUDGMENT, and VIRTUE. Because they are created in the *likeness* of God, they have the potential to become like God.

Ethical reflection in the Roman Catholic Church is known as moral theology. Its principal features are NATURAL LAW, the church, and meditation. Natural law governs human actions. These laws are discernable by means of reason, which then is able to direct human action in morally responsible ways. In actual practice, Catholic moral theology has tended to emphasize natural law more than scripture in formulating ethical systems. The role of the church in moral guidance centers on the pope and the bishops, who possess a special AUTHORITY to set moral standards, prohibiting, for example, the use of contraception. The third feature, meditation, is based on the joining of such theological categories as FAITH and REASON, faith and works, grace and nature divine and human, and so on. Thus the joining of tradition and scripture means that the authorities of the church rule on how the Bible should be interpreted by members. Also, the divine commandments mediate the virtues, which in turn mediate LOVE.

Protestantism emphasizes the primacy of scripture and, in sharp contrast to the Roman Catholic position, the RIGHT of individual Christians to interpret the Bible as they see fit. This freedom enjoyed by Protestants is a reflection of the widespread Protestant emphasis on the freedom that God exercises, acting in and through history as he deems fit. The effect of these liberal views (*see* LIBERALISM)—the emphasis on both divine and human freedom— is great diversity and PLURALISM within Protestantism. At one extreme are fundamentalist Protestants who believe that God revealed in the Bible specific ethical rules and requirements that apply throughout time and across cultures, and which must be obeyed (*see* OBEDIENCE) under all conditions. To fail to do so is to commit mortal sin and be subject to eternal damnation. In contrast to the fundamentalist stance is a twentieth-century approach that departs from

identifying specific sins (such as greed, hatred, stealing, and lying); instead it focuses on the unique conditions of each concrete situation in which a position or action is required. For example, if an innocent person's life is threatened, one is entirely justified in lying to protect that person's life. Known as contextual or SITUATIONAL ETHICS, this approach calls for the creative application of love in each changing circumstance. No matter what the particulars of a situation may be, the ethical requirement is to respond according to the demands of love. Despite its apparent focus on outer conditions, situational ethics requires an inwardness informed by the same spirit that dominated the life of Jesus—selfless, unconditional love.

CHUN-TZU Literally, "duke's son"; the ideal person in Confucianism (pronounced "june-tsu").

By perfecting one's moral qualities, one becomes a *chun-tzu,* or truly noble person. Confucius declared: "For the gentleman, MORALITY is supreme" (*Analects* 17:23). The *chun-tzu* embodies a spirit of BENEVOLENCE, a genuine LOVE for humanity (*see* JEN), and expresses it properly (*see* LI).

Confucius envisioned government under the moral influence and guidance of the *chun-tzu,* one who would constantly uphold the interests of the populace rather than simply those of the ruling authorities. *See also* CONFUCIAN ETHICS.

CITIZENSHIP The status of having RIGHTS and obligations (*see* OBLIGATION) as a member of a nation.

In most cases, a person automatically becomes a citizen of the country in which she or he was born. People may also become citizens of a country by applying for citizenship and fulfilling a number of often demanding requirements.

Citizenship entitles one to special rights and benefits not available to noncitizens. For example, citizens usually have the right to live in their country of citizenship, to be protected by that country's military and legal systems, and in democracies (*see* DEMOCRACY) vote and participate in that country's political process. In return for these benefits, citizens are expected to assume a number of responsibilities (*see* RESPONSIBILITY) and obligations. In the United States, citizens are expected to pledge allegiance to their country and to serve in the military or on a jury when called to do so.

Some ethicists (*see* ETHICS), such as ARISTOTLE and Immanuel KANT, have argued that only individuals, who are willing and able to participate in the political process should be entitled to citizenship. Others have argued that it is important to educate people on the rights and responsibilities of citizenship in civics classes so that citizens not only appreciate the responsibilities of citizenship but also know how to fully take advantage of its benefits. This viewpoint is not always put into action, however, as an educated and demanding citizenry is something that many governments are reluctant to encourage.

CIVIL DISOBEDIENCE

The ACT of protesting against laws (*see* LAW) and social arrangements by deliberately disobeying laws or disrupting patterns of ordinary social life through nonviolent means.

Many people believe that it is morally correct to resist an unjust law, and in essence, this is the primary purpose of civil disobedience. Examples of civil disobedience include refusing to serve in the military (*see* CONSCIENTIOUS OBJECTION), refusing to pay taxes, blocking traffic, or illegally occupying private or government property as a form of protest.

In the twentieth century, civil disobedience has often been used as a strategy for influencing public opinion, which in turn often forces a government to choose between enforcing an unpopular law and yielding to popular demand. Civil disobedience is often thought of as a morally superior form of protest because it is nonviolent. Indeed, those who use civil disobedience as a tactic often seek to establish their own moral worthiness by contrasting their actions with those of a government that uses VIOLENCE to suppress demonstrations. Prominent CIVIL RIGHTS leaders Martin Luther KING and Mohandas Karamchand GANDHI were both passionate advocates but sparing users of the tactic of civil disobedience.

Possibly the biggest ethical DILEMMA facing advocates of civil disobedience is the risk that by resisting some laws, they may encourage others to resist different laws, or even to commit acts of CRIME, terrorism, and violence in the name of the cause. In general, such behavior is not in the interest of protestors, who are simply asking for changes to the system, not the system's complete elimination. Advocates of nonviolent protest therefore often argue that even though it is one's moral OBLIGATION to resist an unjust law, it is also important to accept one's punishment and the legal consequences of one's actions. This demonstrates support for the system itself and a desire to work within it.

CIVIL RIGHTS

The benefits and freedoms, often guaranteed by LAW, that belong to citizens of a particular country by virtue of their citizenship.

Civil RIGHTS generally protect civil liberties such as EQUALITY under the law, FREEDOM of expression, freedom of movement, the right to vote, and the right to participate in the political process. In the United States, these rights are guaranteed by the Constitution, the BILL OF RIGHTS, and several constitutional amendments.

More controversially, some argue that civil rights should also include economic and social rights, such as the right to a job, the right to a generous minimum wage, and the right to become a member of certain social organizations. For example, some believe that restricting women's access to exclusive male-only clubs is a violation of women's civil rights because membership in such clubs is often an important way to make contacts and meet influential people.

Civil rights exist to prevent DISCRIMINA-TION, and therefore those who most publicly demand civil rights protection are members of groups who feel that they are discriminated against. In the United States, minorities, women, homosexuals, and the disabled have all argued for civil rights protection, with various degrees of success. This has resulted in the passage of laws such as the Civil Rights Act of 1964, which specifically prohibits discrimination on the basis of race (*see* RACISM), and the Disibility Act of 1990.

It is important to note, however, that civil rights alone do not guarantee equality, although they may require the elimination of preferential treatment. In the 1970s, for example, it was proposed that the United States Constitution be amended to ban discrimination on the basis of sex. This proposal, known as the Equal Rights Amendment (ERA), was eventually defeated, partially because it was argued that women would lose valuable protections, such as the right to be exempted from compulsory military service.

In the United States, civil rights supporters organized nonviolent protest beginning in the late 1950s in order to contest the racial segregation in the southern states. This movement became known as the Civil Rights Movement. The Civil Rights Movement was sparked in Montgomery, Alabama, when Rosa Parks, a black woman, was arrested after she took a seat on the "whites-only" section of a bus and refused to move. Local minister Martin Luther KING, Jr., led the transformation of this protest into an effective political resistance movement. Through the 1960s the Civil Rights Movement remained a united and peaceful movement that brought together many people in the black community, students, and other supporters from the white community. In 1966, however, many younger members became frustrated with the slow rate of

change and pressed for more radical or militant actions. When King was assassinated in 1968 by James Earl Ray the Civil Rights Movement as an organized, nonviolent group was virtually ended.

CLASS STRUGGLE   Conflict between different economic classes for the fair distribution of social goods.

The principle of class struggle is most clearly articulated in the philosophy of Karl MARX. Marx holds that the most important feature of any society is its economic classes and their relationship to one another. Classes are defined by the relationship of the members in a class to the means of production in a society. For example, in a capitalist society, capitalists own the means of production, and the workers own their work capacity. If you work for an electric company, for example, you do not own the electricity or the means for producing the electricity. Your pay is drawn by exchanging the hours you work for a salary.

Each class tries to secure the best economic benefits for itself. This results in a struggle over scarce goods or over fair wages to buy plentiful goods. In Marx's theory, class struggles are won only through revolution, as any class is reluctant to give up any part of its power peacefully. *See also* COMMUNISM.

CODE   A body of LAW; a system of PRINCIPLES or RULES.

In ETHICS, individuals, groups, organizations, and even entire societies may be said to have codes of behavior—sets of rules by which they live their lives or by which they *think* they should live their lives. Such rules are often explicitly stated, as in a military CODE OF HONOR or a professional code of ethics for physicians or lawyers. In studying cultures, anthropologists try to discover the codes societies live by or profess. Individuals develop their own codes by accepting the rules of a group or society and then modifying them according to their own REASON and JUDGMENT.

A moral code (*see* MORALS) is often thought to be different from other types of codes in that it is considered superior to, or takes priority over, all other considerations. For this reason, a moral code may be said to express a person's most important beliefs or the fundamental VALUES of a group or society. Moral codes are usually intersubjective (*see* INTERSUBJECTIVITY) because they are shared by a number of different people and bind them together in a system of beliefs. People also tend to think of their codes as being grounded in reality, expressing their views about HUMAN NATURE. People do not always live up to or obey the codes they express, but they usually use them to judge the moral behavior of themselves and others.

CODE OF HONOR

Special moral obligations (*see* OBLIGATION) that exist among members of a group, society, or institution.

A CODE of honor often exists in professions, disciplines, and guilds. For example, an army may have a special code requiring that soldiers never leave the dead on the battlefield. In some colleges, a code of honor prohibits students from cheating and requires them to report others who cheat. The goal of a code of honor that prohibits actions such as cheating, stealing, lying, or disloyalty is to create a moral COMMUNITY. In these cases, a code of honor attempts to give further incentive to act morally or to help others. The HIPPOCRATIC OATH, for example, sets an ethical standard for the medical profession.

Some societies have unwritten codes of honor concerning keeping secrets or promises and responding violently to personal insults. Criminal organizations or gangs may have codes that require unlawful actions ranging from conspiracy to protect criminal behavior to murder. In these cases, the code is intended to protect the honor or status of the organization and its members. Codes of honor that transgress ordinary moral RESPONSIBILITY are often thought to be immoral (*see* IMMORALITY).

COERCION

The ACT of forcing someone against his or her WILL; the use of excessive force or pressure on others.

Coercion is most often morally improper. For example, it is considered immoral to coerce another into having sexual intercourse or into signing a contract. Coercion in these instances is considered WRONG because it denies persons the FREEDOM to make choices about their own behavior and to act as free moral agents (*see* MORAL AGENCY). Sometimes coercion is thought to be morally acceptable, as when a parent coerces a young child to behave (*see* PATERNALISM) or when a government forces someone to pay child support.

Often coercion is apparent; a person knows that he or she is coercing or being coerced, as in the case of blackmail. But sometimes coercion can be difficult to detect. For example, a person may join a religious cult and be coerced by subtle types of mind control. Children, who are often ignorant of the group dynamics of peer pressure, may be coerced by friends into activities such as taking drugs. In these and similar cases; it may sometimes be difficult to detect where willing consent begins and coercion ends.

Sometimes, circumstances rather than a person seem to force someone to take a course of action. When a person takes a job out of financial desperation, for example, some people would say that the person was coerced into taking the job. However, the use of the term *coercion* is most properly applied only to the moral activities of human beings.

COGNITIVISM

The belief that all mental behavior is reducible to problem-solving processes.

Cognitivism rests on two claims: first, that humans are able to approach problems because of our capacity to REASON; second, that our reason is based on our ability to think symbolically. In relation to ETHICS, cognitivism suggests that ethical behavior is essentially problem-solving behavior. We begin with simple problems and gradually gain ethical skills as we graduate to more complex problems and develop an ability to match problems with patterns and RULES. Cognitivists believe that ethics can be reduced to rules. Anti-cognitivists believe that moral knowledge does not consist of more definitions. Cognitivism can be understood in opposition to theories of MORALITY based on CHARACTER, MORAL SENTIMENT, or INTUITION.

COHERENCE A method in ETHICS used to establish moral responsibilities (*see* RESPONSIBILITY) and the TRUTH or validity of moral beliefs (*see* MORAL OPINION).

Most people have a sense of RIGHT and WRONG, which includes various PRINCIPLES, RULES, and specified obligations (*see* OBLIGATION). For example, a person's moral sense might hold that harming others is wrong, that people should be allowed to live whatever style of life they find appropriate, that children have an obligation to help parents when in need, and that people should keep their agreements. If a person's moral beliefs contradict one another, we say they are incoherent. This conflict is likely to result in moral conflict (*see* DILEMMA) as the inconsistent beliefs compete with one another.

The method of coherence demands that people examine their beliefs and try to revise them when they conflict. For example, suppose a person's parents need money, and this person believes in the obligation to help your parents when they are in need. Further, suppose that the reason the parents need money is because they ceased showing up for work and were fired. Furthermore, assume that this is the second time in a year this has happened. If our person also believes that you should keep agreements—the agreement between an employer and employee, for example—then a moral dilemma arises. Should the person help the unemployed parents even though they reneged on their agreement to work? In order to decide what to do, it will be necessary to further refine or prioritize the competing principles.

Many ethicists hold that morality rests upon consistency. A moral person should make the same moral decisions in cases that are similar. An immoral person may make an exception of himself or herself when principle dictates an action that is inconvenient or difficult. Holding an incoherent set of moral beliefs allows one to pick and choose moral obligations. People might want to hold others responsible when they break agreements, concentrating only on one part of their system of moral beliefs. When they don't want to keep an agreement, however, they might wish to excuse themselves or construe their situations as importantly different. When a system of beliefs is coherent, then this sort of selective morality is not possible. It is for this reason that those favoring the coherence view of morality insist that we each have a moral responsibility to remove inconsistencies from our moral beliefs.

The theory of coherence can be extended beyond individual moral judgments. MORALITY, many claim, is a social tool used to help people guide their lives so that they can live well together. Morality is thus understood to be communal (*see* COMMUNITY) and is not based on the opinion of one person or another. Coherence, then, is a way to examine a social morality to decide whether or not it dictates consistent actions from all community members. If it does not, then the community must engage in an examination and revision process to achieve a coherent set of moral standards.

COLONIALISM A system in which one country controls another for the purpose of economic EXPLOITATION.

In the past, colonialism has involved explicit political rule by a dominant power, such as Great Britain or France. Some powerful European countries, for instance, took over various Asian nations and then exploited them for their tea, spices, and other valuable commodities. Today, former colonies are by and large free of such rule, which is typically considered immoral (*see* IMMORALITY) because it deprives people of self-governance. Despite this apparent advance in global MORALITY, however, colonialism continues to persist in different manifestations.

Contemporary colonialism is usually limited to the economic exploitation of poor developing countries by wealthy ones. Often, developed economics benefit by exploiting inexpensive labor in poorer countries. In some cases, large companies are able to bribe or otherwise manipulate corrupt governments into giving them extraordinary control over the lives of a developing nation's citizens and free or highly undervalued access to a country's resources.

Colonialism can result in environmental destruction and the theft of irreplaceable resources, and this in turn can make it even harder for a poor country to succeed in improving its situation in the future. Because colonialism often results in further impoverishing an already poor country, it has become an issue of significant moral concern for many ethicists (*see* ETHICS).

COMMITMENT   An agreement to carry out a course of action in the future.

A commitment, like a PROMISE, is a guarantee that one will follow, or refrain from following, a certain course of action. For example, people who marry make a commitment to take care of one another in good times and in bad and to be faithful to one another. Although they cannot know in advance what specifically this commitment will entail, they promise to always act in such a way to honor the commitment to be loyal and loving to each other.

Religious commitments are between people and a church or deity (*see* GOD). The commitment may be to model oneself after church or religious leaders, to bring others into the church, to know and obey (*see* OBEDIENCE) the doctrines of the church, to be responsive to the needs of the church and church members, and to raise one's children in accordance with religious traditions (*see* CUSTOMS). Commitments may also have a political dimension. When a person is willing to make personal sacrifices (*see* SACRIFICE) in order to promote a cause, we describe that person as committed to the cause. A person who is committed to animal rights, for example, might make the commitment to refrain from eating meat. In economic terms, commitments are promises to be responsible financially (*see* RESPONSIBILITY) within the terms of an agreement. This may be a commitment to repay a loan, to support a child or a spouse, or to pay for a product or a service. Most businesses have corporate visions that include a commitment to certain PRINCIPLES of BUSINESS ETHICS. Normally, such a vision would include a commitment to INTEGRITY and FAIRNESS within both the industry and the COMMUNITY and to overall excellence in the production of their product or performance of their service.

Commitments may be enforced through social or family ties, through religious AUTHORITY, or through LAW. The price of breaking a commitment varies. In the case of personal and social commitments the price may be a loss of reputation or the endurance of the displeasure of others. Violating a religious commitment may necessitate some penance or in extreme cases could result in dismissal from a church community. Reneging on financial commitments most often has legal ramifications that may range from a penalty or fee to imprisonment.

COMMON GOOD   The basic material, political, and social needs required so that each member of society can enjoy the maximum possibility for human fulfillment and DIGNITY.

In order to achieve the common good, civil leaders and individuals alike must seek what is good for the whole of society rather than what promotes individual or minority interests. For individual citizens, regard for the common good requires bringing private interests in line with the needs of the COMMUNITY. For civil authorities, regard for the common good requires pursuing only those objectives that are consistent with the essential elements of the common WELFARE.

More specifically, promoting the common good may mean providing employment for as many workers as possible, maintaining the balance between wages and prices, making goods and services available to as many citizens as possible, and ensuring that there are no institutionalized barriers to social mobility (*see* AFFIRMATIVE ACTION).

While some philosophers hold that all political and ethical (*see* ETHICS) arrangements should benefit all people, others point out that in fact almost every moral or political rule we can think of opposes the interest of someone in society. These philosophers challenge the notion that a common good exists and can be approximated.

COMMUNISM   A utopian (*see* UTOPIA) ideal of social EQUALITY through the common ownership and equitable distribution of property.

Communism is inherently idealistic (*see* IDEALISM) because it assumes that it is in fact possible to create a perfectly egalitarian society (*see* EGALITARIANISM) in which no one needs to hoard wealth or exploit others. In contrast, CAPITALISM, communism's main rival, is pragmatic (*see* PRAGMATISM): it assumes that an ideal egalitarian state is impossible because HUMAN NATURE is essentially selfish (*see* SELFISHNESS) and unalterable.

Communism originated during the mid-1800s in the works of Karl MARX and Friedrich Engels. Marx argued that the upper classes use their control over the "means of production," such as land, factories, and other property, to make the lower classes dependent. He believed that the lower classes have little choice but to work for the upper classes in exchange for minimal wages. Any difference between the workers' wages, the cost of production, and income from product sales is kept by the upper classes in the

form of profits—to Marx, a form of EXPLOITATION.

Worse, held Marx, often the only jobs workers can get are boring, repetitive, and unskilled. This leads to feelings of ALIENATION in workers who have no stake in the outcome of their production. For example, workers on a factory line have little incentive to care about what they are doing because what they do rarely provides much opportunity for individuality and because they rarely see the final product of their WORK. A craftsworker, on the other hand, is able to make products from start to finish and can make those products in a way that reflects her or his personality.

Marx believed that this exploitation and alienation created a CLASS STRUGGLE between the upper classes, or bourgeoisie, who were exploiting workers, and the lower classes, or proletariat, who fought back. He argued that inequities in a capitalist system would inevitably result in revolution by the discontented working class, who would then create a communist state in which the means of production was controlled jointly by all workers.

In a communist system, Marx believed, private property should be abolished because it inevitably leads to concentration of wealth in the hands of a minority, who then use the accumulated wealth to exploit workers. Marx summarized his ideal system in the phrase "From each according to one's ability, to each according to one's need."

Communism has acquired many negative connotations in the twentieth century because most, if not all, self-described communist nations have turned out to be massive failures. None of these countries ever achieved the communist ideal, and opponents of communism use this as evidence to support their contention that communism can never work. They argue that communism simply replaces one system of inequalities with another. They also believe that eliminating private property removes any motivation (*see* MOTIVE) to work because someone who works hard ends up with exactly the same lifestyle (*see* LIFESTYLES) as someone who doesn't.

COMMUNITARIANISM
A commitment to moral VALUES arising from an organized COMMUNITY life that balances the needs of individuals and the needs of the community.

Communitarianism is the belief that it is our shared experiences in a community that provide the foundation for sound ethical (*see* ETHICS) choices. This mode of thought is opposed to INDIVIDUALISM, which holds that the individual is the proper locus of moral decision making (*see* JUDGMENT) and moral identity. Opponents to communitarianism claim that communitarians compromise individual *rights* and freedoms (*see* FREEDOM). They argue that an individual is obliged only to refrain from harming (*see* HARM) a community. In this view, individuals cannot be further required to make sacrifices (*see* SACRIFICE) for a community.

By contrast, communitarians believe that we do not determine what is RIGHT or WRONG individually; instead, our sense of right and wrong is largely communal. Our MORALITY comes from our social life or community. Communitarians emphasize the need for members of a community to internalize the responsibilities (*see* RESPONSIBILITY) that come with the privileges of communal life. For example, many people believe that a trial by jury is a fundamental right in the United States, yet are reluctant to serve on one. This reluctance indicates that some citizens want the benefits of a jury system but are not willing to do their share to ensure that one exists. In a like manner, U.S. citizens have a deep sense of entitlement to community services and protection; yet voter turnout in local and national elections is shockingly low.

Communitarians hold that environmental, moral, social, and political order and improvement emerge from restoring communities. Those communities, in turn, must safeguard and enhance the future of its members while preserving constitutional rights and moral traditions.

Communitarians work peacefully within communities to enact changes in values, habits, and polices that achieve the betterment of the community as a whole. Communitarianism has influenced world leaders such as Bill Clinton in the United States, Tony Blair in the United Kingdom, and Jacques Delors in France.

COMMUNITY
A group of individuals unified by common interests in living in a particular place. The term *community* may also refer to the place itself.

A community is a group of people, often having a shared history or shared social, economical, political, or professional interests, who live in mutual OBLIGATION to one another. Community life involves both RIGHTS and duties. For example, if you live in a community that offers police protection, you have a right to that protection. At the same time, you have the duty to obey the law and most likely the duty to pay taxes to support community law enforcement.

SOCIAL CONTRACT theorists hold the agreements of a community to be the substance of ETHICS. Proponents of the social contract theory argue that MORALITY is based on social agreements that serve the best interest of those in the community. As in the example above, members of a community may agree to forgo some activities in order to reap the benefits of the larger resources of the community. For example, if someone steals from your home, you agree to call the police rather than to take revenge on that person yourself.

Certain other communities believe that duty goes beyond the basic social contract. Christian communities (*see* CHRISTIAN ETHICS), for example, follow the teaching, "You shall love your neighbor as yourself," (Leviticus 19:18). In the New Testament, Christians are commanded to love one another even as Jesus has loved them (John 13:34). This commandment includes friends and enemies alike. These directives emphasize the communal and individual nature of morality. They are the basis of a community ethic, one that is not based on biological relationship but rather the recognition of human beings in community. The emphasis is not on the individual believer but rather on a community that represents the living body of Christ as the earthly manifestation of the Kingdom of God.

Jewish ethical formulations (*see* JEWISH ETHICS) also emphasize both individual and communal obligations. Believers are reminded that not only are they responsible for their sins but that their sins may be visited upon their children. Furthermore, the goodness or justness of an individual is related directly to the goodness or justness of the community in which that individual lives. Moral responsibilities cannot be fulfilled in the context of individual relationships alone; rather, they must involve full participation in a defined community.

COMPASSION   Suffering   along   with another person.

Compassion is a deep feeling of sympathy for another person. We say people are compassionate when they are moved by the suffering or distress of others and wish to take some action to relieve that suffering or distress. For example, if you encountered a person who was indigent and felt so moved by that person's plight that you offered assistance, you would be acting out of compassion. Compassion may also be extended to animals and to the environment. In ETHICS, compassion may be the foundation of MORALITY based on MORAL SENTIMENT.

COMPETENCY   Status of a person who has developed a cluster of moral and psychological abilities (*see* MORAL PSYCHOLOGY).

For people to be considered competent to make their own decisions, they must have the following moral and psychological abilities: (1) REASON—ability to comprehend and to weigh evidence. According to LAW, children, the profoundly mentally retarded, and unconscious and comatose people lack reason and therefore are

incompetent. (2) Moral sensitivity—ability to VALUE oneself and others. The law instructs that toddlers, psychopaths, and sociopaths lack this quality and are therefore not competent. (3) Psychic intactness—realization that our thinking self is our acting (*see* ACT) self. (4) Decisional capacity—acting as we decide we should act without psychological compulsion to do otherwise. Psychotic people, such as schizophrenics and those suffering from obsessive-compulsive disorders, are not considered competent because they have neither psychic intactness nor the ability to make decisions.

Some laws treat persons as competent with respect to particular areas of decision making that were prior to the legally established age of adulthood. For example, teenagers are considered competent to drive an automobile, to hold certain jobs, and, in some instances, to seek medical care without parental consent. Usually, people who want to be considered competent prior to adulthood must prove their competence to a judge. Otherwise, competence is presumed upon reaching the legal age of adulthood.

Competency raises moral questions not only regarding the RIGHT to exercise individual liberties (*see* FREEDOM) but also regarding RESPONSIBILITY for actions. When people who are competent commit crimes, society is morally justified in punishing them. In contrast, when a crime is committed by someone who is considered mentally incompetent at the time of the crime due to a psychiatric disorder, the legal system permits that person to enter a plea of INSANITY. Thus, an insanity defense is an admission that the person committed the crime, but it is a denial that the person was responsible for the consequences. Because we do not hold incompetent people to be morally or legally responsible for their actions, we provide psychiatric treatment for them, rather than punish them for committing crimes. Similarly, if a five-year-old child shoots and kills someone, we do not put the child in jail because children are not yet competent to take moral responsibility for their actions. *See also* AUTONOMY; PUNISHMENT.

COMPUTER ETHICS The practice of maximizing the moral uses (*see* MORALITY) and minimizing the immoral uses (*see* IMMORALITY) of computers and computerization.

Computers have an enormous impact on both our personal and professional lives. Like any powerful tool, computers can be used to benefit individuals and society or to HARM them. For example, computers may increase the efficiency of a business and reduce costs to customers. In so doing, however, jobs may be eliminated or employee privacy may be compromised. As a result of computer technology, managers can now monitor employee's keystrokes, e-mail, and personal or business phone calls.

PRIVACY is an important issue in computer ETHICS. Computers can collect, sort, search, store, and retrieve large amounts of information. A great deal of personal, professional, financial, and medical information is accessible through computers. Many are concerned about the ease with which this information can be generally accessed and abused. Although some institutions seek to limit the amount and type of computerized information kept on clients, patients, or employees in order to protect privacy, the trend continues toward gathering and recording as much information as possible. Thus, when privacy is important to protect competitive interests, avoid personal embarrassment, receive loans or credit, or protect oneself from DISCRIMINATION, it cannot always be ensured.

Computer ethics also considers the matter of distribution of social goods. Computers facilitate the exchange of information all over the world. In this way, they may assist in educational, environmental, public health, and financial programs worldwide. On the other hand, computers may simply widen the gap between the "haves" and the "have nots." In order to use computers appropriately, technology, supporting technical systems, and skills are required. Areas that cannot afford to "modernize" and do not have the material and educational resources to compete in a computerized society may simply be left behind. Alternatively, cultures that wish to compete on a less intensive scale may find that they have to compromise their VALUES in order to adapt to the increased pace of work that normally accompanies computer use. For example, in order to remain competitive, businesses in Arab nations have found it necessary to permit Internet access for workers. Consequently, a great deal of material that would normally be censored in that society has become freely available.

Computer ethics is also concerned with copyright and intellectual PROPERTY matters. Computer technologies such as the World Wide Web make it possible to distribute protected text, graphic, and audio materials to millions of users in only seconds and at virtually no cost. Furthermore, the boundaries separating fair use and abuse of copyright are increasingly blurred. When material is not used for profit, the legal status of its use is increasingly complicated.

Because of the relative newness of computer technology and rapid advancement in the computing field, moral precedents may not exist for particular ethical questions. The profession is still in the process of defining the special obligations (*see* OBLIGATION) associated with the use of computers. As in other professions, computer professionals are establishing codes (*see* CODE) of ethics to guide their decisions. The Computer Ethics Institute has outlined ten precepts of the moral use of computers. According to these precepts, computer users should not use a computer to harm others, interfere with others' work, invade the privacy of others' computer files, steal or falsify data, copy proprietary software without paying the appropriate fee, or use the computer resources of others without permission and without providing compensation when requested.

The Association for Computing Machinery (ACM) has also established a code of ethics. In addition to those responsibilities listed in the code of the Computer Ethics Institute, the ACM directs members to act in their profession so as to contribute to social and human well being, avoid harm to others, act honestly, take action not to discriminate, honor property rights, honor confidentiality, and give credit for intellectual property. The ACM also addressed the ethics of maintaining technical competence, acquiring knowledge of laws pertaining to professional work, performing safety and risk analysis on computer systems and notifying all appropriate parties of the results, honoring contracts, agreements and assigned responsibilities, accepting and providing appropriate professional review, and enhancing public understanding of computers and the consequences of computing.

CONFIDENTIALITY The principle (*see* PRINCIPLES) that information is disclosed to a person on the condition that it not be repeated or otherwise disseminated to others.

Many different kinds of relationships between individuals involve the assumption that information revealed in the context of that relationship will not be disclosed to others. Expectations that information will be kept confidential arise either from personal or, more commonly, from professional relationships. Married people, for example, expect their spouses to keep private matters (*see* PRIVACY) confidential. Employers expect secretaries not to disclose business SECRETS. Patients not only expect but consider it a professional OBLIGATION of their doctors to keep their medical information confidential. Penitents hold priests to the same standard of not disclosing their sins (*see* SIN).

Confidentiality traditionally meant that information would never be divulged to any other person. This expectation is clearly unworkable in many professional settings. For example, many people may handle a patient's medical record, an employer's letter of recommendation, or a lawyer's case notes. Assistants, secretaries, and file clerks all routinely handle confidential information, and physicians and attorneys may need to consult with outside experts; so the duty of confidentiality is understood to "trickle down" to and bind everyone working at the direction of the professional.

In extreme circumstances, the duty to preserve confidentiality can be overridden by more important moral duties, as was the finding of the court in *Tarasoff v. Regents of the University of California*. In that case, a psychiatrist failed to warn Tatiana Tarasoff that a deranged former boyfriend intended to kill her. The former boyfriend had disclosed his intention to the psychiatrist during a treatment session, specifically mentioning Tarasoff's name. After leaving the office, the psychiatrist's patient killed his former girlfriend. The court ruled that the duty to protect the lives of innocent third parties overrode a doctor's duty to preserve confidences and that the doctor should have called the police and warned the intended victim.

CONFLICT OF INTEREST The clashing of a public or formal OBLIGATION with a private need or interest.

A conflict of interest makes it more difficult for a person to ACT ethically (*see* ETHICS), either due to willful NEGLIGENCE of duty for personal gain or because of a subtle BIAS. For example, suppose an engineer is hired to draw up a plan to reroute traffic flow in a certain area of the city. As it turns out, the engineer lives in one of the neighborhoods that will be affected by the type of rerouting system chosen. This situation involves a conflict of interest. The engineer may be influenced to choose a solution that benefits his or her neighborhood rather than a solution that is objectively best for the city. Even if the engineer is able to draw up an unbiased plan, the appearance of conflict remains. Because it may be difficult to tell whether a potential conflict of interest will really influence a decision, many agencies and companies demand that individuals disclose any potential conflict of interest. They also have policies against actions that can lead either to actual conflicts of interest, or to the perception of conflicts of interest. *See also* JOURNALISM ETHICS.

CONFLICT RESOLUTION   The solving of differences among individuals or groups through ethical negotiation or mediation.

Conflict is a part of nearly all cultures and cultural institutions. Conflict occurs when one person or group wants something that is incompatible with the wants or needs of another person or group. When conflict is destructive it causes confusion, harm, and even violence or war. When conflict is productive it can lead to deeper understanding and cooperation. Conflict resolution occurs when parties are able to achieve a peaceful solution. Both the solution achieved and the method used to achieve that solution give equal protection to the interests of all parties to the conflict. The solution must also respect the rights of the parties to the conflict as well as the rights of those directly affected by the conflict's settlement. Conflict resolution is used to prevent and resolve labor strikes, to negotiate contracts between institutions and employees, to settle disputes about who own the rights to scientific discoveries, and to negotiate treaties.

Common strategies for conflict resolution include negotiation, refereeing, mediation, and binding or nonbinding arbitration. Conflict resolution depends on four basic conditions. First, the parties in the conflict must want to reach a solution. Because conflict resolution relies on negotiation, it is not effective when parties are unwilling to seek a means to solving their dispute. Second, the parties must agree on exactly who will participate in the negotiations and who will represent the interests of each party. In order for the negotiations to be binding, each party must accept the fairness and authority of their representatives and of the mediators who are negotiating. Third, the parties must agree to

honor and abide by the solution their representatives reach. Finally, the parties must agree to the methods that will govern the negotiations. This includes (a) the strategy that will be used to seek a resolution to the conflict; (b) the time frame in which the resolution will be sought; (c) the place in which the negotiations will take place; (d) the respectful treatment of all parties involved in the conflict resolution process; (e) the genuine consideration of all parties' points of view regarding the conflict; and (f) the conditions, if any, under which a resolution will be imposed by an independent authority in the event that the participants cannot achieve a solution.

CONFUCIAN ETHICS   The standard of conduct for government, society, and interpersonal relations as formulated by the Chinese philosopher Confucius and his followers.

Confucius (551–479 B.C.), or K'ung Futzu, "Master K'ung," did not consider himself an innovator, but rather one who drew from the sages or wise teachers (*see* WISDOM) of the past. His system of ETHICS is founded on T'ien, "Heaven, Sky," the supreme POWER or principle (*see* PRINCIPLES) that governs cosmic processes. He promoted a hierarchic, or graded, system according to which the Way of Heaven (*see* TAO) at the top sets the standard for government. By using these standards in the way it governs, government sets the CODE of behavior for the populace at the bottom of the hierarchy. Confucius identified the five basic relationships of society: ruler and subject, parent and child, older sibling and younger sibling, elder person and younger person, and friend and friend. The subordinate or younger person is expected to demonstrate *hsiao* (pronounced "she-aoh"), "filiality," or respect and concern for the superior or older person, who, in turn, adopts an attitude of guidance and protection toward the subordinate and younger.

An important principle in governance, as well as all forms of communication, is that of "the rectification of names," or the correct and accurate use of words. This means using words according to their true meaning; to employ euphemisms to disguise one's true intent (*see* INTENTION) or the real situation is clearly a form of dishonesty. For example, Confucius would have strenuously objected to saying a couple "made love" if in reality one of the partners was forced to have sex against his or her will.

Another important feature of Confucian ethics is *I* (pronounced "ee"), which means "righteousness or JUSTICE." Confucius connected *I* with what is fitting, RIGHT, and seemly, thus aligning it with LI, or MORALITY. Mo-tzu, a Confucian philosopher, regarded *I* as a CARDINAL VIRTUE and a characteristic of Heaven. Mencius (Meng-tzu), another Confucian philosopher, exalted righteousness and justice to such an extent that he said he would rather forfeit his own life than be guilty of violating *I*.

The ideal person (*see* IDEALISM) in Confucian ethics is the gentleman or humanitarian (*see* CHUN-TZU) whose moral CHARACTER is determined by a spirit of BENEFICENCE and generosity (*see* JEN) and whose behavior is always in accord with the dictates of propriety. Central to morality in Confucianism is *shu*, or the principle or RECIPROCITY. Confucius was once asked if there was a single word that could be serve as a guide to conduct one's life. He replied: "It is perhaps the word *'shu'*: Do not impose on others what you yourself would not desire" (*Analects* 15:24; *see* GOLDEN RULE).

CONSCIENCE A person's beliefs (*see* FAITH) about the rightness (*see* RIGHT) or wrongness (*see* WRONG) of his or her own actions (*see* ACT).

Conscience is sometimes said to be a faculty of the mind that informs individuals about what they should or should not do. It represents a person's considered MORAL OPINION. People are said to act "in good conscience" when they do what they believe is right. They violate their own consciences when they do what they think

is wrong. A person is usually said to have a conscience if he or she has moral scruples, is capable of reflecting upon the MORALITY of his or her own behavior, is capable of feeling GUILT or remorse, and is disposed to do what is right, or to avoid doing what is wrong.

Some philosophies, such as that of Joseph BUTLER, bid us to do what conscience dictates, as if conscience were infallible in the judgments (*see* JUDGMENT) it makes. Others, however, allow that not every conscience is well formed or that conscience can err in what it dictates. People may conscientiously believe that something is right but nonetheless be mistaken in their belief. A problem thus arises over whether people should do what their consciences dictate, what they think is right, or whether they should do what is really right. One might argue that they should do what is really right because their belief might be mistaken. But how could they do what is really right if they do not know what that is? Moreover, it also seems strange to ask people to do not what they think is right but what they believe is wrong. Normally when we think people are wrong, we try to convince them to change their mind. Failing that, we may simply have to oppose them.

Some philosophers distinguish between the *subjectively* right thing to do (*see* SUBJECTIVISM)—namely, what conscience dictates—and the *objectively* right thing to do (*see* OBJECTIVISM)—what is right according to REASON or moral PRINCIPLES. They sometimes argue, as did Thomas AQUINAS, for example, that we are bound by our consciences, or the subjectively right thing to do, but that we also have a duty to improve our reasoning and judgment, to find out what is objectively right. But even then the paradox remains. If a person is morally bound to do what he or she thinks is right, then what one thinks is right really is the right thing to do. We might say that something else would be right if the person knew better, but we could not say that it is right, given that person's beliefs. Objective rightness then appears to be an ideal (*see* IDEALS).

Take, for example, UTILITARIANISM. According to this theory, we should choose that act that, among all the alternatives open to us, has the best consequences (*see* CONSEQUENTALISM). But we do not always know for sure which act will have the best consequences; the act we think will have the best consequences may not be the act that really does. This seems to leave no alternative but to make our decision according to our best judgment, even if it is wrong. Given more experience, we may learn to make better predictions about the future and so become better at choosing right acts. We might then come closer and closer to the ideal, without ever knowing for sure that we have discovered the TRUTH.

CONSCIENTIOUS OBJECTION Objection to an action or policy according to the dictates of CONSCIENCE.

A person may conscientiously object to many things, including ABORTION, RACISM, and pollution of the environment. Conscientious objection becomes a serious moral issue (*see* MORALITY) when someone objects so strongly to a particular LAW that he or she is prepared to break it regardless of the consequences.

Most commonly, the term *conscientious objector* is used to describe a person who refuses to serve in military forces despite being legally required to do so as a result of conscription, otherwise known as the draft. In this sense, conscientious objectors are often pacifists who believe that *all* VIOLENCE and war is WRONG. Such people are often motivated (*see* MOTIVE) by deep moral or religious convictions (*see* RELIGION AND MORALITY). In the United States, these people are usually exempted from military service requirements. Other conscientious objectors are people who object to a particular war or who object to being forced to serve in the military against their WILL. In the United States, this is rarely if ever grounds for an exemption from military service.

In the past, conscientious objectors have been imprisoned or even executed for their beliefs. In modern times it has become more common for governments to allow conscientious objectors to substitute military service for some other form of service, such as working in a hospital as an orderly. *See also* CIVIL DISOBEDIENCE.

CONSENSUS General agreement within a group, political body, or society.

In order to form a consensus, a group must achieve a unanimous or nearly unanimous agreement. There are a variety of methods to achieve consensus. Sociologists, for example, identify different kinds of cultural consensus. Spontaneous agreement may occur in traditional village-based societies where there is little public debate. When faced with a major decision or problem, the tribe thinks together as a whole. In industrialized societies, however, consensus typically occurs after individuals consider various perspectives and then vote or register their opinions. If a nearly unanimous position is reached, then a consensus occurs. Those who disagree with the preferred view defer their opinions for the COMMON GOOD. Central to this kind of consensus is the notion that each person has a say and that no one opinion is more important than another (*see* DEMOCRACY).

The significance of consensus for modern ETHICS lies in the supposed RATIONALITY of moral agreement. According to the rationalist tradition exemplified by Immanuel KANT, rationality entails uniform adherence to universal PRINCIPLES. In this view, a truly ethical commonwealth is one in which all free, rational agents (*see* MORAL AGENCY) accept the same moral principles as their guides.

However, other notions of government demand consensus on fundamental issues but allow for a plurality (*see* PLURALISM) of opinions on other important issues. In the United States, for example, there is consensus on the liberties (*see* FREEDOM) guaranteed in the BILL OF RIGHTS, but there are many other moral issues that are the subject of deep disagreement. This view allows that if there is consensus on basic freedoms, disagreement and debate on other issues actually strengthens a society.

Finally, there are those that argue that universal moral "facts" are illusions. This claim suggests that consensus is strictly contingent on cultural agreement, and not the rational recognition of universal principles, as Kant held. In this view, irreconcilable moral disagreements are simply an inevitable consequence (*see* CONSEQUENTIALISM) of having moral commitments (*see* COMMITMENT).

CONSEQUENTIALISM   The position that the moral (*see* MORALITY) worth of an action is determined by the value of its consequences rather than by the intention of the agent or the principle that motivated the action.

The term *consequentialism* refers to moral theories that hold that an action is morally right if the consequences of that action bring about more good than harm. For the consequentialist, right action is determined solely by a COST-BENEFIT ANALYSIS of an action's consequences. In order to perform this analysis, the consequentialist must first calculate both the good and bad consequences of an action. Next, the agent must determine whether the sum of the good consequences outweighs the sum of the bad consequences. If the good consequences outweigh the bad consequences, then the action is moral. If the bad consequences outweigh the good consequences, then the action is immoral (*see* IMMORALITY).

There are three major branches of consequentialism: ethical (*see* ETHICS) EGOISM, ethical ALTRUISM, and UTILITARIANISM. Ethical egoism holds that actions are moral if the consequences of those actions bring about more good than harm to the individual performing that action. For example, if an ethical egoist is trying to decide whether it is moral to tell a lie, he only need consider the effects that the lie is likely to have for him. Ethical altruism holds that actions are moral if the consequences of those actions yield more good than harm to everyone concerned except

the individual acting. Ethical egoists believe that all people are instinctually motivated to act in their own best interests and that their theory is simply the moral extension of that instinct. Ethical altruists always try to do what is best for others, independent of their own concerns. Utilitarians hold that actions are moral if the consequences of those actions bring about the greatest happiness for the greatest number of people (*see* BENTHAM, JEREMY; MILL, JOHN STUART).

Detractors of consequentialism point out how often consequentialist theories lead us to act against our moral intuitions. For example, acts of lying, stealing, and violence could be deemed ethical as long as they brought about more good than harm. False imprisonment, torture, and slavery might all be justified as long as consequentialists could show that the good for society outweighed the pain of the act of punishment.

CONSERVATISM   The belief that older, traditional ways of doing things are usually better than newer, less-proven ways of doing things.

Conservatives believe that as CUSTOMS have been tried and tested over many years, their success has been proven. They are not against change per se but prefer gradual, small scale change to rapid, radical change. Conservatives generally concede that traditional systems are far from perfect but argue that large amounts of change over short periods of time can have unpredictable and often devastating consequences for society. Therefore, they believe that radical change isn't worth the risk. Opponents of conservatism argue that it is simply a thinly veiled attempt by those who benefit most from existing POWER structures to preserve their own advantages.

In the United States, the term *conservative* is often a label used to describe those who simultaneously favor free-market CAPITALISM and traditional social arrangements. This terminology is potentially confusing because support for free-market capitalism has historically been a principle of LIBERALISM. American conservatives tend to emphasize the importance of religious belief and traditional family arrangements (*see* RELIGION AND MORALITY), including strong government support for these institutions, while also favoring little or no government interference in the economy.

CONSISTENCY Similarity of moral JUDGMENT across similar situations.

Such consistency is often thought to be morally obligatory (*see* OBLIGATION). Thus, if the circumstances in one case are the same as the circumstances in another, then the same moral judgments ought to apply and be consistent in both cases.

Consistency is at the base of Kantian MORALITY (*see* KANT, IMMANUEL), the use of the case method, and CASUISTRY. Some moral PRINCIPLES are also based on consistency. For example, the GOLDEN RULE requires that we only do to others what we would have them do to us. Those who make exceptions of themselves by cheating, stealing, or moving to the front of the line would often would react negatively were they to be hurt by others doing the same thing. In this way they appear to be inconsistent. Some philosophers, such as Immanuel Kant, believed that consistency is the mark of a moral person. To make exceptions by lying when it is personally advantageous, for example, is a sign of IMMORALITY.

Some philosophers counter that it is not always inconsistent to make different judgments. Sometimes a lie may be appropriate. It is not inconsistent, for example, to think on the one hand that it is typically unacceptable to lie and on the other to claim that it is permissible to lie in exceptional circumstances, such as to save a life. But consistency demands that exceptions should be permitted in all relevantly similar cases.

The problem with simple consistency is that it does not tell us which sorts of case features provide the basis for judgments. If two cases are virtually identical, differing only in the eye colors of the people involved, then we claim that the cases are similar because eye color is not a morally relevant trait. But people may disagree on what traits are morally relevant, as in the question of whether a physical disability is a relevant consideration in a particular circumstance. Moral reasoning can be used to determine those traits that should be considered morally relevant.

CONSUMERISM A pattern of behavior driven by a preoccupation with the buying and ownership of goods.

Consumerism emerged from the increased availability of services and the growing number of goods produced in factories and by industry since the 1950s. It manifests itself as the compulsive purchasing of consumer products, with little attention given to whether there is a need for that product, whether the product is of high quality, where and under what condition the product was manufactured, and the environmental costs of its production and disposal. Consumerism establishes patterns of consumption in a society that are not sustainable. Consumerists are inclined to discard goods before they have outlived their usefulness in order to keep up with current style and fashion.

Consumerism is an attitude exemplified by the adage, "Whoever dies with the most toys wins." It is characterized by dependence on private transportation, the necessity of full time WORK, dependence on labor-saving devices, the growing availability of consumer credit and increase in consumer debt, the importation of more and cheaper foreign goods, the collapse of local economies, and increased pollution.

As more and more individuals insist on personal ownership, communal (*see* COMMUNITY) and public systems and services decline. For example, cars are preferred over public transportation in many cities. This practice is more expensive and more damaging to the environment than public transportation systems, but it is considered more convenient by the consumer. The focus on individual consumption also tends to displace spaces that formerly facilitated community action and awareness. For example, malls have become more popular than parks as a place to seek entertainment. Because of the variety and the lower cost of inventory, malls have also displaced many local merchants. This displacement means that the economy of many cities and towns is dependent on corporations that are based in other areas.

Consumerism changes the focus from VALUE based on durability and longevity to value based on acquisition. Consumerists often see people and resources as available for consumption. This attitude has important implications for personal and family relationships. Friendships, family ties, and celebrations become inseparable from gift giving. The commercialization of many holidays, such as Christmas and Valentine's Day, is an example of the consumerist mentality. Consumerists often cast others in the role of competitor. Life becomes a series of competitions to get ahead of others by earning more money and having the FREEDOM to purchase more goods.

Not only are relationships with others weakened when viewed with a consumerist attitude, but consumerism can also be damaging to other areas of an individual's life. The constant drive to work and make money in order to consume or to alleviate consumer debt is physically and emotionally exhausting. The consumerist's creative time and energies are devoted to earning. Furthermore, advertising has deep effects on individual self-image in a consumerist culture. Both children and adults are susceptible to understanding their self-worth in terms of how they look and what they own. For example, individuals in all economic classes may go into debt in order to wear fashionable clothing and drive a prestigious car.

Anticonsumerists advocate voluntary simplicity. This means choosing to reduce the amount of consumption and clutter in one's life. They believe that having fewer things leads to a greater appreciation for the things we have and allows us to cultivate a deeper sense of value. Less consumption also means less distraction from family, friends, community, nature, and education. Anticonsumerists also believe that moving the focus from things to people will assist in solving real problems at home, in their communities, and in the world.

Supporters of consumerism argue that spending is an important way to bolster the economy and keep jobs. In their view it is patriotic to spend, especially on domestic products. They may also argue that people have a RIGHT to spend their money in any way they choose and should not be morally bound to live frugally.

CONTRACEPTION Reducing the chance of pregnancy through mechanical, chemical, or medical means.

Contraception does not present any ethical dilemmas (*see* DILEMMA) in most religious traditions; in fact, the case can even be made that in the modern day, selective use of contraception is actually an OBLIGATION. ABORTION is not a form of contraception because it terminates an existing pregnancy, although abortion is sometimes used as a form of birth control.

The primary opponent of artificial means of contraception today is the Catholic Church. The church teaches that the procreative aspect of sexual intercourse cannot be separated from its unitive, spiritual, and pleasurable aspects and that therefore contraception undermines God's purpose (*see* TELEOLOGY). For this reason, the church's PROHIBITION, does not extend to periodic sexual ABSTINENCE.

Critics of the Catholic position argue that it is too narrow and mechanistic in its definition of sexual intercourse. They argue that apart from procreation, sexual intercourse is also used as an expression of deep union, affection, and LOVE between two committed (*see* COMMITMENT) individuals. The church, therefore, fails to acknowledge an important emotional component of human relationships.

A more limited objection to contraception is that it promotes sexual relationships outside of MARRIAGE and encourages promiscuity. There is no conclusive evidence to support this claim, however.

If it is the case that people will continue to have sexual relations regardless of the availability of contraception, it can be argued that individuals have a RESPONSIBILITY to themselves, their partners, and society to use contraception in order to prevent the spread of sexually transmitted disease (*see* SEXUAL ETHICS). Widespread use of contraception also has the potential to reduce the number of children born to mothers who do not want them or cannot adequately support them. It may also help alleviate problems associated with overpopulation.

CONTRACT   A legally enforceable exchange of promises between two or more parties.

Several complicated legal conditions need to be met before a PROMISE can be considered a binding contract. For example, a contract requires an exchange of some sort. One of the simplest forms of contract is the exchange of money for a product or service.

A contract need not be a written document. It can also be a verbal agreement or even just certain types of behavior. For example, a shop owner who puts goods on display for sale is making an offer to form a contract for sale with anyone who wishes to purchase those goods. The contract is finalized when money changes hands.

CORRUPTION   Abuse of a position of trust for personal gain.

In the past, someone may have been considered corrupt if she or he engaged in behavior considered to be IMMORAL. In the sense that it is used today, however, corruption is most commonly associated with abuses of POWER, such as taking bribes or using favoritism in making decisions that should be impartial (*see* IMPARTIALITY), such as awarding a contract to someone simply because he or she is a friend or relative. Corruption is considered WRONG because it is a breach

of trust (*see* TRUSTWORTHINESS) and can undermine respect for the office or institution the person is supposed to serve.

COST-BENEFIT ANALYSIS   A way to measure the gain of an action (*see* ACT) against what must be paid for it.

Often, people want things that seem good but do not take into account the sacrifices (*see* SACRIFICE) involved in pursuing their goals. Considering the cost of an action seems to be especially important, morally speaking (*see* MORALITY), when one person or group of people does something to or for others. So it might seem especially beneficial for cost-benefit analysis to be used by a government when it imposes policies on others. For example, eliminating pollution in a society is certainly a worthy goal, but policies designed to eliminate pollution may be very expensive. Are the results worth the costs?

The answer to questions about cost relative to benefits are relatively easy when we compare similar things, know how to measure benefits, and apply our standards to a consistent population. When we examine difficult cases such as pollution controls, the calculation of costs and benefits becomes much more complicated. In examining the issue of pollution, for instance, we know that pollution offends and sometimes kills people and that it can be harmful to animals, crops, and property. We also know that fighting pollution is often expensive and may even lead to the elimination of certain jobs. If we save the lives of some animals at the expense of jobs, how do we measure the costs and the benefits? If we save some human lives by eliminating pollution, we may lose others because we have less money to spend on other pressing problems or because of the social harms caused by unemployment.

Cost-benefit analysis is controversial partly because it seems to place price tags on inestimable VALUES, such as the survival of a human being or a species of animals. Nevertheless, spending tremendous amounts of a society's resources for relatively small gains makes little sense. Cost-benefit analysis is designed to prevent such wastefulness.

COUNSELS OF PERFECTION   In the Christian religion (*see* CHRISTIAN ETHICS), teaching of the Apostles regarding unity with Christ.

The counsels of perfection (*see* MORAL PERFECTIONISM) teach the ways in which Christians might emulate Christ and therefore be closer in spirit to GOD. They include such directives as to LOVE one's enemies, to turn the other cheek when insulted or injured, to forgive (*see* FORGIVENESS) others "seventy and seven" times, to cast away PROPERTY, to respect God's name, to be faithful in marriage, to display COURAGE, to forgo thoughts of the present life, and to show HONOR in all things. More generally, counsels of perfection may be any set of teachings regarding moral excellence (*see* MORAL EXEMPLAR).

COURAGE   The ability to meet danger without succumbing to fear. Courage is sometimes used interchangeably with the term *fortitude* by some ethicists.

ARISTOTLE thought courage of sufficient importance to classify it as a VIRTUE. According to Aristotle, the courageous person is neither free of fear nor overwhelmed by fear but has the degree of fear that is appropriate to the situation. A person with courage acts (*see* ACT) according to good JUDGMENT and keeps PASSIONS AND EMOTIONS in their place. For instance, a courageous warrior resists the desire to flee from danger. Courage was later identified in CHRISTIAN ETHICS as one of the four CARDINAL VIRTUES.

Although Aristotle considered courage to be the most purely demonstrated in battle, modern ETHICS recognizes various kinds of courage. A person with intellectual courage, for instance, dares to think in ways that are not authorized by some governing institution, as in Martin Luther's theological objections to central items in Catholic doctrine. A person may show courage in choosing a difficult or unpopular vocation, such as teaching in a ghetto high school. Someone may also show courage in refusing to engage in certain kinds of socially condoned or expected behavior, such as pacifists who go to jail rather than fight. In most cases, the degree of one's courage is measured against the costs of one's actions; persons who risk their lives, for example, are usually held to be more courageous than those who risk mere unpopularity.

COVENANT   A binding PROMISE between individuals, groups, or nations having social, legal, or religious ramifications.

Historically, covenants have been used to create new familial, communal (*see* COMMUNITY), or political relationships. Covenants were used to arrange marriages as well as to dictate the relationships between a conquered society and its conquerors. Covenants were also used to govern newly formed societies. For example, the seventeenth-century Puritans formed one of the most famous covenants in the Mayflower Compact, in which they formed a new society to enact laws (*see* LAW) for the COMMON GOOD.

The central covenant of Judaism, known as *Brit* in Hebrew (*see* JEWISH ETHICS), establishes the relationship between GOD and the Jewish people: "If you obey my voice and keep my covenant, you shall be my treasured possession out of all the peoples." (Exodus 19:5) This is the scriptural basis of the self-understanding of Jews as the "chosen people," a concept that theologically and morally (*see* MORALITY) carries a sense of RESPONSIBILITY rather than privilege.

In Christianity (*see* CHRISTIAN ETHICS) a covenant refers to the allegiance of an individual or people to God. The biblical (*see* BIBLE) covenant is often associated with baptism and related themes of grace. In baptism, a person freely and voluntarily accepts ethical obligations (*see* OBLIGATION) and receives, in return, grace. The metaphor *new covenant* refers to the relationship of JESUS with the church. The new covenant established the AUTHORITY of Christ against both paganism and Judaism. *New Covenant* is also used occasionally as a synonym for the New Testament.

CREATIONISM   *See* EVOLUTION.

CRIME   Any ACT that involves breaking the LAW.

In most cases, laws forbid people from engaging in activities deemed inappropriate by the local COMMUNITY or the government. Often laws forbid activity detrimental to public order and safety, such as loitering or MURDER; activity detrimental to private PROPERTY, such as graffiti and theft; activities that conflict with religious doctrines, such as BLASPHEMY; and activity detrimental to a state, such as treason. In some instances laws also impose an OBLIGATION to act, such as when a citizen is required to register for compulsory military service. Usually someone caught breaking the law will be required to pay a penalty for his or her actions.

In the United States, most crimes must be the result of an intentional (*see* INTENTION; MENS REA) act. For example, accidentally killing someone is not murder. In some cases, however, such as speeding or other instances of negligent (*see* NEGLIGENCE) disregard for public safety, a crime has been committed even though the act was not intentional.

Some ethicists (*see* ETHICS) have argued that it is ethical to break an unjust law or a law that forces someone to break her or his own moral CODE. For example, a religious person may feel justified in breaking a law that forbids them from practicing their religion. Others have argued that laws may be broken if in the aid of a higher principle (*see* PRINCIPLES). For example, in the United States during the 1960s many people fought to end discrimination against minorities. They felt morally justified in peacefully breaking laws that they believed were discriminatory, a tactic known as CIVIL DISOBEDIENCE.

CRITICAL THEORY   A method based on the belief that history and culture play the most important roles in the formation of identity and meaning.

Critical theory is better understood as a loosely bound group of theories or a cluster of themes than as a unified theory or specific doctrine. These theories seek to discredit the notion of a universal, nonhistorical human identity or set of moral laws (*see* LAW). Max Horkheimer, director of the Frankfurt Institute for Social Research founded in Frankfurt, Germany, in 1923, coined the term "critical theory." Other famous members of the Frankfurt School were Theodor W. Adorno, Erich Fromm, and Herbert Marcuse. Marcuse introduced critical theory to the United States in the 1960s.

Critical theory emerged from the study of the theories of Georg Wilhelm Friedrich HEGEL and Karl MARX, who offered an analysis of society based on relations of POWER. Drawing from the work of these philosophers, critical theorists believe that claims to universal moral PRINCIPLES are not objective (*see* OBJECTIVITY) moral facts but rather tools of OPPRESSION. The powerful use these tools in order to enforce behaviors that are advantageous to those in power but exploitive (*see* EXPLOITATION) to those who are not in power. For example, the moral laws that prohibit violence can be used to oppress certain groups, as in Martin LUTHER's belief that rioting peasants must be killed in order to maintain the divinely instituted moral order. Feminist critical theorists such as Julia Kristeva seek to show how traditional forms of thinking and writing assign women a marginal role in society (*see* FEMINIST ETHICS).

Critical theorists seek to abolish social injustices by revealing the power implications of supposedly neutral language. Not all critical theorists, particularly the early theorists of the Frankfurt School, believed that the abolition of social injustice through a critical examination of moral and political language was possible. This concern lends an air of pessimism to much of critical theory.

CRUELTY TO ANIMALS   *See* ANIMAL RIGHTS.

CULTURAL RELATIVISM.   An ethical doctrine claiming that MORAL RESPONSIBILITY is relative to one's own culture.

A thing is relative when its identity depends on its relationship to something else. Whether a person is considered tall or short, for example, depends on the height accepted as average in a given culture. A man who is considered tall in one country might be considered of average height in another. In contrast, ABSOLUTES are defined regardless of context. For instance, we may claim that people need food and water to be healthy and that this claim does not depend on whether a society believes food and water to be healthy.

RELATIVISM is the claim that all moral beliefs are relative to the believer. MORALITY on this view is a matter of individual opinion or conviction. Cultural relativism claims that all moral facts are relative not to individuals but to a particular cultural group or society. Cultural relativism puts stronger criteria on moral beliefs than does relativism. Cultural relativists hold that it must be possible to locate an individual's beliefs within their society. On the other hand, cultural relativism denies that any independent moral facts exist outside of a society. Instead, they maintain that all moral beliefs are proper or improper in relation to a society's CUSTOMS. For example, if one lives in a society where killing older parents who cannot take care of themselves is considered moral, then each person in that society has that obligation. On the other hand, if one lives in a society where such killing is thought to be morally wrong, then each person has an obligation to refrain from such a killing, even if serious sacrifices are required to care for the parents.

In contrast to moral relativism, many believe that morality is absolute and unchanging. Thus, moral PRINCIPLES are held to be the same for all no matter where or when they live (*see* DEONTOLOGY). This claim can be based on the belief that moral RULES are designed to respond to an unchanging HUMAN NATURE or perhaps on the belief that GOD makes moral rules and that they are the same for all people. People who believe morality to be absolute often disagree, however, about what morality demands. For example, some absolutists believe that abortion is wrong, and some believe that people have the right to choose an abortion.

Cultural relativists take note of such disputes and claim that we can only refer to cultural standards, not universalizable ones, to settle moral differences. They recognize and give moral weight to anthropologist's observations regarding different moral CODES among different peoples. Each code is intelligible given its culture of origin. Many see no reason to claim that any one code is morally superior to any other. According to cultural relativism, to proclaim one code as superior to another is to be guilty of cultural chauvinism.

Cultural relativists typically object to the condemnation of people in other cultures. Moral and political JUDGMENT of different cultures has led to war, DISCRIMINATION, and intolerance. Cultural relativists believe that their doctrine instead teaches TOLERANCE and understanding. Absolutists respond that tolerance itself is thus proposed as an absolute standard to be followed by all people at all times. If so, cultural relativists contradict themselves by claiming that an intolerant cultural attitude is immoral (*see* IMMORALITY). Another problem with cultural relativism concerns the issue of the makeup of a culture. One may belong to an ethnic group, a religious group, a particular part of the country, or a particular neighborhood. Each of these groups may have significantly different MORALS. If a conflict in moral beliefs arises, the cultural relativist will have to determine which of these groups is owed his or her moral allegiance.

CUSTOMS   Characteristic and conventional ways of behaving or thinking sanctioned by convention.

A custom is a PRACTICE generally accepted by the tradition of a group. Customs are practices that justify behavior (*see* JUSTIFICATION), and in this sense they are related to MORALS. Customs are usually taught from generation to generation. They gain their validity based on having always been the practice of the group; they are justified based on tradition. Customs are usually relative to the COMMUNITY in which they arise. They are not held as binding to visitors or foreigners, although observance of local customs is considered respectful.

Customs are usually viewed as distinct from morals in that customs are held to apply only to group members for the sake of traditions, while morals are normally held to have a basis other than tradition alone. The relationship of customs to morals is controversial, though. For example, proponents of CULTURAL RELATIVISM might hold that customs and morals are identical in their basis. In this view both customs and morals derive their meaning and validity from community practices. They would be distinct only in carrying different penalties when transgressed. Absolutists (*see* ABSOLUTES), on the other hand, hold that customs and morals are entirely different precisely because customs rely on local community traditions while morals should extend beyond local communities.

D

DEADLY SINS   *See* CARDINAL SINS.

DEATH AND DYING   A category of ethical issues (*see* ETHICS) concerning the end of LIFE, including, for example, ABORTION, AIDS and other diseases, CAPITAL PUNISHMENT, EUTHANASIA, medical criteria of death, MURDER, SUICIDE, and war.

The study of death and dying is called thanatology. Concern with the circumstances of death and the proper treatment of the dead is an ancient ethical issue. Every person must face the awareness of his or her own death, and every culture has some LAW, custom (*see* CUSTOMS), or ritual associated with death. Recent advances in medical technology, the growth of the elderly population, the decline in infant mortality, widespread media attention to abortion and euthanasia, diseases such as AIDS and cancer, and a greater awareness of health and mortality on a global scale have prompted interest in death and dying as an organized field of scientific discussion and ethical inquiry.

Controversial issues in the field of death and dying often concern when, if ever, it is appropriate to take a life intentionally, including one's own. These discussions may center on abortion, euthanasia, capital punishment, questions of whether it is justified to kill in self-defense or war, and suicide. Increasingly sophisticated medical techniques have occasioned controversy over the definition of death and the determination of the appropriateness of life support (*see* BRAIN DEATH). Ethical issues surrounding transplantation also fall into this category. Diseases, epidemics, and starvation raise ethical questions concerning fair treatment, compassionate CARE, and humanitarian aid.

DECALOGUE   *See* TEN COMMANDMENTS.

DECENCY   Adherence to standards of GOOD conduct, or to standards of taste or propriety.

With respect to ETHICS, we use the term *decency* in two senses. In the first sense we refer to actions that bear out a standard of moral conduct (*see* MORALITY), which is fair (*see* FAIRNESS), faithful, and kind. For example, a decent person will fulfill obligations to family members, keep promises, and behave honestly toward strangers. A decent person is one who acts as we believe people should act. In this sense saying a person is decent is a moral commendation.

We also use the term *decent* to refer to speech, actions, or art that falls within a COMMUNITY's accepted sensibility. Speech, actions, or material that falls outside such sensibility may be labeled *indecent* by that community and may, therefore, be subject to CENSORSHIP. For example, pornography is often censored because it is thought to be indecent. Because decency in this second sense is dependent on tastes and sensibilities, there is active controversy over which material is decent versus that which is indecent and should be regulated or controlled.

DECONSTRUCTION   A method of philosophical inquiry based on the principle (*see* PRINCIPLES) that language becomes meaningful against specific social, political, and philosophical conditions and that proper readings of moral and political texts will reveal hidden political agendas in seemingly neutral language.

Deconstruction is most closely associated with the French philosopher and critic Jacques Derrida. In the late 1960s, Derrida began to publish a series of books that criticized traditional Western views about TRUTH, knowledge, ETHICS, and MORALITY. Derrida suggested a new method of understanding these classic texts that challenged their most basic assumptions. Derrida questioned fundamental oppositions that have made Western thought meaningful, such as cause and effect, man and woman, truth and language, presence and absence.

Derrida and the deconstructionists who have followed him employ this method in order to expose what they argue is BIAS in traditional philosophical thought. Deconstructionists expose bias by examining the language in which philosophers make their knowledge claims and revealing how these claims contain veiled political and moral hierarchies. For example, a deconstructionist might strive to show how a moral text that presents itself as absolutely true is better understood as representing the view of a certain gender, class, or race.

Deconstructionists do not believe that there is absolute or universal TRUTH. Thus, they do not believe that language describes a moral reality that exists waiting to be discovered but rather that moral language describes a reality we are creating. A deconstructionist will be at odds, for example, with most religious views of the world that suggest that there is an independent deity (see GOD) who is the source of moral truth (see RELIGION AND MORALITY).

DEFAMATION   Words or pictures that have the effect of damaging a person's reputation.

Defamation is considered morally WRONG if it *unjustly* has a negative effect on the esteem in which an individual is held by the community. For this reason, negative claims that are nevertheless truthful, accurate, or factual are not necessarily morally wrong. A person who unjustly defames another may be subject to criminal penalties and may be required to pay a financial penalty to the victim if successfully sued in civil court. In the law, a distinction is sometimes made between the defamation of a person's CHARACTER through printed words or pictures, known as libel, and the defamation of a person's character through the spoken word, known as slander.

Some people argue that defamation should not be subject to criminal penalties. In their opinion, defamation is only words and cannot really "damage" anyone. This position, however, seems to discount as inconsequential the opinions of others, and negative opinions may have a significant effect on the way we are treated. For example, a sporting hero who is accused of child molestation may lose lucrative contracts and sponsorship deals because the accusation prevents companies from wanting to be associated with him or her.

Others who object to prohibitions on defamation concede that defamation can have consequences but believe that it is important not to criminalize free speech. Indeed, the governments of many countries have used anti-defamation laws to stifle popular criticism and debate. For this reason, the United States has tried to balance these competing interests by outlawing claims that are knowingly false, malicious, and inaccurate, while still protecting the right to engage in political satire and to report on public figures in good faith, even if such reports later prove to be unfounded.

DELIBERATION   A form of reasoning (see REASON) by which people try to determine which ACT they ought to choose.

To answer the question, "Should I attend school today or stay home?" one would deliberate by considering the reasons for and against each of the alternatives. One might consider whether any RULES would be broken by staying home, or one might consider the consequences (see CONSEQUENTIALISM). If one were sick, then staying home might be considered a justified (see JUSTIFICATION) exception to the general rule that students ought to attend school. If a student failed to prepare an assignment, he or she would probably anticipate the consequences of attending class unprepared and compare them with the consequences of missing class entirely. Sometimes one or another alternative is judged (*see* JUDGMENT) to be morally wrong. At other times, all of the alternatives are thought to be permitted (*see* PERMISSIBLE ACT), but a person may still try to determine which is best. One might also determine that one of the alternatives is wrong but do it anyway, choosing to perform an immoral (*see* IMMORALITY) act.

DEMOCRACY   The social and political doctrine stating that governmental decisions should be made by the people, either directly by majority rule or indirectly by electing representatives to make political judgments (*see* JUDGMENT).

A democracy is based on political values such as respect for individual FREEDOM and protection of that freedom. Democracies hold that citizens are equal before the law (*see* EQUALITY), and deserve the equal protection of the law. In a liberal democracy, a citizen has RIGHTS simply by virtue of being a citizen, regardless of sex, race, or religion. Democracies are based on the belief that adults are autonomous (*see* AUTONOMY) and self-directing. This belief is in contrast to other types of government that act paternalistically (*see* PATERNALISM) towards their citizens.

Democracy is often thought of as an ideal (*see* IDEALISM) form of government, but it is not without problems. Direct rule by the people is impractical: too many people are ignorant about important issues, and a general election cannot be held every time something needs to be decided. On the other hand, representatives sometimes act against the interests and wishes of the people who elect them. These problems may be merely technical, as in finding the best way to put into practice the will of the majority. Sometimes, however, serious moral problems arise (*see* DILEMMA). What happens if the majority desires a social policy that discriminates against or harms the minority? Is it fair for an apathetic majority to use its votes to thwart a dedicated minority? What if some groups of people always end up on the losing side of elections, and thus feel they are unrepresented? These problems are sometimes offset by constitutional policy, which makes certain actions, such as racial discrimination, illegal even if desired by the majority.

DEONTOLOGY   In ETHICS, a theory that holds that acts are RIGHT or WRONG in and of themselves because of the kinds of acts they are and not simply because of their ends or consequences (*see* CONSEQUENTIALISM).

According to deontologists, the ends do not justify the means (*see* ENDS/MEANS): A GOOD end or purpose does not justify (*see* JUSTIFICATION) a bad action. For this reason, deontology is usually contrasted with TELEOLOGY, which maintains that actions are justified by ends. Deontologists are also distinguished from utilitarians (*see* UTILITARIANISM), who believe that actions are justified or prohibited (*see* PROHIBITION) on the basis of consequences alone.

For example, a deontologist might argue that a promise ought to be kept simply because it is right to keep a promise, regardless of whether the doing so will have good or bad consequences. A deontologist might also argue that certain acts such as breaking the law ought to be punished because they are wrong and deserve to be punished—not because doing so will serve a purpose, such as deterring others from breaking the law as well. In contrast, a utilitarian will argue that we should keep our promises only when keeping them results in better consequences than the alternatives. On questions of punishment, a utilitarian would appeal to such considerations as crime prevention or the rehabilitation of criminals.

Deontologists fall into two categories, *rule deontology* and *act deontology*. Rule deontologists believe that the MORALITY of actions is determined by moral RULES. For instance, they might argue that it is wrong to lie because lying breaks the moral rule that prohibits lying. The philosophers Immanuel KANT and W. D. Ross are rule deontologists.

Act deontologists, however, such as the early nineteenth-century ethicist W.A. Prichard, have argued that the morality of acts cannot be determined by rules alone, for rules can have exceptions. If rules have exceptions, they reason, the rightness or wrongness of each and every particular act must be intuited (*see* INTUITIONISM). Act deontologists believe that even though rules and even consequences may be considerations, after all factors have been considered, it is still necessary to intuit whether a particular act is right or wrong. Each case must be judged on its own merits, for no case is exactly like any other case.

DESIRE   A strongly held preference.

Ethicists (*see* ETHICS) have made many attempts to explain the connection between desire and ethical behavior. Some, such as Thomas AQUINAS, argued that even though it may not always be obvious, acting morally is always in one's own best interests and that, therefore, all people prefer to act morally unless they are irrational or uninformed. Others, such as Immanuel KANT, argued that an action is moral regardless of whether it is in one's own best interests and that, therefore, someone who knows what is right may still choose to act immorally. Recently some ethicists, such as the emotivists (*see* EMOTIVISM), have suggested that MORALS are simply strongly held desires. In this case, they argue, ethics should primarily be concerned with how to negotiate between the competing desires of various individuals.

DETERMINISM   *See* FREEDOM.

DETERRENCE   The use of negative consequences as a threat to discourage a person or group from engaging in certain activities.

Deterrence is generally considered to be an important justification for PUNISHMENT, on the principle that people will be less likely to engage in certain types of undesirable behavior if there is a possibility that they will be punished as a result.

Deterrence may work either individually or generally. Individual deterrence is often punishment after the fact that is intended to discourage an individual from repeating the same behavior. In general deterrence, punishment is used as a threat to discourage certain behaviors from occurring in the first place. General deterrence might be the threat of a heavy penalty or may take the form of a particularly severe punishment inflicted on one person with the INTENTION that it serve as a lesson to others.

For deterrence to be effective, the threat must be credible; that is, others must believe that the threat *can* and *will* be carried out if the conditions for doing so are met. For example, a parent who threatens to spank a child if the child doesn't stop misbehaving will probably be most effective and convincing if the child has been spanked before and sees that the parent is angry. Threatening to spank the child will be less effective if the parent has threatened the same thing in the past without carrying out the threat.

During the cold war, deterrence was a significant justification for the nuclear weapons buildup. Both sides knew that if they used nuclear weapons, the other superpower would retaliate in kind. This created a lose-lose situation, cleverly dubbed MAD (Mutually Assured Destruction).

DEWEY, JOHN (1859–1952)   U.S. philosopher who tried to integrate the ideas of biology, psychology, and sociology with those of ETHICS, political philosophy, and educational theory.

Dewey's thinking was influenced by many sources, including other pragmatic thinkers (*see* PRAGMATISM), such as Charles Sanders Peirce and William James. His other influences included by his early training in Hegelianism (*see* HEGEL, GEORG WILHELM FRIEDRICH), the impact of the theory of EVOLUTION on thinkers of his time, and writers in the U.S. political tradition such as Thomas Jefferson. As a result of such influences, he placed a great deal of emphasis on the importance of the individual and on DEMOCRACY, as well as on scientific method and the need for social and educational reform.

In ethics, Dewey advocated applying the scientific method to resolve questions of MORALITY. Seeing the universe as evolutionary, he characterized individuals as problem solvers, as organisms who need to make adjustments to their environment in order to survive and prosper. Thus, in his view, genuine thinking of any kind is problem solving, a method of finding means to achieve ends. In this respect, his ethics is teleological (*see* TELEOLOGY), but it differs from many traditional positions in being both pluralistic (*see* PLURALISM) and relativistic (*see* RELATIVISM). As a pluralist, Dewey criticized the idea that there is one and only one ultimate end of all action, whether it be described as pleasure, happiness, or unity with God. In his view, actions have many different ends or purposes, and these ends are relative to the contexts or types of activities in which individuals are engaged. At one time, we may try to start a fire in order to keep warm, and at another time, we may be trying to repair a house, pass a course in school, or find a job. Different ends do not all have some other end in common, although a means to an end in one context may be the end or goal of some other activity. Thus, Dewey speaks of an ENDS/MEANS continuum, in which a means in one context is an end in another, so that nothing is a final end or goal.

Just as the scientific method is a means of testing hypotheses by experiments, ethical reasoning (*see* REASON), according to Dewey, is a means of testing moral beliefs by actions. If one thinks that a problem can be solved or an end reached by acting in a certain way, then one can test the belief by acting on it to see if it produces the desired result. If it does not, then another hypothesis or belief must be considered to see if acting on that belief will be successful.

As conditions change, ideas or actions that worked in the past may no longer be useful and so must be replaced with new beliefs. For this reason, morality, and society itself, must be subject to change as people encounter new problems and devise new techniques for solving them. In this way, Dewey envisioned that ethics could be interwoven with economics or technology, for he saw both as attempts to create a better world. Indeed, in keeping with Hegel, he tried to synthesize moral, social, economic, and political ideas.

DHAMMAPADA   "Path of VIRTUE"; one of the most widely read Buddhist scriptures. The word *dhamma* is the Pali (an early classical language of Buddhism) form of DHARMA. The *Dhammapada* sets forth the basic teachings and practices (*see* PRACTICE) of Buddhism in a readily accessible form. Its opening verse calls attention to the central Buddhist perspective, which states that the mind determines the quality of a person's life. "We are what we think. All that we are arises with our thoughts. With our thoughts we construct the world. Speak or ACT with an impulse mind and trouble will follow you like a wheel follows an ox pulling a cart." *See also* BUDDHIST ETHICS.

DHARMA   "LAW; that which is established"; cosmic, religious, social, and moral order; key term in Hinduism and Buddhism with a range of meanings.

In both Hinduism and Buddhism, dharma names the underlying order and laws that govern all processes: metaphysical (reality beyond what is known through the physical senses), natural, and human. More specifically, dharma identifies the ethical (*see* ETHICS) norms that enable a society to function in an orderly and harmonious manner. These same norms also serve as the moral basis for a PSYCHOSPIRITUAL DISCIPLINE. Depending on the context, dharma can be translated as truth, religion, righteousness, VIRTUE, duty (*see* OBLIGATION), MORALITY, or teaching.

Hinduism names itself *sanatana dharma,* "the eternal religion," by which it means a total way of life. More narrowly, dharma refers to religion, one of the four authentic (*see* AUTHENTICITY) pursuits of human life according to Hinduism. The other three pursuits are pleasure, wealth, and liberation (*see* FREEDOM; MOKSHA). An individual's dharma, in the sense of personal duty to be fulfilled, can only be realized in light of the KARMA that sets the fixed conditions of an individual's life—his or her parentage, genetic makeup, or temporal realities.

In Buddhism, no word has a greater range of meanings than *dharma.* It names the smallest, most elemental particle in the physical world, as well as the most inclusive, essential truth of the metaphysical realm. Dharma is also the second of the three refuges, or foundations, on which Buddhism as a way of life is carried out. These refuges are the Buddha ("Awakened One"), the Dharma (teachings and practices), and the Sangha (the community of Buddhists, monastic and lay). Because dharma as teaching and practice is a reflection of dharma as ultimate reality, as the way things are most fundamentally, it is the means for coming into full accord with this ultimate reality. *See also* BUDDHIST ETHICS; HINDU ETHICS.

DIALECTICS   A method of establishing or refuting a claim by examining the logical consequences of that claim.

The dialectic method is believed to have originated in the fifth century B.C. and is attributed to Zeno of Elea. Generally, the dialectic method refers to the refutation of opponents' claims by showing that those claims lead to contradictory or undesirable ends (*see* ENDS/MEANS). It may also refer to the method of reasoning (*see* REASON) from PRINCIPLES or opinions that are generally accepted to reach a desired conclusion. For example, we might reason from the general principle that overpopulation is undesirable, to the conclusion that we should limit family size. Dialectic reasoning may be employed in a sincere attempt to achieve TRUTH or as a rhetorical ploy to force another to accept a position as apparently logical and therefore necessary. In the latter sense it is associated with the Sophists, who used dialectic reasoning as an instrument for winning disputes without regard to the truth.

SOCRATES, who opposed himself to the Sophists, used a form of dialectical reasoning called elenchus. This process consisted of a series of cross-examinations in which Socrates was able to get his interlocutor to reverse his position by drawing out a consequence that contradicts the opponent's original thesis. Socrates' student PLATO also held dialectics in high regard as the supreme philosophical method. The first systematic account of the dialectic is supplied by ARISTOTLE in his work, the *Topics.* Two other philosophers, Georg Wilhelm Friedrich HEGEL and Karl MARX, employed dialectic reasoning as a means to achieve truth. Marx in particular used a form of dialectics called dialectical materialism to explain history and human development.

Dialectics is an important method in ETHICS because it tests the strengths and weaknesses of opposing points of view. Through dialectical reasoning, ideas, opinions, and principles are pitted against each other in order to get at the truth of a matter. In testing ideas, we often find that some ideas we hold are inconsistent with more important ethical principles. Dialectic reasoning allows us to assess which of our ethical practices or ideas we will keep and which we will reject. Those who oppose dialectic reasoning in ethics may cite its sophistical applications. They may also claim that truths in ethics cannot be revealed through reason and, therefore, that the dialectic method only gives the illusion of achieving ethical truth.

DIGNITY   The state of being honored (*see* HONOR), esteemed, respected, or inherently worthy.

Most of the world's religious and moral philosophies (*see* RELIGION AND MORALITY) recognize the inherent VALUE of the human being. By inherent value, we mean that human beings are regarded as morally valuable simply by virtue of being human. To have dignity is to enjoy the basic moral RIGHTS due to any human being. For example, in the U.S. Declaration of Independence, human dignity is protected in the claim that all citizens are equal, and that simply by virtue of being humans we are entitled to life, liberty, and the pursuit of happiness. Among moral philosophers, Immanuel KANT is well known for arguing that rational (*see* RATIONAL-ITY) creatures have natural dignity and should not be enslaved or manipulated by others.

Dignity is also an important term in the moral concerns surrounding DEATH AND DYING. Here *dignity* usually refers to "a manner befitting a human life." For example, those in favor of euthanasia may argue that a person deserves to choose to die rather than suffer through the final, painful stages of a terminal illness. Opponents of euthanasia might argue that human dignity is compromised by suicide or mercy killing.

DILEMMA A problem that occurs when a person is incapable of meeting all of her or his obligations (*see* OBLIGATION) at the same time. A moral dilemma is one that directly involves issues of MORALITY. It is not the same as a MORAL CONFLICT, which occurs when a person knows the right thing to do but finds that doing so involves sacrifice.

A moral dilemma may occur, for example, if a parent makes a PROMISE to a child that conflicts with an obligation to help a sick relative. If one of these obligations is stronger, the dilemma is not so serious. In fact, many philosophers believe that moral obligations are always "all things considered"—that one is never really obliged to perform inconsistent actions and that the real obligation in any apparent dilemma is whichever is the most serious one. If the obligation to the sick relative is the stronger of the two, then the promise to the child is not an

obligation at all. In this way, some believe that genuine moral dilemmas never really occur.

Other philosophers think that this view is mistaken. If a moral agent (*see* MORAL AGENCY) has two obligations but cannot do both, then one obligation will simply be left undone, and this is always to be regretted. But moral regret may be a GOOD thing: it shows moral agents that they have done WRONG and spurs them to make up for it in the future. In the example of the promise dilemma, the parent may be moved by regret to bring a present to the child.

Often, however, the person caught in the moral dilemma does not know which obligation is stronger. Thus, the agent may act without assurance that he or she is doing the right thing. Ideally, one would put off acting when in doubt; this strategy allows more time to consider what one's responsibilities really are. But delaying an action is not always possible: in the real world, one must sometimes simply choose a path without knowing the right thing to do. In such cases, a genuine moral dilemma is arguably present. *See also* HEINZ'S DILEMMA.

DISABILITY RIGHTS A guarantee of EQUALITY under the LAW for people with physical or mental impairments. This consideration involves prohibiting (*see* PROHIBITION) DISCRIMINATION against those with disabilities, such as by removing physical obstacles and providing them with the assistance they need to have AUTONOMY.

The basic philosophical assumption behind disability rights is that everyone should have equal right to the exercise of FREEDOM and autonomy. Historically, however, policies have been made and buildings constructed without taking the needs of people with disabilities into account. For example, buildings with many staircases can be impossible for someone in a wheelchair to access. Rarely do architects design buildings specifically so that the disabled are denied access, but ignorance is generally not seen as an excuse for significantly and arbitrarily restricting the ability of a group of people to interact freely and equally with others. Whether conscious or not, buildings designed without the disabled in mind discriminate.

Many countries have passed legislation specifically prohibiting discrimination against the disabled by landlords, employers, school officials, and others. In 1990 the United States Congress passed the Americans with Disabilities Act. The act includes provisions that require officials, professionals, and organizations to take the needs of the disabled into account in their planning and decision making. For example, architects are now required to build public buildings with Braille signs and audible elevator signals for people who are blind, and government offices must make sign language interpreters available for communicating with people who are deaf.

Other regulations have been enacted to protect the rights of people with disabilities to training and education tailored to their individual needs and abilities, and courts have intervened to protect people with mental disabilities from violations of their rights, such as including forced sterilization.

DISCOURSE ETHICS The philosophical system that seeks nonviolent, rational, and universal consensual CONFLICT RESOLUTION; also called the Ethics of Conflict.

The term *discourse* implies a specifically argumentative form of communication in which problematic claims of validity become an issue. The discourse is the arena in which such claims are investigated. A discourse takes place in an IDEAL communication community, which is defined by forcelessness, unlimited amount of time for the generation of consensus, and the ability of all participants in the discourse to be able to take on the perspective of any other person involved.

There are two core statements within discourse ethics. First, NORMS are valid when all potentially affected persons involved in the rational discourse would consent to them. Second, the consequences and side effects that may result from the universal obeying of the norm in question must be accepted forcelessly and must be preferred to consequences of all known alternative norms by all participants in the discourse.

Discourse ethics is a communicative ethics. It arises from the belief that ethics can no longer be based on solipsistic, self-rule-making REASON. The transcendental subject (*see* TRANSCENDENTALISM) of Immanuel KANT is replaced by the ideal communication community. Reason takes on a social dimension or interpretation that unfolds in communicative action. Discourse ethics does not want to rely on the basic convictions of people or recommend specific material norms. Therefore, discourse ethics interprets its principles as formal-procedural. The content of justified norms, ethical claims, and decisions to solve conflicts are issues of the practical discourse of all people affected.

Proponents of discourse ethics want all public procedures in which decisions on social and political conflicts are made to obey the principles of the system. Many proponents understand discourse ethics as independent from culture and time, valid for all rational beings. Discourse ethicists are convinced that people have the ability to recognize reasons for the validity of ethical claims and to understand and accept rational solutions. Discourse ethics can be located between the "classical" ethical theories of DEONTOLOGY and TELEOLOGY.

Of course, discourse ethics has not been without critique. Obviously, the ideal communication community is an ideal that never exists in day-to-day life. Critics argue that ethical norms cannot arise out of an ideal community inhabited by ideal individuals. Furthermore, they question why, if the ideal participant is an individual that is able to take on the perspectives of any other participant and if he or she is able to evaluate all perspectives free of interest, there needs to be a dialogue at all: would not the monologue of such a rational being be enough? Another line of critique points to the consensus and the difference between TRUTH and a CONSENSUS of opinion. Discourse ethics is therefore fixed to a procedural criteria of the correctness of norms, not to the content of those norms. Others claim that discourse ethics is a form of RELATIVISM because the RULES of discourse could be different in various societies.

DISCRIMINATION

Treating members of one group differently from members of another in a way that is unfair or harmful (*see* HARM), usually as a result of PREJUDICE.

Discrimination is generally considered WRONG because it categorizes people into groups based on arbitrary considerations, such as a negative stereotype or a fear of the unknown. Even if it could be conclusively established that members of certain groups are more likely to have particular traits than others, this would still tell us nothing about any one individual who may share little in common with others in that category. When people are categorized into classes because of their skin color, country of origin, sexual preference, gender, or anything else, we stop seeing them as individuals with their own unique talents, skills, and beliefs.

To some extent, it is inevitable that human beings will make generalizations about others, but most ethicists (*see* ETHICS) now believe that it is important for us to acknowledge that these generalizations are nothing more than that. Being aware of our faults helps us to see beyond the stereotypes we have created.

In the United States, as a result of the CIVIL RIGHTS and WOMEN'S RIGHTS movements, a number of laws (*see* LAW) have been passed that prohibit certain kinds of discrimination. These include the Equal Pay Act (1963), which guarantees equal pay for men and women doing the same types of jobs, and the Civil Rights Act (1964), which guarantees the right to freedom from discrimination on the basis of race, color, religion, sex, and national origin in voting, employment, and the use of public facilities.

See also AFFIRMATIVE ACTION; BIAS; RACISM; SEXISM.

DISTRIBUTIVE JUSTICE *See* JUSTICE.

DIVINE COMMAND THEORY

The theory that ethical PRINCIPLES or RULES are commanded by GOD.

NATURAL LAW theory generally has been a form of divine command theory in that the natural law has been defined as the law of God as it is understood by humans. Various forms of INTUITIONISM (the view that we have direct insight into our moral responsibilities) and some MORAL SENSE THEORIES are based on the idea that God illumines our minds or souls and that we can therefore find moral truth within ourselves. A priori ideas (*see* A POSTERIORI) are often thought to be innate, or implanted in human minds by God.

The religious belief (*see* FAITH) that the TEN COMMANDMENTS were dictated by God to Moses on Mount Sinai is a popular expression of divine command theory. But philosophers have not usually explained the theory in this literal sense. AUGUSTINE, for example, argues in his *Confessions* that God could not have literally spoken to Moses on top of the mountain. Nonetheless, Augustine believed that God does illumine human minds so that they can understand the truth or the LAW according to which God created the world.

Critics of divine command theory argue that it fails to settle moral disputes (*see* MORAL CONFLICT). In the first place, not everyone believes in God; those who do not are unlikely to be persuaded by appeals to divine AUTHORITY. Even among believers, there is considerable difference of opinion about what is morally RIGHT or WRONG or about what it is that God dictates or requires us to do. Arguably, the fact that many different religions exist suggests that God's demands are unclear and that people interpret them in many different ways. Thus, whether people believe in God or not, they still need to figure out what they should do based on their own REASON; they need to decide whether they will accept the teachings of a religious organization or how they will apply such teachings to their lives.

In his dialogue the *Euthyphro,* PLATO argued that even if what God, or the gods, say is true, it cannot be true simply because God says it. God would not say that something is true unless it were indeed true, independent of God's saying it. Plato made this point by raising the question "Is an act pious because it is loved by the gods, or is it loved by the gods because it is pious?" In Plato's view, things are GOOD in and of themselves and not because somebody, even God, says they are. But, of course, if one *could* know what God commands, then one would know what is right, for God, by definition, cannot be mistaken.

DIVORCE   The legal dissolution of a MARRIAGE.

In most societies marriage is both a legal and a moral COMMITMENT. Moral issues (*see* MORALITY) surrounding divorce concern the RIGHT circumstances under which to end marriage through divorce. These issues may involve religious commitments, legal commitments, keeping a PROMISE, the economic well being of both parties, and the well-being of a couple's children.

Divorce is allowed, with varying degrees of difficulty, in almost every society. Religion is often a major factor in determining the availability of divorce. Where marriage is believed to be a lifelong COVENANT between individuals and GOD, such as in Roman Catholic countries, divorce is difficult to obtain. In Italy, for example, divorce is permitted by LAW but remains unrecognized by the church. In other religions, such as Islam (*see* ISLAMIC ETHICS), marriage is considered a CONTRACT between two adults, and it is considered better to dissolve a bad marriage than to maintain an unhappy state.

Divorce rates have increased dramatically in industrialized countries since World War II. In the United States, divorce rates have risen from 385,000 divorces granted in 1950 to more than 1.2 million divorces granted in 1996. Presently 40 percent of marriages in the United States are expected to end in divorce. Divorce rates are affected by many factors. There tend to be fewer divorces in times of economic hardship and more in times of economic prosperity. Divorce rates are higher in ethnic or religious groups that place less stigma on divorce than those that do not. Divorces are more common early in a marriage than among couples who have been married more than a few years. The ETHICS of divorce often surround the physical and emotional well-being of children. The effects of divorce on children are complicated. The first year after a divorce seems to be the most difficult, with the impact being more severe the younger the child. According to a study by the U.S. National Center for Health Statistics, children from single-parent homes tend to have more social problems, such as dropping out of high school, becoming pregnant as teenagers, developing substance-abuse problems, and encountering trouble with the law. Due to the increased problems suffered by children of divorced parents, some argue that, unless children are in an abusive environment, parents have a moral OBLIGATION to stay married at least until their children reach adulthood.

DOGMA   An official or established doctrine of a religious group, or some other organization or institution, that is regarded as true, usually on the basis of AUTHORITY.

Members of religions, for example, often believe that their FAITH is true because it is authorized by a sacred scripture, such as the BIBLE, and ultimately by GOD. In this sense, the word *dogma* is used respectfully.

The word *dogma* may also be used critically or disparagingly to mean a belief that is held without good reason, the implication being that a dogma is a PREJUDICE. Dogma may also be used simply as another word for *doctrine,* which is a set of teachings or PRINCIPLES held by members of a group, often with deep conviction.

Of course, the mere fact that something is an official or traditional teaching does not by itself tell us whether that belief is true or false.

DOGMATISM   The assertion of a belief as a DOGMA, or an established TRUTH.

Dogmatism is usually used in a critical or disparaging way to mean strongly held or forcefully asserted conviction supported without good reason. In this sense, people who are said to be dogmatic are thought to be unreasonable in that they are unwilling to consider reasons or evidence that opposes their beliefs (*see* FAITH). Because they feel certain they are right, they see no need to consider the possibility that they may be WRONG. In this way, being dogmatic is tantamount to having a closed mind or being prejudiced (*see* PREJUDICE). In contrast, people who are reasonable about their beliefs are willing to examine them, allowing for the possibility that they may be wrong. This does not mean that it is wrong to have strong convictions but only that from a moral point of view (*see* MORAL OPINION), it is normally considered a fault to be unreasonable.

DOUBLE EFFECT   An action that has both good and bad consequences.

Many actions have both good and harmful (*see* HARM) effects. In medicine, for example, a treatment may be risky or involve harmful side effects but may, nevertheless, be thought justified if the benefit is great enough. The principle (*see* PRINCIPLES) of double effect attempts to define when an action with both beneficial and harmful effects is morally justified.

Although scholars differ in their interpretation of the doctrine of double effect, the following conditions are generally thought to apply. First, the action must not be WRONG in and of itself. Second, the harmful result of the action cannot be the intended (*see* INTENTION) consequence of the action. Third, the GOOD that results from the action cannot be the result of the harmful effect of the action. Wrong action should not be chosen in order to produce a good end. For example, the doctrine of double effect would not endorse a murder, even if the consequences of the murder were "good." Fourth, the harm produced by the action must be necessary and unavoidable. If there is a way of producing the good without causing the harm or by causing a lesser harm, then another method should be chosen. For example, self-defense is usually held to be justifiable even if the assailant is wounded or killed. However, if one could prevent harm to oneself or another by negotiation, then one should negotiate instead of using force.

It is sometimes difficult to determine whether all the conditions for a moral action in the case of double effect are satisfied. Some ethicists (*see* ETHICS) dispute whether the doctrine of double effect is morally worthwhile. They argue that killing in war, for instance, is often thought to be justified, although it is intentional and any good effect is the direct result of the harmful effect.

DOUBLE STANDARD   The application of a principle that is unequally based on arbitrary considerations.

Having double standards is generally seen as a undesirable thing because it implies an element of unfairness and irrationality. For example, the term is commonly used in the United States to refer to situations where one gender appears to be treated more leniently than the other. Such a distinction is particularly obvious in traditional sexual MORALITY, where women are expected to refrain from sex until marriage, while promiscuity among men is generally tolerated or even celebrated.

Double standards may also happen in situations where society appears to apply radically different standards to substantially similar circumstances or where standards appear to be unevenly applied. For example, some argue that it is a double standard for violence and murder to be permissible on television, even though they are illegal and undesirable in real life, while nudity is not permissible, even though private nudity and sexual relationships are generally legal.

Another example of double standards is individuals holding others to more stringent standards than they hold themselves to; when, for example, they have one rule (*see* RULES) for themselves and another for everyone else.

DRUG ABUSE   *See* SUBSTANCE ABUSE.

DUBOIS, W. E. B. (WILLIAM EDWARD BURGHARDT) (1868–1963)   An African-American sociologist and black protest leader, one of the founders of the National Association for the Advancement of Colored People (NAACP).

During the early years of his intellectual life, roughly 1895–1910, DuBois studied and wrote about the real material conditions of blacks in America. His work *The Philadelphia Negro* is considered a landmark in the development of empirical sociology. DuBois believed that there were some people who had special talents above others in their race and advocated a special moral role for these individuals. "The Talented Tenth," as he called them, had a moral RESPONSIBILITY to improve the lives of all people, especially those in their own race. This doctrine partly followed from his belief that RACISM was caused by ignorance. Through his studies and writings, he believed he could improve the lives of African Americans, despite the vicious racism he encountered. However, DuBois came to believe that education alone would not adequately overcome such racial evils as lynching, segregation laws, and race riots.

DuBois became an activist and argued that racism stemmed from economic EXPLOITATION, much like that of COLONIALISM. Meaningful social change for African Americans could be accomplished only through aggressive demonstration and their organization into a significant economic force. In this way he differed from the most prominent black leader of the period,

Booker T. Washington. DuBois's opposition to Washington is best articulated in his book *The Souls of Black Folk*. In 1910, DuBois helped to organize the NAACP in order to launch a fight for CIVIL RIGHTS.

DuBois advanced an idea called Pan-Africanism, or the belief that people of African descent had common interests and should work together to achieve their FREEDOM. As the editor of *Crisis*, the NAACP's magazine, he encouraged the development of Afro-American art and literature. He also argued that blacks should fight racism by establishing a strong group economic presence. His ideas were based in part on the ideas of Karl MARX and eventually caused a break with the NAACP. For the rest of his life, his work shed light on race and race conflict in both the African and African-American struggles for freedom and EQUALITY. In 1961 DuBois moved to Africa, where he died in 1963 working for pan-African unity.

DUE PROCESS   The requirement that individuals be free from unfair, biased (*see* BIAS), or arbitrary treatment under the LAW.

Due process is based on the principle that every individual has RIGHTS and should be treated objectively (*see* OBJECTIVISM). It is a principle that is accepted by many countries around the world.

In the United States, the principle of due process is written into the Constitution. It applies not just to court procedure but to all government activity. Both the Fifth and Fourteenth Amendments to the Constitution state that no individual may "be deprived of LIFE, liberty, or PROPERTY, without due process of law." Such protection includes the right of someone accused of a crime to an impartial (*see* IMPARTIALITY) judge and to present evidence in his or her own defense. It has also been used to support the freedoms of free speech and religion guaranteed by the First Amendment. *See also* BILL OF RIGHTS.

DUTY   *See* OBLIGATION.

ECOLOGY   *See* ENVIRONMENTAL ETHICS.

EGALITARIANISM   The belief that all people are equal (*see* EQUALITY) and should have equal RIGHTS and privileges, especially in regard to social, economic, and political rights.

Fundamental to egalitarianism is the belief that individuals are the supreme moral unit (*see* INDIVIDUALISM). Therefore, egalitarianism may be opposed to theories of collective RESPONSIBILITY, such as COMMUNITARIANISM. Egalitarianism is the foundation behind modern DEMOCRACY and was the philosophical basis for both the French Revolution, with its motto of *"Liberté, égalité, fraternité"* (Liberty, equality, fraternity), and the American Revolution, during which Thomas Jefferson's Declaration of Independence declared the "SELF-EVIDENT TRUTH" that "all men are created equal." *See also* HUMAN RIGHTS.

EGO   The sense of self; center of the conscious personality.

In philosophy, the ego represents the experience of the "I" that is other than and not reducible to body, mind, and emotions. It is the central organizing principle of the individual and accounts for the sense one has of being the same person throughout one's life.

In psychology, the ego is that part of the psychic structure that is most concerned with the individual's place in the world. Moreover, especially in Freudian psychology (*see* FREUD, SIGMUND) the ego allows one to balance one's instincts and impulses with one's CONSCIENCE.

In conventional religion, the ego is often blamed when the standards of the faith, especially its moral requirements, are broken (*see* RELIGION AND MORALITY). A person who violates these standards may be said to have acted out of sheer EGOISM—out of SELF-INTEREST alone.

In mystical religion (*see* MYSTICISM), ego is the assumption that one is separate, independent, and more or less self-sufficient in relation to other humans, the natural world, and the Ultimate. In other words, ego is the failure to realize the extent to which one is defined and conditioned by factors outside oneself. When this sense of separation is accompanied by a feeling of inadequacy or deficiency—as it always is to a greater or lesser extent—it can give rise to the impulse to steal, cheat, lie, or murder. Ego as the sense of separateness is also the source of such attitudes and emotions as PRIDE, GREED, anger, and hatred, which have direct bearing on many moral issues (*see* MORALITY). The PSYCHOSPIRITUAL DISCIPLINES of mystical religion are directed toward eradicating the deepest root of IMMORALITY, the sense of being separate and unrelated.

The respective views of philosophy, psychology, conventional religion, and mysticism on the ego are not contradictory but complementary, each depicting an aspect of the ego as seen from the perspectives of its own discipline. *See also* GOD; SIN.

EGOISM   An ethical theory (*see* ETHICS) that maintains that actions (*see* ACT) are and ought to be motivated (*see* MOTIVE) by SELF-INTEREST.

Egoism is often discussed as two related theories: psychological egoism and ethical egoism. Psychological egoism is a description of human behavior in which people always try to promote their own self-interest, which ultimately is the sole motivation for human action. According to this theory, even when people do things for others, they do so only as a means of helping themselves. When people give money to the poor, for example, psychological egoists explain their behavior by claiming the true motivation of the gift was to make the giver feel good. Ethical egoism, by contrast, not only describes but also endorses this behavior as ethical. Ethical egoists maintain that people *ought* to act in their own self-interest; they ought to look out for themselves. Ethical egoists often say it is HUMAN NATURE, or a fact of life, that people act out of self-interest or self-preservation, and thus this cannot be immoral (*see* IMMORALITY).

Critics of ethical egoism usually offer two arguments against the theory. The philosopher Joseph BUTLER, for example, argued that there are at least four distinct motives for action, and therefore the premise that people always act out of self-interest is itself mistaken. Other critics argue that even if psychological egoism is true and people do act only out of self-interest, it does not follow from this fact that we ought to do so (*see* IS/OUGHT DISTINCTION). They argue that humans have a moral OBLIGATION to cultivate a moral CHARACTER or perform moral actions that may sometimes include overriding the impulse towards self-interest.

EIGHTFOLD PATH   Foundational moral and PSYCHOSPIRITUAL DISCIPLINE of Buddhism.

The Eightfold Path completes the FOUR NOBLE TRUTHS and includes the following:

1. Right Views: holding sufficient confidence in the Four Noble Truths to test them in one's life; developing a philosophy that is in accord with reality; wisdom.
2. Right Intentions: orienting one's entire life in the direction or realizing the truths (*see* TRUTH) and VALUES upheld by Buddhism; for example, practicing nonviolence (*see* PACIFISM).

3. Right Speech: speaking only what is truthful and conducive to the WELFARE of others.
4. Right Conduct: upholding basic MORALITY; avoiding such activities as killing, stealing, and illicit sexual relations.
5. Right Livelihood: engaging in a vocation that does not cause one to violate Buddhist precepts; this means avoiding such jobs as bartending, butchering, or manufacturing ammunition and armaments.
6. Right Effort: NIRVANA cannot be realized except by single-minded COMMITMENT and the expenditure of energy.
7. Right Awareness: present mindedness; attending to what is happening inwardly and outwardly as it is happening; essential in the practice of meditation.
8. Right Meditation: penetrating exploration of the mind; cultivation of tranquility and insight (*see* INTUITION).

All the steps on the Eightfold Path are practiced at the same time; each is one part of a total discipline. They are commonly arranged to form the three trainings of Buddhist practice: training in wisdom (1 and 2), training in morality (3, 4, and 5), and training in meditation (6, 7, and 8). *See also* BUDDHIST ETHICS; DHARMA; KARUNA; PRAJNA.

ELITISM   The position that society depends on a particular class—intellectual, social, or cultural—in order to flourish.

Sometimes "elite" refers to a special social class. In some countries, elite status is inherited, as in the case of the monarchy and nobility. In advanced industrial nations, however, an elite is often defined in terms of special knowledge or economic POWER and influence. People with superior or valuable technical skills—engineers, scientists, or doctors, for instance—may be thought of as elite.

Some elitists believe that because of their special status or talents, elites are the most appropriate and qualified people to make decisions for the GOOD of society. They argue that DEMOCRACY is an inefficient and undesirable system because it leaves decisions in the hands of a mass of unqualified voters who are neither intelligent nor knowledgeable enough to make effective decisions. Elitists often argue that because of the importance of their role, elites should be given special responsibilities (*see* RESPONSIBILITY), RIGHTS, privileges, and political powers.

Supporters of democracy respond that elites are rarely qualified to tell others what is best for them. They might argue, for example, that the person best qualified to know if a house is acceptable is not an elite engineer but the people who are supposed to live in it. This explains why elitism has extremely negative connotations in democratic nations such as the United States and has even been called immoral (*see* IMMORALITY).

EMBRYO   *See* FETUS.

EMOTIVISM   A metaethical theory (*see* METAETHICS) that holds that moral words, such as *good* and *bad*, and sentences, such as "stealing is WRONG," merely express emotions.

Emotivism is associated with the twentieth-century philosophic movement known as logical positivism (*see* LOGIC). According to logical positivism, statements of fact (*see* FACT/VALUE DISTINCTION) are said to be genuine propositions because they refer to empirical properties (*see* EMPIRICAL KNOWLEDGE). Such statements are also said to have cognitive (*see* COGNITIVISM) meaning because they are either true or false. They can be verified or falsified by our senses. The logical positivists claim that moral statements, by contrast, do not refer to properties of any kind. They are, therefore, noncognitive, or neither true nor false. Positivists believe, however, that moral terms and statements do have emotive meaning; that is, instead of referring to properties, they express the feelings or emotions of a speaker (*see* PASSIONS AND EMOTIONS).

For example, "This table is brown" is an empirical or fact-stating proposition. It is either true or false, and it can be verified or falsified by observation. But the statement "This table is good," according to logical positivists, is not an empirical proposition. It is not a genuine proposition at all, they claim, because goodness is not a property of any kind. Because "good" does not refer to any PROPERTY, it has no cognitive meaning. Therefore, moral statements that use terms like *good* and *right* are neither true nor false. Saying that something is good is simply a way of expressing an attitude of approval toward that thing. As a consequence, if this position is correct, no one can ever express a true MORAL OPINION or, for that matter, a false one. It would also follow that persons could not logically disagree with one another on moral questions, for according to emotivism there is nothing for them to disagree about.

Emotivism is opposed to OBJECTIVISM, which is the belief that there is moral TRUTH, or that there are moral properties or moral facts. It is also technically opposed to SUBJECTIVISM, the theory that moral terms refer to subjective or psychological properties, such as personal feelings or attitudes. According to emotivists, moral terms do not refer to anything at all, subjective or objective. They express feelings but do not report about them. For example, to say "I have a pain in my back" is to report about how one feels, and such a statement is either true or false. But to say "Ouch!" while holding one's back in pain is not to report about the pain but to express it. According to A. J. Ayer, a British emotivist, saying that something is good or right is like saying "Hurrah!" or "Yippie!" for that thing. It is also an attempt, according to Ayer, to elicit similar feelings in others.

EMPATHY   Imagining oneself in the situation of another to gain an understanding of their problems, concerns, motivations, desires, or feelings.

Some philosophers believe that empathy is the motivation behind acting morally (*see* MORALITY). This is because empathy is more than just treating others as we would like to be treated. It also involves understanding people who may not have needs and desires similar to our own. Empathy gives us a better appreciation for why someone feels a certain way. For example, if a friend is sad, even if we think that the friend is acting irrationally, we nevertheless try to imagine ourselves in his or her situation. As a result we gain a better appreciation for why the friend is feeling sad.

Empathy is sometimes coupled with feelings of sympathy; however, it is also possible to feel sympathy without empathy and to empathize without feeling sympathetic. Sympathy is simply the hearing about the situation of another and the feeling of similar emotions. One may be sympathetic without having any idea why the other is feeling the way he or she does. For example, one may empathize with a murderer without feeling sympathetic toward him or her.

EMPIRICAL KNOWLEDGE   Knowledge acquired through our direct experience of the world.

Empirical knowledge is acquired A POSTERIORI; that is, it is knowledge that we are not born with but that we learn. An empirical fact can in theory be verified or disproved by observation or experiment. Empirical knowledge is opposed to a priori, or innate, knowledge—knowledge that we have in some sense known since birth, even if we have not been aware of it.

ENDANGERED SPECIES   Type of plant or animal whose survival is threatened.

The threat to the survival of species of plants and animals often becomes an ethical issue (*see* ETHICS) when human activities are responsible for such endangerment. For example, unrestricted hunting, the use of pesticides to protect crops, destruction of plant and animal habitats for industrial and residential development, and pollution have all contributed to the radical alteration of plant and animal habitats. Sometimes this alteration can lead to the endangerment of a species or even to extinction.

Some people feel that we have an OBLIGATION to protect endangered species either because they are inherently valuable or because they may be useful to human beings. These beliefs have spawned such legislation as the U.S. Endangered Species Acts of 1966, 1969, 1973, and 1988 that prohibit trade in endangered species and require that federal agencies assess the impact on wildlife of proposed projects. Other legislation includes the Convention on International Trade in Endangered Species. (1973), which regulates trade in endangered species as well as products derived from them. *See also* ENVIRONMENTAL ETHICS.

ENDS/MEANS   The end of an action is its goal; the means is the path to achieving the end.

When something is desired for its own sake, it has INTRINSIC VALUE or is an end in itself. In some moral theories, such as those of Immanuel KANT, we must always treat other people as ends and never as a means to an end. Means are merely the actions necessary to obtain an end. Means have only instrumental VALUE. Thus to treat someone as a means is to regard that person only as a tool to achieve a desired result. The distinction between ends and means also arises in connection with the belief that one should not perform an EVIL action for the sake of a GOOD action (*see* DOUBLE EFFECT). The relationship between ends and means in MORALITY is controversial. The common saying "The end justifies the means" implies that the goal is so valuable that anything done in its service is acceptable. For example, those who believe that all actions are motivated by survival might feel that anything done in order to preserve survival is justified (*see* EGOISM; SOCIAL DARWINISM). As we have seen above, however, others believe that for an action to be ethical (*see* ETHICS) both the ends and the means must be ethical. UTILI-TARIANS believe that it might be acceptable, in some circumstances, to use others as a means to an end if the greater HAPPINESS for all concerned is achieved. Still others suggest that when you desire a certain end, you necessarily desire all the means that led to that end.

ENLIGHTENMENT ETHICS An ethical approach associated with a belief in the EQUAL-ITY of all human beings and an optimism concerning human ability to know the GOOD through their own reason and achieve it through education and social policy.

The Enlightenment is a term that refers to an intellectual movement in Europe in the eighteenth century. The rise of science in the seventeenth and early eighteenth centuries strongly influenced the Enlightenment era. Its ethical views arise from the belief that knowledge about the world and the destiny of human beings was not dependent upon religious revelation but could be achieved through reason. Although Enlightenment thinkers varied in their religious beliefs, secularism with an emphasis on the innate goodness of human nature and the promise inherent in human understanding characterized ETHICS during this period. Enlightenment VALUES center on the equal capacity for reason of each human being and thus their equal VALUE to society and equal right to societal goods. The U.S. Constitution, for example, reflects the belief that all members of society are equal and deserve free self-expression and an equal chance to "life, liberty, and the pursuit of happiness," and this embodies the Enlightenment's ethical views.

ENTITLEMENT   *See* RIGHTS.

ENVIRONMENTAL ETHICS Specialized subject within ETHICS that investigates the nature and extent of human duties (*see* OBLIGATION) toward the planet, its animals, plants, water, and mineral resources as well as its atmosphere.

Traditional ethical theory has focused on identifying what is good for humans and on resolving ethical issues raised by interaction among humans. Some attention has also been paid to issues of ANIMAL RIGHTS, but much of the focus has been limited to cruelty to individual animals, rather than embracing issues of JUSTICE toward entire species.

Environmental ethics, however, is broader in scope than animal rights issues. Environmental ethics proposes two very difficult tasks. The first is to examine whether traditional human-centered (anthropocentric) ethics is a useful and morally defensible framework from within which to examine humans' duties toward the planet and all it contains. Its second task, assuming that a justifiable moral framework can be found for examining these issues, is to ask exactly what humans' duties are toward the planet and all it contains, including, among other things, people's duties toward animals.

In undertaking the first task, ethicists ask whether traditional moral philosophies ought to be used to construct a theory of people's duties toward the planet, its environment, and its contents. One obvious objection to traditional ethics is its heavy bias toward including only humans as members of the moral COMMUNITY and toward human VALUES, especially the value of reason.

One proposal that has been made to escape this bias is known as *zoocentrism,* which focuses on an ethic of animal liberation (*see* FREEDOM). This proposal, however, is too limited to serve as an all-encompassing ethic because it fails to consider nonanimal forms of existence (for example, plant life or ecosystems as a whole) as having a part in the moral community.

Biocentrism, the idea that all biological life forms have INTRINSIC VALUE, is also a problematic theory. It holds that all biological life forms should be preserved and have equal (*see* EQUAL-ITY) value. But in discussing environmental ethics, should people place the same value on other biological forms, such as viruses, as we do on human life? Conversely, should the last living smallpox virus be destroyed in order to protect human biological life forms from pain and death?

Ecocentrism, another environmentalist ethic, focuses on the duty to preserve biological systems that are mutually interdependent and preserving also the environments needed to sustain those systems. It is holistic but permits the use of traditional ethical theories to determine duties that humans have toward one another. However, it does not put human concerns (for example, creating more jobs) ahead of concerns for the biosystem (for example, preserving habitats for endangered species).

Ecofeminism is another environmental ethic, springing partly from those concerns that women have had in common with nature: feminist ethicists hold that both have been undervalued, mistreated, and exploited (*see* EXPLOITATION) by men for men's own needs. Ecofeminism is critical of the traditional view, based on the Bible (Genesis 1, 26–28) that humans have been given dominion (control) by God over nature and therefore are justified in exploiting and even destroying whatever in nature may gratify human needs. Rather, ecofeminists support the "steward" relationship to nature and hold that there is a moral obligation to preserve the planet as we found it and protect it if possible. They argue that not only does contemporary society lack the WISDOM to anticipate the possible catastrophic consequences of destroying the environment but that they also have duties to future generations of humans to conserve the quantity and quality of the planet's resources.

ENVY   The resentment of an advantage, possession, or attribute possessed by another person, often coupled with a DESIRE to possess that advantage, possession, or attribute.

Envy was one of the CARDINAL SINS recognized by the Christian church (*see* CHRISTIAN ETHICS) during the Middle Ages, and many moralists (*see* MORALS) continue to believe that envy is always morally WRONG. This is probably because envy can often only be fulfilled at the expense of someone else. Envy is also more often associated with a desire for "something for nothing" than a desire for self-improvement. It can, however, be argued that envy is sometimes useful because it provides a motivation for action and self-improvement.

EPICTETUS (50–130)   A Roman slave born in Greece who later became free and founded a school of STOICISM.

Epictetus dedicated himself to living and lecturing about a life of VIRTUE, conceived by him to be a life of discipline or SELF-CONTROL. The virtuous life is the life of REASON, and reason dictates that we should not be concerned about things we cannot control but only about things that lie within our POWER. We have no control over the conditions of our own birth, for example, or over the fact that we will die. Nor can we control the workings of nature or the behavior of other people, including what they may think or say about us. However, we can control our own minds or thoughts or our attitudes towards events. People who DESIRE what they cannot attain are unhappy. Happy (*see* HAPPINESS) people are those who limit their desires to what they have or to what they can attain. The goal of life is to attain peace of mind, and this can be reached only by becoming indifferent to the vicissitudes of life or to external conditions. Even physical suffering, Epictetus says, should not affect a person's peace of mind.

EPICUREAN   *See* EPICURUS.

EPICURUS (341–270 B.C.)   An ancient Greek philosopher who taught that people can attain HAPPINESS, or peace of mind, by enjoying simple pleasures and avoiding pain.

Epicurus was an egoistic hedonist (*See* EGOISM; HEDONISM), who believed that everyone naturally seeks pleasure and avoids pain and that pleasure is the ultimate GOOD, or end (*see* TELE-OLOGY), of life. However, he argued that unsatisfied DESIRE can be painful and that, for this reason, people should not desire things they cannot obtain. Therefore, he advocated living a simple life rather than a life of extravagance. He also believed that the pleasures of the mind are superior to the pleasures of the body, for while they may be less intense, they are more lasting. His model of the good life was that of living in his garden, eating and drinking with his friends, discussing philosophy.

Epicureanism is one of the major schools of ETHICS developed in ancient times and, like STOICISM, has had considerable influence on subsequent thought. Nineteenth-century UTIL-ITARIANISM, for example, is expressly hedonistic: John Stuart MILL not only defends the PLEASURE PRINCIPLE but also distinguishes between higher and lower pleasures, as does Epicurus. Hedonism is also a popular philosophy, even today, in some theories of psychology and ordinary discussions of ethics.

EQUAL RIGHTS AMENDMENT   A proposed amendment to the U.S. Constitution intended to prohibit SEXISM—DISCRIMINATION on the basis of gender.

When originally proposed in 1923, the Equal Rights Amendment (ERA) was intended to remove the many legal barriers to women that existed at the time in such areas as education, employment, and PROPERTY RIGHTS. It was opposed not only by people who believed that women were not entitled to the same rights as men but also by people who argued that the ERA would in fact have the effect of invalidating the privileges and protections that women enjoy, such as exemption from compulsory military service and eligibility for various gender specific economic support programs. The amendment was eventually passed by Congress in 1972 but never received the approval of a sufficient number of states and therefore never became a part of the Constitution. *See also* WOMEN'S RIGHTS.

EQUALITY   In ETHICS, the belief that all human beings are morally equivalent, that is, that any one human being deserves the same treatment, consideration, and respect as all others.

In its traditional sense, equality is the state of being the same, identical, and equal. When applied to human beings, however, literal equality is plainly impossible. Human beings differ in many ways. They have different skills and abilities, they have different circumstances and needs, and they even have significant physical differences. There are, however, two things that all human being appear to share: the ability to REASON and the ability to act autonomously (*see* AUTONOMY) as individuals.

Equality in the case of human beings therefore implies that all individuals are morally equivalent and equally worthy, a belief known as EGALITARIANISM. All forms of DISCRIMINATION are morally WRONG by this measure because they limit the ability of individuals to act based on traits that are correctly or incorrectly associated with a group of which they appear to be a member, rather than on an objective evaluation of that person as an individual.

The idea of equality is implicit in many ethical IDEALS. For example, the Bible seems to support implicitly the idea of equality in the passage "Do to others what you would have them do to you" (*see* GOLDEN RULE). DEONTOL-OGY, which argues that an ACT is inherently GOOD or bad regardless of the consequences, also seems to imply equality because it allows no scope for exemptions. For example, certain kinds of killing will be seen as wrong regardless of one's gender, race, status, or career. UTILI-TARIANISM, which seeks to maximize the total HAPPINESS in society, also appears to be egalitarian because no one individual's happiness is necessarily more important than anyone else's.

The extent to which the ideal of equality can be extended further than egalitarianism is a matter of significant contention. Obviously it is impossible to guarantee physical equality. For example, the bodies of men and women will always be different, and few would argue that this is anything but a good thing. Other traits are more easy to equalize, but opinions vary about the desirability of doing so. For example, the guarantee that everyone would receive an equal income could reduce the incentive for individuals to improve themselves; also, the amount would probably be insufficient for some, such as people with a disability. Before any debate on equality can occur, it is therefore important to identify the areas where equality is both possible and desirable.

To complicate matters, it is possible that equality can be achieved even though the benefits or responsibilities involved are not identical. For example, two individuals may be said to have been treated equally if one is given $20 worth of gold while the other is given $20 in cash. But since VALUE is so subjective, the two may not be equal at all. One individual may prefer the glitter of gold and therefore value it more highly than the $20 bill; conversely, $20 in gold may be impossible to spend at a store and therefore would be worthless to a starving person.

This argument—that equality does not require identical treatment—is also problematic because it creates many opportunities for abuse. For example, in the United States during the first half of the twentieth century, the doctrine of "separate but equal" was used to justify racial segregation in schools. The argument was that African Americans and white Americans had different needs and therefore should be educated separately. In 1954, however, the Supreme Court essentially found that segregation was an excuse for discrimination whereby predominantly African American schools were given significantly fewer resources than exclusively white schools.

Another factor that complicates the debate about equality is that sometimes it seems that we must treat people unequally in order to support equality. For example, nonwhites in the United States were historically treated very unequally, even though such discrimination is illegal today. It has been argued that, today, the residual effects of discrimination continue to be felt among members of the affected groups through lower wealth and low self-esteem. Some people argue that as a result, nonwhites need to be given advantages not available to whites until they can overcome the aftereffects of discriminatory policies, an idea known as AFFIRMATIVE ACTION. Others, however, argue that this solution is just as bad as the original discrimination. At the very least, a policy based on groups, and not individuals, incorrectly targets everyone in the group, even though some of them may not suffer from the effects of discrimination in the same way as others, if at all. Also, others not in the group may have equally good claims to preferential treatment.

ETHICAL CODE   *See* CODE.

ETHICS   The study of problems of RIGHT conduct in light of moral PRINCIPLES such as COMPASSION, FREEDOM, GOOD, JUSTICE, RATIONALITY, RESPONSIBILITY, and VIRTUE.

The word *ethics* comes from the Greek word *ethos,* "CHARACTER." Choices concerning what VALUES to hold and how to treat oneself and one's responsibilities to others are matters of character, or of ethics. The term *ethics* is often used interchangeably with the term *morality,* which is derived from the Latin work *mores,* "CUSTOMS." Philosophers sometimes make a distinction between ethics and morality, holding ethics to refer to the cultivation of character and practical decision making while morality refers more generally to the set of practices a society holds to be right or just. Even among those who favor this distinction, a considerable overlap between the fields of ethics and morality is recognized.

Our ethical beliefs help us distinguish right from wrong. They help us to define good and bad and to try to realize our vision of the good in our actions. Ethical beliefs help us sort through differences of opinion over what is good and what is bad. Questions like "What is the right thing to do?" and "Why is this the right thing to do?" are the basis of ethical inquiry. Ethics as a field of study inquires into why we have a sense of right and wrong at all, how ethical views are grounded, and whether or not there are universal ethical principles.

Some philosophers have held that our sense of right and wrong comes from God. Others have believed that it is a natural capacity, like our ability to reason. Still others have argued that our sense of right and wrong arises from our individual experiences in the world. These differences have given rise to various types of ethical theories.

Some philosophers believe that there are definite standards of ethical behavior, that we can know what they are, and that all people have an obligation to act on them. This position may be called ABSOLUTISM. Absolutists may believe that ethical standards are religious in nature (see RELIGION AND MORALITY), or they may believe that the standards are dictated by human reason. In either case this position is characterized by a belief in the ability to universalize ethics.

Another group of thinkers holds that there are definite standards of right behavior but that more than one right standard exists. This position is known as PLURALISM. A pluralist may hold that there are several right courses of action, but the pluralist does not open the door to saying that anything a person feels to be right is necessarily ethical. One form of pluralism is known as CULTURAL RELATIVISM. This theory holds that different standards of right and wrong arise in different cultures. Within a given culture there are distinct standards, but these standards may vary from culture to culture. Cultural relativists hold that no culture is in a position to make ethical judgments about the behaviors of other cultures. Those who subscribe to a more extreme type of RELATIVISM hold that individuals have to decide for themselves what is right and wrong

based on experience and that no one can tell other people what they should do.

The study of ethics is sometimes divided into METAETHICS and normative ethics (see NORMATIVE ETHICS). Metaethics is the inquiry into the meanings of ethical terms like compassion, duty, freedom, good, justice, rationality, responsibility, right, and virtue. Metaethical inquiries are also concerned with what ethical terms have in common, how we know whether ethical judgments are right or wrong, and how we can recognize ethical views as consistent and coherent. For example, the question of whether or not we can claim to derive values from the facts of the world is a metaethical question. Naturalism, COGNITIVISM, INTUITIONISM, EMOTIVISM, and SUBJECTIVISM are all forms of metaethical theories.

Whereas metaethics deals with the meanings and concepts in ethics, normative ethics deals with questions of what to do and how to act. We might think of normative ethics as dealing with norms of behavior. Theories on how we should act are often divided into those based on CONSEQUENTIALISM and those that are based on DEONTOLOGY. Consequentialists hold that we should choose the actions that bring about the best outcomes. EGOISM, for example, holds that we should always act to maximize our own individual interests. UTILITARIANISM, on the other hand, holds that we should act to maximize the happiness of all affected by the action. Deontologists hold that we should choose actions based on their intrinsic worth. Other theories of right action appeal to divine will. SITUATION ETHICS teaches that ethics depends on the situation that calls for action and not on any principle.

APPLIED ETHICS is the branch of normative ethics that deals with questions of professional ethics in fields such as science, engineering, lay, medicine (see MEDICAL ETHICS), business (see BUSINESS ETHICS), and journalism (see JOURNALISM ETHICS). Applied ethics may also raise questions of how to distribute scare resources and services and of ENVIRONMENTAL ETHICS. Ethical issues in new fields such as BIOETHICS and COMPUTER ETHICS concern the ethical uses of new techniques in science and new technologies.

ETHNOCENTRISM   The tendency to see one's own culture as superior, and to evaluate other cultures by exclusive reference to one's own.

Ethnocentrism is generally seen as undesirable in Western societies, and the idea that other societies are somehow inferior or abnormal is now widely discredited. Examples of ethnocentric outlooks include claims that a country is backward because its people live in homes that lack indoor plumbing or that a culture is stupid and unsophisticated because it has not produced great scientific achievements. In neither of these cases, however, is it possible to make a legitimate VALUE JUDGMENT.

Supporters of RELATIVISM argue that all VALUES are culturally relative and therefore believe that it is ethnocentric to use Western concepts of MORALITY to judge other cultures. Ethicists (*see* ETHICS) who believe that there are such things as moral ABSOLUTES find this position problematic. Unfortunately, what constitutes a moral absolute is often difficult to define. For example, are individual rights applicable to cultures with a tradition of collective responsibility? *See also* RACISM.

ETIQUETTE   Conventional manners and ceremonies.

Etiquette concerns the use of GOOD manners, consideration for other people, and observance of often unspoken RULES of behavior for RIGHT conduct in social situations. Etiquette is considered conventional because it is dependent upon the CUSTOMS of a particular social group. Proper etiquette in one group may differ from proper etiquette in another group or in other circumstances. In one society, for instance, etiquette may dictate that people eat only with their hands, while in another forks and knives are preferred.

Typically, etiquette is not thought to have moral significance. If someone is harmed or perhaps more likely offended by improper etiquette, then moral considerations may come into play. The moral impropriety, if any, is dependent on the offensiveness of the action.

EUDIAMONISTIC ETHICS   *See* HAPPINESS.

EUGENICS   A branch of science concerned with the improvement of any species, race, or breed, but especially human beings, by selecting for desirable traits through methods such as selective breeding.

As it is applied to humans, eugenics was first developed by Sir Francis Galton in England in 1869. Galton based his theories on the work of his cousin, Charles Darwin, who only ten years earlier had published his theory of EVOLUTION. Eugenicists believe that if the human race is to advance and survive, genetically inferior people should be prevented from reproducing.

In Galton's time, it was widely believed that a person's social position and economic status were good indicators of that person's genetic fitness. At the time, those believed to be of inferior genetic stock included people suffering from mental illnesses, physical disabilities or epilepsy, criminals convicted of sex crimes, alcoholics, homosexuals, and people in professions considered to be socially undesirable, such as prostitution.

Some eugenics programs simply urge people with desirable, adaptive traits to reproduce. Other programs are more coercive. For example, compulsory serialization laws for individuals deemed to be of inferior genetic stock were passed in thirty U.S. states between 1907 and 1931. Eugenics has also been used to justify various forms of RACISM, such as the United States' IMMIGRATION Restriction Law (1924) which limited the number of immigrants from southern and eastern Europe on the grounds that they were "biologically inferior." Eugenics arguments were also used to justify the retention of 300-year-old antimiscegenation laws that prohibited marriage between people of different races in many southern states of the United States.

Eugenics, however, was most aggressively embraced in Nazi Germany under Adolf Hitler and culminated in Hitler's Eugenic Sterilization Law, which permitted the sterilization of non-Aryan peoples in Nazi Germany and, later, in other countries invaded by the German Third Reich. Theories of eugenics were used to justify the MURDER of six million Jews, Gypsies, and homosexuals by the Nazis during the HOLOCAUST.

Partially because of its history of ELITISM and racism, as well as its association with Nazi Germany, eugenics has come to be seen as morally reprehensible in many Western countries. Eugenics is problematic because it relies on a subjective VALUE JUDGMENT about which traits are "GOOD" and which are "bad." Many of the theories underlying eugenics, such as racial inferiority and the inheritability of criminal tendencies, have also been widely discredited.

In contrast, the voluntary use of genetic science by individuals to avoid suffering is now becoming more widely accepted. For example, parents with a family history of genetically transmittable diseases, such as Tay Sachs and sickle cell anemia, may voluntarily refrain from having children. In addition, in an increasing number of cases, genetic science is now being used to test for potential genetic defects in an unborn fetus, the results of which may be used to justify the termination of a pregnancy (*see* ABORTION). *See also* GENETIC ENGINEERING; PREJUDICE; SOCIAL DARWINISM.

EUTHANASIA   An attempt to bring about a quick and painless death, especially for individuals who are sick or suffering; sometimes also called MERCY killing.

The moral JUSTIFICATION for euthanasia is thought to be the need to relieve intense and needless suffering, especially in cases where the person (or animal) is likely to die soon anyway. Thus, the question of euthanasia usually arises when someone is terminally ill or in a comatose state with little chance of recovery. Those who argue against euthanasia usually hold that it is WRONG to kill another human being deliberately, even for the purpose of relieving extreme pain.

When debating euthanasia, it is sometimes worthwhile to distinguish between active and passive euthanasia. Active euthanasia is the termination of a life by a deliberate act, such as prescribing or administering fatal medication or even a gunshot. Passive euthanasia, by contrast, means not doing something that would keep a person alive, such as withholding medication or even food and drink. In accordance with this distinction, it is sometimes argued that under certain conditions, passive euthanasia is justified while active euthanasia never is.

This distinction is difficult to maintain, however, at least in certain cases. If in a hospital, for example, a person is being kept alive on a machine, would pulling the plug on the machine be active or passive euthanasia? If we suppose that pulling the plug is something actively done to bring about death, then it certainly appears to be active euthanasia. However, it is also a way of withholding treatment, albeit treatment already begun. Some philosophers would argue that it makes no difference in any case. If the INTENTION of the agent is to bring about death, then the intention is the same, whatever means are chosen. Furthermore, if one's emphasis is on consequences, then the consequences—the death of the suffering person—are also the same.

Another distinction may be drawn between people who voluntarily request euthanasia and involuntary euthanasia, which is where the wishes of a dying patient are not or cannot be made known (*see* SUBSTITUTED JUDGMENT). If a suffering person wants somebody else to help him or her to die, the death in this case is sometimes called assisted SUICIDE.

Presumably, it would be MURDER to kill somebody who does not want to die, but in many places assisted suicide is also considered to be unjustified killing and is against the law. Opponents of euthanasia often argue that even if there are cases where the practice is morally justified, it is impossible to guarantee that its legalization would not result in widespread abuses. For example, the child of a sick parent could manipulate the parent into authorizing her or his own euthanasia simply so that child can collect an inheritance. *See also* DEATH AND DYING; MEDICAL ETHICS.

EVIL   Extreme IMMORALITY; something totally incompatible with, and in opposition to, moral goodness.

Evil is not just amoral, that is, the absence of MORALS; it is the complete opposite of GOOD. Evils may fall into two categories, natural evils and moral evils. Natural evils are acts of nature that create misery and suffering. They are events that have terrible consequences but that are not due to an intentional ACT on the part of a moral agent. For example, a catastrophe such as a violent earthquake that results in many deaths may be described as a natural evil. Moral evils, on the other hand, are morally reprehensible decisions made by moral agents (*see* MORAL AGENCY) in the full knowledge that they are doing WRONG.

Few situations are morally unambiguous, and *evil* is therefore a term that is used sparingly and with caution. For instance, most people agree that bank robbery is wrong, but if the person is confused or desperate, most would say that the bank robber is bad but not evil.

EVIL, PROBLEM OF   The problem of reconciling how a perfectly GOOD and powerful (*see* POWER) GOD can create a world with evil in it.

The problem of EVIL refers to the CONSISTENCY of believing (*see* FAITH) that God is supremely good and supremely powerful and at the same time recognizing that evil exists in the world. If God is perfectly good, the argument goes, then God would not create a world with evil in it but rather a world that is perfectly good, and if God is all-powerful, then God could create a world that is perfectly good. Why, then, is there evil in the world? One conclusion is that evil in the world is a sign that God is not all-good or all-powerful because he lacks the WILL or ability to prevent evil. Indeed, the fact that evil exists has been used as an argument against the existence of God: If there were a God, there would be no evil, but there is evil, so there must be no God.

Several philosophers and theologians had addressed the problem of evil. AUGUSTINE, for example, argued that everything God creates is good. Evil is the absence of goodness and so has no creator. The world God creates is good but imperfect because it is necessarily less than God. The seventeenth-century philosopher Leibnitz argued that although this world is imperfect, God creates the best of all possible worlds, one that contains as much goodness as can exist. Only so much goodness is possible in a created world, he held, because the existence of any one thing necessarily limits the existence of other things. The total amount of goodness, however, is always as much as possible.

EVOLUTION   In biology, the process by which the genetic makeup of a population transforms over a long period of time resulting in changes in species and in the emergence of new species.

In the nineteenth century, due largely to the publicity of the work of English naturalist Charles Darwin, theories about human evolution brought into question traditional ways of thinking about ETHICS. Applying the PRINCIPLES of evolution to human beings suggested that human beings evolved from genetic transformation in earlier primates and were not literally created by GOD in his image. This theory challenged the basis for many religious theories about the special moral status of human beings.

Philosophers such as Herbert Spencer attempted to base new ethical theories on the presumed facts of evolution. These theories, often referred to as SOCIAL DARWINISM, emphasize the struggle for natural selection and the priority of the "survival of the fittest." This school of evolutionary ethics justifies social inequalities by arguing that those best fit to survive naturally and deservedly acquire social goods. More modern schools of evolutionary ethics focus on more recent biological discoveries that suggest that ALTRUISM and kin-selection play an important role in species survival. These theories emphasize cooperation and collaboration over aggression and competition. Other philosophers reject the idea that the theories or facts associated with evolution have any bearing on moral thought. They observe the FACT/VALUE DISTINCTION that holds that matters of fact about nature do not necessarily imply ethical or moral values. *See also* SOCIOBIOLOGY.

EXCELLENCE   A quality attributed to people who possess a skill or characteristic to a superior degree.

Excellence can be a standard of goodness (*see* GOOD), as in the case of a MORAL EXEMPLAR or a MORAL SAINT. ARISTOTLE believed that HAPPINESS occurs when individuals excel at traits that are unique to human beings, such as REASON. MORAL PERFECTIONISM is a theory that claims everyone has a moral RESPONSIBILITY to seek human excellence, whether intellectual, artistic, or athletic.

EXISTENTIALISM   A nineteenth- and twentieth-century movement in philosophy, literature, and the arts that investigates the "absurdity" of human existence in a godless, amoral (*see* AMORALITY) cosmos.

Existentialists typically believe that individual human beings are alone in the universe, with no antecedent moral order (*see* MORAL COMPASS) to guide their choices, no transcendent HUMAN NATURE to vouchsafe their desires for COMMUNITY,

and no beneficent deity to oversee their plans. Existentialist authors thus attempt to dramatize the isolation of the human condition in such literary classics as *Notes From Underground,* by Fyodor Dostoyevsky; *The Stranger* and *The Plague,* by Albert Camus; and *Waiting for Godot,* by Samuel Beckett.

Although existentialism is not defined by a single core teaching, its dominant disposition is conveyed by Jean-Paul SARTRE's succinct observation that "existence precedes essence." This slogan suggests that human beings attain their meaning, identity, and VALUE—in short, their "essence"—only by virtue of their very existence and not by virtue of some preestablished nature or destiny. Existentialists consequently identify human subjectivity with FREEDOM itself, with the dynamic capacity to choose and to ACT, which they typically contrast with the brute "unfreedom" of objects and things. Existentialism thus essays a teaching of radical human freedom, which holds each human being ultimately responsible for the shape and course of her or his life. This teaching of radical human freedom is regularly received, however, as both terrifying and onerous. Very few individuals are truly willing (and able) to accept full responsibility for their lives. Friedrich NIETZSCHE reserved the term *übermensch* (or "overman") for such "existential heroes," whereas Søren KIERKEGAARD, a Christian existentialist (*see* CHRISTIAN ETHICS), preferred to call them "knights of FAITH."

The notion of a distinctly existentialist approach to ETHICS is notoriously difficult to convey, for existentialist authors typically disavow any interest in ethics. As a development within the study of ontology, existentialism aims to restrict itself to a factual description of human existence; existentialist thinkers consequently claim not to offer a normative prescription for how human beings ought to shape their existence (see NORMATIVE ETHICS). Moreover, because existentialists view conventional MORALITY as one of the most formidable obstacles to the authentic realization of human freedom, they are wary of providing yet another moral CODE. This is not to say, of course, that existentialist thinkers successfully resist the urge to moralize: they regularly present their theories in a discourse or vocabulary that suggests the likelihood of ethical ramifications.

Insofar as we may speak meaningfully of an "ethics of existentialism," this enterprise would comprise two related projects. First, existentialists prize the disclosive project of debunking religious dogmas, objective verities, and preordained orders. Much of the enduring interest in authors like Dostoyevsky, Nietzsche, and Kierkegaard is attributable to their prodigious iconoclasm, to their ability to expose and explode the saving fictions under which most human beings unreflectively labor. Second, existentialists often imply that a positive "moral" value accrues to the attainment of AUTHENTICITY, which is the closest existentialism comes to an ethical ideal (*see* IDEALS) or standard.

Although authenticity is a difficult concept to define in the writings of most existentialists, it generally conveys a sense of remaining true to oneself in one's radical freedom, of refusing to allow others to define the ambit of one's agency. Because human beings possess no antecedent "essence" or "nature," most existentialists associate authenticity with freedom itself, with the ever-renewing power to express oneself through resolute choices and actions. Existentialists typically believe that human life derives its meaning only from the continuous exercise of one's radical freedom. What one chooses is not so important; that one chooses is sufficient to honor the radical freedom that constitutes human subjectivity.

Those who will not choose the meaning of their existence wallow in inauthenticity, which Sartre has famously called bad faith. Inauthenticity is the condition wherein one chooses to believe that one possesses an essence, nature, or destiny that is impervious to human volition. Human beings live in bad faith when they pretend not to be radically free, by allowing themselves to be defined by religion, history, politics, popular opinion, and other external forces. Those who live in bad faith thus actively deny their own radical freedom, preferring to treat themselves (and be treated by others) as objects or things.

Although existentialism actively eschews all forms of conventional morality and organized religion, several thinkers have attempted to develop a distinctly religious articulation of existentialism. Dostoyevsky depicted the cruel, godless world of human existence as the crucible within which true Christian LOVE and CHARITY are forged (*see* CHRISTIAN ETHICS). Through the protracted experience of exemplary suffering, one might gain a sense of connection and community with other tortured souls. Kierkegaard similarly appealed to the sheer absurdity of human existence as the sole legitimate ground of Christian faith. Only in a world abandoned by GOD could one truly risk the "leap of faith" that would galvanize one's spirituality.

Existentialism is no longer as popular and influential as it was in the 1940s and 1950s. Critics now dismiss it as a faddish movement born of the angst and despair surrounding World Wars I and II. As a potential source of normative ethical teachings, existentialism is often criticized for overstating the bounds of human freedom, for placing an inordinate emphasis on choice and volition, and for failing to develop prescriptions that might enable human beings to derive more determinate HAPPINESS and meaning from their lives. Yet, the enduring appeal of existentialism remains strong, especially as a point of departure for any serious exploration of the loneliness and isolation of the human condition.

EXPLOITATION Taking advantage of the weakness or vulnerability of a person, group, or thing for the benefit of another in a way that is not in the best interests of that person, group, or thing.

The person best known for his discussion of exploitation is Karl MARX. Marx argued that CAPITALISM is inherently exploitative because it concentrates everything a worker needs to survive, except the worker's own labor, in the hands of a small number of elites (*see* ELITISM). The elites then ensure that a worker is vulnerable by creating unemployment through labor-saving technologies. Unemployment creates a pool of unemployed people who are willing to work for next to nothing just so that they can survive, and this drives wages down. The system is exploitative because elites use a weakness on the part of workers—the overabundance of labor—to take advantage of them by extracting profits that far exceed the elites' own contribution to production.

Exploitation can also occur between groups or organizations. For example, rich countries can exploit poorer ones, a practice known as COLONIALISM.

EXTRINSIC VALUE A measure of usefulness ascribed to a person or thing because of its relation to achieving external needs, desires, or goals.

Something has extrinsic value when it is useful as a means to an end that we DESIRE (*see* ENDS/MEANS). This type of value is opposed to INTRINSIC VALUE, when a person or thing is valued in and of itself. For example, a dog kept as a pet may be valued as watchdog for the security of the home. In contrast, other people may value a pet dog because they feel affection for the animal itself, regardless of whether the pet renders any service to the home.

Some philosophers, such as Immanuel KANT, believe that acting morally has intrinsic value, that we ought to do what is RIGHT simply because it is the right thing to do. Kant also believed that we should always treat people as intrinsically valuable and never as a means to an end. Other moral thinkers believe that MORALITY is wholly extrinsic, that morality is needed, for example, to help us gain the kind of social life we want by promoting neighborhoods safe from crime, by promoting the greatest happiness possible, or by helping people to gain a good reputation.

F

FACT/VALUE DISTINCTION The distinction between matters of fact and statements of VALUE.

The fact/value distinction holds that we cannot derive statements of moral value (*see* MORALITY), or "ought statements," simply from matters of fact about the world (*see* IS/OUGHT DISTINCTION). The fact/value distinction strives to keep descriptions of the world and evaluations of the world separate. For example, the fact/value distinction states that just because animals kill, it does not follow that human beings ought to kill. The fact that animals kill is a descriptive fact. It describes the way the world is. It is true or false based on events in the world and not on anyone's opinion. When we say that it is right for human beings, as animals, to kill we are making an evaluative claim. An evaluative claim depends on personal preference, social custom, or a belief about what is good for human beings. The fact/value distinction is often attributed to the British philosopher David HUME.

Other moral philosophers criticize the fact/value distinction arguing that our value judgments (*see* JUDGMENT) color our perception of the facts from the beginning. It is our value judgments that determine which facts we pick out as important and which we decide are unimportant. Thus, they deny that any clear separation between fact and value can underlie a moral theory.

FAIRNESS Achieving the right balance of interests without regard to one's own feelings and without showing favor to any side in a conflict.

Fairness implies IMPARTIALITY or lack of BIAS. To be fair is to favor neither side. To be fair to someone is to gather all the relevant facts, consider only circumstances relevant to the decision at hand, and not be swayed by PREJUDICE or irrelevancies. For example, a judge in a trial is expected to be dispassionate and to make a decision based solely on the facts of the case.

Fairness means being sure that people receive what is due to them and no less. This means giving others the credit that is due them and giving them an honest deal in business arrangements. Favoritism is unfairly awarding honors, jobs, or duties. It may also be considered unfair to gossip or spread rumors that might mislead others about a person's reputation.

FAITH Holding attitudes, ideas, and positions in the absence of proof or of fully convincing evidence.

To have faith is to have conviction or trust even in the absence of proof or assurance. Some thinkers characterize faith as contrary to REASON. Those who do so emphasize that faith is a belief that rests on something other than reasoned knowledge. For example, faith may mean believing in the revealed truths (*see* TRUTH) of GOD. Those who hold that there are doctrines that cannot be understood through reason but only through faith are called fideists. Søren KIERKEGAARD is an example of one thinker whose ethical (*see* ETHICS) and religious views are fideistic. Fideism poses special problems for ethics because the nature of truths of faith is private and is revealed only intimately to those chosen by God. Because others cannot verify or deny these faiths based on reason, they must either accept or reject the tenets based solely on their own faith or on the AUTHORITY of the person who has experienced the revelation.

Still others hold that faith and reason are not contradictory but different and complementary functions that can operate harmoniously. In this view faith and reason simply have different objects. Some ideas are appropriate to the realm of faith, while others fall within the realm of reason. Immanuel KANT, for example, is famous for delimiting the scope of reason so as to make clear the areas that are left to faith.

FALLACY   A flaw or error in reasoning.

In logic, an argument is invalid if its conclusion does not follow necessarily from its premises. Reasoning (*see* REASON) may be flawed in many ways. Typically, a distinction is made between formal fallacies and informal fallacies. Formal fallacies are those in which the form of the argument is flawed or in which the conclusion does not follow from the premises. For example, consider the argument "Socrates is a man. All men are mortal. Therefore, Socrates is mortal." This argument is deductively true because the conclusion follows from, or is demonstrated by, the premises. The argument has the form *A is B, B is C; therefore A is C*. All arguments of this form are necessarily true. Now consider the argument that Socrates is a man and Plato is a man; therefore Socrates is Plato. The form of this argument is *A is B, C is B; therefore C is A* (or *A is C*). This is an invalid argument form. Arguments of this form will never be necessarily true, although it may happen by contingency that they are true. We call this type of flawed reason a formal fallacy.

Informal fallacies are flawed arguments in which the fault in the reasoning does not lie in the form of the argument—or at least not in the form alone. Informal fallacies are usually a result of ambiguity or lack of clarity in what is being said or of irrelevance in cases where the reasons offered to support a conclusion are not relevant to its TRUTH. The standard treatment of informal fallacies relies heavily on ARISTOTLE, but there many variants and new fallacies as well. It is particularly important to beware of informal fallacies in ethical (*see* ETHICS) reasoning because people may seem convincing when in fact their reasoning trades on subtle mistakes or rhetorical tactics. The ability to identify informal fallacies and dispute them is a useful tool in gaining resolution in ethical conflict. Informal fallacies also cause misunderstanding, even when there is no intent to deceive or falsely persuade someone of an ethical position. People may be arguing different points or issues when they think they are arguing about the same issues because they are using the same words with different meanings. There are several frequently committed types of informal fallacies.

In the class of informal fallacies based on ambiguities, the most common is that of equivocation, the use of a word in a single context to mean two different things. For example, consider the argument "The media should truthfully report all matters of public interest. The public is very interested in the personal lives of politicians. Therefore, the media should report all facts about the personal lives of politicians." In this argument there is an equivocation between the term *public interest* meaning the public good *public interest* indicating public curiosity. Although the argument may sound convincing, it is in fact unsound because it relies on two different and noninterchangeable senses of *public interest*.

In the class of informal fallacies based on irrelevancies, there are twelve common types: ad hominem, appeal to pity, argument from authority, argument from the consensus of nations, begging the question, fallacy of composition, fallacy of division, fallacy of false cause, fallacy of complex questions, genetic fallacy, missing the point, and the SLIPPERY SLOPE ARGUMENT.

Ad hominem arguments are personal attacks. A person using an ad hominem argument tries to refute another person's position by attacking that person's CHARACTER, rather than by addressing the argument. For example, suppose a friend argued that you should be more frugal with your money; suppose you replied, "Why should I listen to someone who once bounced a check? You cannot even keep your own finances straight!" This reply, while possibly true, would be an attack on your friend, not a refutation of your friend's argument.

An appeal to pity occurs when a person uses an appeal to sympathy, pity, or COMPASSION in order to support a conclusion. For example, a worker may argue that he should be excused for his lateness because he has a family to support and they would be out on the streets without his job.

The argument from authority occurs when a person improperly appeals to an expert opinion when (a) that opinion is in contradiction with other "expert" opinions or (b) the expert is not an expert in a relevant field. The second type of improper appeal to authority is related to the advertising tactic of hiring celebrities to endorse products that are not necessarily related to their field of success. For example, when a celebrity is a spokesperson for a company or product, there is the inclination to believe that if you like the celebrity you can therefore trust that product.

The argument from the consensus of nations occurs when a person appeals to what "everyone knows" or "everyone believes" in order to support a conclusion. The argument, "People have always killed in self-defense; therefore it must be moral" is an example of the argument from the consensus of nations. The critical thinker must realize that just because people have always engaged in a practice or belief does not make it RIGHT. According to this line of reasoning, for example, slavery would never have been abolished.

Begging the question occurs when someone assumes the important points of the argument in the premises rather than proving them in the conclusion. Consider the following conversation:

"George Washington was a good president."
"Why?"
"Because he made good laws."
"Why do you say that?"
"Because if he hadn't passed good laws, he wouldn't have been a good president."

The first speaker argues that Washington was a good president because he passed good laws. But he supports that claim by returning to the premise of the argument: the laws must be good because Washington was a good president. That Washington was a good president, however, is what the speaker should prove. While Washington may be a good president, no evidence for this fact is given by the first speaker.

The fallacy of composition occurs when someone attempts to argue that because something is true of the parts of a whole that it must be true of the whole. For example, if you take one apple out of a bag and it tastes good, that does not guarantee that each apple in the bag will be good. We could also imagine a situation where the individual parts of a machine were all in good working order, but because of an incompatibility among the parts the machine itself did not work. If we argued that because the parts are all working the whole machine must work, we have committed the fallacy of composition.

The fallacy of division, on the other hand, occurs when someone attempts to argue that because something has certain properties, then each part of that thing must share the same properties. For example, if a football team wins the Super Bowl, that does not imply that every player on the team is the best in the league.

The fallacy of false cause occurs when someone argues that because two events vary together that one must be the cause of the other. For example, it may happen that your best test scores coincide with rainy days. However, this does not mean that you do well on your tests because it is raining. It could simply be a coincidence, or it could be attributed to some other factor.

The fallacy of complex questions occurs when a question presupposes something that should be determined by argument or evidence. For example, the question "Why did you kick your dog?" assumes that you did in fact kick the dog. Unless the person asking the question witnessed this event, he or she is begging the question of whether or not you kicked the dog, implying that it is known that you did and that all that is left to determine is your MOTIVE.

The genetic fallacy occurs when we argue that because a thing originally had certain properties or that because its origin had certain properties, the thing must still have those properties. For example, suppose you knew that you could not drink directly from a source of water. That need not imply that after the proper treatment, you could not drink the water from that source.

The fallacy of missing the point occurs when a participant in an argument does not keep to the point of the argument but argues other more or less related points intentionally or as a diversion.

The fallacy of the slippery slope occurs when someone objects to an action that is not WRONG in and of itself because it is believed that action will lead to other undesirable actions. One of the most famous arguments of this type is waged against euthanasia. Opponents of euthanasia often argue that if you allow some people to choose to end their lives, it will lead to a sequence of events where others who might still enjoy some quality of life will choose to end their lives, and this choice will be sanctioned by the hospital or by the state.

FAMILY VALUES   The belief that the family is an important social unit that should be supported and protected.

In its broadest sense, a family is a group of people, usually involving children, who are related to each other either by blood, adoption, or by legal or de facto MARRIAGE. How a family is made up has much to do with the society one comes from. For example, families in some cultures commonly involve three or more adult partners in a relationship, such as a man with several wives or, less commonly, vice versa. In most Western cultures, however, when one speaks of the family, one is generally referring to the *nuclear* family, which consists of a man and woman who are in a permanent relationship and are the parents or legal guardians of one or more children. In the United States, when one refers to *family values,* one is, therefore, generally referring to VALUES that support and encourage the nuclear family.

In recent years, the term has been appropriated by supporters of conservative, Judeo-Christian political organizations (*see* CONSERVATISM), who believe that permissiveness, irreligiousness, and moral laxity are detrimental to the nuclear family. They argue that tolerance of such things as HOMOSEXUALITY, ABORTION, sexual promiscuity, and PORNOGRAPHY have led to the disintegration of the traditional religious family and to an increase in lawlessness. Others, however, respond that even if this is the case, there is no reason why the traditional family is the ideal, given that it has historically involved highly segregated gender roles, with a job-holding father as head of the household and a mother primarily responsible for child rearing and homemaking. Apart from being sexist, the traditional nuclear family is also arguably no longer practical. In order to maintain a comfortable lifestyle (*see* LIFESTYLES), it has become increasingly necessary for both partners to hold full-time jobs.

FASCISM   A political philosophy that argues that one's own nation state is the single most important moral unit.

Fascists emphasize the need for a strong, centralized government that exercises dictatorial control over its people and encourages and enforces a high degree of NATIONALISM, social cohesiveness, and uniformity. Fascism is a form of authoritarianism, and all members of the state are expected to blindly and unquestioningly follow the dictates of governmental AUTHORITY.

Fascists believe that individuals must be prepared to SACRIFICE themselves for the COMMON GOOD. Indeed, just as an individual is willing to sacrifice a limb to save his or her whole body, the state will sacrifice individual members for what it believes to be the GOOD of the whole. Each part of the state takes its identity from and exists for the whole. In this way, fascists are hostile to notions of HUMAN RIGHTS and INDIVIDUALISM.

Fascist movements usually appear behind a strong, charismatic leader, such as Benito Mussolini, the Italian leader from 1922 to 1943, and later Adolf Hitler, the German leader between 1933 and 1945. Fascists often espouse RACISM, partially because they generally require the appearance of a serious internal or external threat to justify (see JUSTIFICATION) autocratic rule and because of a common nationalist emphasis on the superiority of their country and its dominant racial group.

Interestingly, although fascism is generally seen as being far to the right of the political spectrum, many self described communist countries (see COMMUNISM) of the twentieth century were in practice fascist in all but name.

FATALISM   *See* FREEDOM.

FELICIFIC CALCULUS   An equation intended to compute the greatest HAPPINESS for the greatest number in the UTILITARIAN philosophy of Jeremy BENTHAM.

Bentham believed that the goal of our actions should be to maximize the happiness of those affected by our actions. The amount of pleasure involved in an activity defined the amount of happiness that activity generated. Thus, the MORALITY of an action could be calculated by weighing the pleasures and pains (*see* HEDONISM) caused by an action. This belief rests on the notion that there is a meaningful way to measure pleasure. Bentham believed that pleasures could be ordered by intensity, duration, and proximity. Some pleasures might be dismissed if they arise from actions that are likely to lead to pain or suffering. Based on this method, Bentham believed he could construct an objective system within which we could evaluate different actions by performing the felicific calculus. We could then determine what action would generate the most units of pleasure and thus bring about the greatest happiness.

Those who challenge the validity of the felicific calculus argue that there is no meaningful way to calculate pleasures and pains objectively. They may also argue that happiness is not correctly identified with pleasures or that happiness and pleasure are not the correct basis for morality.

FEMINIST ETHICS   An approach to the ethical theory (*see* ETHICS) that explicitly seeks to identify and correct BIAS against women in traditional (*see* CUSTOMS) moral philosophy.

The term *feminist ethics* refers to a related group of moral issues concerning gender bias in ethical theories, as well as in social and political structures, legal procedures, and general culture. Feminist ethics is not a unified moral philosophy. There are wide varieties of views, including liberal, radical, postmodernist, lesbian, ecofeminist, and other schools of feminist thought. What these variations on feminist ethics have in common are assumptions that (a) subordination of women and (b) devaluation of the common moral experience of women are morally unjustifiable.

Feminist theorists point out that men and women seldom have been similarly situated socially. Men have typically enjoyed greater social status and privilege. That privilege has emerged in both theories and policies that have subordinated women to men. Traditional moral theories concern themselves primarily with "public MORALITY," or the relationship of citizens to each other and to the state, rather than with "personal morality," the relationship of individuals to each other within the family. Historically, however, the domain of citizenship and politics has been the domain of men. The private domain or family has more fully included women, although not necessarily in equal (*see* EQUALITY) standing with men. Because of the emphasis on the public, a sphere in which women were often excluded, traditional ethical theories have often privileged typically male VIRTUES (such as COURAGE) while diminishing typically female virtues (such as COMPASSION).

Feminists ethicists also claim that a bias against women is evident in traditional moral theory's goal to control the PASSIONS AND EMOTIONS through REASON and the attendant implication that reason (which has been historically assumed to be a male virtue) is morally superior to emotion (which has been historically ascribed as a female virtue). Feminist ethicists, including Nel Noddings and Genevieve Lloyd, maintain that traditional theories wrongly devalue and disparage women's interests and women's abilities and wrongly ascribe a set of "lesser virtues" to women (for example, patience, OBEDIENCE, subservience, HUMILITY) than to men (for example, decisiveness, independence, AUTONOMY, PRIDE). Feminist ethicists dispute the traditional assumption that moral theories are objective, unbiased, and able to be universalized, even though they rarely address the social status of women, or women's traditional role in the moral education of children.

Ancient feminist philosophy can be traced to AESARA OF LUCANIA, a Pythagorean philosopher who may have been a contemporary of PLATO. Aesara held that the Pythagorean virtue of *harmonia,* maintaining an appropriate balance among reason and the affective emotions including LOVE, and the WILL, was a virtue for the home (that is, in private, among family members) as well as for the state (that is, in public, in government).

Medieval feminist philosophy is represented in the work of French writer Christine de Pizan, whose *Book of the City of Ladies* was modeled after AUGUSTINE's *City of God.* Pizan's Lady Reason, Lady Righteousness, and Lady Rectitude argue for the moral equality of women with men.

In the modern period, the English philosopher Mary Wollstonecraft published *A Vindication of the Rights of Woman,* in which she urged the leaders of the American and French revolutions to grant equal RIGHTS to women (*see* EQUAL RIGHTS AMENDMENT). English philosopher John Stuart MILL wrote an eloquent essay *The Subjection of Women* (1869) opposing the view of his father James Mill, who held that women did not need to have economic and political rights—their interests would be taken care of by their fathers or husbands.

Contemporary researchers such as Carol GILLIGAN have held that when women make moral judgments they do so in consideration of maintaining close, loving relationships with others rather than in consideration of whether RULES or PRINCIPLES are upheld.

Feminist ethics is not concerned exclusively with women's rights, interests, and issues, nor with the substitution of traditionally feminine for masculine values. Feminist ethics also shows how bias in traditional ethical theories has historically perpetuated RACISM, HOMOPHOBIA, and the EXPLOITATION of animals and the environment. This historically male perspective accounts for the traditional depiction of ANIMAL RIGHTS, CHILD ABUSE, and GAY RIGHTS as issues of conflicts among rights rather than as issues of natural, human care and concern for others; that is, men have historically viewed ethical issues in terms of conflicts of rights, whereas women have historically seen them as pointing out the importance of caring about and being concerned for others. Similarly, male privilege has led to conceptualizing ENVIRONMENTAL ETHICS as dominion over, rather than stewardship of, the planet's ecosystems. For ecofeminists, this bias is also reflected in limiting the domain of moral parties and failing to see the interconnectedness with and duties toward what they considered to be lower forms—so-called primitive peoples, children, members of other species, and the planet. Feminist ethics seeks to develop a more holistic, inclusive moral philosophy.

Critics of feminist ethics argue that even if we assume that the feminist assessment of traditional moral theories is correct, there are still grave problems with the alternatives proposed by feminist ethicists. For example, a critic might hold that to achieve fairness in a society, it is important to adhere to rules and not to consider personal relationships or special circumstances. Other critics object that it is misleading to term care-based approaches to ethics feminine and rule-based approaches male.

FETUS   Medical term describing the stage of human development from nine weeks after conception until birth.

A fertilized ovum is a zygote until it is implanted in the uterine wall (about one week after fertilization) and an embryo until the ninth week after fertilization. From then until birth, the organism is called a fetus. A fetus is not capable of living outside the uterus until it weighs about 500 grams (slightly more than 1 pound) and is 20 weeks past the date of fertilization.

The question of whether the fetus is a person or merely a potential person is at the heart of the ABORTION debate. Some views, notably those of the Roman Catholic Church, hold that moral personhood begins at conception (fertilization). Due to controversy over when human LIFE begins, the legal status of the fetus was unclear in the United States until the 1973 *Roe v. Wade* decision of the U.S. Supreme Court. That decision held that the state's interest in protecting the lives of pregnant women justified (*see* JUSTIFICATION) regulating second- and third-trimester abortions. However, the Court found that because the risk of death to the pregnant woman was lower for first-trimester abor-

tions than it would be for childbirth, the states had no compelling interest in protecting the life of the pregnant woman by regulating or banning abortion during the first trimester. The effect of this decision was that the fetus still had no legal standing in the United States and could not be considered a person until birth. For all legal purposes (such as for qualification for social services and entitlement benefits), legal personhood occurs at birth.

FIDUCIARY   *See* TRUSTWORTHINESS.

FIRST AMENDMENT   *See* BILL OF RIGHTS.

FIVE PILLARS OF ISLAM   The basic FAITH and practices (*see* PRACTICE) of Muslims.

The five pillars find their support in the QUR'AN, the sacred scripture of Islam. The first pillar is the Confession of Faith: "There is no god but GOD; Muhammad is God's messenger." One becomes a Muslim by believing and reciting this confession in public.

The second pillar is prayer, to be recited five times a day (dawn, noon, afternoon, sunset, night), always in the direction of Mecca, the birthplace of Islam. This is a ritual prayer and is usually carried out alone, with memorized words and prescribed body positions. On Friday at midday, devout Muslims make a special attempt to come together for prayer at a mosque.

The third pillar is alms-tax, a legally required portion of one's total economic worth that is used to assist the poor and the sick as well as to support the more explicitly religious work of Islam.

The fourth pillar is fasting from dawn to dusk during the month of Ramadan, the ninth month in the Arab/Islamic calendar.

The fifth pillar is pilgrimage, which is recommended but not absolutely necessary.

Certain circumstances, such as illness, travel, work, and pregnancy, allow for modification, postponement, or substitutions in fulfillment of these pillars. While only the third pillar, the alms-tax, has explicit moral dimensions (*see* MORALITY), Muslims see all of the pillars as contributing to the quality of moral action (*see* ACT). *See also* ISLAMIC ETHICS.

FORGIVENESS　To give up resentment, hurt, anger, or claims to compensation when harmed (*see* HARM) or offended (*see* OFFENSIVE BEHAVIOR).

Forgiveness may be considered a virtuous (*see* VIRTUE) ACT, like an act of CHARITY or GENEROSITY. In CHRISTIAN ETHICS, believers are urged to seek forgiveness from GOD for their SINS and to forgive readily the transgressions of others.

The philosophical problem concerning forgiveness is that to forgive someone seems to result in treating them better than they may deserve or to give them more than their due. Seen in this light, forgiveness is not an act of JUSTICE, although it may be merciful. This problem is sometimes expressed as the paradox of forgiveness, which states that forgiveness is either unjust because it accords people more than their due or pointless because if people deserve forgiveness there is nothing to forgive. Yet, forgiveness is often demanded within ethical systems (*see* ETHICS). To resolve this paradox, a person must see granting people "more than their due" as compatible with RIGHT action in some circumstances. *See also* MERCY.

FORTITUDE　The ability to bear pain, danger, or adversity with COURAGE.

We say that people have fortitude when they are able to ACT courageously in the face of suffering, danger, or misfortune. We would say that someone who bravely fights an illness without excessive complaint exhibits fortitude. Vices that stand in contrast to fortitude are cowardice and self-pity.

In virtue theory, fortitude is considered a VIRTUE, or one of the characteristics of a GOOD person. Fortitude also plays a central role in STOICISM. The stoic philosopher EPICTETUS taught "bear and forbear," meaning that the heart of daily MORALITY was the ability to face what life brings with courage.

FOUR NOBLE TRUTHS　Basic discovery of the Buddha which initiated his enlightenment; also the foundational insight and disciplinary practice of Buddhists.

1. All of life involves *dukkha*. *Dukkha* is usually translated as "suffering," but the word more accurately denotes the common human sense that life is somehow unsatisfactory and that the conditions now existing in one's personal nature, in that of others, and in the world in general are not what they should be. Thus, *dukkha* names the widespread discontent felt with this moment in this place and characterizes the person who thinks the future is going to be better than the present.
2. Suffering is caused by *tanha*. *Tanha* is usually translated as "DESIRE" but more properly characterizes craving or grasping that stems from the sense of inadequacy and insufficiency. *Tanha* is wanting things to be otherwise than they are; it represents a radical (that is, deeply rooted) nonacceptance of the reality of the moment.
3. Suffering ceases as desire ceases.
4. Suffering and desire cease by following the EIGHTFOLD PATH.

See also BUDDHIST ETHICS.

FREE ENTERPRISE　*See* CAPITALISM.

FREE WILL　*See* FREEDOM.

FREEDOM　The ability and possibility to choose between alternative courses of action.

Freedom involves the decision to perform voluntarily one of several possible actions or to choose not to act at all. When making an ethical choice, we say that the alternatives are GOOD or bad, RIGHT or WRONG, or better or worse. Many philosophers have argued that ETHICS presupposes freedom of choice, for if there were no freedom to choose, there would be no point in prescribing one course of action or prohibiting another and no reason for praising or blaming persons for their actions. Without freedom, it would not make sense to hold persons morally responsible (*see* RESPONSIBILITY) for their actions.

Social and political freedom is sometimes called liberty. Sailors are said to be on liberty when on leave from duty because they are then free to do things they would not otherwise be allowed to do. Thus, the word *liberty* is also used to mean justified (*see* JUSTIFICATION) or permitted choice, as in the example of the sailors. In this sense, *liberty* is distinguished from *license,* the freedom to do anything one may wish, whether right or wrong. Moral, social, legal, and political systems (*see* CODE) allow people liberties, the freedom to do what is considered to be right, but they prohibit people from doing what is considered wrong.

Freedoms or liberties are sometimes understood as negative and positive. Negative freedom is the absence of prohibition, constraint, or interference. Positive freedom goes beyond a lack of interference. Positive freedom refers to social or cultural forces that keep people from realizing their hopes or aspirations. In this sense, freedom is an activity or challenge. For example, imagine that there is a piano in your home. Supposing that there are no rules against your playing the piano, you are free to do so. This freedom is negative freedom. If you have had no lessons, however, or unless you are a musical prodigy, you are unlikely to be free to sit down and play in an accomplished fashion. No one is stopping you, but you do not yet have the requisite skills and abilities to perform such a task. When you have gone through the discipline of studying and practicing the piano, you will then be free to play the piano in the positive sense.

Social and political freedom, or liberty, is also a VALUE. It is in this sense that persons DESIRE freedom. Young people seek freedom or AUTONOMY from parents and other authorities; nations have fought revolutions in freedom's name. Depriving people of freedom in this sense is a form of PUNISHMENT. In many traditions (*see* CUSTOMS), freedom is regarded as a fundamental human value, even a RIGHT. The Declaration of Independence, for example, speaks of the rights of life, liberty, and the pursuit of happiness.

Not all philosophers accept the idea that freedom of choice exists or is even possible. Philosophers who deny freedom of choice are called determinists. They believe that because all events in nature, including human actions, are determined by antecedent causes, freedom of choice is impossible. They hold that the future, like the past, is already fixed or programmed by all of the causal factors operating in nature and so that everything happens by necessity. Determinists argue, therefore, that the human WILL is also determined—by whatever is the strongest MOTIVE for action. They usually allow that persons may have greater or lesser freedom, or liberty, in the social and political sense. To be free, according to determinists, usually means to be free from external constraints, that is, to be able to do what one wills, even though the will itself is determined by other forces. Indeterminists, on the other hand, maintain that even though people are limited in their choice, we are still free to choose among alternatives and to act effectively on those choices. Still other moral philosophers make a distinction between self-determination and determination by another, regarding self-determination as freedom. EXISTENTIALISM places a great deal of emphasis on choice and the necessity of choice in human life.

In theology, freedom is often contrasted with PREDESTINATION or Divine Providence: GOD, understood to be the creator of the world, causes everything that exists, and everything happens according to God's plan. It is, thus, impossible for anything to happen that is not predestined, and there can be no freedom of choice. But if freedom of choice is not possible, people cannot be held responsible for their actions, and punishment and reward are unjustified. Some leaders of the Protestant Reformation advocated the doctrine of predestination, holding that persons are elected by God for salvation: they do not earn salvation by choice or good works. The orthodox position of the Catholic Church has been that people are both predestined and free. Thus, Catholic theologians, such as AUGUSTINE and Thomas AQUINAS, have tried to reconcile these beliefs.

FREE RIDER   A person who benefits from his or her own improper behavior precisely because other people behave correctly.

Free riders get away with SELFISHNESS because it is usually difficult to detect or guard against and because its overall social impact is nearly unnoticeable. For example, during a water shortage people may be asked to save water by not watering their gardens or washing their cars. Someone who continues to water a garden while others cut back on their own water consumption is a free rider. Because authorities cannot continually monitor every house in a large city, the actions of the free rider are difficult to detect. Furthermore, the water used by the free rider will not noticeably decrease the total amount of water available to everyone. It is only through the combined actions of many people that an effect is noticeable. In our example, because of the sacrifices of others, free riders get the benefit of a water supply that lasts longer than it otherwise would without having to make the same sacrifices themselves.

Free riders present a problem for ethical systems such as EGOISM, which posits that to act morally (see MORALITY) is to act in one's own SELF-INTEREST. Although the benefits of acting with the majority are large for society as a whole, the costs to an individual of doing so appear to exceed the benefits gained. If everyone was to make the same decision, however, then everyone loses. This dilemma is famously illustrated in the article "The Tragedy of the Commons" by Garrett Hardin (*Science,* 162, 1968) and in the PRISONER'S DILEMMA.

FREUD, SIGMUND (1856–1939)   Viennese physiologist, medical doctor, psychologist, and founder of psychoanalysis, one of the most influential thinkers of the twentieth century.

Freud is famous for his theories of the unconscious, of infantile sexuality, and of repression. These theories were the basis of a new frame of reference for understanding human psychological development, as well as for the treatment of neuroses. He is also well known for proposing the model of the mind as made up of id, EGO, and superego. Finally, Freud's insight that actions, dreams, and artifacts can all be interpreted to reveal important information about both individual human beings and human culture has been extremely important for aesthetics, anthropology, philosophy, and psychology. Many cite *The Interpretations of Dreams,* published in 1901, as Freud's greatest work. Freud's essay "Civilization and its Discontents" has also been influential for understanding human moral relationships in society.

Freud's work is important for moral philosophy because of the light it sheds on MOTIVE as a factor in human behavior. Freud argued that states of the unconscious determine human behavior and that these states are often repressed in response to childhood trauma. While it is very common for us today to think of our actions and attitudes as shaped by early childhood events, it was not common in Freud's lifetime. Freud's work challenged the notion of free will, suggesting that past experiences and hidden mental processes over which we may have little control determine our behaviors. This has important implications for theories of moral action and RESPONSIBILITY.

Initially, Freud's theories were not well received. This may be due in large part to the role played by sexuality in his thought. Today, criticisms include claims that Freud's theories are logically flawed, that they are unscientific, and that psychoanalysis does not in fact help those suffering from neurosis.

FUNDAMENTALISM In religion, the belief that certain core religious VALUES are threatened and need to be reaffirmed or aggressively defended.

In general, fundamentalists believe in interpreting holy scriptures and commandments very literally, although they are often selective in what passages, commandments, and RULES they identify as fundamental. Fundamentalists are primarily reactionary and tend to organize in response to what they believe is a threat to their interpretation of holy scriptures are the way of life that they believe those scriptures demand. Such a reaction is sometimes violent and aggressive, but in most cases fundamentalists are simply highly vocal in expressing their opinions, choosing to support their beliefs through CONSCIENTIOUS OBJECTION and CIVIL DISOBEDIENCE.

In modern times, fundamentalists have been motivated by the increasingly international nature of culture, including the influence of foreign television and the media, which they believe is a contaminating influence on society. They also object to the increasing influence of RELATIVISM around the globe. Relativists generally argue that holy scriptures are symbolic and metaphorical; therefore literal readings are not always appropriate. They believe that religious texts are best understood with reference to modern cultural norms (see NORM) and circumstances, and they argue that individual CONSCIENCE should dictate how such texts are interpreted. Relativists also tend to be far more tolerant of dissenting viewpoints and other religious traditions (see CUSTOMS) than are most fundamentalists.

FUTILITY Uselessness, ineffectiveness, or hopelessness.

Actions (see ACT) are said to be futile when they cannot produce desired results. The term *futile* has a special meaning in MEDICAL ETHICS: medical procedure or treatment is deemed futile when it cannot effect a cure or improvement in the condition of a patient. In futile cases, additional treatment may only prolong the process of dying (see DEATH AND DYING) without providing any identifiable benefit to the patient.

Several ethical issues (see ETHICS) are associated with medical futility. First, there is no generally agreed-on application of the principle (see PRINCIPLES) of medical futility or futile treatment. Even among well-trained professionals, the determination as to when more HARM than GOOD occurs is a JUDGMENT call, and judgments may differ. Moreover, the physician's judgment may be at odds with that of the patient or the patient's family, which raises ethical issues surrounding a patient's AUTONOMY. To further complicate matters, when considering harm, ethicists do not limit themselves to physical harms. Moral harms, such as the violation of patient DIGNITY, the violation of a patient's RIGHT TO DIE, and the infliction of pain and distress must also be weighed.

Decisions concerning futile treatment can be linked to passive EUTHANASIA, in which treatment is withdrawn so as to bring about a merciful death.

FUTURE GENERATIONS People yet to be born.

Moral decision making is often concerned with duties (see OBLIGATION) toward others. Many people argue that moral considerations must include the needs or rights of the people who are yet to be born into our societies. UTILITARIANS, for example, would argue that in calculating the greatest happiness for the greatest number, we should attempt to include the happiness of future generations where we can be reasonably sure that they will exist and have a direct interest in the decision. For example, our use of the planet's resources will affect the happiness of future generations. In ENVIRONMENTAL ETHICS, our obligations to future generations are discussed with a great deal of care. In discussions of just uses of the planet's resources, questions of our obligations to future generations are most immediate.

Ethical (*see* ETHICS) problems arise when thinking about what, if anything, we owe to future generations. Egoists (*see* EGOISM) might argue that we owe nothing to the future. Other critics argue that RIGHTS can only be ascribed to actual people, not to people who may never be born. Among moral theories that acknowledge some duty to protect the interests of future generations, there is debate as to how heavily the interests of future generations weigh in comparison to the needs of existing people.

G

GANDHI, MOHANDAS KARAMCHAND (1869–1948)

Hindu practitioner (*see* HINDU ETHICS) of NONVIOLENCE, who was instrumental in gaining India's independence from Great Britain in 1947. He has been called the prophet of nonviolence in the twentieth century and was the catalyst for movements against COLONIALISM, RACISM, and VIOLENCE worldwide.

Gandhi is commonly known as Mahatma, "Great Soul." After studying law in England and working on behalf of fellow Indians in South Africa, he returned to India and concentrated first on improving the position of those in the lowest scale of the CASTE system and then on FREEDOM from British rule. He founded his movement for independence on the twin principles of *satyagraha,* "TRUTH force," and *ahimsa,* "nonhurt," or nonviolence. These principles were applied by boycotting British goods and services and by active, though nonviolent, resistance to British governance.

Gandhi was frequently imprisoned for refusing to obey the British laws that he regarded as unjust. He led an ascetic (*see* ASCETICISM) life that endeared him to the masses of India, who were poor. Gandhi was able to empathize with the poor by personally adopting the poverty and simplicity that marked their lives. Yet he also reached the wealthy and politically influential. His voluntary poverty and self-denial added credence and moral POWER to the truth he advocated. He extolled HUMILITY as a foundational principle of LIFE and MORALITY.

Gandhi promoted the VALUE of all religions, believing that each is an authentic path to the Ultimate. He was greatly admired by Albert Einstein, who believed that Gandhi's principle of nonviolence offered a possible redemption from the violent power released by the atom bomb, and he deeply influenced U.S. CIVIL RIGHTS leader Martin Luther KING, Jr. Gandhi was assassinated in 1948 by a Hindu fanatic who objected to the Mahatma's appreciation and affirmation of Islam.

GAY RIGHTS

The assertion of equality under the law for homosexuals.

Gay RIGHTS activists argue that DISCRIMINATION against people because of their sexual preferences is a violation of their CIVIL RIGHTS. Sexual preference, they argue, is a personal matter that is irrelevant to one's ability to perform a job or otherwise interact with others in society. Supporters of gay rights do not demand preferential treatment for homosexuals but simply the right of homosexuals to choose their own LIFESTYLES without fear of being discriminated against as a result.

Traditionally (*see* CUSTOMS), Western societies have been highly intolerant of and prejudiced toward homosexuals. This has resulted in a number of laws that have the effect of discriminating against, or criminalizing, HOMOSEXUALITY. Such laws have included, and continue to include, bans on homosexuals working in certain jobs, sodomy laws that criminalize sex between consenting same sex adults, laws denying homosexuals the right to adopt children, and laws denying same-sex adults the right to marry. Homosexuals have also been disadvantaged by corporate and government policies that benefit only heterosexual couples, including the provision of employment benefits (such as family health insurance) that only opposite-sex partners can take advantage of.

Those who continue to support such discrimination often argue that homosexuality is detrimental to society and the COMMON GOOD in some way. They believe that homosexuality is a deviant and unnatural lifestyle and that appearing to condone it by treating homosexuals equally undermines traditional cultural, religious, and FAMILY VALUES.

Supporters of gay rights, on the other hand, tend to be more egalitarian in their outlook (*see* EGALITARIANISM). They argue that these policies, based on unfounded stereotypes, fear, and PREJUDICE, are unfair and misinformed. Indeed, like the color of one's skin, there appears to be no obvious reason why homosexuality should make any one person less qualified to perform a job, look after children, or benefit from legal protections and advantages offered to couples through marriage. *See also* EQUALITY; HOMOPHOBIA; PRIVATE AND PUBLIC MORALITY.

GENEROSITY   Freely giving of oneself and sharing in an unselfish manner.

Although generosity is usually thought to be a VIRTUE, if taken too far, it could turn into a VICE. According to ARISTOTLE'S doctrine of the GOLDEN MEAN, generosity stands between giving too much and giving too little. If a person gives too much, in terms of time, money, or goods, and is thereby unable to live up to personal obligations (*see* OBLIGATION)—for example, to family, friends, profession, or school—then what appears to be a virtue is really a vice.

Whether a person is generous depends on that person's intentions (*see* INTENTION) and means (*see* TELEOLOGY). A person who gives in order to appear to be a GOOD person is not thought to be generous, and a wealthy person who gives a small percentage of his or her wealth is considered less generous than a poorer person who gives less in absolute terms but more as a percentage of income and wealth.

Giving to CHARITY is often thought to be a moral obligation; for example, Immanuel KANT claimed that we have a duty to give but not a duty to give to any particular cause.

In the past generous giving was essential to prevent harm and promote freedom and opportunity because governments did little to help those in need. Today, with large governmental programs dealing with everything from unemployment to medical research, the apparent need for generous donations to charities seems less significant. However, we still know that many people and organizations have real needs that are not dealt with by government—for example, a sick person's need for good company. Governments do not adequately handle other needs, such as the need for medical research. On a worldwide scale, with millions of people starving to death each year in less developed countries, the need for generosity remains great. *See also* VIRTUE ETHICS.

GENETIC ENGINEERING   The intentional manipulation, modification, and recombination of deoxyribonucleic acid (DNA) in order to change an organism or population.

Every cell of a living organism contains many genes arranged as chromosomes. Genes are the hereditary materials that determine how an organism will grow and develop. Genes are comprised of deoxyribonucleic acid (DNA), a threadlike molecule that contains genetic information. In the 1970s, scientists developed methods that allowed for the formation of new genes by isolating a DNA fragment, changing that fragment, and then reintroducing the DNA into the original organism or introducing the DNA into a new organism. This technique is called genetic engineering.

Genetic engineering can be applied to microorganisms; to plant, animal, or human cells in culture; to whole plants; to whole animals; or to humans. Genetic engineering has many positive applications. Genetically engineered microorganisms can be used in agriculture to improve the health and proliferation of crops and to protect them from damage caused by frost or insects. Genetic engineering has the potential to help the developing world meet its needs for food and fuel by improving the food content of plants, the resistance of plants to disease, and the storage life of food.

Animals can be genetically engineered to improve their weight gain, speed their growth, improve their resistance to disease, and increase their fertility. Genetically engineered sheep have been able to produce the human protein alpha-1 antitrypsin in their milk, which is used in treating the lung disease emphysema. Genetically engineered animals, especially rodents, play a large role in biomedical research.

Through recombinant DNA techniques, we have been able to synthesize human insulin for the treatment of diabetes and have created a vaccine for hepatitis B. We are better able to treat pituitary dwarfism with genetically engineered human growth hormones. Through prenatal diagnosis, parents can be informed as to whether a FETUS has genetic abnormalities. In the future we may be able to address genetic diseases by replacing genes that cause disease with "normal" genes.

Along with these possibilities, however, come many ethical concerns (see ETHICS). Some fear that in altering genes we may introduce harmful elements into plants, animals, or people—or that we may unwittingly create bacteria or viruses that we cannot resist. Some opponents to genetic engineering argue that we have no right to alter animals for human ends and purposes (see ANIMAL RIGHTS; TELEOLOGY). Environmentalists (see ENVIRONMENTAL ETHICS) argue that we may destroy natural ecosystems by upsetting the balance of the food chain. For example, genetically engineered carp may expand their natural habitat into colder waters, displacing normal fish by depleting their supplies of food.

As more human genes involved in various hereditary diseases are identified, some fear that prenatal diagnosis of diseases or possible genetic disorders will lead to an increase in ABORTION. While the overall health of the population may be improved, many people with genetic complications still lead full lives. Some ethicists question whether it is moral (see MORALITY) for a society to decide that physical disability is a bad thing. Still others fear that we will attempt to create a "master race" by genetically engineering "perfect" individuals. See also EUGENICS.

GENOCIDE   The deliberate killing of a whole people, or all members of an entire nation.

The term was first applied to Nazi Germany's almost successful attempt to exterminate all Jewish people in Europe during World War II, an event now known as the HOLOCAUST. More recently, the Bosnian people have suffered expulsion and expatriation from their homes, have been subjected to inhumane and life-threatening conditions, and have in many cases been summarily executed by the Serbs in the Republic of Bosnia and Herzegovina. Because of the horrendous loss of life involved, genocide is considered by most to be a gross moral WRONG. Furthermore, the moral seriousness of genocide is thought to go beyond the loss of individual lives—itself a moral TRAGEDY—because genocide also destroys a way of life, an entire culture.

Genocide is seen as justified (see JUSTIFICATION) by its practitioners (usually, but not always, a government or dominant racial group) because they believe that a people or culture threaten or are incompatible with their own culture and way of life. Such a belief is a form of PREJUDICE and RACISM.

Genocide is sometimes applied in a figurative way, as when a social policy tends to result in widespread death or impoverishment for people of a given ethnic or racial background, even though most people are not killed. See also ANTISEMITISM.

GILLIGAN, CAROL (1936–   )   A professor of psychology who developed a theory of moral psychology based on the experiences of women.

Gilligan's *In A Different Voice* (1982) reported the results of research in which she studied women's moral JUDGMENT processes, particularly regarding the decision to have an ABORTION. From the responses given by her research subjects, Gilligan concluded that women's moral judgments are based primarily on their concern for maintaining and strengthening caring (*see* CARE) relationships, rather than on consideration of PRINCIPLES of EQUALITY or JUSTICE.

In Gilligan's view, women are more likely than men to see MORALITY not in terms of principles and RULES but in terms of responsibilities (*see* RESPONSIBILITY) to people with whom they have developed caring attachments and loving (*see* LOVE) relationships. Although both men and women use care and justice rationales, women tend to ACT according to COMPASSION and concern for concrete individuals, whereas men tend to follow rules and principles. Generally, men's moral judgments reveal that they hold as VALUES equality and FAIRNESS, while women's moral judgments reveal that they hold as values inclusion in a nurturing relationship and protection from HARM.

Gilligan's research with women subjects challenged the validity of cognitive MORAL DEVELOPMENT theory as previously developed by Lawrence KOHLBERG. Kohlberg had developed a psychological test of moral reasoning (*see* REASON) called the Moral Judgment Interview. For nearly fifty years Kohlberg studied the rationales given by thousands of research subjects to moral dilemmas (*see* DILEMMA) concerning truth-telling, honesty, loyalty, and justice. He concluded that advanced levels of moral development are marked by reasons that appeal to highly abstract moral principles, such as justice.

In Kohlberg's early research, males generally scored higher on tests of moral judgment than females. His later research showed that sex differences were minimal, but men and women who were in traditional male occupations (law, theology, philosophy) scored higher than other test subjects. However, the Moral Judgment Interview itself was based on Kohlberg's prior research that included only males. Gilligan claimed that this created a BIAS that made the validity of Kohlberg's Moral Judgment Interview results questionable.

Despite concerns for the validity of Gilligan's research methods, her work triggered a re-examination of the possibility of male gender bias in the development of moral psychology and moral philosophy. Although Gilligan's work is an analysis of the psychology of feminine or woman-centered moral reasoning, it has also spurred recent philosophical inquiry into FEMINIST ETHICS.

GLUTTONY To eat or drink greedily (*see* GREED) and to excess.

Gluttony is discouraged in almost all cultures and was one of the CARDINAL SINS recognized by the Christian church (*see* CHRISTIAN ETHICS) during the Middle Ages. Gluttony is seen as hedonistic (*see* HEDONISM), wasteful, and decadent and is also extremely unhealthy. There are numerous possible ethical objections (*see* ETHICS) to gluttony because of the many social and personal problems it can create. In particular, excessive alcohol consumption has been discouraged and even banned in many cultures at one time, including the United States, at least partially because it tends to loosen inhibitions and, therefore, can also loosen one's objections to other moral wrongs (*see* WRONG).

GOD Central reality in polytheistic (many gods) and monotheistic (one God) religions; ultimate source of POWER and GOOD; focus of worship as creator and ruler of the universe.

Among those who recognize the validity of religion, God is usually regarded as the supreme or highest being. Typical positive attributes of God include omniscience (all-knowingness), omnipotence (all-powerfulness), omnipresence (everywhere present all the time), holy, just, personal, and loving (see LOVE). Those with the most profound—that is, the most comprehensive and inclusive—conception of the Ultimate typically affirm that anything that can be said about God is necessarily limited, inadequate, and misleading, as we cannot capture God's greatness within the limits of human language and understanding. Such thinkers often distinguish between kataphatic theologies that describe God in positive terms and apophatic theologies that use negative terms, defining God by what the Ultimate is not. Typical negative characterization includes eternal (not touched by time), infinite (not limited), absolute (not relative), one (not multiple or divided), all (not part), and impersonal. MAIMONIDES, for example, favored negative theology, asserting that absolutely nothing can be known literally about God. At the same time he made considerable use of the BIBLE's imagery in characterizing God, maintaining, however, that the attributes and qualities commonly ascribed to God must be understood as metaphors or analogies and not as literal propositions. The two approaches to the nature of God—positive and negative—complement each other, but the latter is seen as somewhat more adequate, especially by philosophers and mystics (see MYSTICISM).

FAITH in a single God is seen by many as necessary to the notion of a single TRUTH, a single LAW, and, therefore, a single, universal MORALITY that is applicable to all humans (see ABSOLUTES). Without such a basis, different gods and moralities would exist for different peoples, and CULTURAL RELATIVISM would ensue. Many fear that universal harmony and peace is unattainable without the uniform ethical base of a monotheistic religion.

Because not all people accept the existence of God, some philosophers and theologians attempt to demonstrate through rational (see RATIONALITY) argument that God does exist. One of these arguments, known as the ontological argument, characterizes God as that being which no greater or more perfect being can be conceived. The argument then contends that this being must exist, otherwise it would lack the perfection of existence. Another argument is the cosmological argument, which concludes on the bases of the incontestable reality of the existing cosmos that an eternal and self-existent creator must be its ultimate source. As creator, or source of being, God is sometimes said to be "beyond being" because that which causes everything cannot itself be one of the things it causes. Others hold that belief in God is a personal, private, mystical, or transformative experience. Conversion may happen by divine inspiration, or REVELATION, but does not occur by rational argument. These and other arguments continue to be refined and debated by philosophers and theologians.

GOLDEN MEAN   The midpoint between two extremes.

It has been argued, most notably by ARISTOTLE, that VIRTUE is often, but not always, a median point between excess and insufficiency. For example, the virtue of prudence is the ideal point between foolhardiness (not thinking things through) and indecision (thinking about things to the point of paralysis). The idea of the golden mean is also found in Buddhism's FOUR NOBLE TRUTHS, which states that NIRVANA, or enlightenment, can only be achieved through moderation—a mean between overindulgence, or GLUTTONY, and self-deprivation, or ASCETICISM.

GOLDEN RULE   The principle (see PRINCIPLES) that we should treat others as we would like to be treated ourselves.

The Golden Rule is found in most religious traditions in one form or another and is a central precept of Christianity (see CHRISTIAN ETHICS). To most Western readers, the most familiar rendering of the Golden Rule is found in the BIBLE as "Do unto others as you would have them do unto you" (Luke 6:31) or "In everything do to others as you would have them do to you" (Matthew 7:12). Examples from other religions include "Do not do to others as you would not want done to you" (Judaism, from Rabbi Hillel), "No one really believes unless he wants for his brother what he wants for himself" (Islam), "Do not do to others that which, if done to you, would cause you pain" (Hinduism), and "Do not impose on others what you do not desire yourself" (Confucianism). See also CONFUCIAN ETHICS; HINDU ETHICS; ISLAMIC ETHICS; JEWISH ETHICS.

GOOD A general term used to assign positive VALUE to something.

Almost anything may be said to be good: a good person, a good car, a good vacation, a good counterfeiter, a good year. Obviously, not all uses of the word *good* are moral (*see* MORALITY) uses. To say that somebody is a good person usually means good in a moral sense, but a person may be a good thief or a good money-maker without being morally good. Indeed, a person may become a morally worse person the better he or she becomes at thieving. Thus, being good often means being *good at* something or *good for* something, even if what you are good at or good for is not itself a very good thing to do. When we ask, "Is this good?" we often mean "What is it *good for?*" and, in this sense, we are talking about *good* in this instrumental sense or about things that are good as a means to something else (*see* ENDS/MEANS). So a thief may be very efficient at his or her craft and so be a good thief, even if thieving is not a good thing to do.

Philosophers have often distinguished between things, or acts (*see* ACT), that are good as means to ends and things that are good as ends in themselves (*see* TELEOLOGY). Their interest in understanding the meaning of *good* has been focused primarily on what it means for something to be good as an end, good in itself, or intrinsically good (*see* INTRINSIC VALUE). Money, for example, may be good as a means of providing a livelihood, but it is not good in itself or intrinsically good, as life seems to be. Money has value because of what it is good for or what it can buy, but aside from its exchange value, it is just paper or metal. Life, however, seems to have intrinsic value, or to be good in and of itself, and not simply good as a means to something else.

G. E. MOORE, a twentieth-century British philosopher, claimed that the meaning of *good*, in its intrinsic sense, is the most fundamental question of ETHICS. In fact, throughout history, moral philosophers have tried to analyze the idea or concept of *goodness* because it is so fundamental. According to most views, goodness is the goal of moral LIFE.

How is the good determined? As SOCRATES or PLATO would say, "Not what kinds of things are good, but what is goodness itself?" What does *good* mean? The answer to this question differs according to theory: In HEDONISM, for example, *good* seems to be synonymous with *pleasure*. Other theories define *goodness* as satisfaction or SELF-REALIZATION. An American philosopher, Charles Leslie Stevenson, defined *good* as any object of interest, and emotivists (*see* EMOTIVISM), such as A. J. Ayer, have said that the word *good* simply expresses a positive attitude or emotion toward something and that *good* does not refer to any PROPERTY at all. Plato and Moore both held, for somewhat different reasons, that *good* is indefinable.

In much of ancient and medieval philosophy in the Platonic and Aristotelian traditions, goodness was thought to be convertible with *being;* that is, things were said to be good to the extent that they have being, and to have being to the extent that they are good. On this view, some things are better than others because they occupy a higher level of being. Plants, say, are better than rocks, animals are better than plants, and humans are better than animals because the latter form of being in each case is higher. In this hierarchy of being, GOD was often supposed to be the highest being and, hence, the greatest good—the source of all other being and goodness. Individual things or people were also said to be better or worse as they realized or failed to realize the mature form of their species. A person could be more or less of a human being and, therefore, more or less good as he or she developed or failed to develop human talents or capacities. This kind of theory of goodness or value may be said to be ontological, meaning that it locates goodness or value in things themselves and not in the feelings or attitudes we have about them. Such theories may also be said to be objectivist (*see* OBJECTIVISM) for this reason.

In the theories of ARISTOTLE and Thomas AQUINAS, the adjective *good* takes its specific meaning from the kind of thing it modifies according to what is appropriate to that kind of thing. Thus, *good* does not refer to the same properties in the expression *good car* as it does in the expression *good person,* for the qualities needed to make a good car are different from the qualities needed to make a good person. In other types of theory, however, *good* has been supposed to have the same meaning in all of its uses. In hedonism, as we have said, *good* is taken to mean "pleasure"; according to this theory, when a person says something is good, no matter what it is, he means it is pleasurable. Such a theory may be said to be subjectivist (*see* SUBJECTIVISM) or psychological rather than ontological, for it locates goodness in the feelings of a human subject. Yet, there is a sense in which even hedonism is objective, for it is a fact that somebody likes something or receives pleasure from it, and no one could be mistaken about that fact. People are, of course, less likely to be mistaken about their own feelings, but they could easily be mistaken about whether something is good, in the sense of being pleasurable, for someone else.

Subjectivist theories of value do not locate goodness in things but in people's feelings or attitudes toward things, such that things do not have goodness so much as they have goodness conferred upon them. One might argue, however, that there are qualities in things that elicit or evoke subjective feelings of pleasure or approval, such that, in a sense, the goodness of things really is in the things. Goodness might then be said to be a relational property, such as redness that comes into being only when a certain kind of subject comes into contact with a certain kind of object. As Aristotle would say, when the eye, capable of seeing, comes into contact with an object, capable of being seen, under appropriate conditions, actual seeing takes place. Thus, things themselves may be pleasurable, just as they are visible, for they are capable of giving pleasure, just as they are capable of being seen.

Some twentieth-century objectivists, however, like Moore, seem to have believed that goodness is an objective property which things have in addition to any and all other properties: that goodness cannot be identified with being, or pleasure, or anything else. His argument for this was that goodness cannot be defined by being or pleasure or any other property and so must be a different property. He called this supposed quality of goodness, which things may or may not have, a "nonnatural property" because it could not be identified with or reduced to natural properties of any kind. Emotivists, in turn, argued that *good* does not refer to any property, subjective or objective, natural or nonnatural, because, according to their analysis, the word *good* does not refer to anything. In their view, *good* merely expresses feelings; it does not report about them. They concluded, therefore, that statements about the goodness of things are neither true nor false.

It may be true, however, contrary to Moore and the emotivists, that *good* is used to refer to natural properties but that it is not always used to refer to the same properties. According to John DEWEY, an American pragmatist (*see* PRAGMATISM), the meaning of *good* changes from one context to another, such that what we mean by *good* in one context may be different from what we mean by *good* in another context. Nonetheless, we can identify what we mean by *good* in these different cases and empirically test whether or not things are good in the senses intended. If what we mean by saying that somebody is a good runner is that the person is fast, we can find out whether our belief is true or false by testing that person.

Questions about the meaning of *good* are classified by philosophers as metaethical (*see* METAETHICS), for they are not questions about what is good but about what *good* means or about how the word *good* functions in moral discourse (*see* DISCOURSE ETHICS) and reasoning (*see* REASON). The answers to these questions have substantive import, however, for they bear upon the question of whether any MORAL OPINION is true or false and upon how anyone might know it is.

GOOD SAMARITAN LAW Legislation that protect individuals who help others in good FAITH, particularly in the event of a medical emergency, from lawsuits for improper CARE.

The name *Good Samaritan* is derived from a story in the BIBLE (Luke 10:30–37) in which a person from Samaria helps an injured traveler on the roadside. Without Good Samaritan laws, bystanders in emergencies have sometimes been reluctant to help for fear that they might be blamed for resulting death and injury. Sometimes Good Samaritan laws specify that legal protection only extends to those who are certified to provide medical aid.

In most common law legal systems, including that of the United States, bystanders are not required to render assistance in emergencies. If someone were drowning, for example, you would be under no OBLIGATION to help, even if you could do so without fear for your own safety. However, some states and countries also have "bad Samaritan" laws. Under such laws, people are required to help in emergencies if that help can be provided at little personal cost, but

For example, lifting a drowning child out of small backyard swimming pool typically requires little effort. Under bad Samaritan laws, a person who refuses such help could be held criminally liable.

GRACE *See* CHRISTIAN ETHICS.

GREED The excessive DESIRE to acquire wealth, money, goods, or even personal attainment; avarice.

A greedy person may be miserly and accumulate excessive wealth for no reason other than to hoard it. The greedy may also crave other's possessions, a SIN in Christianity (*see* CHRISTIAN ETHICS) known as covetousness. Greed is the opposite of GENEROSITY. It is generally seen as WRONG because like any craving, the desire is so strong that it overwhelms other considerations, such as DECENCY, and therefore may lead to immoral (*see* IMMORALITY) or criminal behavior (*see* CRIME). Greed is such a strong desire that it also tends to overwhelm other things and hamper one's development in other areas, such as interpersonal relationships.

GUILT The state of having done something WRONG, either legally or morally (*see* MORALITY). The term is also applied to the feelings of remorse people experience, typically after they have done something wrong.

A sense of guilt does not always attend wrong action (*see* ACT). Often, people feel guilt when they have done nothing wrong or when they believe that they *might* have done something wrong. For example, people may feel guilt if they believe they have hurt or angered another person, even if the hurt or anger experienced by the second person is unjustifiable. Sometimes people who believe that their actions are justified (*see* JUSTIFICATION) do not feel guilt, even though others believe the action was wrong. Sometimes guilt is unproductive, causing people to suffer when they shouldn't. For example, a parent might feel guilty if a child is hurt in an automobile that was purchased by the parent for the child. In this case, the parent had little control over the outcome and should not feel guilt.

Guilt, felt in response to actual wrongdoing, can serve as an enforcer of morality. Cultures may use guilt in order to enforce their CUSTOMS. Sigmund FREUD argued that guilt plays an important role in the formation of a sense of RIGHT behavior. If no guilt feelings arise after acting immorally, there may be little self-motivation encouraging proper moral behavior.

Other philosophers have argued that there are better ways to encourage moral behavior, ranging from rewards for good actions to social disapproval for bad actions. Some philosophers, such as Immanuel KANT, believe that the only way to ensure proper behavior is based on respect for morality, a desire to do the right thing regardless of the way one feels when the wrong actions are performed. Utilitarians (*see*

UTILITARIANISM) believe that feeling guilty is appropriate when it leads to greater happiness by, for example, causing people to act in morally appropriate ways. However, such feelings may lead to good results even when people are not guilty of offenses. Guilt feelings themselves are painful, so under the utilitarian view, greater happiness must be accomplished in order to justify attempts to instill feelings of guilt.

Some philosophers believe that all people in a society should feel guilt for some wrong acts committed earlier in the history of the society. For example, those who benefit from the legacy of slavery in the United States might appropriately feel guilt. Such guilt is sometimes called collective guilt. Others believe that guilt should only be attributed to those who benefit from actions wrongly done in the past because they hold that people should only be responsible for actions under their own control. On this view, those who did nothing to promote racism should feel no guilt and are not guilty. *See also* SHAME.

H

HABITS   The effects of repeated actions (see ACT).

Habits arise when we repeat actions or reactions and thus develop a tendency to always act or react in the same way without conscious thought. Once ingrained, habits can be difficult to change and are often described as "second nature." This expression implies behaviors so deeply embedded that it would feel unnatural to depart from them. Habits may involve physical activities or routines, such as diet, sleep patterns, or exercise, or they may refer to attitudes, thoughts, or points of view.

Habits may be formed by a lack of attention, as "to fall into the habit" of slumping in a chair, or they may be formed by discipline, as to create the habit of practicing the piano daily. Because habits learned at an early age tend to be strong, many moral thinkers (see MORALITY) have stressed the importance of teaching proper habits to children. In Aristotelian ethics (see ARISTOTLE), for example, cultivating proper habits is considered essential to cultivating proper moral character.

HADITH   Collection of MUHAMMAD's words and actions, second in AUTHORITY only to the QUR'AN, the sacred scripture of Muslims.

If Muslims do not find guidance on FAITH or PRACTICE in the Qur'an, they look to what Muhammad actually said and did on specific occasions. This information has been recorded in the work known as the Hadith.

Because Muhammad is regarded in Islam as the best possible MORAL EXEMPLAR, devout Muslims base their lives on how Muhammad lived his life. Thus, Muhammad is for Muslims the premier model for determining moral perspective and outlook. AL-GHAZĀLĪ once declared (as translated by L. Zolondek in Book XX of al-Ghazālī's *Ihyā' 'ulūm ad-dīn*): "We ask ALLAH to help us imitate Muhammad's CHARACTER, action, qualities, and sayings." Another Muslim writer, Abū Saʿīd, once confessed: "I modeled my actions, outward and inward, upon the practice of the Prophet, so that habit (see HABITS) at last became nature."

HALAKAH   The legal system of Judaism and main integrative force of the religion and culture; originating from the eighth century B.C.

Basing itself on the Hebrew BIBLE and the TALMUD, Jewish LAW developed three written authoritative forms: codes (see CODE), commentaries, and *responsa*. Codes are systematic presentations of otherwise random Talmudic material according to specific topics, thereby establishing the norms (see NORM) of Jewish conduct in a manner more accessible to students, rabbis, other religious leaders, and judges. MAIMONIDES produced one of the most influential codes. Commentaries provide further clarification and attempt to reconcile disparate opinions found in the Talmud. *Responsa* are applications of the Talmudic clarifications found in codes and commentaries to new historical situations as they occur. The repository of *responsa* has continued to grow throughout Jewish history, with additions from Jewish communities (see COMMUNITY) throughout the world. *Responsa* are written, for example, when new discoveries in science (for example, electricity and its use on the Sabbath) and medicine (for example, artificial insemination) require a

Jewish position that conforms to traditional legal standards.

Major topical divisions of Halakah include ritual law, family and personal law, civil law (for example, treating property issues), criminal law, and laws relating to non-Jews.

Orthodox Jews adhere strictly to Halakah. Conservative Jews regard Halakah as inspired and still open to continual development. Reform Jews consider Halakah when making decisions but do not feel necessarily bound by its precepts.

Even though Halakah purports to govern all aspects of Jewish personal and communal life, there is no Jewish community in the world today where Halakah is the sole basis of government. In many instances, in fact, it is subordinate to secular or other religious systems of law. *See also* JEWISH ETHICS.

HAPPINESS Defined in different ways by different moral theories, but usually involving pleasure or a balance of pleasure, VIRTUE, achievement, and GOOD fortune.

Happiness plays a role in most moral theories. It is defined in different ways: as a life of pleasure by hedonists (*see* HEDONISM), as peace of mind by stoics (*see* STOICISM), and as the actualization of potentiality by SELF-REALIZATION theorists. Different ethical (*see* ETHICS) views also accord a different role to happiness—in the moral LIFE, it is considered variously the ultimate end of all action (*see* ACT), one goal in life, or the fortunate by-product of other goals.

According to hedonists, people are happy or unhappy according to the amounts of pleasure or pain they experience in their lives. But other philosophers have argued that pleasure, or freedom from pain, is not the goal of the moral life, for there are such things as bad or immoral pleasures. PLATO, for example, specifically argues against the PLEASURE PRINCIPLE, as does ARISTOTLE, Immanuel KANT, and G. E. MOORE.

Aristotle's ethics is centered on *eudaimonia,* which we translate as "happiness." *Eudaimonia* comes from the Greek *eu,* meaning

happy or well, and *daimon* refers to a person's spirit. Happiness, understood as flourishing or well-being with virtue, is the ultimate end of all action. Kant, by contrast, held that happiness is not a moral criterion at all. He argues that we do not, or should not, judge actions to be either good or bad, right or wrong, because they produce happiness. Good people, Kant pointed out, are frequently unhappy, or at least less fortunate than immoral people. In Kant's view, people are often required to sacrifice their own happiness or the happiness of others in order to do what is morally right. In the utilitarian view (*see* UTILITARIANISM), happiness plays an important role in the moral life. Utilitarians such as Jeremy BENTHAM and John Stuart MILL held that moral actions were those that produced the greatest happiness for the greatest number.

Happiness is sometimes regarded as a secular goal (*see* SECULAR ETHICS), attainable in the natural world, and sometimes as a religious or supernatural goal, attainable only by unity with GOD. Utilitarianism is an example of a naturalistic philosophy (*see* NATURALISTIC ETHICS) in this sense, as happiness is something that can be measured and achieved in this life. Religious philosophers, however, frequently speak of unity with God as the ultimate happiness, viewing the happiness of this world as imperfect or incomplete. AUGUSTINE, for instance, speaks of what might be called the restless-heart phenomenon, namely, his belief that persons will find no rest until they find rest in God. The philosopher Søren KIERKEGAARD, in turn, characterizes a life without religious faith as one of anxiety and despair, in contrast to the happiness or peace of mind that faith can bring.

HARM Bodily injury, or injury to a person's basic, legitimate interests.

Harm is a difficult concept to establish. In its least controversial sense it involves physical injury. Someone who is assaulted, for instance, has suffered harm. In its morally relevant sense, harm carries with it some connotation of seriousness or permanence. For example, if Ronnie falls and scrapes his knee, he has hurt himself, but he has not suffered harm in the relevant sense. If, however, Ronnie is pushed and then falls and breaks his knee, he has suffered harm. Financial harm is also relatively uncontroversial, although certain areas of question do exist. If a person's money is stolen, we say that person has been harmed. If the supporter of a family deserts that family, we say that the family has been harmed and the deserter is accountable.

More controversially, harm includes emotional harm, psychological harm, and harm to reputation. These sorts of harm can be more difficult to establish. For example, a child whose parents never strike him but who yell viciously and call that child derogatory names may be viewed as harming that child, although no physical or financial injury results. In less-severe cases a person may suffer discomfort, insult, nuisance, or offense, for instance, from the language of a coworker. For the last two decades there has been a building trend to take this class of harm more seriously, for example, in the case of SEXUAL HARASSMENT, but there is still dispute as to whether harm has occurred.

Because avoiding harm to others plays such an important role in many moral theories, such as UTILITARIANISM, it is important to be able to delimit this concept. Moral and legal philosophers continue to seek improved definitions of *harm* and related concepts.

HATE CRIMES   Acts of VIOLENCE or destruction motivated by RACISM or other forms of PREJUDICE.

Many countries have laws imposing higher penalties for hate crimes than for crimes not motivated by prejudice. It is argued that hate crime is more morally reprehensible than regular CRIME because it is effectively an offense against a whole group rather than just the immediate victim. Hate crimes will often have the effect of breeding fear among members of the target group and may encourage other prej-

udiced individuals to commit similar acts. Many acts of intolerance have started out as small events but then snowballed as the COMMUNITY became desensitized to them. In Nazi Germany, for example, early acts of random ANTISEMITISM eventually led to the HOLOCAUST.

Supporters of the RIGHT to free speech often oppose hate-crime legislation because it effectively criminalizes certain types of speech and expression. Because the motivation for a crime is often only obvious from the language used by the attackers, such as racial slurs, or the symbols they wear, such as the swastika, it is the language and symbols that lead to the higher penalty. Opponents may also argue that truly heinous crimes are already outlawed by existing criminal codes (*see* CODE) and that the courts in most cases already have the discretion to impose harsher sentences because of aggravating circumstances. *See also* HOMOPHOBIA.

HEDONISM   An ethical theory (*see* ETHICS) based on the PLEASURE PRINCIPLE.

Hedonists maintain that the ultimate GOOD in life is pleasure and the ultimate EVIL in life is pain. This ethical theory appears to be based on a psychological theory, or a theory about HUMAN NATURE, which holds that people naturally seek pleasure and avoid pain. It does not deny that people desire or avoid other things, but it claims that they do so because they find those things pleasurable or painful or because other things are a means to a pleasurable end (*see* TELEOLOGY) or a means of avoiding pain. Hedonism also allows that persons may choose painful means to pleasurable ends if the pleasure outweighs the pain (*see* ENDS/MEANS).

Some hedonistic theories, such as Epicurianism (*see* EPICURUS), are egoistic (*see* EGOISM), holding that persons desire pleasure and avoid pain for themselves, or as a matter of self-interest, and that they do good for others only as a means of bringing pleasure to themselves. However, classical UTILITARIANISM, as advocated, for example, by Jeremy BENTHAM and John Stuart MILL, appears to hold that people are also capable of desiring pleasure for others not only as a means to an end but as an end in itself (*see* ALTRUISM; BENEVOLENCE).

Critics have questioned whether hedonism is an adequate theory of human motivation, arguing that persons may have other motives (*see* MOTIVE) or ends. They have also called attention to the difference between psychological or descriptive theory, which maintains that people do, as a matter of fact, seek pleasure and avoid pain, and an ethical theory, which maintains that they should or ought to do so (*see* IS/OUGHT DISTINCTION). The criticism is that ethical theory cannot be derived from the psychological theory, for it does not follow from the fact that something is done that it ought to be done. Indeed, if everyone always did seek pleasure and avoid pain, there would be no point in saying that they ought to.

Although, historically, many hedonists were not aware of these criticisms and so did not respond to them, it is quite possible that they did not intend to hold the theory in either its so-called psychological or its ethical form. What they might have meant simply is that the ultimate good in life is pleasure because that is what *good* means and that people ought to choose, as a means, whatever is necessary to achieve that end. This form of hedonism is called analytic or metaethical hedonism (*see* METAETHICS), for it is a theory that analyses the meaning of *good*. This is the form of the theory criticized by G. E. MOORE, who argued that pleasure does not define *good*.

There is also a distinction between quantitative hedonism and qualitative hedonism. A quantitative hedonist is one who maintains that only the quantity of pleasure should be considered in determining the MORALITY of an action and that so-called qualitative distinctions are reducible to quantitative ones. Thus, in the quantitative view, some pleasures may be said to be better than others because they are more intense or because they last longer, but these are quantitative considera-

tions. A qualitative hedonist, by contrast, would maintain that some pleasures, such as mental pleasures, are superior to other pleasures, such as bodily pleasures, and that these qualitative differences are not reducible to quantitative distinctions alone. Among the utilitarians, Jeremy Bentham was a quantitative hedonist and Mill a qualitative hedonist.

HEGEL, GEORG WILHELM FRIEDRICH (1770–1831) A German philosopher who based his philosophical system on the notion of self-conscious or fully rational FREEDOM.

For Hegel, freedom was not merely the lack of interference from external forces. In his view freedom was achieved only when people lived fully self-conscious lives within a rationally organized COMMUNITY or state. Although some critics have charged that Hegel favored a totalitarian state, this criticism is misleading. It was essential to Hegel's thought that the state meet very strict conditions, one of which was the rational consent in GOOD CONSCIENCE of its members.

Hegel believed that history was progress towards freedom. He is known for his dialectical method (*see* DIALECTICAL REASONING), according to which he viewed history as a struggle of ideas wherein competing ideas, or antithesis, are reconciled progressively in syntheses. Each synthesis of opposing ideas, in his view, becomes a new thesis, opposed by another antithesis. These theses will be again synthesized into a new thesis. Hegel sees ideas, or the very thought process of civilization, as growing or developing throughout history, coming closer and closer to the absolute TRUTH (*see* ABSOLUTES).

Hegel described this process as a movement from bare, abstract, universal ideas to a concrete realization of those ideas in actual life. Justice, for instance, in the abstract is a formula that says similar things should be treated similarly until society develops laws that specify in particular what kinds of things are just or unjust and provides protection against unjust acts. Until the idea of justice is concretized in social institutions, it is a mere aspiration and not a reality. RULES of justice, according to Hegel's notions, should change over time, approaching closer and closer to the ideal of justice. Abstract ideas take on meaning in the course of history.

Likewise, Hegel's concept of the *self* is a bare abstract idea, devoid of content, until it takes on meaning through historical process. Knowing that, "I am" is not very informative. As one begins to see the self in relation to other things, the self begins to take on content: I am so-and-so's child or parent; I am a student or a teacher. Understanding this progression helps us to understand the social nature of self-consciousness. The VALUE I have in my own eyes will be largely defined by the value I have in the eyes of others. Hegel addresses the master/slave relationship in society and the need for reconciliation and EQUALITY. He holds that both master and slave benefit from some aspects of the relationship, but both also suffer certain disadvantages. According to his analysis, the opposition between them can be reconciled, ultimately, only when they learn to treat one another as equals or when society or the government institutes laws that guarantee equal rights.

Hegel attempted to synthesize the philosophies of his predecessors; he also had a strong influence on the development of subsequent philosophy, especially during the nineteenth century. The American literary philosopher Ralph Waldo Emerson was influenced by Hegelian ideas, as were some of the American Pragmatists (*see* PRAGMATISM) such as Josiah Royce and John DEWEY. Karl MARX took from Hegel his idea of dialectical reasoning, but he claimed to have turned it upside down, speaking of it in materialistic rather than idealistic terms. Friedrich NIETZSCHE, as well as Marx, also appears to have been influenced by Hegel's discussion of the master/slave relationship. EXISTENTIALISM is both an outgrowth of and a reaction to Hegelianism.

HEINZ'S DILEMMA   A hypothetical moral problem developed by psychologist Lawrence KOHLBERG. This thought experiment was later used by moral psychologist Carol GILLIGAN to investigate MORAL DEVELOPMENT. Heinz's DILEMMA is constructed as follows:

Heinz's wife is near to death from a rare kind of cancer. There is only one drug that might save her life, and it was discovered by a druggist in the town where Heinz lives. The druggist paid a small amount for ingredients in the drug but is charging a large sum for a small dose of the drug. Heinz approaches everyone he knows to attempt to borrow money and has tried every other legal means available to him, but he is only able to raise half of the drug's selling price. Heinz appeals to the druggist and explains that without the medication his wife will die. Heinz asks the druggist to sell him the drug less expensively or to let Heinz pay for the drug on an installment plan. The druggist refuses and stands by his price. Heinz is now considering breaking into the drug store and stealing for his wife. Should he do it?

Mapping responses to Heinz's dilemma can be a useful way of understanding the moral framework a person is using. For example, someone who answers that Heinz should steal the drug because saving his wife will cause more GOOD than the HARM done to the druggist might be said to be using a UTILITARIAN framework. On the other hand, someone who answered that Heinz should not steal because stealing is always WRONG is appealing to a deontological framework (*see* DEONTOLOGY). Kohlberg asked children to decide what Heinz should do and used their answers to attempt to determine their stage of moral development. In his findings, boys, who tended to adhere more strictly to moral RULES, achieved higher stages of moral development than did girls. Gilligan challenged Kohlberg's gender-biased findings and argued that they are an inadequate account of women's moral development. She proposed that women's moral development is better understood as motivated by an ETHICS or CARE (*see also* FEMINIST ETHICS). Heinz's dilemma is also interesting in that it exhibits the common trend to construe moral issues as conflicts (*see* MORAL CONFLICT) between two parties with the solution framed as either/or. In this case, either Heinz steals the money or his wife will die of cancer. In contrast, it may be argued that most moral issues are more than a choice between two alternatives.

HELOÏSE (1101–1164) Medieval French philosopher and poet.

By age 16, Heloïse was known as the most learned woman in France as a result of the quality of her writing. An unordained cleric named Peter ABELARD was hired to teach Heloïse moral philosophy. Heloïse's writings on moral philosophy are found in her *Problemata* (*Problems*) and *Epistolae* (*Letters*).

Heloïse's ETHICS has two major components. The first component, adapted from the Roman philosopher Cicero, places a high VALUE on the VIRTUE called disinterested LOVE. This conception of love holds that true love for another is completely unselfish and asks nothing. The person who loves (the "lover") loves the other person (the "beloved") unconditionally for who the beloved is. The lover wants only to support the beloved in achieving goals and realizing his or her own potential. In an ideal loving relationship, the beloved feels the same way about the lover and has no selfish desires.

The other major component of Heloïse's moral philosophy concerns the MORALITY of intent. This theory relies on a distinction similar to one made by ARISTOTLE regarding the different types of causation. If a person's actions cause another to die, those actions are the material cause of death. If the person did not understand that his or her act might cause death, the death is unintentional, and the person would not be considered morally responsible (*see* RESPONSIBILITY) for it. According to Heloïse, a person is not morally responsible for an action if he or she lacks an EVIL INTENTION.

HEROISM To display bravery or COURAGE above others, particularly in dangerous or trying circumstances.

The idea of heroism is derived from the hero character. Originally a warrior, the hero acted with courage, strength, fortitude, and bravery in war in a way that distinguished him from other men. The term *heroism* came to be applied to the actions of any person, male or female, who displays this characteristic either in actual battle or metaphorically in overcoming seemingly insurmountable obstacles, such as fighting a terminal illness or helping people trapped in a burning building.

HETERONOMY Acting on desires (*see* DESIRE) that are not dictated by REASON.

The term *heteronomy* can be traced back to the Greek words meaning "other" and "LAW." In the moral philosophy of Immanuel KANT, heteronomy is opposed to AUTONOMY. While to act with autonomy means to be self-governing through practical reason, a person acting heteronomously is one whose actions are determined by forces other than a person's reason, such as emotion or inclination. Kant believed that such actions were nonmoral, that is, neither moral (*see* MORALITY) nor immoral (*see* IMMORALITY).

HILDEGARD OF BINGEN (1098–1179) Medieval German Benedictine nun and abbess who was widely respected as a theologian, philosopher, and prophet.

Although Hildegard wrote and preached on the subjects of cosmology (theories of the universe), theology, politics, and ethics, she never considered herself a theologian or a philosopher. She claimed instead that as a weak and untaught woman she had been given visions throughout her life that proclaimed God's teachings for the people of her time. Called by God to preach these divinely revealed ideas, she believed herself the exception to the church's decree that women were not to preach publicly. Unlike most mystics of the Middle Ages, her visions were not ecstatic. In addition, she did not believe that God was speaking to her personally, but instead that God was preaching through her, using her as a vessel by which God might teach the corrupt and arrogant leaders of the 12th-century church and state. In addition to the knowledge she gained by direct revelation, Hildegard claimed that all other knowledge is obtained by the illumination of the mind by the light of God.

Politically, Hildegard upheld the feudal society of her time, preaching that God had ordained certain people to rule over others, even as one class of angels ruled over the next. However she denounced the aristocrats as well as the leaders of the church whenever she believed that they had abused their power or failed to be obedient to the will of God.

Feminists today are taking a new interest in Hildegard. While she upheld the medieval belief that women in general are inherently weaker than men physically, intellectually and morally, she also proclaimed that men and women, both created in the image of God, complement each other. She taught that they must treat each other with mutual love and respect, and together rule and care for the planet over which they had been given the throne. Environmental ethicists find in Hildegard's writings a great respect for nature as the creation of God that humans must foster and protect.

In the field of ethics, Hildegard believed the most serious vice was that of pride. She described pride as the sin that first severed Lucifer from God and caused him to seduce Adam and Eve from paradise. Pride, the feeling that one has no need of God, is based on self-deception, and thus is the greatest threat to an authentic and happy human life. Contrarily, humility and the love of God inspire true knowledge of one's self as a creature of God. She believed that God had chosen her, "a wretched women," as a prophet to shame the men of her time into proper humility. She also taught the importance of self-discipline,

courage, mercy, justice, and wisdom. Because she held to the Christian doctrine of original sin, she also reminded her listeners of the necessity for penitence, for no human is exempt from wrongdoing.

In addition to proclaiming the wisdom given in her visions, Hildegard made great contributions in the fields of botany and medicine—especially gynecology—composed widely popular hymns and liturgies, and illustrated her writings with full-color paintings.

HINDU ETHICS Attitudes, guidelines, principles (see PRINCIPLE), and codes (see CODE) of conduct setting the tone and form of interpersonal relationships for Hindus.

According to traditional Hinduism (see CUSTOMS), individual life unfolds in four stages, each dominated by a particular concern or central objective and a corresponding moral framework. The demands of MORALITY become increasingly stringent and refined with each stage.

The first stage covers the first twenty or so years of life and is that of the *student*. The VALUE uppermost in the mind and heart during this period is pleasure and enjoyment. This is a period of relative indulgence, with more attention given to sensual satisfaction than to self-curtailment for the sake of a larger RESPONSIBILITY.

Increasing self-restraint occurs, however, with the second stage, that of the *householder*. Attention now shifts to marriage, the establishment and raising of a family, service to the COMMUNITY, and the accumulation of enough wealth to achieve these ends.

While formal religion is an important aspect of life in stages one and two, in the third stage it becomes focal. Having fulfilled filial and social duties (see OBLIGATION), the *forest dweller*, or wandering mendicant, turns attention now to reading religious and philosophical texts, seeking WISDOM from sages and saints, and meditating. DHARMA, or the pursuit of deep religious understanding, becomes the controlling passion (*see* PASSIONS AND EMOTIONS). If the third stage proves satisfying, it flows naturally into the last, that of the *sannyasin,* "the renuncient," who makes a final transition from exoteric, or conventional, religion to esoteric, or mystical, spirituality (*see* MYSTICISM). Satisfaction now lies wholly in MOKSHA, oneness with Brahman, transcending SAMSARA, the bondage and limitations inherent in ordinary life. The renuncient will adopt an even more ascetic lifestyle (*see* ASCETICISM) than that of the previous stage and will spend even more time reflecting on the scriptures and engaging in MEDITATION.

The Hindu way of life, including the four stages and their corresponding values (as mentioned above), is founded on *Atman* as the essential nature of both humans and the divine. *Atman* is often translated as "soul" or "Self" (capitalized to distinguish it from the ordinary self of EGO). The UPANISHADS, one of the major categories of Hindu scripture, make two remarkable declarations: (1) Brahman is Atman, and (2) each human being is Atman. The highest aim of human life for the Hindu is to discover this deeply embedded identity with the Ultimate.

Atman is hidden in the manifest forms of both humans and the gods. These constitute MAYA, or that which distorts perception, and must be penetrated in order to discover this deepest reality that is single in essence though multiple in manifestation. Maya is unveiled, and identification with the Ultimate occurs by disidentifying with all that is not the Ultimate; that means everything that makes up one's objective and subjective nature. This process of disidentification reaches its culmination in meditation.

Without meditation there is no full realization. Therefore, every aspect of the comprehensive and intensely demanding PSYCHOSPIRITUAL DISCIPLINE practiced by the forest dweller/renunciant prepares for and culminates in meditation. Meditation is essentially an exploration of consciousness that calms and purifies the mind so that the wisdom that is inherent in and common to humanity may come into awareness. All of the

mystical traditions, including esoteric Hinduism, affirm that this wisdom is one of discovering the unity of oneself with the Ultimate and with mankind. This profound "seeing" has the effect, among other things, of motivating a life that is incapable of harming another because this would be tantamount to harming oneself. Because all sense of separate self has vanished, to violate another is to violate oneself. No possible ulterior motive or objective can exist. Morality becomes implicit in the very being of the liberated person. *See also* BHAGAVAD GITA; BHAKTI YOGA; YOGA.

HIPPOCRATES (fifth century B.C.)   Greek physician called the father of medicine because he is the author of the HIPPOCRATIC OATH, taken by most Western physicians.

Hippocrates is reputed to be the first physician to treat the body as a unified organism rather than focusing on individual ailing parts of the body. Although it is difficult to determine the authenticity of the sixty works surviving under his name, all the works are characterized by their emphasis on observation and their rejection of supernatural explanations. Hippocrates is most famous for his treatise on MEDICAL ETHICS from which the Hippocratic oath is derived. This oath directs physicians to heal rather than to harm their patients. Hippocrates intended the oath for physicians who were practitioners of physical medicine, including pharmacy but not including surgery. The original oath required physicians to swear not to perform surgery because it was considered too risky at that time.

Hippocrates' standards, amended to incorporate the progression of medical technologies, have defined professional conduct for 2,000 years. The contemporary versions of the oath omit several features of the original, including mention of the gods Apollo, Asclepius, Hygenia, and Panaceia. The contemporary oath also includes promises to prescribe appropriate diet and drugs, to act to benefit the sick, to keep confidential information about patients, to avoid sexual contact with patients, and to refrain from other unjust and mischievous behavior toward patients.

HIPPOCRATIC OATH

CODE of professional behavior for physicians attributed to fifth century B.C. Greek physician HIPPOCRATES that has defined professional conduct for 2,000 years.

The original Hippocratic oath is translated:

I swear by Apollo Physician, by Aesculapius, by Health, by Heal-all, and by all the gods and goddesses, making them witnesses, that I will carry out, according to my ability and judgment, this oath and this indenture: To regard my teacher in this art as equal to my parents; to make him partner in my livelihood, and when he is in need of money to share mine with him; to consider his offspring equal to my brothers; to teach them this art, if they require to learn it, without fee or indenture; and to impart precept, oral instruction, and all the other learning, to my sons, to the sons of my teacher, and to pupils who have signed the indenture and sworn obedience to the physicians' law, but to none other. I will use treatment to help the sick according to my ability and judgment, but I will never use it to injure or wrong them. I will not give poison to anyone though asked to do so, nor will I suggest such a plan. Similarly I will not give a pessary to a woman to cause abortion. But in purity and in holiness I will guard my life and my art. I will not use the knife on sufferers from stone, but I will give place to such as are craftsmen therein. Into whatsoever houses I enter, I will do so to help the sick, keeping myself free from all intentional wrongdoing and harm, especially from fornication with woman or man, bond or free. Whatsoever in the course of practice I see or hear (or even outside my practice in social intercourse) that ought never to be published abroad, I will not divulge, but consider such things to be holy secrets. Now if I keep this oath, and break it not, may I enjoy honor, in my life and art, among all men for all time; but if I transgress and forswear myself, may the opposite befall me.

The contemporary versions of the oath omit several features of the original, such as promises to teach medicine free of charge and promises not to perform abortions. The contemporary version of the Hippocratic oath reads:

I SWEAR in the presence of the Almighty and before my family, my teachers and my peers that according to my ability and judgment I will keep this Oath and Stipulation.

TO RECKON all who have taught me this art equally dear to me as my parents and in the same spirit and dedication to impart a knowledge of the art of medicine to others. I will continue with diligence to keep abreast of advances in medicine. I will treat without exception all who seek my ministrations, so long as the treatment of others is not compromised thereby, and I will seek the counsel of particularly skilled physicians where indicated for the benefit of my patient.

I WILL FOLLOW that method of treatment which according to my ability and judgment, I consider for the benefit of my patient and abstain from whatever is harmful or mischievous. I will neither prescribe nor administer a lethal dose of medicine to any patient even if asked nor counsel any such thing nor perform the utmost respect for every human life from fertilization to natural death and reject abortion that deliberately takes a unique human life.

WITH PURITY, HOLINESS AND BENEFICENCE I will pass my life and practice my art. Except for the prudent correction of an imminent danger, I will neither treat any patient nor carry out any research on any human being without the valid informed consent of the subject or the appropriate legal protector thereof, understanding that research must have as its purpose the furtherance of the health of that individual. Into whatever patient setting I enter, I will go for the benefit of the sick and will abstain from every voluntary act of mischief or corruption and further from the seduction of any patient.

WHATEVER IN CONNECTION with my professional practice or not in connection with it I may see or hear in the lives of my patients which ought not be spoken abroad, I will not divulge, reckoning that all such should be kept secret.

WHILE I CONTINUE to keep this Oath unviolated may it be granted to me to enjoy life and the practice of the art and science of medicine with the blessing of the Almighty and respected by my peers and society, but should I trespass and violate this Oath, may the reverse be my lot.

Besides the Hippocratic Oath, there are other historic medical oaths including the Caraka Samhita (first century, Indian), the Oath of Asaph (third—seventh century, Hebrew), the Advice of Haly Abbas (tenth century, Persian), the Five Commandments and Ten Requirements (seventeenth century, Chinese), A Physician's Ethical Duties from Kholasah al Hekam (eighteenth century, Persian Islamic), Moses Maimonides' Daily Prayer of a Physician (eighteenth century, Egyptian Jewish), and the Code of Ethics of the American Medical Association (nineteenth century, American). Today, all health-care professions, including nursing and dentistry, have codes of ethics or codes of professional RESPONSIBILITY. *See also* MEDICAL ETHICS.

HOBBES, THOMAS (1588–1679) A prominent British philosopher who is considered to be one of the founders of the SOCIAL CONTRACT theory.

Hobbes believed that people act mainly out of emotions. He also believed that people have unlimited desires, and that without strong laws to stop them, they would have little motivation to respect the property or lives of others. Without organized social POWER, Hobbes thought, people are destined to live brutal lives. When people live free of social power, they live in what Hobbes called a "state of nature." This state is characterized by perpetual inclination to warfare, given that nothing restrains the natural

GREED of human beings. In his famous work, *Leviathan,* Hobbes stated that life in the state of nature would be "solitary, poor, nasty, brutish, and short." Thus, out of fear for their own safety, Hobbes believed that people living in the state of nature would consent to a government strong enough to protect LIFE and property. He also believed that the only effective government—one strong enough to keep avaricious people in line—would have nearly absolute power. Only by joining together and establishing a government with an overwhelmingly strong police power can some structure and safety be brought into people's lives.

Hobbes is often criticized for his support of dictatorship and absolute monarchy, though he is sometimes praised for his belief that the legitimacy of government ultimately rests on the consent and needs of the people. *See also* ENLIGHTENMENT ETHICS.

HOLOCAUST, THE   The systematic MURDER of up to 11 million Jews, Gypsies, blacks, homosexuals, the disabled, and others by Germany (*see* NAZISM) during World War II.

The 20th century has seen many instances of GENOCIDE, including in the former Soviet Union under Stalin, in Kampuchea (now Cambodia) under the Khmer Rouge, in East Timor after the Indonesian invasion, the massacre of the Tutsis in Rwanda, and the "ethnic cleansing" of Muslims in Bosnia, to name a few. The Holocaust is notable, however, because of the huge number of people killed and because of the calculated way in which the Nazis went about their mass slaughter. The Holocaust was not the result of random VIOLENCE, ANARCHY, or lawlessness. It was a bureaucratic undertaking in which killings were orchestrated for maximum efficiency in much the same way as a factory production line. The murders were justified (*see* JUSTIFICATION) by the government as a way to avoid contamination of the German gene pool and culture through contact with those with genetic traits and social preferences perceived to be undesirable.

For an episode that is almost universally condemned today as a horrific EVIL, it is surprisingly difficult to allocate blame for the Holocaust. In addition to those who directly participated in and authorized (*see* AUTHORITY) the killings, several hundred thousand other individuals were also indirectly involved, from the train drivers who drove the victims to their deaths to the many ordinary Germans who knew what was going on and either encouraged the policy or at least failed to do anything to stop it.

Additionally, many people who participated in the Holocaust later claimed to have done so because they were under orders and feared for their own lives should they disobey. This argument was not accepted as a defense in later WAR CRIMES trials; yet it continues to perplex ethicists (*see* ETHICS). Clearly there were cases where perpetrators of the Holocaust did legitimately fear for their own lives; yet many ethicists believe that self preservation cannot be the only motivation for action—sometimes other moral VALUES take precedence.

Possibly the most important lesson that can be learned from the Holocaust is the ease with which supposedly civilized people can be induced to commit barbaric, hateful acts. The Holocaust is an example of the consequences of PREJUDICE and RACISM when taken to their ultimate, logical conclusion. *See also* ANTISEMITISM; EUGENICS; HATE CRIMES.

HOLY WAR   A conflict fought in defense of, or in the name of, religion.

A holy war is one in which the participants are deemed to be sanctified by GOD with a religious righteousness. Participation in a holy war is seen as virtuous and is often assumed to result in spiritual reward, such as ABSOLUTION from SIN or benefits in the afterlife. A holy war may be the result of a scriptural commandment or the edict of religious authorities, or it may simply be a spontaneous movement by individuals who believe that they are responding to religious REVELATION.

Not all religious conflicts are holy wars. In Northern Ireland, for example, Protestant and Catholic VIOLENCE is more political than religious, resulting from centuries of conflict between different religious communities. In this case, the conflict is largely about generations-old grudges, PREJUDICE, and DISCRIMINATION and is not sanctified by the Protestant or Catholic churches.

Christianity does, however, have an extensive history of supporting holy wars. Between the eleventh and thirteenth centuries, for example, the Catholic Church in Rome authorized no less than eleven separate crusades against Muslims and other "heretics" in the Holy Lands of the Middle East. Islam also has a tradition of holy wars to protect and extend the FAITH, although this tendency is often been exaggerated in Christian cultures. The Islamic term *jihad*, often translated as "holy war" by Westerners, is more correctly translated as "struggle" or "endeavor." In Islam, the *jihad* is about protecting and extending PRINCIPLES of the faith. War is only appropriate when the faith is seriously and directly threatened.

HOMOPHOBIA   Irrational fear and loathing of HOMOSEXUALITY and homosexuals.

Although GAY RIGHTS activists often incorrectly label all opponents of homosexuality *homophobic,* homophobia is more correctly applicable to individuals who suffer from an acute and exaggerated anxiety about homosexuals and homosexual behavior. Homophobes believe that homosexuals represent a very real threat and are hypersensitive to any behavior that may be interpreted as typical of a homosexual. As a result, homophobes will often behave in exaggerated and stereotypically heterosexual ways in the false belief that such behavior will make it clear that they are not homosexual themselves. Typically, homophobes are convinced of the TRUTH of irrational and negative homosexual stereotypes and may react to stereotypically homosexual behavior in a forceful, aggressive, and sometimes violent way. At its most extreme, homophobes may engage in "gay bashing," the targeting of individuals believed to be homosexual for beatings and abuse, sometimes resulting in their death. Homophobia is usually associated with PREJUDICE and DISCRIMINATION against those believed to be homosexual and is similar to forms of RACISM, such as ANTI-SEMITISM. *See also* HATE CRIMES.

HOMOSEXUALITY   Sexual   attraction towards members of one's own sex.

Historically, attitudes towards homosexuality have varied widely. In ancient civilizations, such as Greece and Rome, for example, homosexuality was often seen as noncontroversial and even encouraged. SOCRATES appears to have been a homosexual, and PLATO suggested that homosexuality in the military may be highly desirable because of the bonds that would form between soldiers. Today it seems more common for the public to view homosexuality as immoral (*see* IMMORALITY).

Typically, beliefs about homosexuality are confused by misinformation, bigotry, PREJUDICE, and HOMOPHOBIA. Many people falsely believe, for example, that homosexuality is synonymous with pedophilia (*see* CHILD ABUSE). Similarly, others falsely believe that children and even adults in regular contact with someone who is homosexual might be brainwashed or "recruited" into adopting a homosexual lifestyle (*see* LIFESTYLES) themselves. Some even fear that they might catch homosexuality, as if it were contagious. Clearly, perceptions such as these are unfounded—aside from their sexual preference, people who are homosexual are no different from any other members of society.

Commonly, more educated opponents of homosexuality use a NATURAL LAW argument to explain their opposition to it; that is, they argue that homosexuality is unnatural and therefore a "CRIME against nature." This position, however, is premised on the assumption that the only natural outcome of sexual activity is procreation.

Such an assumption is highly controversial, however, because it appears to ignore the many undoubted psychological benefits of expressing affection to another human being. It also implies that other forms of sexual expression, such as masturbation or anal sex—regardless of the sex of one's partner—are equally WRONG. Indeed, extending the argument to its logical conclusion, it might also imply that many things human beings currently do are unnatural and therefore wrong, such as flying in an airplane, because humans were not designed with wings for flight.

Some people who support a person's RIGHT to a homosexual lifestyle do so on utilitarian grounds (*see* UTILITARIANISM). They argue that something is good if it maximizes the total happiness in society. Therefore, because the only people affected by homosexual behavior are the individuals who enjoy it and consent to participate in it, it can only be good. It has also been argued that FREEDOM of sexual expression is a CIVIL RIGHT that should be defended just as rigorously as the right to any other form of cultural or political expression.

In any case, if, as many scientists believe, homosexuality is not a matter of personal choice but of an unalterable biological predisposition, it could be argued that homosexuality is not a moral issue at all. In such circumstances, it is argued, one should not be praised or blamed for something that one is not responsible for (*see* RESPONSIBILITY) and cannot control. At the very least, homosexuality would presumably not be in conflict with natural law because the preference is itself a natural imperative. *See also* GAY RIGHTS.

HONESTY   To refrain from LYING, CHEATING, stealing, or deception.

An honest person is widely regarded as a moral person (*see* MORALITY), and honesty is a central concept to ETHICS as the foundation for a moral life. Western culture in particular tends to be more concerned with the attribution of moral blameworthiness than moral praiseworthiness. The Western legal system, for example, is not concerned with rewarding moral acts, only the PUNISHMENT of immoral acts. Similarly, a figure such as Robin Hood, who stole from the rich to give to the poor, is today likely to be described as immoral, while an honest banker would generally be regarded as moral.

The importance of honesty to any one individual will have a lot to do with what ethical system they subscribe to, as will the exact way that honesty is interpreted. Deontologists (*see* DEONTOLOGY), for example, tend to see behaving honestly, in the sense of TRUTH telling, as a fundamental requirement of morality. Utilitarians (*see* UTILITARIANISM), on the other hand, do not believe that honesty is always the best policy. They believe that in some cases, apparently dishonorable behavior, as in the case of Robin Hood, can in fact lead to great GOOD. Finally, existentialists (*see* EXISTENTIALISM) tend to believe that acting in a way that is authentic (*see* AUTHENTICITY), or true to oneself, is a form of honesty and basic to morality.

HONOR   The esteem, respect, and recognition in which one is held by others.

Honor is a problematic concept in ETHICS because the qualities that each society deems especially worthy of respect are often somewhat arbitrary and idealistic (*see* IDEALISM). The CODE OF HONOR known as chivalry, for example, defined chastity as essential to a woman's honor, while honorable men were required to defend the honor of the women they cared for. Such codes continue to this day, and it is not uncommon for fights to be provoked by one man insulting the girlfriend, wife, or female relative of another—the implication presumably being that if one is not prepared to fight in her defense, the slur must be true. At the very least, a man is still seen as dishonorable if he does not publicly support the honor of the women he cares for.

In the past, discussions about honor were important to ethical discourse. ARISTOTLE, for example, believed that it was important to be seen to perform honorable deeds. Today, however, most ethicists believe that actions are best evaluated objectively in terms of one's INTENTION and deeds, whether public or not, and not through the subjective perceptions of others. For this reason, the concept of honor is today rarely seen as an important part of moral discourse (*see* DISCOURSE ETHICS). *See also* CHARACTER; DIGNITY.

HOPE   The DESIRE for something coupled with the expectation of obtaining it.

Hope is generally considered a capacity of the WILL or feeling and is often a part of an optimistic disposition. To hope is to believe that something GOOD will come to pass in the future that does not exist in the present. Having hope often helps one be morally stronger, as it is possible to believe that a bad situation will improve.

In the Christian religion (*see* CHRISTIAN ETHICS) hope is a divine VIRTUE, along with FAITH and CHARITY, because it is implanted directly in the soul by GOD and has God as its object. The believer expects, through God, to achieve eternal salvation.

HUBRIS   Excessive PRIDE or self-confidence; aspiring to be a GOD or godlike.

Hubris may be a characteristic of a single person or of a group of people or a country. It is considered to be one of the CARDINAL SINS, as it is an extreme form of pride. Hubris may bring danger to the sufferer and to others. The hubristic person has an exaggerated sense of control and may attempt feats, both physical and political, that are well beyond the abilities of any human. When human beings seek to make decisions concerning the life and death of others, they are often accused of hubris. For example, the advancing research into GENETIC ENGINEERING is called hubristic by its critics because they argue humans are attempting to intrude into the domain of God.

Hubris is usually overcome only by suffering. Suffering often occasions self examination and the need to confront the limits of one's abilities.

HUMAN NATURE   The characteristics belonging to all humans, and only to humans, and forming the basis of what it means to be a human being.

In ETHICS, human nature is used to explain the type of moral and psychological nature we have and what the parameters of MORALITY can be. For example, it is true of all human beings that we exist in space, but this does not capture the sense in which the term *human nature* is used. To note, however, that humans have the capacity to reflect would indicate a morally significant fact about human nature. Because of our capacity to think, we can expect a level of morality from human beings that we would not expect from animals. Different moral theories have held that it is our nature to be selfish, to strive for survival, to be aggressive, to be benevolent, to be social, to be able to speak, and to desire immorality.

Some philosophers, for instance ARISTOTLE, have argued that human nature is basically fixed, and the most we can do is train and control it. Morality in this case becomes a matter of knowledge and discipline. During the Enlightenment (*see* ENLIGHTENMENT ETHICS), it was believed that we could appeal to the common rational nature of humankind to found a secular ethics based on self-interest, sympathy, and benevolence. Others have argued that human nature is changeable and largely determined by our environment. Georg Wilhelm Friedrich HEGEL held that our natures were shaped by our historical and social circumstances. Still others claim that there is no such thing as human nature and that while we have certain biological features in common, everything beyond that is socially constructed. FEMINIST ETHICS, for example, often argues against the idea that there is an essential female nature and an essential male nature. The differences between men and women are not due to a difference in basic qualities, they hold, but rather due to the differences in their roles in raising children, the type of work available in a society, and power relations.

HUMAN RIGHTS   The basic freedoms and benefits that all human beings are thought to be entitled to.

Fundamental to human rights is a belief in, and respect for, individual human DIGNITY and worth. Most important, this includes the right of each individual to live free from the threat of arbitrary execution or death at the hands of the government. Additionally, human rights are thought to encompass the right to AUTONOMY, FREEDOM of CONSCIENCE, and bodily INTEGRITY. Practices incompatible with human rights include such things as TORTURE, SLAVERY, and many forms of DISCRIMINATION. Other violations of human rights include attempts to interfere with an individual's freedom to practice religion, express opinions, or participate in the political process.

The relatively modern idea of human rights can be traced back to French and American revolutionary movements in the eighteenth century, which in many ways culminated in the United Nations' Universal Declaration of Human Rights in 1948. Signed by most national governments, the Universal Declaration of Human Rights is an extensive document that lists a range of rights, including those discussed above, but also, more controversially, the right to such things as education, employment, and an adequate standard of living. Supplementing this treaty are a number of specific, regional human rights treaties, such as the [Latin] American Declaration of the Rights and Duties of Man (1948) and the European Social Charter (1961), as well as a number of treaties concerned with human rights as they apply to specific groups such as refugees, children, workers, and women.

Despite all the international activity in this area, it should be noted that it is rare for any country to respect human rights fully because there are few international mechanisms in place to adjudicate on human rights disputes and virtually no mechanisms to enforce those decisions. In fact, even the United Nations recognizes that individual nation-states are entitled to decide for themselves what human rights they will respect and under what circumstances. *See also* BILL OF RIGHTS; CHILDREN'S RIGHTS; CIVIL RIGHTS; WOMEN'S RIGHTS.

HUMANISM   A belief in, and celebration of, the individual worth of humans and humanity.

All humanists share a belief in the human capacity for AUTONOMY and REASON and hold that human JUDGMENT provides the best foundation for finding moral guidance. Beyond its human-centered core, however, *humanism* is a term that has historically encompassed a wide range of interpretations and beliefs.

One influential version of humanism is known variously as scientific, naturalistic (*see* NATURALISTIC ETHICS), or philosophic humanism. It emerged during the early twentieth century and is closely associated with ATHEISM. Scientific humanism asserts that human beings are the central moral unit, independent of any creator or "higher" being. Another version of humanism is known as Christian humanism. Christian humanism stresses the importance and centrality of humans as creations in the image and likeness of GOD.

Humanism was the subject of much development and debate during the first half of the twentieth century and has roots dating back to classical times; however, it is most closely associated with the European Renaissance during the fourteenth, fifteenth, and sixteenth centuries.

HUME, DAVID (1711–1776)   Scottish naturalist philosopher (*see* NATURALISTIC ETHICS) and essayist pivotal in the Enlightenment (*see* ENLIGHTENMENT ETHICS).

Hume's writings concern the foundations of ETHICS, politics, and economics. His most important works are the *Treatise on Human Nature* (1739, 1740), *An Enquiry Concerning Human Understanding* (1748), *An Enquiry Concerning the Principles of Morals* (1751), and *The Dialogues Concerning Natural Religion* (published posthumously in 1779).

In the *Treatise on Human Nature,* Hume considers the philosophical topics of space, time, causality, external objects, the passions (*see* PASSION AND EMOTIONS), free will, and MORALITY. His views are highly original, and he was among the first to attempt to bring the experimental method to the study of the human mind and experience. Today the *Treatise* is regarded as an important philosophical work, but it was not well received during Hume's lifetime.

Hume's *Enquiry Concerning Human Understanding* is a more accessible version of the ideas published in the first part of the *Treatise.* The *Enquiry* also addresses religious belief (*see* FAITH) with skepticism, beginning to lay the groundwork for a morality that is based on sentiment and utility rather than REASON or metaphysics. The *Enquiry Concerning the Principles of Morals* further establishes a moral theory of utility. Jeremy BENTHAM, the founder of UTILITARIANISM, was directly influenced by Hume's work.

Hume's moral thought is naturalistic. He rejected any a priori or religious moral framework, viewing morality instead as the expression of sentiments (*see* MORAL SENTIMENT). Hume believed these sentiments evolved from natural human dispositions such as the disposition to form family groups, to share feelings, to have positive and negative reactions to the actions of others, and the tendency to form RULES. As we strove to work together in society in order to meet the demands of nature, he held, we began to form systems of approval or disapproval based on a combination of our needs for survival and our natural sympathies.

Hume further distinguished between natural and artificial virtues (*see* VIRTUE). Natural virtues always produce GOOD and are always approved of by society. Artificial virtues arise from the necessities of a circumstance. For example, according to Hume, benevolence is considered a natural virtue, whereas justice is considered an artificial virtue.

HUMILITY   The recognition and acceptance of one's limitations; the acceptance of PRINCIPLES and forces that we cannot control.

Humility is often engendered as a result of experiences of gratitude, awe, or reverence. For example, one might feel humbled by the generosity of a friend or by the beauty of a sunset. Humility may also arise during trying times or periods of struggle when we experience the limits of our resources or abilities. Those with humility usually listen well to others and are accepting of them. A humble individual is usually unselfish, dependable, flexible, and adaptable. A person with humility can succeed in all environments and is not concerned with status or material success. A life without humility may be characterized by PRIDE, ENVY, arrogance, SELF-RIGHTEOUSNESS, and excessive ambition.

In the Christian tradition (*see* CHRISTIAN ETHICS), humility is a VIRTUE that is acquired when one voluntarily submits one's life to GOD's WILL. Divine grace, strength, and forgiveness are promised to the humble. Humility is often coupled with other virtues, such as patience.

HYPOCRISY   Encouraging others to believe that one has higher moral standards than one in fact does.

Hypocrisy is a form of LYING. It is more than just a moral lapse on the part of a virtuous person (*see* VIRTUE); it requires a conscious effort to deceive others. For example, a politician would be behaving hypocritically if he or she were to engage in an adulterous relationship in private, while publicly declaring a commitment to family values and the sanctity of marriage. On the other hand, that same politician would not be hypocritical to declare a commitment to family values if his or her only transgression was a previous divorce that he or she now regrets.

Hypocrisy is a breach of trust (*see* TRUSTWORTHINESS) because we generally assume that individuals represent themselves as they really are. It is therefore common to feel a sense of betrayal when hypocrisy is discovered. Additionally, hypocrisy may cause us to question the motives of all apparently virtuous people and to lessen the respect in which such people are held by the COMMUNITY. For example, although many politicians are trustworthy, hypocritical actions by some have undermined respect for all politicians and the institutions that they serve. *See also* DOUBLE STANDARD.

HYPOTHETICAL   In ETHICS, an imaginary set of circumstances used to illustrate or identify a moral PRINCIPLE.

Hypotheticals enable ethicists to explore moral issues that may be difficult to understand without the use of examples. Furthermore, because real life issues often require a complex mix of INTUITION, JUDGMENT, and knowledge to resolve, it is sometimes only through the use of hypotheticals that we can isolate particular moral principles that would otherwise be difficult to see separately and objectively.

For example, although most of us believe that killing is wrong, we might want to find out if exceptions are possible. In this case, we could ask others how they would react to a hypothetical situation, such as where a terrorist is about to explode a nuclear weapon in a major city and the only way to stop this is to kill the terrorist. The question is useful because it presents an unusual situation that many people may not consider if they were asked simply, "Is murder always wrong?"

Some people object to the use of hypotheticals because they are often unrealistic. For example, our hypothetical allows only two possible outcomes: the terrorist is killed and millions of people saved, or the terrorist is not killed and millions die in a nuclear explosion. In real life, we are likely to have other options, such as trying to disarm the terrorist or alert authorities. We use this hypothetical because it is only by restricting the circumstances that we can easily separate people who believe that killing should only be used as a last resort from those who believe that murder is never justified.

HYPOTHETICAL IMPERATIVE A conditional command.

A HYPOTHETICAL is a proposition that claims that one thing is so if another condition is supposed or is to be met. Hypotheticals are often called conditionals and usually have the form "If . . . , then . . ."—for example, "If we are going to get to the movie on time, then we should leave now."

The hypothetical imperative is a conditional command; for example, "If you want to go to the moon, then you should build a rocket ship." In moral theory, a hypothetical imperative tells people how to ACT if they want to bring about a certain result. The claim, "If you want people to respect you, then you must tell the truth," is an example of a hypothetical imperative. In the view of some philosophers, MORALITY is simply a system of conditional statements like these.

Other philosophers, most notably Immanuel KANT, argue that morality is a matter of categorical, rather than hypothetical, imperatives (*see* CATEGORICAL IMPERATIVE). On this view moral imperatives are absolute (*see* ABSOLUTES) and are not contingent a material outcome. Given the hypothetical imperative, "If you want people to respect you, then you must tell the truth," it is possible to reply, "But I don't care if people respect me; therefore I do not have to tell the truth." The categorical imperative, "Tell the truth," does not allow for such exception.

I

IDEAL OBSERVER An impartial and perfectly informed moral judge, otherwise indistinguishable from a normal human being, who makes moral judgments (*see* JUDGMENT) on the basis of gut reaction.

In a very real sense, the ideal observer is more than just an impossible, imaginary entity created by ethicists (*see* ETHICS) to help us decide moral dilemmas (*see* DILEMMA) but an ethical system in its own right. Underlying the idea of the ideal observer is a naturalistic (*see* NATURALISTIC ETHICS) assumption that RIGHT and WRONG are functions of how human beings react to the world. According to this theory, the unbiased and objective observer is motivated by feelings of EMPATHY, or at least sympathy, for both the initiator of the act being evaluated and for those affected by that action. In addition, it is essential that the observer is fully aware of all facts and knowledge relevant to that act, including the circumstances and consequences of the act. Finally, assuming that all these conditions are met, if the overall reaction elicited from the ideal observer in response to the act is approval, then the action is right; conversely, if the reaction is disapproval, then the action is wrong. *See also* IMPARTIALITY.

IDEALISM The position that reality is fundamentally constituted of mind or spirit.

There are several forms of philosophical idealism. Objective idealism holds that material objects do exist but rejects the idea that VALUES have emerged from material things. Subjective idealism is a stronger view and holds that material objects exist only dependent upon human thought. In daily life, idealism refers to those who base their moral standards on pure ideas, such as TRUTH, goodness, beauty, and JUSTICE.

PLATO is usually considered the first Western idealist philosopher because of his doctrine of Forms. For Plato, the universal idea of the *good* was more real than any particular good action. The idea of the *Good* has a spiritual dimension. It is universal and does not change, where as particular actions are impermanent and changing.

The eighteenth-century Irish philosopher George Berkeley was one of the strongest proponents of idealism. Berkeley is famous for his immaterialism, or the claim that the external world does not exist. The only reality, he held, was the mind and its ideas. The individual and his awareness are the basic units of reality. Thus, any ethical view (*see* ETHICS) will also have to be centered in the individual and the RATIONALITY of his ideas. This position automatically minimizes an ethics based on COMMUNITY, the body, or the environment.

Immanuel KANT held a position called transcendental idealism (*see* TRANSCENDENTALISM). In Kant's view we cannot have knowledge of the world by REASON or sense experience alone; rather, knowledge is dependent on the transcendental self, or the universal structure of all subjects. This view also lays the groundwork for an ethic based on reason, ideas, and rules rather than, for example, the experience of particular individuals, the body, or passion.

IDEALS Standards of EXCELLENCE or perfection.

The concept of an *ideal* is crucial to many different kinds of discourse. For instance, someone may refer to another as an ideal friend, mate, musician, or teacher. In each case, the person is said to manifest the characteristics that one should aspire to possess. An ideal guitarist is everything that a guitarist should be. The term *ideals,* however, usually refers to beliefs about how the world or some aspect of the world should be. To say of someone that he or she has certain ideals is to say that he or she has fixed opinions about what should be.

The difficulty with ideals is that they often come into conflict with reality. For example, a baseball player may enter the major leagues with certain ideals about what professional baseball should be. If the players learns that major league baseball is more difficult than anticipated, or more stressful, or more competitive, or more corrupt, the player may come to see a gap between original ideals and reality. We then may say that those ideals have been shattered, meaning that the player has seen how reality falls short of what it should be.

Ideals may be nonmoral, but they usually have a moral component. An example of a nonmoral ideal is the belief that college should be a time to explore many different interests without being distracted by financial worries. Examples of moral ideals may be beliefs about how adults should behave when playing competitive sports or about how married people should treat one another. Regulative ideals are moral ideals that may be unrealizable in full but may nonetheless govern behavior. For example, the belief that everyone should live in peace may be presently unrealizable in full, but many believe we should always strive to realize this goal as closely as possible. One may also have political ideals, as in the belief that everyone in a democracy has a chance to participate in governing the country.

Related to the concept of someone with ideals is that of someone who is idealistic. People who are idealistic do not see the extent to which reality fails to conform to their vision. For instance, someone who expects the poor to be pleased by the donations of charities may ignore the sense of shame that people may feel when accepting such gifts. An idealistic social worker may be shocked, for instance, to find people responding with resentment or anger. An idealistic person is said to have high ideals, in contrast to a person of low ideals who expects less from the world. Typically, to say of people that they have either high or low ideals is a pejorative judgment: it is to say they expect too much or too little from the world.

IDEOLOGY   A collection of VALUES and beliefs that structure the way in which the world is interpreted.

Ideology was a term originally coined to describe any set of ideas and beliefs and the relationships between them. Nowadays it more commonly refers to any system of beliefs that is accepted uncritically by a group or society at large. Examples of common ideologies include CAPITALISM, COMMUNISM, CONSERVATISM, and LIBERALISM. Because ideologies are accepted largely on faith, they are arguably a form of BIAS.

Ideologies may shape the way in which an issue is examined and presented. In capitalist countries, for example, when we say that a country is doing well, we generally mean that it is wealthy, not that the citizens are healthier or happier. This may be because wealth is the primary measure of success in capitalist countries, for we could just as easily say that a country is doing well when overall community satisfaction is high, although we generally do not. Capitalists may also prioritize wealth because they incorrectly assume that good health and happiness follow automatically from it, although the wealth may in fact be created for people too stressed from overwork to enjoy it.

An inequitable ideology that is widely and uncritically held may come to seem natural or just, consequently legitimizing the status quo. Furthermore, ideologies may only serve the interests of a powerful elite (*see* ELITISM) who have the resources to influence popular opinion. Karl MARX was possibly the biggest champion of this idea, pointing out that capitalism's emphasis on the sanctity of private property is of primary benefit to those who have a majority of the wealth.

IMMIGRATION   The movement of people into a new country of residence.

During the nineteenth and twentieth centuries, the world's wealth became increasingly concentrated in a small number of countries, primarily in Europe and North America. Today, although these countries represent only 20 percent of the world's population, they control 80 percent of its wealth. Under the circumstances, it is not surprising that many of the poorer 80 percent of the world's population DESIRE the affluent LIFESTYLES enjoyed in Western countries and see migration to those countries as a way of obtaining that sort of lifestyle.

Immigration clearly benefits Western countries in a number of ways; for example, many employers cannot fill low paid, labor intensive jobs with local workers, and immigrants are often the only ones prepared to do such jobs. Furthermore, immigrants from different cultures can serve to enrich their new countries, bringing with them ideas and traditions (*see* CUSTOMS) that may broaden a COMMUNITY through different languages, exotic new foods, or simply a different perspective on life (*see* MULTICULTURALISM).

Although opponents of immigration are sometimes motivated by RACISM, there is a clear limit to the number of migrants any country can accept. New immigrants require schools and education, housing, and other forms of support to ease their transition to their new society, and this costs money. Furthermore, large-scale immigration can cause social disruption as older residents learn to cope with the influx of new migrants, and new migrants take some time to become comfortable with a new language and new ways of doing things.

Even if there were not benefits associated with immigration, however, it can be argued

that the affluence of the West leaves it with a moral OBLIGATION to accept RESPONSIBILITY for the poor and needy in the world, especially as many migrants are fleeing severe deprivation and political prosecution.

IMMORALITY   Acts (*see* ACT) or thoughts opposed to, inconsistent with, or in violation of moral LAW.

Unlike amorality (*see* AMORALITY), which is the absence of MORALITY, immorality involves the specific violation of a morally prescribed principle (*see* PRINCIPLES). Whether something is considered immoral or amoral depends very much on the system concerned. For example, a consequentialist (*see* CONSEQUENTIALISM) is likely to believe that it is immoral to tell the truth when lying would relieve someone of pain, while it is amoral to tell a "white lie" that neither hurts or harms anyone. A deontologist (*see* DEONTOLOGY), on the other hand, is likely to see lying as immoral regardless of the consequences because for the deontologist it is the act that is important, not the consequences. *See also* EVIL.

IMPARTIALITY   The absence of BIAS or PREJUDICE; not favoring one side over another.

Almost all ethical theories (*see* ETHICS) presuppose that, ideally, moral decisions should be made free from personal bias; yet, it is practically impossible for us to fully disregard our own biases because we are often unaware that they exist. For this reason, several principles have been suggested to help us minimize bias in our decision making, including the principles of reversibility, the ability to universalize, and the "veil of ignorance."

According to the principle of reversibility, one is acting impartially if one would make the same decision if the relevant roles are reversed. For example, José must chose between two different sites on which to build a new dam. The first site will result in the flooding of his hometown, and the second will result in the flooding of a neighboring town. In this case, assuming

José chooses the second site for the new dam, José is acting impartially if he would have made the same decision even if the town in the second site was his hometown.

According to the principle of the ability to universalize, a decision is impartial if the decision maker is comfortable advocating that others use exactly the same decision-making principles in similar circumstances. In this case, José would be acting impartially if he would be comfortable with any other person in a position of AUTHORITY using the same principles to make their decisions.

According to the "veil of ignorance" principle, a decision is impartial if the decision maker acts rationally (see RATIONALITY), but as if she or he has no special knowledge or personal preferences in the matter, even regarding her or himself. In this case, José would be impartial if he acted as if he didn't know which of the townships was his hometown.

Although perfect impartiality is impossible to achieve, one can come close by inviting someone who does not have a personal interest in any particular outcome to make controversial decisions. In our example, this might involve José asking a colleague from outside the area to make a final decision on the site of the dam. *See also* FAIRNESS; IDEAL OBSERVER.

INCEST   A sexual relationship between people who are closely related genetically.

The taboo (*see* TABOO) against incest remains one of the strongest prohibitions (*see* PROHIBITION) in Western society, but it is not entirely clear that incest is always a moral WRONG.

Incest is most clearly undesirable when it takes the form of CHILD ABUSE, occurring between an older relative and a young child. In such cases it is very easy for children to be manipulated into doing something that they don't understand and can't realistically be said to have consented to. Furthermore, because of strong laws and social taboos against the practice, chil-dren are often pressured into suppressing what is going on, often with threats. This can lead to low self-esteem, strong feelings of GUILT, and developmental problems.

In other cases of incest, however, such as between two consenting adult siblings, the rationale for its prohibition is less clear. It has been argued, for example, that the prohibition exists to prevent "inbreeding," the possibility of regressive, undesirable traits appearing in a couple's offspring, although many modern geneticists now refute this argument. It has also been argued that all human beings are naturally born with a fundamental aversion to incest; however, the evidence suggests that the aversion is learned and not inbred—there are numerous recorded instances of incest in which those involved have suffered no apparent psychological damage as a result. Others object to incest because they believe that it may cause role confusion and, consequently, a possible breakdown in the structure of the family, although the likelihood of this is unclear. When all arguments are examined, however, the strongest argument against the social acceptance of incest remains that it may encourage the abuse of relatively powerless and impressionable children.

INDIVIDUALISM   The view that the individual human being is the most important moral unit.

Individualists generally see concepts such as the *community* as fictions. They argue that ideas such as the *common good* are only valid to the extent that they represent the needs of individuals. For example, the need for community safety is relevant only in that it represents the aggregate of the need for safety that each individual feels independently. For this reason, individualism is often in conflict with COMMUNITARIANISM, which defines community as the most important moral unit and therefore implies that the good of the community must always take precedence over the GOOD of the individual.

Individualists also tend to oppose the belief that people sometimes need to be protected from themselves, a doctrine known as PATERNALISM. Although paternalists may argue that dangerous activities such as rock climbing should be banned, individualists believe that individuals must be allowed to decide for themselves what risks they are prepared to accept.

Over time, individualism has taken a variety of forms. Egoists (*see* EGOISM), for example, believe that all human action is essentially selfish (*see* SELFISHNESS), and that one's only MORAL RESPONSIBILITY is to look after one's own SELF-INTEREST. Other individualists, such as libertarians (*see* LIBERTARIANISM) and many anarchists (*see* ANARCHY), believe that although people should be as free as possible to make decisions about their own lives, some laws (*see* LAW) are necessary to stop people from harming (*see* HARM) each other.

Individualism has been criticized for implicitly downplaying the importance of social bonds, although most people feel a strong need for such ties. Additionally, virtually everything each human being does undermines the AUTONOMY of others in some way, for as the English poet John Donne wrote, "No man is an island." If each individual is inseparable from the people around him or her, then perhaps it is not community but individualism that is the unnatural fiction. In any case, the distinction between individual and community may simply be arbitrary and unrealistic, as is illustrated in the problem of the FREE RIDER.

INFANTICIDE   Killing an infant at birth.

Historically, infanticide has been practiced for religious and social reasons. Egyptian, Greek, and Roman records all refer to religious offerings of newborn babies. Ritual SACRIFICE of a firstborn child was also common among some tribal groups in India through the 1800s. People who live in harsh physical environments, such as the Eskimo and the Aborigines of Australia, are also known to practice infanticide to control the size of their tribes.

Infanticide is most often practiced on female infants, especially in war-prone cultures or cultures where hunting is a main source of food. Cultures that especially prize male children as a status symbol also have high rates of female infanticide. In some cultures, sick or deformed infants are also subject to infanticide. As historically practiced, infanticide was a group practice; that is, recognized by a social group as necessary to its survival. Today, infanticide is not sanctioned (*see* SANCTIONS) by any country, but it is still practiced in some areas. In some parts of India, for example, a second female child will not be tolerated by local tribes because they cannot afford to raise her. In China, female infants are in danger of surreptitious infanticide because there are restrictions on the number of children a family may have, and male children are considered to be more prestigious.

In contemporary debate over ABORTION, infanticide is sometimes used by antiabortion activists to describe any termination of pregnancy. They hold that human LIFE begins at conception; therefore, abortion constitutes infanticide. This use is highly rhetorical, and although increasingly common it deviates from the traditional understanding of infanticide.

INFORMED CONSENT   In MEDICAL ETHICS, the state where a patient or research subject agrees to specific medical procedures in full knowledge of all relevant facts.

The concept of informed consent is grounded in the ethical doctrine (*see* ETHICS) that each person has a RIGHT to self-determination as a reasoning (*see* REASON), autonomous (*see* AUTONOMY) being and that this right should be respected. Implicit in this principle is the belief that no person should be touched or interfered with unless they have specifically consented to such interference in advance.

Before patients can be said to have given their informed consent to a medical procedure, it is essential that they fully understand the full implications of that procedure. Information such as the risks associated with treatment, realistic alternatives to the proposed treatment, and the potential consequences of nontreatment are all highly relevant to a person's decision. It is, therefore, insufficient for patients to simply express a willingness to undergo treatment or to sign waivers, because this alone will not guarantee that their decision is truly in their own best interest. Similarly, and for this reason, the use of pressure or COERCION by a doctor in obtaining consent to a procedure also violates the principle of informed consent.

Because each person is different and has different priorities, many believe that it is impossible for doctors to say what is best for individuals. For example, there is a small risk of death associated with even the most minor operations, and, therefore, a person may need to evaluate whether the condition that the operation is purported to cure is inconvenient enough to justify taking such risks. Similarly, even with terminal illness, a person may have to weigh the risk of death on the operating table against a guaranteed final few months of life to wind up their affairs and say good-bye to their families.

The belief in informed consent is a relatively recent phenomenon in Western society. Historically, society was far more paternalistic (*see* PATERNALISM)—it would have been unthinkable for many patients to question the WISDOM of doctors, who seemed much better qualified than the average patient. Such a belief has fallen into disfavor because, aside from the fact that doctors cannot know any individual's personal priorities, there were many instances in the 20th century in which doctors, motivated by GREED, curiosity, or simple arrogance, performed untested and unscientific treatments to the detriment of trusting patients.

All adults are presumed to be competent (*see* COMPETENCY) to give their informed consent to medical treatment unless there is strong evidence to the contrary, such as in the case of

mental illness. Other exemptions exist where a person is incapacitated and emergency treatment is required. In these cases, if a patient's opinions regarding treatment have been previously expressed, those opinions take priority. If it is impossible to discover a patient's opinion, however, the doctor may proceed with treatment if a reasonable person would agree to such treatment in similar circumstances. Exemptions also exist in the case of children, where the guardian or guardians are the ones required to give informed consent, with the provision that their decision must not obviously conflict with the child's best interest. *See also* BIOETHICS.

INSANITY Mental illness; an irrational state of mind.

Many ethicists and legal scholars believe that the insane, like small children and the mentally retarded, should not necessarily be seen as blameworthy or morally accountable (*see* ACCOUNTABILITY) for the consequences of their actions (*see* ACT). This is because mental illness can affect a person's JUDGMENT, causing her or him to act irrationally, and may even interfere with the sufferer's ability to understand the difference between RIGHT and WRONG. A person who is affected in this way would lack the so-called "guilty mind" (*see* MENS REA) that is essential for allocating moral blameworthiness in most ethical systems.

Unfortunately, unlike the case of young children or the retarded, not everyone who is suffering from a mental illness is necessarily impaired to the extent that they cannot make rational decisions for themselves. In these cases, for example, someone who is mentally ill but is still able to distinguish between right and wrong may be held morally and legally accountable for his or her actions. Conversely, however, particularly in criminal trials, those who are judged to meet the legal definition of insanity may be found not guilty—not accountable for their actions. This has led some defendants in criminal cases to claim falsely and immorally to be insane in the belief that an insanity defense will enable them to avoid accountability for their actions. In response, it should be noted that people found not guilty of a CRIME by reason of insanity are rarely automatically set free. In fact, mentally ill offenders are usually compulsorily confined to a mental institution for treatment, a fate that may seem worse than prison for many criminals. This may also give some explanation to why insanity is rarely used as defense in criminal trials.

One's position on insanity may also depend on whether one is a retributivist (*see* RETRIBUTION) or a consequentialist (*see* CONSEQUENTIALISM). Retributivists believe that PUNISHMENT is something that should automatically follow from criminal acts simply because particular acts justify particular responses by society. Retributivists, therefore, tend to be unsympathetic to the insanity defense. Consequentialists, on the other hand, tend to support punishment only when it is for the purpose of a greater GOOD, and in the case of insanity, many common consequentialist justifications for punishment seem less valid. For example, consequentialists often argue that punishment will help deter a person from reoffending (*see* DETERRENCE); yet, the mentally ill are often unable to act rationally in their own SELF-INTEREST. Similarly, although punishment is sometimes justified as a form of REHABILITATION, in the case of the mentally ill, trying to cure their mental illness would seem to be a more productive way of achieving this goal.

Regardless of one's position, however, few disagree that some form of confinement for particularly dangerous offenders is often necessary to protect society from danger, be it in a psychiatric institution or prison.

INTEGRATION   *See* SEGREGATION.

INTEGRITY   CONSISTENCY of belief (*see* FAITH) and action (*see* ACT); uncorrupted VIRTUE.

Integrity is an important component of GOOD CHARACTER and virtue and is essential to HONESTY. A person who has integrity is someone who has strong moral principles (*see* PRINCIPLE) and will successfully resist the temptation to compromise those principles. For example, a person who does not believe in lying might be said to have integrity if she or he refused to lie, even if doing so would be at great personal cost. Integrity is opposed to behavior such as inconsistency, prevarication, and HYPOCRISY. Implicit in integrity is the notion of moral identity, that is, a consistent wholeness of self that can be corrupted (*see* CORRUPTION) or violated by certain actions.

Integrity is not necessarily a virtue in itself because it is also important that the VALUES one holds are themselves moral (*see* MORALITY). An employer might be said to have integrity, for example, if he or she is morally committed to racist beliefs and refuses to hire workers who are members of ethnic groups he or she disapproves of, even at the cost of going to prison. *See also* VIRTUE ETHICS.

INTENTION   The choice to ACT in a specific way, believing that it will bring about a particular result.

Many ethicists (*see* ETHICS) believe that we should not be held accountable for acts that we do not intend on the basis that acts we are unconscious of are out of our control. For example, a person who accidentally injures another is not generally held accountable for that injury. As a result, unintentional acts are often seen as neither praiseworthy nor blameworthy.

For one to intend something, one must both resolve to achieve a particular outcome and then act in some way that will help attain that outcome. In the case of a praiseworthy act, for example, one might resolve to help the poor, and therefore, donate money to CHARITY. On the other hand, accidentally leaving a $20 bill on the street would not generally be seen as either praiseworthy nor blameworthy, even if it was picked up by someone who was poor.

In most English-speaking countries, the legal system does not generally hold people accountable for acts that are apparently unintentional. Exceptions exist, however, such as in the cases of statutory rape and negligent disregard for public safety. In these cases it is believed that people have a RESPONSIBILITY to avoid acting in a way that may lead to accidental HARM. For example, a person may be guilty of NEGLIGENCE if he or she causes an accident while speeding, even if he or she legitimately believed that there was little or no chance that such an accident could occur.

INTERNATIONAL LAW   The collection of treaties, agreements, and informal CUSTOMS that regulate the way countries interact with each other.

Ethicists have traditionally devoted little time to the study of international MORALITY. Of those who have, some ethicists such as Thomas HOBBES and Niccolò MACHIAVELLI deny that morality is applicable to the international realm. These philosophers generally argue that a country's RESPONSIBILITY is first and foremost to the well-being of its own citizens. Indeed, it may be arbitrary and unnatural to assume that the nation is even a morally significant thing because it is an artificial entity with arbitrary boundaries and no unified physical existence and is run by individuals subject to their own personal morality. Others believe that states should be constrained by morals similar to, or the same as, those applicable to individuals. Still others believe that the international realm is subject to moral laws (*see* LAW) that are fundamentally different from conventional morality.

What all commentators seem to have in common, however, is the concession that the international system is essentially anarchial (*see* ANARCHY) and that international law, where it exists at all, exists primarily because of reciprocal SELF-INTEREST (*see* RECIPROCITY). It is, therefore,

important not to overstate the importance of international law to the conduct of international affairs. In fact, there are relatively few laws governing the behavior of nation states and relatively few mechanisms for enforcing those laws.

Countries that contend that international law has been violated have a relatively limited set of options for having their concerns heard. Most commonly, countries will seek the support of other countries to apply pressure on the violator, either through simple diplomatic maneuvering or through more severe action such as sanctions and embargoes. More formally, a country may seek a JUDGMENT on the issue through MEDIATION, diplomatic negotiation, or an international panel of jurors, such as the International Court of Justice. In no case, however, is there a superior AUTHORITY to enforce the decisions of such bodies; therefore, JUSTICE is not always served while large, powerful countries (*see* POWER) such as the United States can easily resist the pressure of international condemnation.

INTERNATIONAL   RESPONSIBILITY
Moral and political obligations (*see* OBLIGATION) to people living in other nations.

Today, more so than ever before, the world is a complex, interconnected, and interdependent place where modern technology has given us the means to both help and hurt communities (*see* COMMUNITY) far distant from our own. In this world of staggering opulence and shocking destitution, citizens of affluent countries in particular have increasingly been forced to consider their moral RESPONSIBILITY to the rest of the planet. Affluent countries not only consume the vast majority of the world's resources but also produce the vast majority of the world's pollution. In such circumstances, many argue, rich nations have a responsibility to try to mitigate the damage that they are doing to the planet, as well as to help the citizens of destitute countries achieve at least a minimum equitable standard of living.

Of course, not everyone believes that we have a responsibility to those in other countries. Many communitarians (*see* COMMUNITARIAN-ISM), for example, believe that our primary moral responsibility is to our own community. Other people object to international assistance because historically it has often been counter-productive. For example, giving food to poor countries has sometimes served to support authoritarian dictators and to create dependence by driving out the businesses of local food producers who cannot make a profit when food is being supplied for free. These problems, however, might be mitigated if international-aid efforts were motivated by ALTRUISM and not by political considerations, as they often are today.

INTERSUBJECTIVITY   Beliefs (*see* FAITH), attitudes, or feeling shared among members of a COMMUNITY.

Ethical theories (*see* ETHICS) based on inter-subjectivity take a middle ground between SUB-JECTIVISM, which holds that MORALITY is based simply on the emotional impulses of individuals and is therefore relative, and OBJECTIVISM, which holds that there is a one true universal morality independent of individual circumstances. Intersubjectivists believe that TRUTH and morality are based on a widespread CON-SENSUS of opinion that may vary between communities but which is not dependent on individual factors.

Intersubjectivism avoids a number of criticisms of subjectivism, including the claim that subjectivism is simply a form of EGOISM, insep-arable from SELF-INTEREST. Intersubjectivity also retains a degree of flexibility unavailable to objectivists and needs to be less concerned with solving difficulties, such as BIAS—difficulties associated with attempts by inherently subjective actors to identify objective moral VALUES. Inter-subjectivity, however, has its own problems, such as the facts that it assumes that people are capable of transferring information between themselves with a high degree of accuracy, and also that it is actually possible to say that all minds are truly in agreement.

INTERVENTION   An attempt to change the beliefs or behavior of an individual through the use of pressure that includes mental and, sometimes, physical COERCION.

Interventions create a number of moral dilemmas (*see* DILEMMA) for ethicists (*see* ETHICS) because although they are ostensibly in the best interests of the person that they are focused on, they are essentially a way of forcing someone to think or act differently. This appears to be a violation of the moral principle that we should respect the AUTONOMY of others and is, therefore, a potential violation of HUMAN RIGHTS. Interventions are a form of PATERNAL-ISM because they assume that to some extent the subject is incapable of making a rational (*see* RATIONALITY) decision for her- or himself.

In some cases, people will freely subject themselves to an intervention in the belief that this will change behavior that they cannot otherwise seem to control. For example, people who cannot stop themselves from consuming alcohol may ask friends to prevent them forcibly from giving in to this desire should they appear to be about to do so.

In other cases, intervention may be used even when a person does not consent. For example, a criminal may be required to undergo psychological adjustment intended to stop her or him from reoffending. Similarly, it is some-times argued that people require interventions (or "deprogramming") when they have appar-ently been brainwashed into believing seem-ingly illogical or personally harmful ideas, such as the belief that they must commit criminal or immoral acts on behalf of a cult leader. For the most part, ethicists see consensual interventions as morally acceptable, while it is much harder for many to justify coercive interventions.

INTRINSIC VALUE   The worth (*see* VALUE) arising solely from the nature of a thing.

We say a thing has intrinsic value if it is valued as an end in itself or if it is worthy of being valued in and of itself and not as a means to another goal (*see* ENDS/MEANS). For example, health may be considered intrinsically valuable or good in and of itself. We need no further reason to desire to be healthy than the goal of health itself. By contrast, a thing has instrumental value if it is valued as a means to another end. For example, if health is intrinsically valuable, then a proper diet might be considered instrumentally valuable in achieving health.

INTUITION Immediate awareness of a concept or TRUTH that is achieved without perception, memory, or reasoning (*see* REASON).

A moral theory of intuition holds that we can only apprehend moral truths, principles, or laws through intuition; that is, moral truths are indefinable and cannot be understood through reason. Other variations of this theory hold that intuitive moral knowledge can supplement moral knowledge gained through reason or perception or that we can distinguish between RIGHT and WRONG actions through intuition as well as reason. For example, the notion that health is good can be achieved both through intuition and through reason. Some mystical thinkers (*see* MYSTICISM) have held that GOD can be apprehended through intuition. When we claim that certain truths are SELF-EVIDENT, we are claiming that they are apprehended through intuition and that we simply recognize them to be the case. For example, when the U.S. Declaration of Independence states, "We hold these truths to be self evident, that all men are created equal . . .," it intends that we should be able to apprehend these truths immediately and should not need reason or argument to establish them.

Some psychologists have argued that intuition refers to thought processes that are too subtle or occur too quickly for people to be aware of them. Thus, what we call intuition is really a rapid form of reasoning. Other thinkers are skeptical about intuition and regard the notion only as indicative of where true reflective understanding stops.

INTUITIONISM A metaethical theory (*see* METAETHICS) that holds that, ultimately, VALUES can be known only by INTUITION.

Some intuitionists speak of moral intuition as if it were a special human faculty, analogous to faculties of sense perception, by which persons can discover moral TRUTH by direct apprehension, without reasoning (*see* REASON). Intuition is regularly contrasted with reasoning or inference because the fundamental claim of intuitionists is that we cannot know what is GOOD or bad, RIGHT or WRONG, by reasoning alone. In their view, reasoning, which is a process of inference from one idea to another, needs to get started somewhere, beginning with some truth or knowledge that is not itself a product of reasoning—hence the need for direct awareness or intuition.

Intuitionists are objectivists (*see* OBJECTIVISM) because they believe that judgments (*see* JUDGMENT) about values are either true or false. They deny that values are relative to or dependent on anyone's personal feelings or opinions. If something is good, objectivists hold, it has the PROPERTY of being good, whether or not anyone thinks or feels it is, just as a physical object may be hard or round, whether anyone knows it or not. Likewise, actions (*see* ACT) are right or wrong regardless of our opinions or feelings about them. Objectivists argue that moral judgments cannot be subjective (*see* SUBJECTIVISM)—that is, dependent on personal feelings or opinions—for if they were, everyone would be right or, more accurately, there would be no distinction between correct and incorrect opinions (*see* RELATIVISM). Objectivists insist on making a distinction between someone's thinking that something is good or right and its really being so.

There are different kinds of intuitionists, according to what they think the proper objects of intuition are. Some, like G. E. MOORE, have held that the goodness of things can be discovered only by intuition, whereas H. A. Prichard, an act deontologist (*see* DEONTOLOGY), has argued that the rightness or wrongness of acts must be intuited. For Moore, a teleologist (*see* TELEOLOGY), *good* is a more fundamental concept than *right* because he believed that the rightness or wrongness of acts is a function of good or bad consequences (*see* CONSEQUENTIALISM). Prichard believed that the rightness or wrongness of acts could not be so derived and so must be known directly.

Prichard held that the rightness or wrongness of particular acts must be intuited, for he tried to show that the values of particular acts could not be derived, by a process of reasoning, from moral principles or rules. Because principles and rules can have exceptions, Prichard held that there is no way of knowing what is right or wrong in particular cases by principles and rules alone. In ordinary discussions of ETHICS, people sometimes express an opinion similar to this one when they say that they decide moral issues on a "case-by-case" basis, deciding each case on its own merits and not according to any general rule.

Other philosophers have argued that rules are known by intuition and that judgments about particular acts should be derived from these. W. D. Ross, for example, a rule deontologist, argued that moral rules are known by intuition. He, too, allowed that rules may have exceptions, but, unlike Prichard, he believed that moral rules determine what is right or wrong in particular cases.

Intuition, however, if viewed as a way of knowing, appears to be no guarantee for truth, for it would seem that all ways of knowing are subject to error. Because one person's intuitions may be different from another's, the intuitionist is faced with the problem of distinguishing correct from incorrect intuitions and so must appeal to reasoning of some sort in order to make this distinction. Intuitionists could appeal to the COHERENCE or incoherence of intuited

beliefs, but then not simply intuition but coherence must be recognized as a test of moral truth.

IN VITRO FERTILIZATION   Reproductive technology in which human eggs (ova) are retrieved from a woman, fertilized by sperm in a laboratory, and then transferred into a woman's uterus to establish pregnancy.

In vitro fertilization indicates that the ova is fertilized in a test tube, or in vitro, rather than in a woman's body. Babies born of this technique are sometimes called test-tube babies. In vitro fertilization is sometimes used to treat certain types of infertility and, more recently, has been employed as a way to "prolong" fertility by storing frozen embryos in liquid nitrogen for later implantation.

There are several moral and legal issues associated with in vitro fertilization and embryo freezing. To suggest just a few: What is the moral status of an embryo that is formed in a laboratory and not yet developing within a woman's body? Do we have the same RESPONSIBILITY for such an embryo as we may have toward a FETUS or embryo that developed in the normal way? What should be done with frozen embryos if the parents die? Who retains custody of embryos in the case of divorce?

Some moral philosophies entirely reject in vitro fertilization and related reproduction technologies, arguing that they are unethical. The Catholic Church, for instance, issued a statement in 1987 that condemns in vitro fertilization and the related practices of SURROGATE MOTHERHOOD and embryo freezing.

ISLAMIC ETHICS   The ethical principles (*see* PRINCIPLE) and CODE of conduct followed by Muslims.

Islamic ETHICS is based on and drawn from SHARI'A, which in turn is based on and drawn from QUR'AN, HADITH and two distinctive ways of working with Qur'an and Hadith, namely, reasoning from analogy and reaching CONSENsus. By means of these two written sources and the two procedures for working with them, the Muslim COMMUNITY is able to establish standards for RIGHT belief (see FAITH) and behavior. Nothing ranks higher for Muslims than divine REVELATION, where GOD makes known both himself and his WILL for humankind. Although the Qur'an is the premier revelation of God in written form, nature is also seen as a means by which God reveals himself. Thus, Islam denies any essential conflict between the natural world, including HUMAN NATURE, and divine expectation. GOOD science and right religion are in accord. The role of religion is not to deny or repress human nature but to place sufficient restraint and guidance on it to permit the fulfillment of God's INTENTION for each human. M. Z. Khan, in *Islam: Its Meaning for Modern Man* writes: "Islam teaches that natural instincts and tendencies are converted in to moral qualities through their proper regulation and adjustment by the exercise of REASON and JUDGMENT."

The interiority of Muslim MORALITY is attested to by AL-GHAZĀLĪ (as translated by L. Zolondck in *Book XX of Al-Ghazālī's Ihyā' 'ulūm ad-dīn*); "Actions are rooted and originate in the innermost thoughts of the heart."

Al-Ghazālī was building on the Prophet Muhammad's earlier declaration, reported by Shems Friedlander in *Submission: Sayings of the Prophet:* "Vice is thoughts which if, known by others, would be shameful." (In this statement, Muhammad is affirming the same position, though stated more generally, that was asserted by JESUS when he said that lust is equivalent to adultery committed in the heart.) In Arthur Jeffrey's *A Reader in Islam,* Muhammad is seen to have expanded his understanding into a universal moral guideline: "If it does not cause you to be ashamed, do whatever you wish." Islamic ethics depends on CONSCIENCE—shaped by religious, societal, and family standards—to provide the inner voice that enables the sensitive, that is, the conscientious, Muslim to discriminate

between right and WRONG. While humankind is innately good (Islam recognizes no original SIN), this goodness only reaches fruition as drives and capacities are directed toward worthy ends. This directing begins with intention, *niyya* in Arabic, by means of which one integrates mind and body, thereby making an action either moral or immoral (see IMMORALITY). The Qur'an (33:5) declares: "There is no sin for you in the mistakes you make unintentionally, but what your heart proposes (knowing to be sinful, that will be counted sinful)." Reuben Levy, in *The Social Structure of Islam,* reports that Muhammad once said: "The intent of the believer is more important than the action" (see INTENTION).

The most important Muslim text on philosophical ethics was written by Miskawayh, a Persian who died in 1030 A.D. Drawing from PLATO, Miskawayh identified three CARDINAL VIRTUES—WISDOM, COURAGE, and TEMPERANCE—which when harmonized give rise to a fourth, JUSTICE. The corresponding vices (see VICE) are ignorance, cowardice, GREED, and VIOLENCE. Drawing next from ARISTOTLE, Miskawayh argues that each virtue represents a "GOLDEN MEAN" between extremes. It is central to his ethical system because the opening chapter of the Qur'an (1:5/6) identifies Islam as "the straight path," that is the path that does not lead astray into one extreme or another.

Miskawayh argued that happiness is realized by avoiding vice and cultivating VIRTUE. Happiness is the supreme goal of humankind and of two kinds: worldly and divine. Though divine happiness is higher and more noble, it nonetheless, according to Miskawayh, builds on worldly happiness, which, among other things, consists of health, success, and honor. The truly happy person is one who combines temporal and spiritual happiness and as a consequence internalizes morality to such an extent that all action is performed for its own sake, for the sake of the virtue and goodness inherent in the action itself, and not for any ulterior end (see DEONTOLOGY). Morality ceases not only to be code but even principle; it becomes one's nature, the only way one can be.

ISOLATIONISM   The belief that one's country ought not be dependent on any other country or unduly concern itself with international affairs.

Isolationists are opposed to notions of INTERNATIONAL RESPONSIBILITY, reject the AUTHORITY of international organizations such as the United Nations, and believe that their country should not be bound by INTERNATIONAL LAW. Isolationists see independence from the outside world as a form of strength, for if their country is dependent on another for something, it is also vulnerable to that country. For example, if the United States is dependent on the Middle East for its oil supplies, Middle East countries may be able to demand concessions from the United States by threatening to withhold oil. Similarly, isolationists believe that their country should be militarily self-sufficient, free from the need for military alliances; they disagree with international activities not obviously in their own country's national interest, such as peacekeeping missions in defense of human rights.

Those who reject isolationism claim that isolationism is both undesirable and impractical in an increasingly interconnected world. Nowadays, problems such as the environment, ethnic conflict, and terrorism have little regard for national boundaries. Furthermore, it is often the case that problems that appear to be outside a country's national interest soon become the opposite if left unchecked; for example, although the United States attempted to remain independent at the start of both World War I and II, it eventually was forced to become involved as the conflict spread. In any case, few ethical systems see a distinction between our RESPONSIBILITY for those inside and those outside our own COMMUNITY.

IS/OUGHT DISTINCTION   A differentiation or contrast between what is the case and what ought to be done, usually made with the intention of indicating that moral obligations cannot be derived from facts. This distinction is much like the FACT/VALUE DISTINCTION, bringing with it similar considerations and problems.

When we talk about what *is* the case, we are talking about facts. What *ought* to be the case involves VALUES. If we say that racial strife exists, we are making what we take to be a factual claim. It should be empirically verifiable (*see* EMPIRICAL KNOWLEDGE). But, if we claim that there ought to be more racial harmony, we are making a value JUDGMENT.

The problem involving moral theory is that people often attempt to derive what ought to be the case from the facts alone. For example, it is a fact that there has historically been slavery. Some have argued based on this fact that there *ought* to be slavery because it has always been a way of life. This is/ought distinction counters that we cannot derive what we ought to do solely from what is the case. Someone making this distinction would argue that the fact that there is or has been slavery does not mean that there ought to be slavery.

While the principle (*see* PRINCIPLES) behind the is/ought distinction seems clear, we have to consider that what we take to be an objective fact (*see* OBJECTIVISM) may be colored by our own values. While the is/ought distinction attempts to show that values are subjective and facts are objective, the value we put on some things, such as good health, seems objective, even though we might not be able to derive it from any facts. For example, the judgment that a long healthy life is better than a short, less-healthy life is a value judgment. Even what a healthy life *is* thoroughly involves human values. Many claims that seem objective are actually based on value judgments. Observations such as these tend to diminish what appeared to be a hard and fast distinction between facts and values. Once the distinction is blurred, it seems more likely that moral values are, or can be, objective.

J

JAIN ETHICS The ethical system (*see* ETHICS) and moral PRACTICE of the Jain religion of India, which was founded on an especially high regard for all forms of life.

Jainism was founded in the sixth/fifth century B.C. by Vardhamāna (known as Mahāvira "Great Hero"). The tradition (*see* CUSTOMS) shares numerous features with Hinduism and Buddhism, such as SAMSARA, KARMA, and MOKSHA, though its interpretation may be somewhat different. For example, Jains envision karma as an actual material substance that "adheres" to the soul, thereby weighing it down and thus causing continual rebirth.

A single, comprehensive perspective informs all of the main features of the Jain moral and spiritual path. Mahāvira declared: "One who disregards earth, air, fire, water, and vegetation disregards his own life since it is intertwined with these" (*Life Force: The World of Jainism,* Michael Tobias [Berkeley: Asian Humanities Press, 1991], 7). Jains attribute maximum regard to the life force, which they see permeating all of nature. This life force is most concentrated in humans who have a mind and five senses. It extends down through a hierarchy of animals with sense ranging from five to two and ends in vegetation with only one sense, namely, touch.

The Jain reverence for life takes the form of *ahimsa,* "nonhurt, noninjury" (*see* NONVIOLENCE), which attempts to inflict the least amount of pain of living creatures as possible. Because animals represent a higher form of life than vegetation, Jains refuse to eat meat and fish (*see* VEGETARIANISM). They also avoid that which gives rise to life, eggs, as well as such fruits as figs, which contain high concentrations of seeds.

Because of its extraordinarily high respect for all forms of life, Jainism has developed a MORALITY based on the attempt to reduce injury to a minimum. It is, thus, a morality of restraint. Jains refrain from partaking of meat, alcohol (fermentation destroys countless organisms; intoxication beclouds the mind and activates the passions), honey (myriads of microorganisms are annihilated when honey is extracted from the comb), and several varieties of figs. They also refrain from false speech, theft, and illicit sexual activity. They attempt to limit their possessions, as well as travel. A life of voluntary simplicity, even ASCETICISM, is considered most desirable.

The Jain morality of restraint evolves to a spirituality of renunciation. Now the principles of noninjury, noninvolvement, and nonattachment become internalized. This inwardness is seen in the ideal expressed by a Jain saint: "Equanimity toward all beings; SELF-CONTROL and pure aspiration; abandonment of every thought which is tainted by desire or aversion" (*The Jaina Path of Perfection,* Padmanabh S. Jaini [Berkeley: University of California Press, 1979], 221f).

For monks and nuns, the life of the soul takes increasing precedence over the life of the body. This process culminates in a practice unique to Jainism. Elderly Jain saints, convinced that their earthly life is nearing an end, sometimes voluntarily, and with inner tranquility and clear conviction, undertake a fast that ends only with death or, as it is commonly said in India, with "dropping the body." Jain morality has particular relevance in the context of ecology and the environment (*see* ENVIRONMENTAL ETHICS). The Jain way of life, given its deeply ingrained sensitivity to all life-forms and its voluntary restraint from consumption and EXPLOITATION, is far less destructive of nature than perhaps any other ethicoreligious tradition. *See also* GANDHI, MOHANDAS KARAMCHAND.

JEALOUSY   Overly desirous (*see* DESIRE) and resentful regarding the goods or accomplishments of another; demanding exclusive LOYALTY. It is considered a VICE.

Jealousy has two forms. In the first, a person is excessively concerned about keeping control over his or her possessions. This is often evident in interpersonal relations. A man dating a woman might want to control that woman, always afraid that she might show interest in others. The person must be excessive in such concern to deserve the label *jealous*.

The second form of jealousy occurs when someone is resentful or envious of the gains of another. If a person buys a new fancy car, his or her neighbor may be upset, wishing that he or she could have it instead. Perhaps it is normal to want nice things and to feel bad when we cannot have them. Jealousy, however, takes such feelings to a more extreme form. It is often difficult to decide why a person is jealous of another, but jealousy follows from GREED, insecurity, or hostility. The vice of jealousy establishes a disposition to act in morally unacceptable ways (*see* IMMORALITY); for example, a jealous person may try to curtail the freedom of his or her mate. *See also* PASSIONS AND EMOTIONS; SEXUAL ETHICS.

JEN   (Pronounced "run") "Humaneness," "LOVE of fellow humans"; central VIRTUE in Confucianism.

Jen is the most important quality in the *CHUN-TZU*, the ideal person according to Confucianism. The pictogram, or symbol, used in pictorial writing systems such as Chinese, for *jen* is the sign for *a human being* and the sign for *two*; thus, *jen* stands for the attitudes and behaviors that contribute to harmonious relationships between people. When asked about the nature of jen, Confucius replied that it is love for one's fellow human beings. *See also* CONFUCIAN ETHICS.

JESUS   Founder of Christianity; recognized as a great teacher in Judaism and as one of the greatest prophets in Islam; highly respected in all religious traditions.

Jesus was born between 6–4 B.C. and died between A.D. 27–30. Nearly all of what is known about him comes through the interpretive vision of his followers, whose writings (*see* BIBLE) were composed throughout the second half of the first century. One of the most vigorous forms of current Christian scholarship focuses on the distinction between the Jesus of history and the Christ of FAITH.

Both the name *Jesus* and the title *Christ* signify for Christians the saving activity of Jesus' life, death, and resurrection. Christians believe that this salvation is available to everyone through repentance of SIN and submission to Jesus the Christ as Savior and Lord. As the Son of GOD, Jesus is wholly human and wholly divine and an integral member of the Trinity, a doctrine that equates Jesus as Christ with God and the Holy Spirit.

Jesus' active public ministry is variously estimated to have extended from several weeks to the traditional three years. During this time, Jesus adopted a simple lifestyle (*see* LIFESTYLES) and roamed the eastern Mediterranean, teaching, preaching, healing physical and spiritual ills, and gathering disciples, who carried on his ministry after his death. Because of his violation of some Jewish precepts and radical interpretation of others, he found considerable opposition from the authorities (*see* AUTHORITY) of his time. He lived and advocated a radical life and was crucified by Roman authorities who feared him as a revolutionary idealist (*see* IDEALISM).

The ETHICS preached and exemplified by Jesus was as radical and revolutionary as any known at the time. He called for total submission to and trust in God, thereby withdrawing reliance either on one's own strength and cleverness or on other human beings, including religious and governing authorities. For Jesus, MORALITY was not simply a matter pertaining to interhuman relations; it was a matter founded in God. As in Judaism (*see* JEWISH ETHICS), morality is a dimension and expression of holiness. Jesus' ethical teaching, though found throughout the New Testament and especially in the Gospels is summarized in the Sermon on the Mount (Matthew 5–7). Its radical character is seen in the Beatitudes; for example, "Blessed are the meek, for they will inherit the earth" and "Blessed are those who are persecuted for righteousness' sake, for theirs is the kingdom of heaven."

Jesus' ethics called for a fundamental transformation of the heart and not simply conformity to a CODE of behavior. He shifted the focus of morality from actions (*see* ACT) to inner attitude. For example, he taught that to feel lust—sexual desire directed at another person—is the equal to actually committing adultery. INTENTION is crucial; action performed to impress others is totally without spiritual VALUE.

Jesus knew that the inner person is shaped by the environment and therefore warned against exposing oneself to TEMPTATION and sinful influences. Morality is first and foremost a matter of shaping one's own life and not of passing JUDGMENT on others, as Jesus expressed in the book of Matthew (7:3): "Why do you see the speck in your neighbor's eye but do not notice the log in your own eye?"

LOVE is the foundation of Jesus' ethics. He called for love to be extended even to one's enemies. Finally, Jesus taught that it is not enough to simply hear moral principles enunciated; one must act on them inwardly and outwardly at each opportunity. *See also* CHRISTIAN ETHICS; GOLDEN RULE.

JEWISH ETHICS   The ethical system and CODE of the Jewish people.

Jewish ETHICS, rooted in the BIBLE (or Tanakh) and TALMUD, finds its fullest statement in HALAKAH, the Jewish legal system, where it is made clear that moral perspective and action (*see* ACT) are derived from OBEDIENCE to GOD. Judaism is sometimes called ethical monotheism but is more accurately Torah monotheism, thereby indicating that its ethical basis is Torah, God's will for the Jewish people and ultimately for humankind.

Traditionally, Judaism makes no distinction between the SACRED and profane. Therefore, ethics is subsumed under holiness (*see* KADOSH). Holiness includes but sets a higher standard than mere JUSTICE (TZEDAKA) or goodness (*see* GOOD). Leviticus 19, part of the Torah God gave to Moses, opens: "You shall be holy, for I the Lord your God am holy." This chapter addresses what might be called ritual and moral holiness. It repeats some of what is found in the TEN COMMANDMENTS and also adds specific moral injunctions, such as not harvesting all of one's crops so that the poor can glean what is left behind. It also includes such broad moral principles as "You shall love your neighbor as yourself."

Judaism recognizes two tendencies in every human being: One is centered in a "me-first" drive and is aggressive, grasping, and sexually unrestrained; the other is informed by CONSCIENCE and manifests as LOVE, EMPATHY, and GENEROSITY. Accordingly, the purpose (*see* TELEOLOGY) of Jewish MORALITY is to place appropriate restraint on the instinctual, impulsive drives and to encourage and facilitate development of the higher inclinations.

One of the earliest works to emphasize the development of the higher inclinations was Bahya ben Joseph ibn Paquda's eleventh-century *The Duties of the Heart*. According to Bahya's scheme, any act involving the body or senses is unspiritual; thus, even prayer and religious study are excluded from the truly spiritual because they entail physical action. Spiritual precepts are carried out entirely "within the heart." Thus, the legal commandments (*see* MITZVAH) that involve physical action have no VALUE for one's religious life. A physical deed can only have religious value if it is accompanied by sincere INTENTION or spiritual concentration. It is only the "action" of the heart that gives value to the deed. Bahya's radical position, based on his absolutistic (*see* ABSOLUTES) distinction between body and heart, between physical and spiritual, represented a departure from Jewish tradition and LAW.

A more systematic and balanced treatment of ethical issues was formulated by MAIMONIDES. Drawing from ARISTOTLE as well as Arab philosophers, Maimonides formulated a Jewish ethical system around the GOLDEN MEAN in which VIRTUE lies in the middle position between two extremes, each of the latter representing VICE. Maimonides believed that it is possible to develop one's spiritual nature to the extent that one internalizes the commandments of the law so thoroughly that one's holiness makes it impossible to commit a wrongful act (*see* WRONG).

JIHAD   *See* HOLY WAR.

JIM CROW LAWS   Statutes passed by southern states in the U.S. in the late 19th century that effectively created a racial CASTE system.

Jim Crow laws (*see* LAW) were named after an antebellum minstrel-show character. Although SLAVERY had been abolished, it was still common for white citizens to believe that nonwhites were undeserving of citizens' RIGHTS. The constitutionality of the Jim Crow laws was challenged by Homer A. Plessy. Plessy, an African American, chose a seat in a "white-only" car on a train departing from New Orleans. Plessy was ordered to move, and refused. He was then arrested. Plessy took his case to the Supreme Court in *Plessy v. Ferguson* (1896) arguing that

his right to equal protection under the law (the Fourteenth Amendment) was violated by the Jim Crow Laws. The Supreme Court ruled against Plessy, and following that ruling each southern state passed a law that created two "separate but equal" societies (*see* EQUALITY), one for whites and one for nonwhites.

This division was maintained through Jim Crow laws—a collection of poll taxes, literacy requirements, and grandfather clauses that made it veritably impossible for nonwhites to perform the duties of CITIZENSHIP. Nearly every part of society was segregated (*see* SEGREGATION), including hospitals, schools, restaurants, transportation, and churches.

Jim Crow laws remained in place until the Supreme Court's landmark decision in *Brown v. the Board of Education* (1954). This decision declared unconstitutional the practice of segregating public schools. The Jim Crow legal legacy was not completely dismantled until the CIVIL RIGHTS legislation of the late 1960s.

JOURNALISM ETHICS   RIGHTS and responsibilities (*see* RESPONSIBILITY) that pertain to news reporting in both the print and electronic media.

The media is a tremendously powerful force in modern society, through its ability to control what information the public hears about and its ability to influence public opinion through misleading and biased (*see* BIAS) reporting. As a result, a number of principles (*see* PRINCIPLE) have emerged that attempt to guard against the abuse of this POWER. Many of these principles were formalized in the influential Canons of Journalism, adopted by the American Society of Newspaper Editors in 1923.

The Canons of Journalism state in part that: (1) Although newspapers have a RIGHT to make a profit, journalists should not use their power for "selfish or unworthy purposes," or to undermine the public interest; (2) FREEDOM of the press must be protected; (3) Journalists must be independent and must not publish private news releases or promotional material without identifying the source; (4) All material published must be as truthful as possible; (5) Journalists must be impartial (*see* IMPARTIALITY); (6) Journalists should not publish material detrimental to someone's reputation (*see* DEFAMATION) without allowing that person a right to respond and only where the public has a legitimate right to know; and (7) Journalists should not promote sensationalism.

In reality, not all journalists subscribe to these principles, and a large media industry, often described as the "tabloid press," exists to promote rumor and sensationalism. In this case, there appears to be a conflict between what much of the public is interested in buying and the standards that many journalists believe should be upheld. Commercial pressures on news sources are significant, and, therefore, it is arguable that in many cases today news has become increasingly indistinguishable from entertainment, particularly on television.

An ongoing conflict in journalism is between the public's right to know and the methods used to gain that knowledge, which may be unethical, deceptive, or even illegal. One such method, known as entrapment, involves the use of undercover or disguised journalists or their informants to trick individuals into revealing information that they otherwise would not. For example, journalists might gain employment at a workplace to research allegations of unsafe or illegal practices, or they might have a concealed tape recorder in a conversation that is supposed to be confidential (*see* CONFIDENTIALITY).

Also related to this issue is the debate on whether journalists have a legitimate right to report on the private lives of public figures (*see* PRIVACY). Many argue that such knowledge is mostly irrelevant and that such attention discourages well-qualified people from seeking positions of influence. Others respond that the public has a right to know about such things as a politician's extramarital affairs because this is directly relevant to assessing a person's CHARACTER and suitability for public office.

The use of anonymous sources creates another ethical DILEMMA for journalists. On the one hand, journalists may be unable to convince some individuals to cooperate with them without a guarantee that the individual will not be identified. On the other hand, the use of anonymous sources is open to much abuse because it limits the public's ability to assess the source's credibility. In these cases, there is often no way of telling whether the source is a janitor, a senior diplomat, or simply a journalist LYING to create for her- or himself a sensational story.

Related to this is the belief, commonly held among journalists, that the names of anonymous sources should not be divulged, even under court order or else individuals will be discouraged from providing them with essential information, thereby hindering their ability to research stories in the public interest. Others, including the United States Supreme Court, disagree, arguing in part that journalists are not above the LAW and that protection of confidential sources can interfere with the ability of legal authorities to prosecute criminal activity. *See also* PROFESSIONAL ETHICS.

JUDGMENT   A person's capacity to formulate sound decisions, or the decision of a court of LAW.

A judgment is an affirmation of the way the world is or a decision about what course of action (*see* ACT) ought to be pursued. We say a person is using GOOD judgment when he or she is able to interpret events and their likely course accurately and is able to make wide decisions concerning states of affairs. For example, drivers who slow their speed in less than ideal driving conditions are often described as using good judgment. We say that a person is using poor judgment when he or she acts without considering the consequences of those actions or when people act in such a way as to bring about undesirable consequences when those consequences could most likely have been foreseen. We would say that a driver who exceeds the speed limit in icy conditions is using poor judgment.

In a different sense, judgments are decisions rendered by courts of law. A judge or a JURY considers the evidence of a case and decides what resolution is just and FAIR. This resolution is the court's judgment. Judgments are considered the final word on disputes brought before the court, unless the decision is appealed to a higher court. The judgment of a higher court supersedes the judgment made by a lower court.

JURY A randomly chosen body of people brought together to decide on the verdict in a legal trial.

Juries are based on the principle that, by encouraging a group of average citizens to decide on the verdict in legal cases, common sense and community standards will prevail, ensuring that justice is done. In reality, juries are never wholly representative of their communities because of broad exemptions to jury service for professionals and others and because jury-selection procedures are widely abused by lawyers who attempt to select members who are sympathetic to their own arguments.

Juries are also intended to act as a check on the abuse of POWER by government and judges and may theoretically refuse to convict someone if they disagree with the LAW. In practice, of course, jurors are rarely allowed to participate in cases involving laws that they disagree with.

It is important to note that because juries are intended to represent a cross section of their community, they are not necessarily impartial (*see* IMPARTIALITY). For example, juries from communities where prejudice such as racism is common are likely to be influenced by that prejudice when deciding on their verdict. It is also important to note that jurors are expected to know little or nothing about the information that they will be judging, even when that information is highly technical and specialized. In fact, prospective jurors familiar with the details of a case that they have been selected to sit on or people with technical skills relevant to that case are almost always dismissed from jury duty.

JUST-WAR THEORY The theory that seeks to detail when it is proper for a state to go to war and to outline conduct acceptable during war.

The PRINCIPLE of a just war states that war should only be waged as a last resort and after all nonviolent options have been exhausted. Just-war theory also holds that a war is just only if it is waged by a legitimate AUTHORITY. No matter how honorable (*see* HONOR) a cause, war waged by individuals or groups other than a society's legitimate authority is not considered just. Just wars can only be fought in self-defense or to redress a wrong. Wars fought with ulterior motives, for example, to redress a wrong but also to gain strategic land, are not just. A just war can be fought only when there can be some realistic expectation of success. Lives may not be endangered and lost when there is no hope of winning a war. A just war must ultimately establish peace, and the peace established after the war must be better than the circumstances before the war.

Regarding acceptable tactics in a just-war, the just-war theory states that the force used in the war must be proportional to the injury being redressed. The weapons used in war must discriminate between combatants and noncombatants. Civilians are never permissible targets of war, and every effort must be taken to avoid killing civilians. The deaths of civilians are justified (*see* JUSTIFICATION) only if they are unavoidable victims of a deliberate attack on a military target.

JUSTICE A key moral concept involving fair treatment.

Justice is central in MORALITY because it deals with human interaction—with what people should receive and give in their association with others. More technically, justice concerns the proper allocation of the benefits and burdens of human interaction.

In ETHICS, philosophers offer theories about what *justice* means. Most agree that justice involves giving to each what he or she is due. But what is due to a person? In day-to-day life, the answer seems easy enough: we expect to ACT and be treated fairly according to established RULES (*see* FAIRNESS). If someone agrees to work for another, he or she expects to be paid according to LAW or according to a CONTRACT. If a teacher announces a grading policy and a student lives up to the requirements, the student expects to be graded accordingly.

On another level, issues of justice become much more difficult. We must determine if the rules themselves are fair. If rules say that only those with money can receive good health care, many feel this is not just. Should people have access to health care based on their need for it or based on their ability to pay for it? Deciding such a matter is a question of distributive justice. Should we change the rules so that all in need receive adequate health care? Some have argued that in a just society, each person should get what they need or at least should have enough to meet their basic needs—for food, clothes, shelter, and health care. The distribution of goods based on need is an essential aspect of Marxian justice (*see* Karl MARX). If people cannot provide these things for themselves, then they should be provided by government.

Others, however, including the contemporary American philosopher Robert Nozick, argue that justice requires that each person should receive income or wealth in relation to his or her contribution to society. Those who contribute much to society should receive much. Injustice occurs when those who contribute little receive much.

Philosophers have also argued that a society is just only when all people have equal opportunities. Opportunity plays a key role in John RAWLS's theory of justice. It is unfair to reward people for contributions when some are denied the means to contribute. If a person cannot find a job because of poor education, a disadvantaged upbringing, or discrimination, a system of rewards based only on how much a person accomplishes is considered unjust by such philosophers.

A central debate over the nature of justice exists between those who claim that people are entitled to all they rightly earn and those who argue that people are fairly treated only when they are equal. Those who argue in favor of EQUALITY are called egalitarians (*see* EGALITARIANISM) and include such thinkers as Kai Nielson and R. H. Tawney. Those who favor the first view understand that coercion, discrimination, and deceit invalidate entitlements. Those who favor equality claim that coercion is often subtle and sometimes impossible to detect. Only when people are equal can we know that they are fairly treated. The problem is that *equality* is a difficult concept to define. Is equal opportunity enough? Is complete racial, gender, religious, and ethnic equality enough in a just society? Or, more radically, does justice require complete equality? Such issues are at the heart of contemporary political and moral debate.

JUSTIFICATION Reasoning (*see* REASON) that is used to show that an action (*see* ACT) or type of action is just (*see* JUSTICE), morally permitted, or correct (*see* PERMISSIBLE ACT).

People try to justify actions to themselves or others by giving reasons for what they do or wish to be allowed to do. In seeking justification, they may also be trying to win acceptance for or approval of their actions or beliefs. In so doing, they usually appeal to reasons that other people will accept, such as social RULES, traditions (*see* CUSTOMS), or common practices (*see* PRACTICE) and may also try to change the beliefs of those who disagree with them by convincing them that they are wrong. A teen, for example, may try to convince his or her parents that there is nothing wrong with staying out late at night in order to win permission to do so. The reason offered would be given to justify the behavior. The parents, in turn, may offer reasons for thinking that it is not justified for the teen to stay out late at night.

Not all the reasons that we may give are GOOD reasons. Justification is an attempt to show that there are *good* reasons for action. Wanting to commit suicide because of a pimple on the nose on prom night would seem to be an insufficient reason to justify the act. People sometimes claim that they have a right to do whatever they want with their own bodies; if that were true, this would justify suicide, even for no reason at all. Others claim that people do not have a general right to kill or mutilate themselves, and people are normally considered unhealthy if they attempt such actions. So philosophers have been concerned with trying to answer the questions: What kinds of reasons are good reasons? What kinds of reasons are needed to show that an act is justified?

People often try to justify acts by showing that they conform to a moral PRINCIPLE or rule.

Thus, an act may be said to be justified if it does no harm or because it is fair. At other times acts are justified by showing that they are similar to other acts that are allowed or deemed to be right or good (*see* CASUISTRY). Because logically, the VALUE of reasoning is tested by CONSISTENCY, reasons are thought to be good if they can be applied consistently across cases (*see* COHERENCE). Thus, if something is justified in one case, it should be justified in other similar cases as well, for the same reason.

Substantive ethical theories are attempts to clarify and explain principles and methods of justification. UTILITARIANISM maintains that acts are justified by their consequences (*see* CONSEQUENTIALISM), and rule DEONTOLOGY claims that acts are justified by moral rules. Cultural relativists (*see* CULTURAL RELATIVISM) argue that acts are justified by the rules of society or by conventional norms (*see* NORM). In everyday life, all of these methods may be used. People are usually satisfied if they can reach CONSENSUS or agreement, whatever method is employed.

K

KADOSH In Judaism, "holiness"; designates the kind of life GOD expects of His people according to the COVENANT; the agreement that bound God and the Jews together.

Kadosh suggests something or someone consecrated, that is, set apart from the ordinary by RIGHT of being dedicated for a life of holiness. The Jewish people are expected to emulate the attributes of God. As God is merciful (*see* MERCY), forgiving (*see* FORGIVENESS), just, and kind, so his people must be merciful, forgiving, just, and kind. *See also* JEWISH ETHICS.

KANT, IMMANUEL (1724–1804) An influential German moral theorist known for his development of a strict DEONTOLOGY.

Kant's ETHICS centers on obligations (*see* OBLIGATION) regardless of consequences. Thus he stands in opposition to UTILITARIANISM. Kant rejects any attempt to make an exception of oneself and insists upon treating all people with respect. The basic question in the development of Kantian MORALITY concerns when a person deserves moral praise. Kant's view is that only actions (*see* ACT) that are done because they are our duty deserve moral praise. Acting for any other MOTIVE does not deserve moral praise. For example, although it is good to help those we love because we love them, this, according to Kant, does not deserve moral praise. Actions done from love are not done from a sense of moral obligation. He argues that morality does not concern happiness or the desire to obey God's command but rather must be grounded in REASON. Thus, only actions done out of true respect for the moral LAW and not done only in obedience to it are morally good.

Kant describes two types of imperatives given to us by reason: the HYPOTHETICAL IMPERATIVE and the CATEGORICAL IMPERATIVE. The hypothetical imperative describes what one must do to achieve a certain end, while the categorical imperative dictates what one must do because of its rightness and necessity. The categorical imperative is the basis of Kant's moral system and may be formulated as follows: "Act as if the maxim of your action were to become through your WILL a general NATURAL LAW."

In *The Groundwork for a Metaphysics of Morals* (1785), Kant discusses three main formulations of the categorical imperative expressing the moral requirements of respect, AUTONOMY, and the ability to universalize. The three main formulations of the categorical imperative dictate that an action is morally good only if we can will all persons to do it, if it enables us to treat other persons as ends in themselves and not merely as the means to our ends (*see* ENDS/MEANS), and if it allows us to see other persons as mutual lawmakers in an ideal "Kingdom of Ends."

The first expression of the categorical imperative keeps us from making ourselves an exception to the moral RULE. Kant reasons, for example, that we cannot lie for we cannot consistently will that everyone should lie. The second formulation of the categorical imperative states that we should always treat other persons with respect and recognize their INTRINSIC VALUE and DIGNITY. Thus, it would be wrong to pretend friendship to someone only in order to meet that person's sibling, for this reduces the first person from someone of VALUE to a part of a plan.

The third formulation of the categorical imperative demands that we recognize our own autonomy and that of others. Kant's ethical ideas are the extension of his belief in the autonomy of the individual as outlined in the *Critique of Practical Reason* (1788). Autonomy is based on the idea of self-government, which means the FREEDOM consciously to obey one's own reason. In Kant's view, each person's health and well-being was an end in itself, and all moral laws should seek to realize that end.

KARMA   In Hinduism, Buddhism, and Jainism, the principle (*see* PRINCIPLES) that the consequences of our actions (*see* ACT) are reflected back on us in the future, either in this life or in future lives; also, the actions that cause such effects.

The idea of *karma* is based on the principle that MORALITY is integral to the LAW of the universe, in which all actions create immutable natural effects that reflect back upon the individual. All circumstances are the result of previous acts, either earlier in life or in a previous life. For example, a person born into a high CASTE is thought to have accumulated good karma during a previous life, while a person who experiences a personal tragedy is thought to be reaping the effects of bad karma from earlier on in their life, or in a previous life. In essence, karma is an application of the principles "one reaps what one sows" and "what goes around, comes around."

It is possible to accumulate karma though virtually all human activity, from specific actions and deeds, to intentions, emotions, and thoughts. Accumulating good karma by living a worthy life is seen as highly desirable and guarantees a favorable reincarnation. In general, however, the highest state of attainment is achieved when one is able to escape the cycle of rebirth by avoiding the accumulation of karma altogether. This is because the karma creates bondage and OBLIGATION, regardless of whether it is to higher or lower realms. A karma-free life

is extremely difficult, however, and is possible only through the most rigorous PSYCHOSPIRITUAL DISCIPLINE.

On the surface, karma seems to leave little room for FREEDOM of action, if all circumstances are the deserts of previous actions. This need not be true, however, if one accepts that although one's circumstances are previously determined, how one reacts to those circumstances is a matter of personal choice that, in turn, can create good karma, bad karma, or no karma at all.

INTENTION determines the moral quality of karma. If one intends something morally WRONG but is not able to carry it out, bad karma is nonetheless accrued. If one intends something good but is not able to carry it out, good karma is accrued. According to Hinduism, a deed is devoid of karmic implications only if it is carried out without attachment, without any sense of personal gain or loss. In Buddhism, a deed is devoid of karmic implications only if it is carried out without any trace of GREED, hatred, or delusion. These three are understood by Buddhists to be the core defilements of the human EGO. Operating in numerous and often very subtle forms, greed, hatred, and delusion are the roots of all IMMORALITY and keep one bound to SAMSARA, that is, the natural world of constant cycles and endless reincarnation. *See also* BHAGAVAD GITA; BUDDHIST ETHICS; CONSEQUENTIALISM; HINDU ETHICS; JAIN ETHICS; MOKSHA; NIRVANA.

KARUNA   COMPASSION; one of the two CARDINAL VIRTUES or highest realizations of Buddhism.

Compassion in Buddhism is founded on the awareness that the distinction that we perceive between ourselves and others is largely illusory (*see* MAYA). There are, therefore, no rational grounds (*see* RATIONALITY) for distinguishing between our own desires and interests and the desires and interests of others. In reality, we should relate to others solely as we would want others to relate to ourselves (*see* GOLDEN RULE).

Buddhists understand compassion to be connected integrally with PRAJNA, or "WISDOM." Indeed, as Buddhists see it, true compassion is impossible without wisdom. The Buddhist who is motivated (*see* MOTIVE) by compassion and wisdom is thought to be without any sense of self-preference (*see* EGO) and, consequently, can only ACT morally (*see* MORALITY). *See also* BUDDHIST ETHICS; DHARMA.

KIERKEGAARD, SØREN (1813–1855)

A Danish philosopher and theologian, sometimes referred to as the first existentialist (*see* EXISTENTIALISM).

Kierkegaard wrote that he was primarily concerned with what it meant to be a Christian (*see* CHRISTIAN ETHICS) and how people might attain the HAPPINESS that Christianity promises. A Protestant, born into a Lutheran family, he emphasized the individual's direct relationship to GOD and was critical of the institution of the church. Indeed, he was also critical of his contemporaries who claimed to be Christians but who were not, in his opinion, genuine Christians at all.

In his ETHICS, Kierkegaard did not lay down a set of RULES but, instead, tried to characterize different modes of life. In so doing, he emphasized the need for choice (*see* FREEDOM) in determining the kinds of persons we will be. In his work *Either/Or*, he pointed out how we can choose to live our lives either on what he called the aesthetic level or on an ethical or even religious level. He used the character of Don Juan to illustrate what he meant by an aesthetic life: a person who pretends to be a lover but loves no one in particular; a person who avoids COMMITMENT by shunning marriage; and a person who lives his life extensively rather than intensively, counting how many times or how well he makes love but not how much he loves. According to Kierkegaard, such a person is bored and constantly seeks variety in new activities to relieve boredom and even despair. Life is boring because it is the simple repetition of one thing after another, with no particular involvement in any one thing.

A person who lives an ethical life, by contrast, loves individual people and not men or women in general, becomes committed to those persons, and so takes chances or risks that the aesthetic person is afraid to take. The ethical person is involved in the things that he or she does and, hence, is interested in and appreciative of life.

Kierkegaard sometimes spoke of the religious level as if it were continuous with the ethical, but at other times he seemed to regard it as being distinct. The religious level is attained when a person makes a "leap of FAITH," believing in God with mind and soul, loving and trusting in God unconditionally. Such faith, LOVE, and trust give a person the peace of mind needed to live life fearlessly, without anxiety or despair. One can then pluck the flower of the day, so to speak, and not worry about the consequences.

According to Kierkegaard, faith goes beyond REASON, in that faith in God cannot be acquired by reasons or proofs. It is because God's existence cannot be demonstrated that a leap of faith beyond reason is required. Indeed, he said that belief in Christianity is belief in the absurd, for it is absurd to believe in the Incarnation: the idea that God became man. Yet, subjectively, he argued, people can be united with God by their faith. Such faith may even rise above ethics, as in the case of Abraham, where God asks Abraham to sacrifice his son. In *Fear and Trembling*, Kierkegaard pointed out that Abraham obeys, not because ethics dictates he do so but because he believes it is the will of God.

KING, MARTIN LUTHER, JR. (1929–1968)

Leading figure of the CIVIL RIGHTS movement in the United States.

Martin Luther King, Jr., was a Baptist minister and activist for the poor and racially oppressed. King, influenced by the teachings of Mohandas Karamchand GANDHI, advocated nonviolent CIVIL DISOBEDIENCE. In 1963, King organized the March on Washington, a multiracial civil rights march to demand social EQUALITY, poverty relief, and an end to DISCRIMINATION, and gave his famous "I Have a Dream" speech. King was instrumental in inspiring minorities and the poor to register to vote and to enter into mainstream politics. He recognized the important relationships among social equality and POVERTY and wealth.

King received the Nobel Peace Prize in 1964. He was assassinated in Memphis, Tennessee in 1968 where he was supporting striking sanitation workers. James Earl Ray was convicted of Dr. King's murder, although people continue to speculate as to whether Ray acted alone or as the agent of a group who disagreed with Dr. King's effective political action. James Earl Ray died in custody of liver failure after serving 28 years of a 99-year prison term. Among those with doubts about Ray's ability to mastermind or carry out the assassination were King's widow, Coretta Scott King, and one of King's four children, Dexter King.

KOHLBERG, LAWRENCE   (1927–1987)
American psychologist who applied the developmental approach of Jean PIAGET to the field of MORAL DEVELOPMENT.

Kohlberg studied children and the differences in their reasoning (*see* REASON) about moral problems. He developed a psychological test for moral reasoning called the Moral Judgment Interview. For nearly fifty years, Kohlberg studied the rationales given by thousands of research subjects to moral dilemmas (*see* DILEMMA) concerning TRUTH telling, HONESTY, LOYALTY, and JUSTICE. Kohlberg concluded that advanced levels of moral development are marked by reasons that appeal to a highly abstract moral PRINCIPLE, such as justice. In Kohlberg's early research, males generally scored higher on tests of moral JUDGMENT than females. His later research showed that sex differences were minimal but that men and women who were in traditional male occupations (law, theology, and philosophy) scored higher than other test subjects. Kohlberg's major work in MORAL PSYCHOLOGY is *Essays on Moral Development* (1981).

Kohlberg's theories have been challenged by feminist psychologists (*see* FEMINIST ETHICS), most notably Carol GILLIGAN, who pointed out that the Moral Judgment Interview was developed based on interviews with male subjects only.

KORAN   *See* QUR'AN.

L

LAW The principles (*see* PRINCIPLE) and RULES that govern human conduct.

Ethicists sometimes distinguish two senses of law: human law and moral law. Human laws are rules and regulations set down and enforced by a legitimate AUTHORITY, such as the government. Moral laws, on the other hand, are fundamental ethical principles that apply irrespective of the existence of human laws and are usually dictated by individual CONSCIENCE. From a practical standpoint, moral laws define what is RIGHT and WRONG, while human laws define what authorities believe should and should not be permitted.

Another difference between moral law and human law is that while human law changes with individual circumstances, depending on practicalities and political considerations, moral laws are often seen as immutable and constant. Furthermore, although human law is often built on a moral foundation, human law and moral law do not always overlap. For example, although both human law and moral law may prohibit theft, only moral law is likely to demand that one respect one's elders, and only human law is likely to say much about taxation.

In some cases, moral law and human law conflict, leaving one with a DILEMMA about which to obey. For example, a human law may prohibit specific types of worship required by moral law. In these cases, most ethicists believe that moral law automatically takes precedence over human law. The penalties associated with disobeying human law may be significant, however, and in these cases, individuals may be forced to examine their own consciences for solutions. In some cases, the choice made may

be to disobey the law conscientiously while accepting the consequences, thereby affirming support for both the rule of law and moral law (*see* CONSCIENTIOUS OBJECTION).

Some ethicists prefer to avoid the term *moral law* entirely, using instead terms such as *moral rule* or *moral principle*. The term *moral law* is generally associated with religious and NATURAL LAW traditions of morality and may therefore imply connotations that one does not subscribe to. Additionally, the term *moral law* may imply a universally applicable system of principles, something that subjectivists (*see* SUBJECTIVISM), among others, deny exists.

LEX TALIONIS Latin phrase meaning "law of retaliation"; commonly associated with the saying "an eye for an eye, a tooth for a tooth."

Lex talionis is based on the principle that the appropriate PUNISHMENT for those who commit crime is to have the same thing done to them in return. *Lex talionis* has its origins in primitive legal codes (*see* CODE), most notably in the Code of Hammurabi from the eighteenth century B.C. and the Law of Moses (Exodus 21:22–25).

There are a number of problems associated with *lex talionis* that make it difficult, if not impossible, to apply in practice and, in particular, to anything other than simple cases of assault. It is difficult to see how it might be possible, for example, to apply *lex talionis* to instances of crimes against the state, crimes against public decency, forgery, corporate crime, and even theft in cases where the thief owns nothing.

Even in the case of assault, however, *lex talionis* often proves to be an unsatisfactory method for achieving equitable outcomes. Most problematically, because no two events can ever be truly equal, *lex talionis* is justly criticized for being an extremely arbitrary standard. For example, the terror of a hardened boxer about to be whipped is hardly the same as that of a young child who was previously subjected to the boxer's wrath. Similarly, the arthritic arm of a hardened criminal is arguably quite different from the arm of a famous baseball pitcher. In fact, in some cases, an equal exchange might not even be possible, as in the case of a blind person who causes another to lose an eye.

Furthermore, *lex talionis* seems to allow little room for mitigating factors; for example, should the penalty be the same for both murder and manslaughter? In both cases someone is killed, but in the first case the death is intentional (*see* INTENTION), while in the second, accidental.

Finally, some object to *lex talionis* because it appears to permit the infliction of cruel and sadistic punishments. For example, a rapist or torturer would have to be raped or tortured for her or his crimes. This, however, is something that many people would view as both uncivilized and abhorrent.

LI A term from CONFUCIAN ETHICS meaning "RIGHTS, CUSTOMS, MORALITY" (pronounced "lee").

Li represents the types of behavior that are thought to contribute to harmonious interpersonal relationships. Li governs a wide range of behaviors, including good manners and the correct performance of religious rituals. Li is ideally accompanied by suitable reverence for both the spirits and our fellow human beings (*see* JEN). The pictogram (the picture representing a word in a pictorial writing system) for li consists of a mark indicating communication with heaven and another mark depicting a sacrificial vessel, thereby indicating that li rests on a religious foundation.

LIBEL   *See* DEFAMATION.

LIBERALISM   The doctrine that all individuals have an inalienable RIGHT to AUTONOMY and self-determination.

Liberalism is an applied version of INDIVIDUALISM and holds that all individuals are entitled to a core set of RIGHTS that guarantee individual freedom. Preferably, liberals believe, these rights should be protected through constitutional and legal means. Core elements of liberalism emerged during the seventeenth century, in particular through the works of John LOCKE, and later during the nineteenth century in the works of John Stuart MILL. Since that time, liberalism has been extensively developed by many prominent and influential philosophers, including the twentieth-century philosopher John RAWLS. Liberalism is arguably the most-dominant philosophy in the Western world today and in the United States in particular.

A central tenet of liberalism is that the individual should be free from concentrations of POWER that restrict individual opportunity, regardless of whether the power lies in government, the aristocracy, or big business. Seventeenth-century liberals were generally supportive of CAPITALISM and the free market and skeptical of government, a position known as classical liberalism. Classical liberals were also mostly concerned with the elimination of de-jure (institutional or official) barriers to self-actualization and less concerned with the elimination of de-facto (unofficial or practical) barriers to self-actualization. In practice, classical liberals tended to assume that the rights they discussed were only applicable to a select group of white males.

Classical liberals, however, could not have predicted many twentieth-century developments, such as the accumulation of vast power and wealth by a small number of companies. Modern liberalism has therefore been forced to concede that government intervention is sometimes necessary to assist those harmed by huge income disparities (*see* POVERTY), RACISM, SEXISM, and other forms of OPPRESSION. Many of these problems have causes far more-complex than simple legalized DISCRIMINATION, and therefore modern liberals are likely to be equally concerned with eliminating both de-jure and de-facto barriers to self–actualization. This modern development in liberalism achieved widespread public support throughout the middle part of the twentieth century, in particular in the progressive New Deal policies of U.S. President Franklin Delano Roosevelt.

Critics argue that liberalism is simply a form of EGOISM, glorifying SELF-INTEREST, and therefore indirectly supports the inequalities created by market forces. Others argue that liberalism is an illusion that can only work in communities with a strong preexisting communitarian ethic of mutual obligation and tradition (*see* COMMUNITARIANISM). Despite this, liberalism has proven to be a remarkably resilient doctrine that remains widely accepted in Western societies, despite the fact that the label *liberal* has itself fallen out of favor in U.S. political debate.

LIBERTARIANISM

The doctrine that radical INDIVIDUALISM should be the dominant organizing force in society, free from the constraint of government interference and as expressed through the ownership of private property.

Libertarians strongly believe in the ability of market forces to regulate and distribute capital and goods most efficiently (*see* CAPITALISM). According to libertarians, compulsory taxation is a form of theft. They believe that if government can be justified at all, it should exist only to the extent that is necessary to provide those services that would be difficult or impossible to organize through other means. They might argue, for example, that social security should be provided for individually through retirement accounts and voluntary charitable organizations such as the Salvation Army. Indeed, government might not even be necessary for such things as national defense and local policing, as these could potentially be provided by a citizen militia of interested volunteers or through a voluntary levy.

Libertarians are also strongly opposed to government PATERNALISM and see no justification in restricting what consenting adults choose to do in their homes and private lives. In particular, they see no reason for prohibiting "victimless crime," such as drug use, prostitution, voluntary EUTHANASIA, HOMOSEXUALITY, and ABORTION.

Libertarianism has strong roots in ANARCHISM and LIBERALISM, but in practical terms, those professing to be libertarians tend toward the right-wing, free-market side of politics. Radical individualists with a more left-wing emphasis, on the other hand, generally describe themselves as anarchists.

LIBERTY *See* FREEDOM.

LICENSURE

A system whereby the government prohibits individuals from engaging in particular activities without specific approval.

Because licensure places restrictions on the ability of individuals to act freely, individualists (*see* INDIVIDUALISM) believe that the onus is on the government to justify the use of such restrictions. Licensure is arguably a form of PATERNALISM as it often is invoked as a way of protecting individuals from themselves.

A number of justifications are given for the use of licenses. Sometimes, licensing is simply a form of "user pays" taxation. For example, fishing and pet ownership is often restricted to those who hold fishing or pet-owners' licences, although sometimes the only qualification for receiving these licences is payment of a fee. In these cases, the payment may go toward upkeep of river systems or provision of facilities for stray animals.

In other cases, licensing is intended to protect the public by restricting certain activities to those who are able to demonstrate a degree of proficiency in the activity or an understanding of the responsibilities required of one who engages in that activity. Automobile drivers, for example, are required to demonstrate driving proficiency and a familiarity with road rules before they are allowed to drive on the road. This is because drivers who are unable to control their cars or who have an insufficient understanding of the road rules may present a significant danger to other drivers, pedestrians, and themselves. Other examples of common activities that are often deemed to require licensing for similar reasons include the right to work in certain fields, such as medicine or elevator repair, and the right to own and safely store hazardous materials.

LIFE   The natural functioning of an organism.

One of the most fundamental biological and moral questions concerns when and how life begins. Some hold that life is a result of a supernatural or mystical event that is usually connected to the idea of a creator or GOD. This position suggests that the origin of life cannot be known through science but may perhaps be known through religion. Alternatively, there are those who hold that life originated on Earth by a series of chemical reactions that we can come to understand through modern science (*see* EVOLUTION).

Nearly all moral systems and traditions accord a fundamental VALUE or GOOD to life becase all other experiences or appreciation of other values depends on it. RULES prohibiting (*see* PROHIBITION) the taking of life and encouraging the protection or preservation of life are found in every major civilization. Standards differ, however, in their recognition of human life, animal life, and vegetative life (*see* ANIMAL RIGHTS; ENVIRONMENTAL ETHICS). Many traditions hold that people have a RIGHT TO LIFE, meaning that others have a duty or OBLIGATION not to deprive them of it. This respect for peoples' lives is the basis of the moral MAXIM, "Do not kill." Life may be understood in either a broad or narrow sense. When people speak of killing they are usually speaking of ending life in the biological sense. By life, however, one might mean a person's total life experiences, thoughts, plans, and memories. Life may be

harmed or improved in both or either of these senses not only by killing, but also, for example, by depriving people of opportunities.

Some theories, however, maintain that the duty not to kill can be overridden by other considerations. In hedonistic theories (*see* HEDONISM) killing can be justified in cases when a person's life is so painful that the person determines that it is no longer worth living. Even in NATURAL LAW theory, where it is generally thought to be WRONG to kill a human being intentionally (*see* INTENTION) for any reason, distinctions may be drawn to justify killing in war, or in cases capital punishment or self-defense. Questions concerning the beginning and ending of life are morally controversial and motivate the debate over the ETHICS, of ABORTION, CAPITAL PUNISHMENT, EUTHANASIA, and SUICIDE.

LIFESTYLES   The ways in which people live and express their preferences and beliefs.

Our lifestyles are a concrete manifestation of the VALUES we believe in and can affect the way that we view the world. Eastern lifestyles, for example, tend to emphasize nature and the continuities and commonalities between all things, and they are therefore relatively communitarian in outlook (*see* COMMUNITARIANISM). Western lifestyles, on the other hand, tend to view the world as consisting of discrete components, only indirectly related to each other, and are therefore relatively individualistic in outlook (*see* INDIVIDUALISM).

All lifestyles have a structure of priorities that specifies which ideals are important and which are less important, or discouraged. In Western countries, for example, profit and individual fulfillment are dominant values. In other countries, values such as contentment and spirituality are much more highly prized.

Within the lifestyle of a dominant culture, there are often various minorities who live their lives with alternative priorities to those of the mainstream. Alternative lifestyles may be simply passing fads, they may remain minority preferences, or they may gradually come to be adopted by society at large.

It is not uncommon for people to be critical of others who have different lifestyles to their own. This is because lifestyles are the overt expression of deeply held beliefs about the way that the world is and should be. When evaluating the lifestyles of others, however, it is important to avoid the trap of ETHNOCENTRISM. Just because we personally have strongly held beliefs and principles does not automatically imply that these beliefs (*see* FAITH) are correct or that others should agree with us. *See also* CUSTOMS; IDEOLOGY.

LOCKE, JOHN (1632–1704) English moral and political philosopher who inspired the Enlightenment (*see* ENLIGHTENMENT ETHICS) in England and France and whose work influenced the authors of the United States Constitution and its Declaration of Independence.

Locke's greatest contribution to philosophy are his works *Essays Concerning Human Understanding* (1690) and *Two Treatises on Government* (1690). In the *Essays*, Locke explores questions concerning the nature of the world, the human being, God, and our ability to have knowledge of these things. The key notion is that of an "idea." By "idea" Locke intends the object of our understanding. Locke holds that all of our ideas come to us through experience. In this view, he stands in opposition to those who argue that we have some innate ideas impressed on our minds or souls. In this Locke includes moral ideas, arguing that there are no innate moral principles (*see* PRINCIPLES.) Locke maintains that our natural disposition to seek pleasure and avoid pain (*see* HEDONISM) was not enough to give us moral knowledge. Locke believes in universal moral principles but holds that we can achieve them only through reasoning about our experience.

In the *treatises,* Locke expounds upon the relationship between man's capacities for knowledge, his actions (*see* ACT), and the proper principles of government. The *Treatises* first appeared anonymously in 1690. Locke acknowledged authorship only in his will in which he listed his anonymous works. In the second of the treatises, Locke posits that people are originally in a state of nature. In this state, people are free (*see* FREEDOM) to act in any way they choose within the NATURAL LAW without asking permission from any AUTHORITY. Natural law dictates that people can, through REASON, know the fundamental principles of MORALITY. Thus, in the state of nature it is the RESPONSIBILITY of each individual to preserve mankind, to achieve peace, and to refrain from hurting one another. Violating the natural law is the same as declaring war on others, and anyone who does so may be punished by any other individual as long as that PUNISHMENT is in proportion to the offense.

Because of the difficulty of living in the state of nature, where each individual is responsible for constantly guarding freedom, LIFE, and PROPERTY, the people form a SOCIAL CONTRACT. This contract is the basis for a single civil government. The key characteristic of this contract for Locke is that it is an agreement between free and equal (*see* EQUALITY) citizens, not an agreement between ruler and ruled. If anyone attempts to gain absolute POWER, that person is considered to be at war with the people and the contract is broken.

LOGIC   The art of science of REASON; the study of arguments for the purpose of discovering principles (*see* PRINCIPLE), RULES, and techniques that can be used to determine validity or invalidity.

An argument is valid if its conclusion follows necessarily from its premises; in other words, the conclusion must be true when the premises are true. The conclusion to an argument is the statement or proposition it seeks to prove, and the premises are the reasons offered to prove it. When an argument is valid, its conclusion is said to follow from its premises; if it is invalid, the conclusion does not follow. The same point is sometimes made in ordinary language by saying that something does or does not make sense. It is valid, or makes sense, to argue that SOCRATES is mortal because all men are mortal, and Socrates is a man. But it is not valid, or does not make sense, to argue that because snow is white and sugar is white that, therefore, sugar must also be snow. To argue validly is normally what is meant by being logical, while to offer an invalid argument is to be illogical.

If an argument has true premises and a false conclusion, it must be invalid. But arguments can be shown to be valid or invalid by their forms alone without knowing the truth or falsity of the premises or the conclusions. For example, any argument of the form "All A is B, all B is C, and therefore all A is C" is a valid argument, no matter what the argument is about. Thus, rules for determining validity can be developed by discovering valid argument forms. Any argument that follows a valid rule or has a valid argument form is a valid argument. Invalidity is sometimes more difficult to demonstrate because an argument that does not conform to one valid form may conform to another. Nonetheless, some forms of argumentation are said to be fallacious (*see* FALLACY).

In ETHICS, questions of logic arise over the validity or invalidity of particular arguments offered by people to justify their positions (*see* JUSTIFICATION). For example, somebody might argue that capital punishment is wrong because killing is wrong and capital punishment is killing. This argument structure is valid. The conclusion follows from the premises. If one wanted to challenge a valid argument of this sort, one would need to challenge the TRUTH of the premises in an attempt to show that it is unsound. All invalid arguments are unsound, and a valid argument with false premises is also unsound because the premise on which the argument is founded is untrue. So one might challenge the argument in the above example by pointing out that not all killing is wrong. One might then back up this claim by producing a counterexample, for example, by pointing out that killing in self-defense is

not necessarily wrong. One would then be producing another argument intended to supplant the original argument.

In theoretical ethics, there are also questions about how and even whether it is possible to prove, by an argument or a process of reasoning, that any moral JUDGMENT is either true or false. Substantive ethical theories are theories about how persons can logically demonstrate, on the basis of moral rules and principles, that actions are right or wrong or that judgments about actions are either true or false. Some metaethical theorists (*see* METAETHICS) have argued that it is not possible to reason in ethics or at least that reasoning in ethics can never be conclusive. Emotivists (*see* EMOTIVISM) claim that in ethics there is nothing to reason about because moral sentences are merely expressions of emotion. Others appeal to intuition (*see* INTUITIONISM), not reason, as a way of knowing what is right or wrong.

Logic is held in high esteem among most moral philosophers, so much so that they usually assume that what is right is rational (*see* RATIONALITY) and what is rational is right. The dictates of MORALITY in this view are the dictates of reason or of logic as it applies to practical affairs or to the problems of daily life (*see* ENLIGHTENMENT ETHICS). The same assumption is often made in ordinary conversations when people accuse others of being illogical or when they claim that their own position is supported by reason.

LOVE   A feeling of strong affection for and devotion to another based on family relationship, personal ties, admiration, respect, BENEVOLENCE, or common interests.

Love is considered a central VIRTUE in all religious traditions and many moral traditions. It is normally characterized as unselfish and loyal (*see* LOYALTY), and carrying with it a deep concern for the GOOD of another.

Three Greek terms may be used to identify different qualities or degrees of love. *Eros* indicates strong DESIRE and is sometimes equated with sexual drive, erotic love, and even LUST. It names the passionate urge (*see* PASSIONS AND EMOTIONS) that seeks its own ends and satisfaction. *Philos* implies RECIPROCITY and names the love that prevails in friendship. Here there is a mutuality, give and take, and sharing. Finally, *agape* refers to divine love. *Agape* is selfless love, love that expects nothing in return. It is sometimes called unconditional love.

In religious traditions love may be modeled on the concern of the divinity for human beings or the concern of the great religious teachers for fellow beings (*see* JESUS; MUHAMMAD). According to Christianity (*see* CHRISTIAN ETHICS), love identifies the ideal quality in all vital relationships. It is the central quality out of which GOD relates to humankind: "God so loved the world that he gave his only Son" (John 3:16). It is the central quality by which humans are to relate to God: "You shall love the Lord your God with all your heart, and with all your soul, and with all your mind" (Matthew 22:37; Deuteronomy 6:5). According to both Judaism (*see* JEWISH ETHICS) and Christianity, love names the way in which humans should relate to each other: "You shall love your neighbor as yourself" (Leviticus 19:18, Matthew 22:39).

One of the most compelling expressions of *agape* was written by the Apostle Paul: "Love is patient; love is kind; love is not envious or boastful or arrogant or rude. It does not insist on its own way; it is not irritable or resentful; it does not rejoice in wrongdoing, but rejoices in the TRUTH. It bears all things, believes all things, hopes all things, endures all things. Love never ends" (I Corinthians 13).

Contrary to SIN, which is essentially an estranging, divisive force, love is said to unite. It dissolves alienating forces (*see* ALIENATION). In all instances of love, there is a coming together of that which is otherwise separate. This coming together ranges from joining of physical bodies to the merging of identities (*see* MYSTICISM). *See also* BUDDHIST ETHICS; KARUNA; NONVIOLENCE

LOYALTY A feeling of faithfulness (*see* FAITH) or allegiance to a person, cause, ideal, institution, custom, or government.

Although most of us recognize loyalty when we see it, loyalty is nonetheless not easy to define. Typically, loyalty is characterized by the CHARACTER or INTENTION of the person who performs an action rather than by the action itself. We say a person is loyal when that person is willing to put the interests of another person or institution before his or her own, even when that person may be harmed. If, for example, you stand by a friend who has made an unpopular choice, you would be acting out of loyalty. However, if you support that same friend because you believe that friend will owe you later, you would be acting not from loyalty but rather from self-interest.

Loyalty, whether to a friend, team, group, or job, includes respecting our duties (*see* OBLIGATION), but it more than mere dutifulness. Loyalty involves affection or sentiment. Loyalty often involves gratitude to those who have extended help in time of need. Loyalty usually involves PRIDE. If we are proud of a person or group, we are likely to be loyal to them as well. Loyalty affects how we respond to other people and their needs. It affects our sense of FAIRNESS and JUSTICE. Loyalty is the product of a relationship. We grow into it, like friendship.

However, loyalty can also be excessive. A person's loyalty might inspire immoral action (*see* IMMORALITY). Perhaps a friend asks us to cover for him while he is away from work without permission, or perhaps a roommate asks to lie on the phone to a parent or friend. Loyalty is a strong motivator (*see* MOTIVE), but it does not always attach itself to worthy people or worthwhile objects. People may attempt to misuse a person's loyalty by demanding unfair treatment or practices.

Therefore, it is necessary to use good JUDGMENT when developing loyalties. Ethically (*see* ETHICS), loyalty demands what is due the person or object of loyalty. It does not demand absolute (*see* ABSOLUTES) compliance or complete OBEDIENCE. We cannot revoke loyalty when there is a CONFLICT OF INTEREST. At the same time, we must be able to recognize when a situation cannot be redeemed and we have reached the limits of true loyalty.

How can we decide who deserves our loyalty? Loyalty often motivates us to suspend virtues (*see* VIRTUE) such as PRUDENCE and good judgment, which would help us to make a good decision about our allegiances. Inherent to the idea of loyalty is the reality that a loyal person will sometimes exhibit a readiness to set good judgment and OBJECTIVITY aside. Sometimes loyalty demands what MORALITY would demand anyway. For example, we would not steal from an organization to which we were loyal. However, sometimes loyalty demands that we act imprudently. Perhaps we loan money to a friend out of loyalty, even though it is money we need and we doubt that the money will be returned promptly.

"GOOD" loyalty inspires COURAGE, HONESTY, gratitude, and dutifulness. It promotes an atmosphere of justice and fairness and can lay the groundwork for other ethical decisions involving ACCOUNTABILITY and INFORMED CONSENT. However, all loyalty is not good. Loyalty can also inspire chauvinism, DISCRIMINATION, and other forms of unfairness. For example, a manager who promotes only Caucasians in a racially diverse workplace might be loyal to a group but might not be acting morally.

One rule of thumb for determining when loyalty is good is that actions inspired by loyalty should be related to the character and worth of the object of loyalty. For example, loyalty to a person who is inept or corrupt will often lead us into unethical behavior. However, loyalty to a person who is honest and skillful more often leads to pride and success.

LUST   Intense DESIRE, especially sexual desire.

The term *lust* is used to describe an uncontrolled, intense longing or desire. Lust usually has a sexual connotation and is often used in opposition to the idea of LOVE, although the two certainly need not be exclusive. When one person craves another sexually, we say that person lusts after the person he or she desires. Lust is normally characterized as beyond a healthy passion and has in that sense traditionally been considered a VICE.

LUTHER, MARTIN (1483–1546)   German theologian, professor, pastor, and leader of the Protestant Reformation.

Luther, first trained as an Augustinian monk and later as an Old Testament theologian, is perhaps best known for his theological rediscovery that one is made righteous before God not because of one's justifying works but solely because of God's gracious gift in Jesus Christ. It is one's belief in this truth, one's FAITH, that makes one right with God. Faith comes, reasoned Luther, when one hears the Word of God and grows, in the Holy Spirit's help, to believe that God is telling the truth. As faith grows, love must also grow, because, states Luther, faith is always active in love. They are bound together they like heat and light are bound to fire. Good works, in the end, are not a means to God, but an expression of faith in God.

This simple theological insight drove Luther to profound changes in church and society. It was necessary, for example, to reform the church's sacraments and preaching so they better conveyed the grace of God and built up faith. In writings such as the *Babylonian Captivity of the Church* (1520), *The Freedom of a Christian* (1520), *The Blessed Sacrament of the Holy and True Body of Christ,* and the *Brotherhoods* (1519), Luther attacked the ecclesiology of the church and the form of the liturgy, but also confronted a popular "piety of achievement," and a "mathematics of salvation," in which good works were believed to merit salvation for the believer. Luther's place as a theologian and pastor compelled him to speak on matters of faith and the church first, but his insights always moved to society. For example, as Christ is present for all in His body and blood during the Eucharist, we too, describes Luther, are formed into a community of love that is really present for each other. Luther's reforms in Word and Sacrament were, therefore, responsible for extensive social welfare reforms in church and community ordinances throughout Reformation Germany.

Luther was a voracious writer and preacher. At the high point of the Reformation 1520–30 he published some 360 original works, fueled by the advent of the printing press, and often preached twice a day. His balance of the intellectual and pastoral made him famous and notorious in his native Germany. Luther saw himself as a reformer within Roman Catholicism. In his mind his theology was decidedly Christian, never Lutheran. Luther's vocational theology opened him to his marriage to Kathrine of Bora, and his later family, which continued to fuel him with theological insights from everyday life.

LYING Issuing statements characterized by falsehood.

When people lie, they are speaking or behaving in such a way as to intentionally deceive others. In most moral theories, the INTENTION to deceive is the crucial factor. For example, if a person unknowingly speaks the truth when the intent is to deceive, the act is still considered dishonest. In a like manner, a person who intends the truth but unknowingly gives false information is more aptly thought to be incorrect than to be lying. Lying is in opposition to the VIRTUE of HONESTY.

Lies may be overt, or by omission. False statements are lies, but it may also be a lie to withhold important information or pretend not to have relevant knowledge. Moral theorists disagree as to when, if ever, it is acceptable to tell a lie. In *The Republic,* PLATO indicates that it is sometimes allowable for a statesman to lie for the good of the city or for a doctor to lie to a patient. ARISTOTLE, on the other hand, held that it was never allowable to tell a lie. Neither does Immanuel KANT allow a lie under any circumstances. UTILITARIANISM would allow a lie if that lie served to bring about the greatest happiness of the greatest number of people (*see also* CONSEQUENTIALISM).

One of the most difficult moral cases arises when the duty to be truthful conflicts with the OBLIGATION to keep a secret (*see* SECRETS). In this case, most moral thinkers advise silence unless that silence will betray the secret. If silence is as telling as a spoken remark, some philosophers argue that a person should reply with a question such as, "Why do you need to know something like that?" or should simply reply with a statement such as, "I cannot discuss that with you." Others hold that it is permissible to lie or withhold information if the person requesting that information has no right to it or if it is a matter of self-defense or the preservation of another's life.

M

MACHIAVELLI, NICCOLÒ (1469–1527)

Influential Italian political philosopher of the Renaissance.

Machiavelli's writings on politics redefined much of political theory in his time and continues to influence modern thinking about political RIGHT and WRONG. Machiavelli's work departs from other political works of that period in that he is not interested in defining the basis of a just government but rather the strategies that are necessary to retain POWER. This means that Machiavelli is more interested in ethical norms (*see* NORM) that are based on what humans do rather than those based on an ideal of what humans *ought* to do. Machiavelli held that a political leader has the right to do whatever is deemed necessary in order to retain power for the state. This means that the state acknowledges no higher moral AUTHORITY and that any ACT that furthers its ends is by definition acceptable. Machiavelli redefined *virtue* in terms of those qualities needed to govern effectively. He argued that those qualities that allow a sovereign to govern effectively were right, irrespective of moral or religious teachings (*see* RELIGION AND MORALITY). In fact, he concludes that many of the commonly held virtues such as HONESTY or MERCY or GENEROSITY will lead to the destruction of the state, while "vices" (*see* VICE) such as deception will strengthen it. Therefore, it may be virtuous for a sovereign to lie (*see* LYING) or even to steal. However because the state is only stable if the sovereign is perceived to be virtuous, a sovereign must always appear to be merciful, honest, humane, upright, and moral (*see* MORALITY). Thus, Machiavellian's political morality allows for the deception of the public by a sovereign when the sovereign deems it to be in the best interest of the state. These views are most famously expressed in Machiavelli's book *The Prince (Il principe)*, published in 1513.

Machiavelli was not concerned with the GOOD or EVIL in actions but only with their political effectiveness. However, some have taken his writings to mean that cruelty or WICKEDNESS is more effective than good in political rule. This misunderstanding is the basis for the term *Machiavellism*. Although Machiavelli does argue that traditional ethical norms can be overturned for the good of the state, he does not actively advocate OPPRESSION. Machiavelli believed that the business of states was growth and expansion, not the enforcement of justice. This belief does not, however, automatically translate into permission for any act of oppression by a government. *See also* ENDS/MEANS.

MAIMONIDES (1135–1204)

Jewish rabbi, biblical commentator, codifier of Jewish LAW, communal leader, philosopher, and physician.

Maimonides, also known as Moses ben Maimon, was born in Spain, and lived most of his life in Egypt. He was a contemplative, scholarly man who also served the sick and played a leading role in his local Jewish COMMUNITY. Indeed, the life of Maimonides exemplifies his view that the superior leader is one who combines intellectual mastery with practical leadership and moral VIRTUE.

Maimonides' continuing influence rests partly on his open-mindedness and RATIONALITY.

He believed that TRUTH should be acknowledged wherever found, and he knew much from ARISTOTLE, the Greek philosopher, and al-Farabi, the Muslim thinker. Maimonides also believed that REVELATION, the divine truth conveyed in holy scripture, and REASON are entirely compatible. In his work, reconciling secular philosophy (*see* SECULAR ETHICS) and religious law, he occasionally used symbolic or allegorical methods of scriptural interpretation in order to uncover the hidden significance beyond the literal reading.

Maimonides' integration of belief and PRACTICE, philosophy and law, Judaism (*see* JEWISH ETHICS) and Aristotelianism, formed the basis for further developments in Jewish philosophy and law. He contributed extensively to HALAKAH, the Jewish system of law that addresses all aspects of life. His major presentation on law, *Mishnah Torah* (*Mishnah* refers to oral law, established about 200 A.D., a source of the Halakah), was unprecedented in rabbinic literature and remains unequaled to this day.

Maimonides' ETHICS draws from Aristotle, the BIBLE, the TALMUD, which is an extensive commentary on the Bible, and of course, Halakah. Like Aristotle, Maimonides founds his ethical system on the soul and the soul's various powers. Central to this reasoning is the theory of the GOLDEN MEAN, which is a moderate or central position between two extremes. For Maimonides, virtues are the psychological traits that fall between too much and too little. This means, for example, that the mean between lust and insensibility to pleasure (each an extreme which Maimonides called a moral VICE) is a moral virtue. Other examples of the golden mean include: HUMILITY (the mean between haughtiness and abasement); GENEROSITY (the mean between prodigality and stinginess); contentment (the mean between GREED and laziness); and modesty (the mean between impudence and shyness).

Maimonides' most widely recognized work, *Guide for the Perplexed,* was written to resolve apparent contradictions between philosophy and religion. Maimonides hoped to communicate these resolutions and insights to persons who valued both disciplines, without needlessly disturbing those who are familiar only with the perspectives of traditional religion. The *Guide for the Perplexed* was not written for the philosopher who denigrates religion, nor for the simple religious believer; rather it addressed the person who has a high regard for reason and a corresponding distaste for literal readings of scripture. Consequently, Maimonides' interpretive approach in the *Guide* is to resolve perplexity by means of analogy, metaphor, and symbol. For example, GOD is not literally a father but in some ways is *like* a father.

Eight centuries after his death, Maimonides remains one of the most illustrious and influential Jewish thinkers of all times.

MALPRACTICE   Service provided by a professional that is not in keeping with standards of PRACTICE in that profession and that leads to HARM to the client.

Malpractice starts with the understanding that an agreement has been made between professionals and their clients: that professionals will help clients to the best of their abilities and in keeping with STANDARDS OF CARE that are accepted in that profession (*see* PROFESSIONAL ETHICS.) Malpractice requires a willful neglect of these standards in a way that results in harm to the client. If there is no harm done, then there is no malpractice, regardless of the actions (*see* ACT) of the professional. If the professional could not have foreseen or avoided an adverse reaction, no malpractice has been done. If the practice of the professional was in keeping with standards of practice at the time the service was performed, no malpractice has occurred, even if the actions result in harm to a client.

In the medical profession, a blood transfusion that resulted in acquiring the AIDS virus before testing for the virus was available would be an example of harm done to a patient without malpractice. If a blood transfusion was given after the test was available, the test was not run, and the patient did not acquire the virus, malpractice did not occur. But if a patient acquired the virus from untested transfused blood after the test was available, malpractice did occur.

A malpractice suit is a legal claim brought against a professional by a person who claims to have suffered injury. Medical malpractice suits are often cited as the reason for skyrocketing costs in health care. Damages awarded in malpractice suits have been as high as tens of millions of dollars. As a result physicians may feel it necessary to practice "defensive medicine," protecting themselves by ordering more tests, more procedures, and more consultations. These additional steps increase the overall cost of health care. Additionally, malpractice insurance increases the cost of health care passed onto patients.

Professionals most often cited for malpractice are in the fields of health care and LAW.

MALTHUS, THOMAS (1766–1834)   British economist and social thinker who contributed substantively to theories of population.

Thomas Malthus's theory of population holds that populations tend to grow geometrically. Imagine a pond with a population of lily pads that doubles each day. If you have two lily pads on the first day and four on the second, on the third day you will have eight, and so on. One day you will find the pond half full of lily pads. On the very next day, the pond will be entirely full.

In 1798 Malthus published his *Essay on Populations* in which he argues that populations tend to grow more quickly than the supply of food that is available for them. Thus, in human populations we see the ethical problems of hunger, POVERTY, and starvation. This view was a severe challenge to ENLIGHTENMENT ETHICS, which argued that humans tend naturally toward progress.

Malthus's arguments raise moral controversy (*see* DILEMMA) because they suggest that

giving food and other aid to starving populations only stimulates further population growth, resulting in greater poverty, famine, disease, or even war. This challenges traditional ethical beliefs that we have an OBLIGATION to perform works of CHARITY for the poor.

MARRIAGE   The socially recognized joining of two persons as a union of husband and wife.

Marriage involves a social, legal, and moral CONTRACT between a man and woman who intend (*see* INTENTION) to share a life in common. In many cases, marriage is also considered a religious ceremony in which both partners PROMISE a union for life in the presence of GOD. Marriages may be either monogamous, in which each spouse has only one partner, or polygamous, in which a man has multiple wives (or, more rarely; a woman has multiple husbands). Polygamy is illegal in many countries and states. Marriage usually implies fidelity, although rates of ADULTERY are reportedly high in Western societies. In some cultures, marriage is only appropriate sanction for sexual activity (*see* SEXUAL ETHICS). Marriages are ended by the death of a spouse or by annulment or DIVORCE.

Controversies surrounding the marriage contract include when, if ever, the dissolution of a marriage should occur and whether same-sex partners should be allowed to marry.

MARX, KARL (1818–1883)   German political philosopher and economist; an inspiration for many forms of socialism.

Marx believed that human thought was shaped by social and economic forces. His doctrine of historical materialism states that our material conditions, such as our means of providing food, shelter, and other goods for ourselves, are of ultimate importance in shaping our thoughts and identities. Therefore, he argued, we must have social and economic JUSTICE in order to provide the conditions most befitting human beings. Marx put forth a method of analysis called dialectical materialism that described how changes in society occur as a result of social and CLASS STRUGGLE.

Marx's most famous work is *The Communist Manifesto,* written with Friedrich Engels and published in 1848. In this work, Marx and Engels argue that all of history is the history of class struggle. *The Communist Manifesto* is a moral (*see* MORALITY) and political critique of CAPITALISM and false forms of socialism and a call to revolutionary action in order to improve the lives of working people. Marx argues that within capitalist societies human labor itself becomes a kind of capital to be bought and sold. People exchange their time and work for money. In a real sense, people are exchanging a portion of their daily lives for money.

Marx noted that there were many laborers but only a few people who owned most of the capital or resources. The fact that the people who perform the most labor tended to reap the lowest benefits from that labor troubled Marx, who argued that those who owned the means of production profited excessively at the expense of the working masses. Marx believed that to treat people as commodities was unethical and disregarded their basic human DIGNITY. He described a sense of ALIENATION that arises when people feel a radical discord in themselves, between themselves and their lives, or between their work and the rewards they reap from that work.

Marx believed that the struggle between the working class, or proletariat, and the owning class, or bourgeoisie, would result in a new communist society (*see* COMMUNISM). In this new society the means of production would be owned in common by the people, and private ownership of the means of production would be abolished. People would divide their working lives roughly into thirds: one-third of the time would be spent in the labor necessary to keep a community running, one-third of the time would be spent in a profession chosen by the worker, and one-third would be spent in continuing education and learning new talents and skills. Thus, everyone would have a share in the jobs that are necessary to a community, and everyone would have the chance to pursue special interests and talents. Both the burdens and rewards of work would be shared. Only thus, Marx believed, would the EXPLOITATION of the workers end. Marx's ideal communist state has never been realized.

The collection of philosophical and social ideas that have developed from Marx's works is called Marxism. Marx himself would not have approved of the idea of Marxist philosophy, as he considered philosophy to be a class-biased enterprise. Marx believed his analysis was a purely historical one, although he recognized its moral implications. Marx hoped that the revolution he foresaw would end philosophy and bring people back to the material realities that define their well-being.

MAXIMAL VS. MINIMAL ETHICS The debate as to whether moral behavior demands the highest possible action (maximal ethics) or adherence to a minimum standard of human respect with all above regarded as CHARITY or some other VIRTUE (minimal ethics).

The PRINCIPLE of maximal ETHICS suggests that our moral duties (*see* OBLIGATION) require the most excellent or positive action (*see* ACT) possible. For example, "love thy neighbor" is a maximal moral standard. The principle of minimal ethics suggest that moral behavior consists in CODES that determine noninterference. "Do not kill," for instance, is a NORM in minimal ethics. Minimal ethics is sometimes characterized as negative, meaning that its principles usually prohibit action (*see* PROHIBITION). "Do not steal" and "Do not lie" are further examples of maxims in minimalist ethics. Maximalist ethics, on the other hand, is characterized as positive and tends to direct us to greater action. In contrast to the directive not to steal, maximalist ethics might direct us to give to the poor or feed the hungry.

MAXIM   A basic rule (*see* RULES).

A maxim is a guide for action (*see* ACT) that is simple and easy to remember. Maxims are often associated with folk sayings. For instance, "a stitch in time saves nine" or "an ounce of prevention is worth a pound of cure" are maxims that teach that work done in advance will save greater effort later on.

In moral theory, the term *maxim* is often associated with the philosophy of Immanuel KANT. Kant terms maxim as those rules or principles (*see* PRINCIPLE) that guide people in determining what to do in moral situations. For example, "lying is wrong" is a maxim that might guide our actions if we are faced with a situation in which we are tempted to lie. Kant held that we should act so that the maxim, or guiding rule, of our actions could guide everyone's actions. *See also* CATEGORICAL IMPERATIVE.

MAYA   A Sanskrit term meaning "illusion," or more specifically, the subjective, illusory nature of the world of our perceptions.

Maya is a central concept in Hinduism and Buddhism and is an important barrier to discovery of ultimate reality—known in Hinduism as *Brahman* and in Buddhism as NIRVANA. Discovery of ultimate reality is the supreme goal in both religions and is thought to lead one to a thorough understanding of how one is interconnected with, and inseparable from, everyone and everything that constitutes the world.

Maya does not imply a denial of the commonsense world of appearance but simply emphasizes that below the indeterminacy of the world we perceive is an essential, unchanging and absolute (*see* ABSOLUTES) reality. This reality, however, is not grounded in the physical universe, in the sense that we might describe a table as having an objective existence of atoms and scientific properties, but rather it exists as an holistic aggregate with both material and spiritual aspects. *See also* BUDDHIST ETHICS: HINDU ETHICS.

MEANS   *See* TELEOLOGY.

MEANS/ENDS   *See* ENDS/MEANS.

MEDIATION   A method of settling disputes between two or more factions by appealing to a neutral and impartial party (*see* IMPARTIALITY).

The word *mediation* comes from the Latin *medius,* which means "middle." Central to the concept of mediation is the notion of a party or person who interposes between conflicting persons or groups. The aim of mediation is to allow for a reconciliation or compromise that cannot be achieved by the parties themselves. For example, because divorce is often a difficult and emotional process, it is sometimes difficult for partners arguing between themselves to agree to an equitable division of family assets. In these cases, the use of a rational, impartial mediator may assist both parties to avoid expensive and drawn-out legal battle.

Mediation may be accomplished in two ways. In the first, conflicting parties agree to allow the mediator to act as a guide but without giving up the right to reject any proposal. In the second, parties agree to abide by the decision of the mediator. In this case, the mediator acts as a judge, that is, as someone with the power to issue a ruling that must be accepted by all disputants. For the process to be successful, the mediator must be neutral and impartial with regard to the conflicting parties. Theoretically, the presence of someone who is not emotionally involved allows the parties to see perspectives that they may otherwise have been unable to see.

MEDICAL ETHICS   The code (*see* CODES) of behavior that dictates appropriate interactions between physicians and their patients. Medical ethics covers the gamut of interactions among health-care institutions, health-care providers, and health-care consumers (or patients). It should not be confused with STANDARDS OF CARE, which concerns the level or intensity of the medical care that is given.

Medical ethics concerns the appropriateness of behavior and medical CARE for an individual.

It naturally embraces the entirety of the medical field, but there are several important areas: PHYSICIAN-PATIENT RELATIONSHIP, INFORMED CONSENT, physician impairment, unnecessary treatment, experimental medicine, and guarantees in medicine.

Physicians are required to ACT in the best interest of their patient. Physicians occupy a unique role in a patient's life as confidant, advocate, and advisor. It is not ethical for a physician to use this unique position to gain an advantage over the patient, whether for professional, personal, financial, or sexual gain. For example, a patient who confides that his or her business is causing sleepless nights because it is failing can reasonably expect that the physician will not share this information with the patient's business competitor.

With the rapid advances in medical technology, Western society increasingly believe that any and all means that are available to keep a person alive should always be used, no matter what the personal or financial cost. However, this may not be what a given patient wants. It may not even be in the patient's best interest. Because it is not usual for patients to be trained in medicine, they are not always able to make complete decisions even when the alternative choices, risks, and benefits are explained to them in an effort to obtain informed consent. This may be because of education, language barriers, or state of mental functioning at the time the decision needs to be made (*see* BRAIN DEATH). At these times a health-care provider must act as the patient's advocate, making decisions for or with the patient and the patient's family in an effort to follow a patient's wishes. This must be in a manner consistent with accepted medical ethics. At times this may mean using any and all medical means available to prolong life or to change the course of a disease. In another instance it may mean to withhold such care. The actual definition of ethical care in medicine can be nebulous, and it can change rapidly. Many larger hospitals have medical ethicists on staff. These

people work with patient-care teams (such as nurses, doctors, and social workers), hospital lawyers, and patients and their families to reach a group consensus when care decisions are more difficult to solve. The goal is not to convince patients and families to agree with the doctor but rather to have everyone talk about the options that are available and their benefits where this one patient is concerned so that everyone involved can feel comfortable with the decisions that are made.

An impaired physician is anyone who from medical illness, mental-health illness, or drug and alcohol dependency is not able to practice medicine at a level consistent with accepted standards of care. The ethical course for impaired physicians is to identify their problem, remove themselves from patient care, and seek professional help of their own. When physicians have received appropriate care and their personal physician releases them to work, they are considered able to resume their medical practice.

Any care that will not change the course of a disease or illness, will not increase the patient's level of health or aid in diagnosis, or will HARM a patient is considered unnecessary care. Cosmetic care in cases of trauma or surgery are deemed necessary. Cosmetic care is otherwise deemed optional, not unnecessary. In general, it is felt that unnecessary care is provided for the financial gain of the health-care provider. There are cases in which differing medical opinions may deem certain types of care, such as alternative medicine, unnecessary care. In these cases, however, it is medical standards of care that are the overriding determining factor of necessity, not personal opinion.

As in any science, advances in medicine begin with experiments. When experimental treatments are used, informed consent must be obtained in a clear manner so that the patient is aware that the treatment is meant for the advancement of medical science, not for the actual treatment of their disease.

It is considered unethical to give guarantees of results for any medical treatment, medication, modality, or diagnostic procedure. Human biology and variations in response to treatment do not allow for such guarantees. It is not unethical to allow patients to purchase a product and to guarantee they will want to keep the product or receive their money back, as is the case in many types of hearing aids. In this case it is felt that no guarantee is being made that the device will actually work, only that patients become able to try such a device for a limited time without heavy financial OBLIGATION.

MENS REA   Latin for "guilty mind."

Mens rea is a legal term synonymous with *criminal intent* (*see* INTENTION). In most ethical systems people are not seen as morally blameworthy for actions (*see* ACT) that are committed either accidentally or inadvertently. Similarly, unless the law specifies otherwise, perpetrators may not be found guilty (*see* GUILT) of committing a CRIME if it can be shown that they were unaware of what they were doing. For example, a person would not generally be convicted of theft if she accidentally took another person's purse, thinking it to be her own. It is important to note, however, that criminal intent does not require knowledge of the LAW, only intention to commit the act itself. This is largely because such an exemption would create a loophole that criminals could use to avoid prosecution.

In some cases, such as bigamy (marrying more than one person) or statutory rape (having sex with an underage person), the law waives the requirement that mens rea be proved. This is partially because of a desire to encourage people to take extra precautions in order to avoid contravention of particular statutes and also because in these cases it is sometimes difficult, if not impossible, to prove intention.

MERCY   Leniency or compassion toward another.

To show mercy means to show COMPASSION, especially when one has POWER or AUTHORITY over the person or group in question. Mercy suggests giving up a RIGHT to inflict HARM on another or giving up one's power to do so. Thus, a merciful soldier may elect to spare an enemy, or a merciful judge may mercifully reduce a prisoner's sentence. Mercy also suggests caring treatment of those in need or distress, as in merciful works for the poor or hungry. In this sense, mercy is related to CHARITY and BENEVOLENCE.

Mercy is distinct from JUSTICE. Whereas justice implies giving people what is fair or due to them (*see* FAIRNESS), mercy means to forgo or reduce punishment even when justice may demand a greater punishment. Acts of mercy may spawn ethical controversy (*see* ETHICS). If PUNISHMENT is meant to stabilize a society or improve an individual, an ACT of mercy could be argued to undermine these aims. Furthermore, if mercy is shown to some individuals and not others, the question of injustice arises. Others argue that to be merciful is an essential characteristic of moral goodness (*see* GOOD).

Some philosophers question whether we can ever say that someone deserves mercy or whether mercy should be seen as a gift. In this sense, it raises moral questions similar to those raised by FORGIVENESS.

MERCY KILLING   *See* EUTHANASIA.

MERIT   An admirable quality or VIRTUE.

A merit is a positive quality. A merit may be a capacity, such as intelligence, or a physical attribute, such as strength or beauty. Talents such as artistic or musical ability or a capacity for diplomacy may also be considered merits. Moral virtues such as BENEVOLENCE, MERCY, TEMPERANCE, HONESTY, and FAIRNESS are merits.

Some thinkers, sometimes called meritarians, believed that social goods should be divided according to merit rather than dividing them based on need or dividing them equally among a social group. They argue that merit rather than RIGHT, utility, CONTRACT, or need should serve as an organizing social PRINCIPLE. For example, two people may badly need a certain job, but only one of those people may merit or deserve it. Meritarians hold that the more meritorious person should receive the job, regardless of who needs the job more. A similar argument could be made with respect to college admissions. A meritarian would argue that those with the most impressive applications should be admitted to a college, irrespective of other factors such as age, race, or sex. A meritocracy is a society in which all social advancement is determined by talent and achievement, and not by nepotism or popular opinion. In a meritocracy, only relevant qualifications and performance are considered relevant criteria for employment or reward. Meritarians differ in whether they believe that merits bestowed by MORAL LUCK are importantly different than those achieved through effort.

Meritarians are opposed by those who argue that all people, regardless of obvious talent or ability, have the same rights to social goods and deserve equal consideration for employment. Proponents of AFFIRMATIVE ACTION, for example, argue that meritarians unfairly ignore the fact that an unequal distribution of social goods, such as education, denies some people the opportunity to compete fairly with others for material necessities. They also raise the question of who is qualified to judge which merits are most relevant. For example, until the 1920s women are not allowed to vote in the United States because they were not considered to have the requisite merits of reason or in some cases of property. *See also* VIRTUE ETHICS.

MERITARIANISM   *See* MERIT.

METAETHICS   A field of philosophic investigation that analyzes the meanings of moral terms and the nature of moral reasoning (*see* REASON).

Metaethics is not specifically concerned about what kinds of things are GOOD or bad, RIGHT or WRONG. Neither is it specifically concerned about people's actions (*see* ACT); rather, metaethics is concerned about what we mean by saying something is either good or bad or right or wrong and whether it is possible to demonstrate that any such judgments (*see* JUDGMENT) are either true or false. For example, to say that lying is wrong is to make a moral judgment. Whether or not lying is truly wrong is said to be a substantive or normative moral issue and not a metaethical issue. However, what it means to say "lying is wrong" is a metaethical issue. Metaethical theories are theories about the meanings of such terms as *good* and *bad, right* and *wrong*. Metaethics also addresses the question of whether ethical statements can be shown to be true or false by a process of reasoning and whether those statements are subjective or objective (*see* SUBJECTIVISM; OBJECTIVISM).

In ancient times, PLATO explored what philosophers today call metaethical issues when, in his dialogues, he sought to define moral terms. In seeking a definition of *justice,* he said he was not looking for examples of just acts but rather for a characteristic or set of characteristics that acts must have in order to be just. Other traditional philosophers, such as hedonists (*see* HEDONISM), may have been doing metaethics, even if they did not call it by that name, by defining *good* as pleasure or *right* as productive of pleasure and *wrong* as productive of pain.

Subjectivist ethical theories hold that moral terms express or refer to subjective or psychological properties, such as human feelings or attitudes, while objectivist ethical theories hold that moral terms refer to properties of things, acts, or states of affairs in the external world, outside our minds. Both of these theories may be said to be *cognitive* theories because they claim that moral terms refer to properties of some kind, whether subjective or objective.

EMOTIVISM, by contrast, holds that moral terms do not have cognitive meaning because moral terms do not refer to any property. According to the subjectivist or objectivist models, moral judgments are either true or false, but according to emotivism, moral utterances are neither true nor false. If moral statements are neither true nor false, MORALITY would not be a matter of reasoning but of some other faculty.

Metaethicists work to determine means of verifying whether moral statements can be said to be true or false. Traditionally, we attempt to determine the worth of a moral statement by applying moral principles and rules to particular cases. A particular act of cheating may be wrong, for instance, because it violates the rule "Do not cheat." If one asks, "What's wrong with cheating?" or "Why do we have a rule against cheating?" the answer might be "Because cheating is unfair" or "Because cheating is harmful." A moral principle, namely a principle of justice or a principle of NONMALEFICENCE, could be cited to justify the rule. If all unjust acts are wrong and cheating is an unjust act, then cheating is wrong.

The problem arises, then, as to how to establish moral principles or rules. Teleological theories (*see* TELEOLOGY) argue that principles are established by appealing to the ends or consequences of actions (*see* CONSEQUENTIALISM). For example, because what hedonists mean by *good* is pleasure, they argue that acts that are productive of pleasure are, to that extent, good and that acts that produce pain are bad. Deontological theories (*see* DEONTOLOGY) appeal to RATIONALITY or intuition. Immanuel KANT, for example, would argue that it is irrational to apply rules differently to different people; hence, cheating is wrong because it violates rules that apply to everyone in the same way. W. D. Ross, a rule deontologist, argued that moral rules can be known only by INTUITION.

Questions about the relativity of moral rules and principles are also metaethical. Cultural RELATIVISM, for example, is really a theory about the limits of moral reasoning. It holds that we can reason from the rules of society to determine which acts are right or wrong, but it denies that we can reason to the rules of society from higher, universal principles. Theories such as UTILITARIANISM, however, are absolutistic (*see* ABSOLUTES) in holding that there are universal principles, in this case the maximization of happiness and the minimization of suffering, that determine what is right or wrong in all cases, regardless of how individuals or societies may differ in their beliefs.

MILITARISM   The glorification of war or military might.

War has not always been viewed as necessarily a bad thing. It can encourage great acts of bravery, HEROISM and self-sacrifice; it can spur great technological advances; it can stimulate a national economy; and it can provide opportunities for building national pride (*see* NATIONALISM). Of course, war can also devastate lives, countries, and in today's nuclear age, the world itself. Is it possible that there are instances where war is morally desirable and even necessary?

There are two common schools of thought when it comes to militarism. On one hand, the liberal tradition (*see* LIBERALISM) of philosophers such as Immanuel KANT, John Stuart MILL, and Jean-Jacques ROUSSEAU sees war as an EVIL to be eradicated. On the other hand, the conservative tradition (*see* CONSERVATISM) of philosophers such as Georg Wilhelm Friedrich HEGEL, Thomas HOBBES, Niccolò MACHIAVELLI and Friedrich NIETZSCHE views war as a necessary and sometimes worthy aspect of human life.

Militarism is usually associated with strong nationalist sentiment, a central feature of NAZISM, FASCISM, and nineteenth-century COLONIALISM. In practice, however, the glorification of war has been present to some extent in almost all world cultures, although this has begun to change over the last few decades. This occurred first with the invention of the nuclear bomb and later with the invention of television. In the first case, human beings were suddenly forced to consider the possibility that war could now totally extinguish all life on the planet. In the second case, the transmission of wartime images into homes around the world suddenly made war's horrific costs undeniable in a way that had never been possible before. *See also* PACIFISM.

MILL, JOHN STUART (1806–1873) An English ethical and political philosopher and leading liberal thinker, who helped defend and develop UTILITARIANISM.

Mill wrote widely in the areas of economics, politics, ETHICS, religion, and logic. In ethics, Mill is best known for his treatise *Utilitarianism* (1861). Mill's philosophy is empiricist (*see* EMPIRICAL KNOWLEDGE), meaning that he sought to build a system in ethics and politics based on experience and observation, much as people do in science. Mill's philosophy is also consequentialist (*see* CONSEQUENTIALISM). Mill argues that an ACT is good or bad based on its consequences and not based on the intentions (*see* INTENTION), motives (*see* MOTIVE), or CHARACTER of the person who performs the action. Thus, Mill rejects VIRTUE ETHICS.

In *Utilitarianism,* Mill expanded the ethical views of his father, James Mill, and utilitarian proponent Jeremy BENTHAM. In *Utilitarianism,* Mill writes that, "Actions are RIGHT in proportion as they tend to promote happiness; WRONG as they tend to produce the reverse of happiness." By *happiness,* Mill means both the "higher" pleasures of the intellect and the "lower" sensual pleasures. He classifies these as higher and lower because he believes that there is a sense of human DIGNITY that should urge us toward the intellectual over the sensual, although both are present in the good life. Knowledge and aesthetic enjoyments, for example, are higher or more preferable than the pleasures of eating or drinking.

The distinction between higher and lower pleasures was meant to defend utilitarianism against charges of HEDONISM. Critics of utilitarianism claimed that it was an ethics based on pleasure alone. Mill advocated a qualitative interpretation of the PLEASURE PRINCIPLE, instead of a purely quantitative interpretation. This distinction means that it is morally relevant to consider the type of pleasure achieved by an action and not only the amount of pleasure. Who decides which pleasures qualify as higher pleasures and which as lower? Mill held that competent judges (*see* COMPETENCY) who had experienced both were in a position to make that determination. A person who had experienced both higher and lower pleasures, Mill believed, would prefer the higher. Thus, one of the goals of MORAL EDUCATION would be to teach people to enjoy the higher things in life. Critics of Mill's position argue that one person's JUDGMENT, even that of a well-educated expert, should not decide for others which pleasures are most valuable. Modern critics point out that there are many important characteristics that Mill does not acknowledge—such as age, ethnicity, and gender—that might influence the types of things that yield pleasure (*see* FEMINIST ETHICS).

Mill also argued that deontological ethics (*see* DEONTOLOGY), normally held to be in opposition to consequentialism, was really only a form of consequentialist ethics. According to this argument, deontologists such as Immanuel KANT calculate the good or bad consequences of an action to decide if the action is moral (*see* MORALITY) and then raise the MAXIM of that action to a rule (*see* RULES; CATEGORICAL IMPERATIVE). Although Mill did not use the term *rule utilitarianism,* we might say that in his view deontologists were really rule utilitarians.

MITZVAH In Judaism, "commandment"; a biblical or rabbinic injunction.

In its actual practice, Judaism is a religion of OBEDIENCE to divine commandment. Orthodox Jews (*see* ORTHODOXY) attempt to live by the commandments—613 are traditionally numbered and believed to be set forth in the Hebrew BIBLE. They are divided into 248 positive and 365 negative mitzvoth. The mitzvoth are believed to correspond to the 248 bones and 365 muscles of the body, emphasizing the connection between LAW and LIFE.

Because no count of the biblical commandments exactly totals 613, scholars have set forth various principles for determining which biblical laws to include in the 613 mitzvoth. MAIMONIDES, for example, in his *Book of Commandments*, lists 14 controlling standards that help to decide precisely which laws should be included to yield 613. His ninth principle offers a fourfold classification that is widely used: (1) laws governing belief (*see* FAITH) and opinion (e.g., confessing the unity of GOD); (2) laws covering action (e.g., offering SACRIFICE); (3) laws on VIRTUE and character (e.g., expressing LOVE for one's neighbor); and (4) laws pertaining to speech (e.g., praying).

In addition to the biblical commandments, other directives are developed in the TALMUD. The importance of the commandments is reflected in the view that every human act is also an act of obedience to God. *See also* JEWISH ETHICS.

MOKSHA   State of ultimate liberation (*see* FREEDOM) in Hinduism; final release from the birth, life, death, rebirth cycle.

Moksha is the fourth and final objective or goal of life in Hinduism. (The other three are HAPPINESS, financial security, and righteousness.) It represents release from SAMSARA, that is, from entrapment within the wheel of perpetual life and death. According to Hinduism, this state of ultimate realization typically occurs only after many lifetimes of dedicated involvement in a PSYCHOSPIRITUAL DISCIPLINE.

A liberated person is one who has ceased to identify himself or herself with the body-mind and knows his or her deepest nature to be essentially *atman,* that is, not different from the Ultimate. This constitutes a radical egolessness

(*see* EGO) that enables the liberated person to genuinely regard others as fully equivalent to herself or himself, all sense of self-preference having disappeared. Consequently, immorality is impossible.

A *jivan mukta* is one who gains liberation while still alive. Liberation in the fullest sense occurs only at death, after which the individual is no longer trapped in the rebirth cycle but becomes totally one with the Ultimate, Brahman, who is transcendent to the entire time-space continuum, the world as ordinarily perceived. *See also* HINDU ETHICS.

MONOPOLY   The situation in which a single individual or company is the exclusive supplier of goods or services in a specific market.

A basic tenet of CAPITALISM is that the free exchange of goods and services between competing interests leads to increased efficiency and cheaper goods and services. Monopolies, by their nature, contravene this principle because where no fair competition is possible, there is little incentive for companies to improve their products or reduce their prices. In systems based on principles other than capitalism, monopolies may be tolerated and even encouraged, particularly when controlled by a supposedly altruistic (*see* ALTRUISM) national government. In a capitalist system with little government regulation, however, a monopoly can theoretically charge consumers an exorbitant amount for products or provide atrociously bad service, safe in the knowledge that customers have no alternative.

In traditional forms of capitalism, such as that envisaged by Adam SMITH, most transactions occur between a very large number of small entrepreneurs, skilled tradespeople, and family businesses. In these situations, monopolies are easy to spot and relatively easy to control. Today, however, there has been an increasing trend toward a few large corporations controlling up to 80 percent or more of a world market among them. These cases create special problems because although there is no single, exclusive market supplier, it is relatively easy for those involved to collude with each other in order to create a de facto monopoly. At the very least, opportunities for new players to usurp huge existing companies in such situations are extremely limited. In these cases, there is very little that an upstart company can do when faced with a huge opponent with enough financial resources to undercut competitors' prices for as long as is necessary to drive them out of business. *See also* BUSINESS ETHICS.

MOORE, G. E. (GEORGE EDWARD) (1873–1958)

An English philosopher who, in *Principia Ethica*, made contributions to both METAETHICS and substantive ethics. In metaethics, Moore was an intuitionist (*see* INTUITIONISM), while he was a utilitarian (*see* UTILITARIANISM) in substantive ETHICS.

In metaethics, Moore was primarily interested in the question of whether *good* can be defined, for he thought that this was the most fundamental question of ethics. He argued, however, that *good* cannot be defined, for no other concept is synonymous with *good* and no other PROPERTY is identical with goodness. *Good,* Moore claimed, refers to a unique, unanalyzable property. Because goodness cannot be inferred from any other property, it must be intuited. This means that goodness cannot be known by a process of reasoning (*see* REASON) but only by direct awareness or apprehension. It is like the color red, which cannot be defined by or inferred from any other property but can be known only by direct perception. We do not know that something is red because we know that it is square or heavy; rather, we know this because we *see* that it is red. Likewise, we cannot know that something is good because it is pleasurable but only if we intuit its goodness.

In Moore's so-called open-question technique, he said that an open question could be applied to any property whether or not the property is good. "Is pleasure good?" he asked and commented that this question is always significant because pleasure, like anything else, may or may not be good. Because no property or set of properties is always or necessarily good, none of them can define the meaning of *good*. Goodness is property *superadded* to other properties because it does not follow logically or necessarily from them. Moore called the identification of goodness with some other natural property, such as pleasure or strength, the NATURALISTIC FALLACY. Goodness, he claimed, is a *nonnatural* property.

As a utilitarian, Moore differs from previous utilitarians in rejecting HEDONISM. He is called an idealistic utilitarian because he spoke of IDEALS such as beauty as being intrinsically good (*see* INTRINSIC VALUE) or as being the ends of human life (*see* ENDS/MEANS). Although Moore did not think that the meaning of the term *good* could be analyzed, he held that the meaning of the term *RIGHT* could be analyzed or defined in terms of what is good. Indeed, he defined the right ACT as the act that maximizes goodness. Like other utilitarians, he thought that everyone has an OBLIGATION to produce the greatest amount of good or the greatest balance of good over HARM that is possible. Moore differed from earlier utilitarians in his OBJECTIVISM, holding that both goodness and rightness are objective properties. He did not think that intended (*see* INTENTION) or anticipated consequences determined the rightness or wrongness (*see* WRONG) of actions because these are merely subjective beliefs (*see* SUBJECTIVISM). Acts are right or wrong, he claimed, according to their actual consequences (*see* CONSEQUENTIALISM), whether or not intended or foreseen.

MORAL

When used as a noun, an ethical lesson (*see* ETHICS) or theme embodied in a literary or dramatic work or derived from a lived experience.

The term *moral* in the sense of *moral of the story* describes the core ingredient of the MORALITY PLAYS of the middle ages. Although such plays are no longer in fashion, we often use stories in MORAL EDUCATION both formally and informally. In addition, many novels, television shows, and motion pictures use plot and character to illustrate a moral teaching. For example, the principal theme of the popular movie *Jurassic Park* concerned the need for bioengineers to consider the moral ramifications of their work. The moral of the story is "Be cautious when you tamper with nature." In the Bible, the parable of the good Samaritan is specifically used by Jesus to preach a message of compassion. Ancient Greek tragedies such as *Oedipus Rex* were often concerned with illustrating the horrific consequences of arrogance and pride.

The concept of moral education through moral stories is interesting to ethicists because it appeals to a means of communicating moral VALUES other than learning a set of RULES. Although the moral of the story may reflect a moral rule such as "Do not lie," it teaches this rule by illustrating what we ought to do when faced with a difficult situation. Many ethicists feel that teaching through stories is the best way to shape MORAL SENTIMENT. Situational ethics (*see* SITUATION ETHICS), for example, advocates a picture of MORALITY as based on concrete social situations. These situations can be represented in moral stories. Along with this shift from rules to situation is a shift from CODE to story as the principal mode of moral instruction. Other moral philosophers argue that stories alone cannot provide the coherent moral vision necessary for responsible action (*see* RESPONSIBILITY).

MORAL AGENCY   To be capable of moral action (*see* ACT).

An agent is someone who acts. A moral agent is a person who performs a moral (*see* MORALITY) or immoral (*see* IMMORALITY) action. When we speak of moral agency, we are speaking of the capacity to act morally or immorally. RATIONALITY is generally agreed upon as a criteria. Human beings can be moral agents, while animals cannot. Animals may have the right to be treated ethically (*see* ANIMAL RIGHTS), but we do not hold them morally accountable (*see* ACCOUNTABILITY) for their actions. Among human beings, those who are deemed incompetent (*see* COMPETENCY) are usually not considered moral agents. Such people do have moral status in the COMMUNITY and deserve moral treatment but are not held morally responsible (*see* RESPONSIBILITY) for all actions. Philosophers differ on some aspects of the characteristics of moral agency. For example, some hold that an individual must reach a certain age to be considered a true moral agent. Others hold that we can be held morally responsible for certain decisions at a young age, while not for others.

MORAL CODE   *See* CODE.

MORAL COMPASS   A person's general sense of RIGHT and WRONG.

A compass is an instrument that allows people to find their bearings, information that is especially useful if they do not know where they are. It also allows them to keep their bearings in unfamiliar situations. A moral compass is one's ethical sense of direction (*see* ETHICS). The idea of a moral compass is closely related to the idea of a CONSCIENCE. To lose your moral compass is to no longer know what is right or wrong, not just in a particular case, but in all. For example, in times of war the warlike environment may be so foreign from anything the soldiers have experienced before that they may lose their moral compass and perform actions that they would not do otherwise, even actions beyond self-defense or defense of country.

MORAL CONCEPT   The idea that stands behind our use of a moral term.

A moral concept is that to which moral terms refer. For example, when we use the term *good*, we are referring to something that is named by that term or a moral concept. We mean to name an existing entity that is *goodness* and to which the description *good* applies.

Some thinkers hold that moral concepts are really existing entities, independent of our ability to think about them or know them. For these thinkers, the term *good* names a concept that exists outside of our idea of the good and outside of cultural agreement about the good (*see* OBJECTIVISM). Others discuss moral concepts as simply the ideas behind the moral language we use to describe those ideas. For these thinkers, the term *good* refers to the idea of *goodness* but that idea may be determined subjectively (*see* SUBJECTIVISM) or culturally (*see* RELATIVISM).

MORAL CONFLICT   A clash of principles (*see* PRINCIPLE), either within a single person or between groups of people.

A moral conflict arises when an individual is torn between more than one course of action (*see* ACT) or when two or more groups DESIRE different, incompatible courses of action. Moral conflicts are related to moral dilemmas (*see* DILEMMA) but are different in that a dilemma is a choice between two courses of action, whereas a moral conflict may involve a choice between multiple courses of action. A moral dilemma is a form of moral conflict, but not all moral conflicts are moral dilemmas.

Individuals may experience at least two different forms of moral conflict. First, an individual may feel conflict between a moral principle (*see* MORALITY) and an immoral (*see* IMMORALITY) or nonmoral principle. For example, suppose we are asked to lie for a friend. We may feel conflicted between our sense of loyalty to that friend and our desire to tell the truth. Both loyalty and truthfulness are morally valuable, but lying is generally held to be wrong. These tensions generate moral conflict.

Second, an individual may feel moral conflict when there is no clearly RIGHT course of action or when faced with more than one right course of action. Suppose that two family members were both in need of a loan for equally good reasons, but you could only help one. A moral conflict arises as you decide which family member to assist.

Moral conflicts arise between groups of people when they desire incompatible courses of action. In the controversy surrounding abortion, for instance, one group argues vehemently for the right of a fetus to exist while the opposition argues equally vehemently for the ultimate right of women to control their own bodies. Deeply held principles on both sides have contributed to a moral conflict that has escalated to instances of MORAL OUTRAGE.

MORAL COUNSELING   The practice of giving advice in moral matters.

Moral counseling often comes into play when someone faces a moral DILEMMA. For instance, a person may have to choose between participating in an immoral war or violating a deeply felt patriotic duty. In such cases, people may seek out others who are able to clarify the problem, point out aspects that might have been overlooked, or offer advice as to which alternatives are best or morally RIGHT.

There is no CONSENSUS on who is able to offer moral counseling. For religious people, priests, teachers, rabbis, or other religious figures are usually considered sources of moral insight. The Roman Catholic institution of confession, for example, is a ritualistic type of moral counseling in which the sinner is able to both confess SIN and seek advice on how to avoid sin in the future. Parents, friends, and mates are often relied on as sources of moral advice for both religious and nonreligious people. Persons in need of moral counseling may seek out a role model or MORAL EXEMPLAR. Moral counseling may also be given when it is not sought, as when a parent observes a child playing a game unfairly and explains to the child why such behavior is wrong.

Moral counseling requires sensitivity to the needs of the person experiencing a moral problem. In some cases, those who seek moral counseling are seeking COMPASSION and insight rather than to receive instructions on what to do or how to behave. Not only the giving of advice but also listening and understanding are required in effective moral counseling.

MORAL DEVELOPMENT The course or stages during which individuals mature in their perceptions of themselves and the manner in which they judge others (*see* JUDGMENT).

According to a number of psychological theories, children and even adults pass through certain stages of moral development, although theories differ over the number of such stages and the characteristics of each. Eric Erikson, for example, in his theory of personality, speaks of various character traits that are developed by proper nurturing—for example, trust, AUTONOMY, initiative, industry, BENEVOLENCE, and INTEGRITY. He mentions mistrust, SHAME, GUILT, inferiority, and isolation as some of the characteristics of improper development.

According to the Swiss psychologist Jean PIAGET, children pass through two stages of moral development. In the first of these, children up to about age seven judge their own actions and the actions of others according to consequences (*see* CONSEQUENTIALISM), as these actions meet with approval or disapproval. They learn, for example, that it is wrong or bad to break things, but they do not distinguish between intentional and unintentional harm. In the second stage, when children mature, they begin to judge actions by motives (*see* MOTIVE) or intentions and not simply by results. They might recognize, at this stage, that someone did something wrong, but they might also point out that they did not mean to do it. Thus, adolescents are often more concerned about whether an act was done accidentally or on purpose than about whether the act had good or bad consequences.

Lawrence KOHLBERG's theory of moral development distinguishes six separate stages, although these stages are also classified under three more general categories: the preconventional, the conventional, and the postconventional. The first two stages, included in the

preconventional category, are characterized by reaction to AUTHORITY and EGOISM; the second two, in the conventional category, are characterized by a need for recognition and a respect for moral RULES; the last two stages, in the postconventional category, by an understanding of the social benefit of LAW and an understanding and application of absolute (*see* ABSOLUTES) ethical principles (*see* PRINCIPLE), such as JUSTICE and EQUALITY.

Kohlberg's preconventional level corresponds roughly to Piaget's first level. *Right* is understood as following orders that are sanctioned by punishments (*see* PUNISHMENT) and rewards. Although children at this stage are aware of the interests of others, their primary motivation is SELF-INTEREST. At the conventional level, *RIGHT* means conforming to the rules of society or the rules of some organization or group, such as a religious organization or political party. At this stage, individuals are motivated by social approval and LOYALTY to other people or groups. Egoism is modified by a consideration of the wishes and needs of the larger group. At the postconventional stage, individuals are not only aware of what the rules of society require but also of the reasons for the rules or laws: namely, justice and human WELFARE. People who reach this level of moral development are able to criticize the rules of society on the basis of human rights and to perceive contradictions in rules. At the highest level, they are motivated by a DESIRE to make a contribution to society by, among other things, attempting to change rules and institutions.

Other psychologists have criticized Kohlberg's theory of moral development. Carol GILLIGAN, one of Kohlberg's critics, observed that his studies were based mainly on questions asked of males about hypothetical dilemmas. She observed that Kohlberg's theory produced quite different results than a theory based on interviews with females facing real life dilemmas. The latter theory is characterized not so much by the application of RIGHTS, rules, and principles but by an attempt to preserve relationships. Gilligan claims that concern about rights and IMPARTIALITY predominate in men, while concerns about responsibilities (*see* RESPONSIBILITY) based on affective ties predominate in women; both models of moral reasoning (*see* REASON), however, are found in both sexes.

Theories of moral development are, in a sense, both descriptive and normative. They are descriptive in the sense that the stages are based on an examination of the opinions and reasons offered by individuals at different ages in response to tests designed to confirm or refute the theorist's hypotheses. However, if accepted as true, a theory of moral development might be used to judge individuals in an attempt to determine whether they are morally mature.

MORAL DILEMMA   *See* DILEMMA.

MORAL DISCOURSE   *See* DISCOURSE ETHICS.

MORAL EDUCATION   Formal or informal teaching of moral principles and behaviors; also referred to as character education.

Moral education concerns the various ways in which we learn about ETHICS and ethical behavior. Moral education may be formal, as in the moral lessons we learn in our homes, through civic groups such as Boy Scouts or Girl Scouts, or through a religious organization. Moral education also occurs informally, as in the lessons we learn from observing other people's behavior, from watching movies and television, and from our daily experiences with others.

In its formal sense, moral education is concerned with systematic instruction in moral VALUES. Parents, for example, may try to teach children not to steal by consistently correcting children whenever they try to take something that is not theirs. It is important that moral education be consistent in order for values to be learned. Churches and other religious organizations are also dedicated to moral education.

Here moral education may take the form of the study of religious texts or of learning the stories of MORAL SAINTS or MORAL EXEMPLARS.

A highly controversial point in moral education is what role, if any, the public schools should assume. Some argue that because all children are in school until age sixteen that this is the best place for moral education to take place. Proponents of this argument feel that this is the only way to ensure moral education for children who may not receive any formal moral instruction elsewhere. Opponents to this view argue, however, that moral education is the RESPONSIBILITY of the family and that the public school is neither the appropriate place nor is it properly equipped to teach moral issues. They agree that it is a problem that many children do not receive moral education at home, but they disagree that the solution is to take time away from the school curriculum to teach moral principles at school. Many also argue that there is no way to agree on which moral principles to teach at school and that in order to preserve each family's right to educate their children morally, moral issues have little, if any, place in public school curriculum.

One reason the issue of moral education in school is pressing is that moral education also occurs informally in all of our daily interactions. Whether we refer to it as moral education or not, our values are shaped as we watch how people treat one another and how they regard themselves. Thus, some argue that not teaching moral principles in school is itself a kind of teaching. They also argue that not teaching moral principles in school ignores the informal moral education that is always taking place.

Informal moral education also takes place through interactions with friends. The influence of one's companions is a reason why so many parents are concerned about the friends their children make and also why adults are concerned about each other's friends. Television programs and movies teach moral lessons by showing certain forms of life as attractive, profitable, or glamorous. This has spawned additional moral controversy about the types of programming that should be available to be viewed by children. Many feel, for example, that programs that glorify violence should not be shown during prime viewing hours or in shows such as cartoons that are particularly appealing to young children. The movie industry has responded to consumer concerns by adopting a rating system that indicates when material in movies may not be suitable for viewing by young children or by teenagers. Many record labels are following suit, acknowledging that music is another strong factor in informal moral education.

MORAL EXCELLENCE   *See* EXCELLENCE.

MORAL EXEMPLAR   A moral example to others.

A moral exemplar is a person who possesses moral EXCELLENCE. Such a person may show great COURAGE, extraordinary CHARITY, FAIRNESS, or COMPASSION and may make great personal sacrifices (*see* SACRIFICE) in order to help others.

Some ethical theories (*see* ETHICS) hold that MORALITY is learned not by following RULES, or not by following rules alone but instead by following the example or inspiration of a moral exemplar. Examples of morally praiseworthy aspects of people's lives, those actions that go well beyond the ordinary demands of morality, are considered helpful in teaching about morally proper behavior. In VIRTUE ETHICS, for example, moral education depends on developing a good character, and emulating a moral exemplar is one of the surest ways to do this.

A MORAL SAINT is a moral exemplar. However, a moral exemplar may also differ from a moral saint, who always or almost always does what is morally RIGHT. Moral exemplars may be ordinary, even morally bad in some ways, but morally commendable in other ways. For example there are a number of cases of people who are excellent public officials but commit adultery. In this case we might follow their example

in civic virtues but not in sexual ethics. Oskar Schindler was a German industrialist who saved thousands of Jews from the Holocaust and yet had what many people take to be moral flaws. So it is only appropriate to think of him as a moral exemplar in terms of some aspects of his life and not others.

MORAL FIBER   Moral CHARACTER, especially GOOD character.

Persons are said to be of strong moral fiber when they manifest a virtuous disposition (*see* VIRTUE). In particular, moral fiber is constituted by FORTITUDE, one of the CARDINAL VIRTUES. A person demonstrates moral fiber by resisting TEMPTATION or by sticking to principles in a difficult situation. For example, people who risk their jobs in order to support a just but unpopular policy could be said to have strong moral fiber. On the other hand, if a person was susceptible to gossip, rumor, and innuendo we might say that person displays weak moral fiber.

MORAL GOODNESS   *See* GOOD.

MORAL GUIDEPOST   *See* MORAL COMPASS.

MORAL HABITS   *See* HABITS.

MORAL IMPERATIVE   An ethical command (*see* ETHICS) or directive.

An imperative is a command, such as "Shut the door." A moral imperative is an ethical command, such as "Tell the truth," or "Do not steal." In the Kantian sense (*see* KANT, IMMANUEL), a moral imperative is a moral LAW that must be followed by the necessity of logic (*see* CATEGORICAL IMPERATIVE). For example, Kant held that the imperative "Tell the truth" was binding on all people who follow reason.

Ethicists who subscribe to prescriptivism hold that all moral commitments can be expressed as either the giving or following of moral imperatives. Difference in MORAL OPINION is expressed in giving different moral imperatives, while inconsistency is indicated by giving contradicting moral imperatives.

Religious ethicists hold that moral imperatives come from GOD. The TEN COMMANDMENTS, for example, are a set of moral imperatives.

MORAL INTUITION   *See* INTUITION.

MORAL JUDGMENT   *See* JUDGMENT.

MORAL LUCK   A situation in which luck makes a moral difference.

The idea of luck is akin to that of fortune. We say we are lucky when something GOOD happens to us that we are not responsible for (*see* RESPONSIBILITY). For example, finding a stray animal that turns out to be a loyal pet may be lucky—both for the finder and for the pet. On the other hand, we may say we are unlucky in situations where something bad occurs even though we have worked hard and planned well. If you prepared a research paper and not only lost the computer disk on which you saved it but experienced a hard-drive crash as well, we would say that you had been unlucky.

Moral luck describes a situation where luck has moral importance. This importance may derive from a personal characteristic, for instance, native intelligence, or it may derive from a set of unforeseen circumstances, as when a careless action turns out to have a highly beneficial outcome. Moral luck poses a problem for many philosophers. Apparently, chance often makes a difference in moral situations. Moral luck may affect the situations for which we are held morally accountable (*see* ACCOUNTABILITY). It may also affect the regard or esteem others give us. Yet, if ethical worth is meant to be determined by effort, INTENTION, or WILL, moral luck seems to disrupt the order of things.

How can we deal with the role of luck in affecting success and HAPPINESS? In his book *Moral Luck,* Bernard Williams argues that morality is affected by luck and that realizing this must force us to rethink morality altogether. If moral success is sometimes affected by luck, then we cannot see MORALITY as ultimately rational (*see* RATIONALITY) or absolute (*see* ABSOLUTES). Even moral JUSTIFICATION, Williams argues, is often a matter of luck with respect to the consequences or success of the events in question. Williams argues that the traditional conceptions of morality as offered by ARISTOTLE and Immanuel KANT as well as by utilitarians (*see* UTILITARIANISM) should be replaced with a notion of *the ethical,* which puts less emphasis on RULES and more emphasis on the activities and projects that people pursue.

In response to Williams, Thomas Nagel defines *moral luck* as situations in which we treat people as objects of moral respect, even when what they do depends on factors beyond their control. Conversely, we may hold them in low moral regard based on actions or circumstances beyond their control. The idea that people may be praised or blamed for actions they did not control seems to be at odds with our traditional notions of morality. Thus, for Nagel the problem of moral luck is the contradiction between the notion that luck should not play a role in morality and the observation that it often does.

Nagel identifies four types of moral luck: constitutive luck, the luck involved in having a certain character traits like patience or intelligence; circumstantial luck, the luck involved in what kinds of problems arise in one's life; causal luck, the luck involved in what environmental influence shape a person (*see* FREEDOM); and resultant luck, the extent to which luck is involved in the success or failure of one's efforts. Nagel senses a deep paradox in the idea of morality. Luck should not, but does, affect moral decisions, outcomes, and judgments (*see* JUDGMENT).

In response to the problems outlined by Williams and Nagel, philosophers have attempted to provide a variety of arguments. This first is to argue that while luck does occur in morality, there is nothing wrong with this.

They place the emphasis on the development of character and our ability to face our circumstances. The second is to argue that while luck may seem to play a role in morality, in fact it does not. They argue that while luck may affect what others think of us or the difficulties we face, it does not affect our true moral standing.

MORAL MAJORITY   Conservative Christian activist group founded in the United States by Rev. Jerry Falwell.

The Moral Majority was founded in 1979 to organize conservative Christians politically so that they could effectively support laws (*see* LAW) that upheld fundamentalist VALUES, such as opposition to ABORTION, HOMOSEXUALITY, PORNOGRAPHY, and the EQUAL RIGHTS AMENDMENT (*see* FUNDAMENTALISM). The Moral Majority also fought for allowing prayer in public schools, teaching creationism (*see* EVOLUTION), and increasing military spending and preparedness. In 1986 the Moral Majority became the Liberty Federation. However, the term *moral majority* still persists as a label for any group of people holding conservative moral values.

MORAL OPINION   An appraisal rooted in MORALITY.

A moral opinion is a view concerning a particular ethical problem or situation (*see* ETHICS). The strength of moral opinions may vary. Some people use the term *moral opinion* to suggest RELATIVISM. A person might claim, for instance, that in her opinion abortion is wrong but that people should decide this issue for themselves. This position might be said to differ from the conviction that abortion is wrong not just for the person who holds that conviction but for all people. Others use the term *moral opinion* to mean a belief (*see* FAITH). This usage may indicate a more firmly held moral COMMITMENT. The statement "In my opinion, capital punishment should be abolished" indicates that person's belief that capital punishment is wrong for him or her and for others as well. In this case,

the person offering the opinion is usually willing to support that opinion with further JUSTIFICATION. Positions that can be completely justified or that seem SELF-EVIDENT are usually discussed in terms of moral knowledge, not moral opinion.

MORAL OUTRAGE   The passionate and usually widespread response to an ACT of exceptional IMMORALITY.

Moral outrage is distinguished by its severity and an intensity from reaction to a commonplace immoral behavior. Important to the notion of outrage is the concept of proportion. To spend five years in jail for petty theft seems excessive; to be executed for such a CRIME is morally outrageous. Moral outrage may channel itself into vehement ethical discussion (*see* ETHICS), as well as civil protests and social, political, and judicial changes, as in the CIVIL RIGHTS movement, or it may in turn engender further immoral action. For instance, many considered the beating of Rodney King by the members of the Los Angeles Police Department in 1991 a moral outrage. People were outraged by the VIOLENCE against King in conjunction with the lack of JUSTIFICATION for such violence. The officers were acquitted of wrongdoing in 1992 in spite of the fact that a bystander had recorded the beating on video. This verdict fueled further community outrage, which led to five days of rioting. While the original verdict in the King case was a moral outrage, the riots that resulted from this moral outrage were also considered immoral.

MORAL PERFECTIONISM   The position that MORALITY consists in perfecting one's CHARACTER, abilities, talents, and conduct.

Moral perfectionists believe that there is a regulative ideal (*see* IDEALS) guiding us to be the best people we can possibly be. Morality consists in striving in every action (*see* ACT) to attain that ideal. Moral perfectionists understand that absolute (*see* ABSOLUTES) perfection is unattainable, but that does not diminish the demand that we strive to become as perfect as possible. Thus, moral perfectionists focus on issues of their own characters. They are not primarily interested in the consequences of their actions (*see* CONSEQUENTIALISM), except in so far as their actions lead to an improvement in their own characters. They are far less interested in judging (*see* JUDGMENT) other people's moral actions than in examining and improving their own actions. They are not strictly speaking deontologists (*see* DEONTOLOGY) either, as they put a great deal of emphasis on developing GOOD judgment rather than on following RULES.

Moral perfectionists differ in what they hold the moral ideal for a person to be. The Stoics (*see* STOICISM) held that moral perfection consisted in achieving the proper balance of reason over emotion. Other moral perfectionists attempt to model their lives on a MORAL EXEMPLAR. This may be a person who is held to be morally wise (*see* WISDOM), such as SOCRATES; a person who is held to be of special religious VIRTUE, such as a MORAL SAINT; or a religious leader, such as JESUS or MUHAMMAD. Some moral perfectionists are intuitionists (*see* INTUITION) who believe that we intuit the good and then model our lives upon it. Moral perfectionists may also be mystics (*see* MYSTICISM) who believe that the good is revealed (*see* REVELATION) to them through a mystical relationship with the divine. *See also* VIRTUE ETHICS.

MORAL PRINCIPLE   *See* PRINCIPLE.

MORAL PSYCHOLOGY   The study of the human mind and behavior as related to RIGHT and WRONG action (*see* ACT).

Moral psychology is the branch of ETHICS that seeks to understand, from the point of view of human psychology, those appetites, passions (*see* PASSIONS AND EMOTIONS), and drives that affect our moral JUDGMENT and behavior. This study includes an investigation of CHARACTER, choice, emotion, WILL, and perhaps most importantly the criteria for MORAL AGENCY. A better understanding of the ways in which our environment does or does not determine our behavior can sharpen our conceptions of moral ACCOUNTABILITY and RESPONSIBILITY. For example, some moral psychologists will argue for leniency in cases where individuals who have committed wrongdoing have been subjected to prolonged abuse. They argue that these individuals are not morally responsible for their action in the same way as an individual who has not suffered such abuse. This suggestion raises ethical controversy concerning moral responsibility, FAIRNESS, and JUSTICE. Other moral psychologists argue that while environmental factors are strongly influential concerning moral actions, people are still able to make morally free choices (*see* FREEDOM) excepting the most extreme of circumstances.

Moral psychology may also pursue questions of MORAL DEVELOPMENT. In this area, moral psychologists study how humans mature morally and whether different races, sexes, or classes of people follow different paths of moral development. *See also* GILLIGAN, CAROL; KOHLBERG, LAWRENCE; PIAGET, JEAN.

MORAL PURPOSE   *See* TELEOLOGY.

MORAL REALISM   In METAETHICS, a position committed to moral OBJECTIVITY.

Moral realism argues that there are really existing moral facts and properties independent of people's MORAL OPINIONS or beliefs. Thus, it is contrasted to many forms of RELATIVISM, which holds that MORALITY consists in personal or cultural views about what is RIGHT or WRONG, and to NIHILISM, which holds that there are no moral facts. Moral realism also stands in contrast to SUBJECTIVISM, which holds that morality resides in attitudes, beliefs or emotions. There are several varieties or moral realists. Some hold that morality is grounded in HUMAN NATURE. Others may hold that the reality behind morality is divine. The common theme, however, is the realists' claim that morality is based on some objective and existing fact or entity and not in human subjectivity.

MORAL RESPONSIBILITY Answerability or ACCOUNTABILITY for actions (*see* ACT).

The word *responsible* (*see* RESPONSIBILITY) has several different but related meanings. In one sense, to be responsible for an act means simply to have performed that act. In this sense, to ask "Who is responsible?" means "Who did it?" However, people are said to be morally responsible only if they are free in making moral choices (*see* FREEDOM), know what they are doing, and are competent (*see* COMPETENCY) to distinguish RIGHT from WRONG. Thus, a person who did something under physical threat or something whose consequences (*see* CONSEQUENTIALISM) cold not be foreseen would not normally be held morally responsible. But when persons are held responsible for their actions, they're subject to praise or blame, PUNISHMENT or reward. If they feel responsible, they may feel happy or proud (*see* PRIDE) for being GOOD or may feel SHAME or remorse for doing EVIL.

People are also said to be responsible for actions that they have a duty or OBLIGATION to perform. Every competent person under normal circumstances has duties not to do certain kinds of things: the duty not to kill, for example, or the duty not to steal. But most people also have positive duties to do certain kinds of things according to their roles or positions in life. Hence, they are said to be responsible for doing these things. Firefighters are responsible for extinguishing fires, and parents are responsible for raising children. If they do not do these things as they should, they are subject to blame or censure. If they do them well, they are deserving of praise or commendation. In this sense, some responsibilities are held by all people by virtue of membership in society, while other responsibilities can be assigned to different people, as in a division of labor, where people have different jobs to do.

Being responsible may also mean being answerable or accountable to somebody—to some AUTHORITY who has the RIGHT to review actions or behavior. Employees, for instance, are responsible to employers; members of a congress are answerable to their constituents, the voters; all citizens are answerable to the LAW. In this sense, people may not only have responsibilities or jobs to do, but they may also be held responsible for doing those jobs by having to answer for or give an account of their behavior. The enforcement of RULES is one way of holding persons responsible for what they do. They may be held responsible not only by punishment and reward but by being asked to explain their behavior or give a reason for it.

Persons may also accept responsibility by taking a job that needs to be done, as when no one else will do it or by helping someone who is overburdened with responsibilities. Thus, accepting responsibility may mean doing one's share. Accepting responsibility for action may also mean admitting that one performed an action and not attempting to blame others for one's mistakes or failures. The root words in *responsible* mean being willing or able to respond. This may mean not only a willingness to help others but also a willingness to cooperate with them in doing what needs to be done. It means being answerable to them in the literal sense of giving explanations or reasons for one's behavior or in discussing reasons with them. In this sense being responsible relies on our ability to REASON. Responsibility also means being responsive in acting on errors or on others' concerns. This may entail not only listening and discussing but also being ready to take whatever steps necessary to solve problems that may arise.

MORAL SACRIFICE *See* SACRIFICE.

MORAL SAINT A person who always chooses to perform actions (*see* ACT) that are as morally GOOD as possible.

A moral saint is someone who deserves elaborate praise because of extraordinary moral CHARACTER and behavior. When it is easy to do good, many people will. What distinguishes a moral saint from everyone else is that a moral saint does good even when doing so is difficult or seemingly impossible. Mother Theresa, for example, was considered by many to be a moral saint.

A moral saint may be different from a religious saint, a term that applies to a person who shows piety as well as moral rectitude. A moral saint is also different from a MORAL EXEMPLAR; to be a moral saint, a person must lead a completely, or nearly completely, good life. A moral exemplar may be morally good in some exemplary way while leading an ordinary life, morally speaking, in other ways.

Some thinkers believe that the idea of a moral saint should be held as a regulative ideal (see IDEALS). This means that moral sainthood is a standard that is never fully attained but one that should inspire and guide moral actions.

MORAL SENSE THEORY   An ethical theory (see ETHICS) that claims that our moral judgments (see JUDGMENT) arise from a specific sense or faculty.

The moral sense theory holds that humans possess a sense, to be distinguished from REASON, that governs MORALITY. It is related to senses such as sight or hearing in that it is a part of the makeup of most people. Moral sense theory relies on the idea of moral perception, which might be likened to our ability to perceive beauty. When we observe an action, our moral perception allows us to detect the GOOD, just as our sight allows us to detect beauty. Like sight, the moral sense can be trained.

Moral sense theory is attributed to the eighteenth-century English philosophers Francis Hutcheson and David HUME; Hutcheson is considered to be the founder of moral sense theory. The theory arose largely in response to the writings of Thomas HOBBES, who tried to reduce all morality and government to SELF-INTEREST. Hutcheson attempted to demonstrate that morality and self-interest are not the same. Although it is true that emotions such as benevolence give us pleasure, it does not follow that we are benevolent only in order to get pleasure for ourselves. Further, Hutcheson held that Hobbes's view of humans as essentially selfish does not account for how we can express moral approval for enemies or for people who do not directly affect our lives.

Moral sense theory is also opposed to the rationalist school (see RATIONALITY), which claimed that we determine what is RIGHT by means of reason. Hutcheson argued that reason does not motivate us to ACT; rather, he held that our goals are determined by our passions: We want something and then use reason only to figure out how to get it. Our passions, which Hutcheson called "exciting reasons," motivate us to act. In contrast, "justifying reasons" consist in our moral approval or disapproval. Justifying reasons have their home in a distinct moral sense, hence "moral sense theory." Finally, moral sense theory also stands in disagreement with UTILITARIANISM, which sees morality as the path to maximizing goodness.

Moral sense theory heavily influenced the moral philosophies of Hume, Adam SMITH, and Joseph BUTLER.

MORAL SENTIMENT   A JUDGMENT or opinion regarding MORALITY, based on feeling or INTUITION as opposed to REASON.

Theories of moral sentiment hold that we make moral judgments based on the feelings or sentiments aroused in us when confronting a moral issue. For example, we may privilege our family and friends in our moral decision making because of our kinship to them. David HUME is generally acknowledged to have put forth the first modern theory of moral sentiment.

Contemporary theories of moral sentiment acknowledge that we tend to give highest moral recognition to those entities that are most like us or to which we can best relate. Thus, moral sentiment tends to be most strongly aroused by members of one's own family or social group, by other human beings, by mammals, and to a lesser extent by other animals and plants. This acknowledgment has given rise to an emphasis on narrative or storytelling as a form of MORAL EDUCATION because through narrative we are able to identify sympathetically with a wide range of persons and situations.

MORAL VICTORY   Keeping to one's principles (*see* PRINCIPLE) in the face of adversity, even if one suffers material loss.

A victory is usually considered to be a "win" or the overcoming of an opponent. The opponent may be a physical challenge such as disease or another person or group of persons in an adversarial situation. A moral victory is a situation in which we adhere to our moral principles even when the situation seems unfair, when we are outmatched, or when the opponent is amoral or immoral (*see* AMORALITY; IMMORALITY). Suppose that a high school wrestling team is competing against a team that is believed to use steroids. There may be some temptation for "clean" team members to use steroids in order to compete. However, if they refrain and compete to the best of their ability, we call this a moral victory, regardless of whether they win or lose the match.

MORALITY   Beliefs (*see* FAITH) and practices (*see* PRACTICE) related to the notion of RIGHT conduct or GOOD CHARACTER.

Most philosophers make some sort of distinction between morality and ETHICS, although the difference can be subtle and difficult to disentangle. One popular distinction defines *morality* as a set of principles (*see* PRINCIPLE) of right conduct, while *ethics* is defined as the study of moral judgments (*see* JUDGMENT). On this conception, a person may have a morality but have no interest in ethics. For example, one's morality would be a more-or-less coherent set of codes, such as "Do not lie" or "Help others whenever possible." Ethics, on the other hand, would be inquiry into why those moral principles are valid and whether or not they are binding to everyone. In everyday language, however, the concepts of *morality* and *ethics* are often used interchangeably.

At the heart of any conception of morality are notions of right conduct. Most moralities also include notions of VIRTUE, the good life, or HAPPINESS. To have morality or to be moral is to have some sense that certain actions (*see* ACT) are better than others or that certain kinds of people are more virtuous than others. Similarly, most moralities have a notion of a well lived or desirable life.

Morality is a broad concept covering many differing, and sometimes conflicting, belief systems. Eastern morality, for example, is very different than Western morality. Within a culture there may be a unified morality, or what is more likely, the culture may exist in a state of moral PLURALISM. Small, preliterate tribes often exhibit an extremely unified vision of what is right and WRONG. In contrast, industrialized nations are usually morally pluralistic with persons and groups with quite divergent moralities coexisting under one LAW.

Philosophers have long sought a proper definition of morality without reaching agreement. The ancient Greeks, for example, typically conceived of morality in terms of harmonious character. The Judeo-Christian moral tradition casts morality in terms of OBEDIENCE to GOD's commandments. Thomas HOBBES, an influential English philosopher, argued that morality was based on a SOCIAL CONTRACT designed for self-protection. David HUME countered that morality consisted in emotional approval, or MORAL SENTIMENT, of people or actions. Immanuel KANT, one of the most influential moral thinkers of all time, defined *morality* in terms of RULES ascertained by REASON, stressing the importance of willing what is right. Utilitarians (*see* UTILITARIANISM) in turn defined *morality* as that which contributes to the greatest social good, thus viewing it as teleological (*see* TELEOLOGY) or as a means to an end (*see* ENDS/MEANS). Existentialist philosophers (*see* EXISTENTIALISM) offered an alternative vision of morality as FREEDOM or self-creation.

Along with problems attending the proper definition of *morality* come challenges regarding the desirability of morality. Why be moral? In a famous passage from PLATO's *The Republic,* Glaucon argues in opposition to SOCRATES that justice is only worthwhile if it produces social approval; only a fool would be just if he or she could get away with being unjust. Socrates, Plato, and ARISTOTLE argue that morality consists in virtue and that virtue is mainly or completely its own reward. Others argue that we should be moral because we have been commanded to do so or because it is rational (*see* RATIONALITY). Still others maintain that morality is a means to the end of happiness. Friedrich NIETZSCHE offered a famous refutation of traditional morality, arguing that the dominant European morality was a "slave morality," a morality created by the weak to make themselves seem superior, because of their ability to bear suffering, to the strong.

One of the biggest areas of contention in ethics concerns the status of moral claims. Are moral claims valid for everyone for all times? Are they valid in some cultures only in certain times? Is morality a private matter for each individual to determine? What are we to say when two or more people, groups, or societies disagree about what is right? Absolutists (*see* ABSOLUTES) and deontologists (*see* DEONTOLOGY) hold that moral rules are universal and apply to all people in all times. Another dominant tradition in ethics considers any moral disagreement to be a factual dispute—that is, only one sort of action can be right; hence, when disagreement about the nature of right action occurs, someone must be mistaken in the facts. RELATIVISM holds that all versions of what is

right are equally (*see* EQUALITY) acceptable. On this view, what is right for one person may not be right for another, and each person's MORAL OPINION is sovereign for that person. Pluralists hold that there are multiple morally right positions but that not all moral positions are right.

MORALITY PLAYS   Popular dramas from the Middle Ages, in which VIRTUES or other abstractions were the principal characters.

The original MORALITY plays, as their name suggests, aimed at illustrating a MORAL, or lesson. They descended from the medieval mystery plays, which in turn developed out of the Christian liturgy, or church service. Common themes included the CARDINAL SINS and the fall from innocence into SIN. The dramas were usually performed by professional troupes that would travel from town to town. The most famous morality play is *The Summoning of Everyman,* a fifteenth-century English work that dramatizes the Christian's need to face death and judgment.

Although morality plays originally dealt with a narrow range of religious topics, their structure and themes grew more complex over the years. Their influence can be seen in the works of such notable playwrights as Christopher Marlowe and William Shakespeare. In contemporary society, morality plays often take the form of made-for-television movies, sitcoms, and cartoons. As in their medieval ancestors, these stories usually feature two-dimensional characters—an honest banker, a lonely widow, an angry alcoholic, and so forth—and an important moral lesson, such as "It never pays to lie," which is revealed through the plot. Moral controversy has surrounded children's television programming in the United States, which often mixes elements of morality plays with a glorification of violence in programming aimed at children or aired during prime viewing hours.

MORALLY NEUTRAL   To be devoid of moral VALUE; AMORALITY.

When something is morally neutral, it is neither GOOD nor bad in and of itself, although it may be used for good or bad purposes by others. For example, some people argue that guns are morally bad because they can only be used violently. However, others argue that guns have no moral status in and of themselves; instead, guns may be used for moral purposes, such as to protect a life, or for immoral purposes, such as to take a life without justification. In either case, proponents of the second argument hold that motives (*see* MOTIVE) and actions (*see* ACT) of the persons in question have moral value but that the gun itself has no moral value or is morally neutral.

MORALS   Principles of right conduct.

Typically, morals are beliefs or attitudes about ethical behavior (*see* ETHICS). They define our duties (*see* OBLIGATION) toward ourselves and others in a civil society. For many, they also define their duties in a religious COMMUNITY. Taken together they comprise a moral CODE, which dictates correct behavior. When we speak of our own MORALITY or that of another person, we are speaking of what is held to be morally RIGHT and WRONG.

Philosophers differ in their views concerning how we acquire morals. Some believe we are born with innate moral faculties. Others believe that morals are the logical outcome of sound reasoning (*see* REASON) about human relationships. Some religious thinkers believe that moral LAW is given to us by divine commandment and that our morals reflect our ability to follow that law. Still others hold that our morals are simply behaviors that facilitate our survival. Finally, it is commonly held that morals are learned through observing the behavior of others around us (*see* MORAL EDUCATION.)

A similar but distinct use of the concept, *morals* refers to a person's actual behavior rather than to his or her beliefs. To say of people that they have "loose morals," for instance, sometimes means that they break moral norms regarding sexual conduct, honesty, or loyalty, regardless of whether they believe in or try unsuccessfully to obey those norms—that is, people may be said to have loose morals even though they hold beliefs that do not allow for loose conduct.

It is important to recognize that morals may conflict with one another (*see* MORAL CONFLICT). The moral principle of loyalty, for example, may come into conflict with that of honesty. If this happens people then have to privilege one moral principle over another, creating a type of hierarchy of morals. Many moral thinkers believe that this hierarchy should be consistent (*see* CONSISTENCY) and unchanging. Others allow that the privilege of morals will change over time and due to social circumstances (*see* RELATIVISM).

Another important aspect of the concept of morals is the way in which it allows for gradations. A person may have strict morals or loose morals, high morals or low morals. The distinctions usually involve the extent to which moral rules are considered to be absolute (*see* ABSOLUTES). Someone who believes that it is never permissible to lie, for example, might be termed a person of high morals. In contrast, someone who believes that an occasional lie is justifiable may be considered to have lower morals. A third person who believes that lying is morally wrong only when it causes direct and severe harm to another may also be said to have low morals. Although these are common uses of the terms *high morals* and *low morals,* it should be noted that these judgments really originate from a deontological position (*see* DEONTOLOGY) in which moral RULES are considered primary. Whether the morals in each case are in fact low or high depends on the extent to which exceptions are allowed for the general principle "Do not lie." A utilitarian (*see* UTILITARIANISM), for instance, may argue that it is wrong *not* to lie if that lie will produce the greatest amount of HAPPINESS for the greatest number of people. On the utilitarian view, this lie would not be a sign of low morals but of correct moral action.

MOTIVATION   *See* MOTIVE.

MOTIVE   Something that causes a person to ACT.

Motives are those desires (*see* DESIRE), emotions (*see* PASSIONS AND EMOTIONS) or acts of WILL that cause actions. Moral thinkers are concerned with motives because they are concerned to understand why people perform the actions they do and also how people can best be motivated to perform GOOD actions. Moral theories hold various beliefs (*see* FAITH) about what motives are appropriate to ethical action (*see* ETHICS): hedonists (*see* HEDONISM) hold that pleasure and the avoidance of pain motivates behavior, while egoists (*see* EGOISM) maintain that ethical behavior is motivated by SELF-INTEREST. Many religious philosophies hold that actions should be motivated by LOVE or OBEDIENCE to divine LAW.

Ethical theories also differ in the importance they assign to motives in assessing the worth of moral actions. Ethical theories based on CHARACTER, such as VIRTUE ETHICS, assign a significant role to the motive behind actions. Thus, a person who happens to perform an action with a good outcome is not virtuous (*see* VIRTUE). However, a person who is striving for moral EXCELLENCE and succeeds is virtuous. Deontological ethics (*see* DEONTOLOGY) also place great emphasis on the motive for ethical action. For example, Immanuel KANT held that motive was all important in determining the value of action and that all actions must be willed to be in accordance with the moral law.

Consequentialist theories such as UTILITARIANISM, by contrast, are concerned only with the outcomes of actions and not the motivations for performing them. For example, suppose a person is running down the sidewalk and happens to knock someone out of the way inadvertently saving that person from a falling tree limb. Consequentialist theories would hold this to be a good act as it has produced good consequences, even though the motives of the agent may have been impatience and rudeness. Deontological- or virtue-ethics theories would not assign this action moral virtue as it motivation was selfish and showed a disregard for the other person, although the consequences in this case were fortunate.

MUHAMMAD (570–632 A.D.)   Considered the greatest of all Islamic prophets (see ISLAMIC ETHICS).

In 610 A.D. Muhammad had a vision from Allah (*see* GOD) that directed him to become a prophet. This was the first REVELATION of many to come to Muhammad up until his death in 632, and the collected revelations constitute the text of the QUR'AN. Muhammad's teaching that there is only one God, in contrast to the Arabic tradition (*see* CUSTOMS) of polytheism, brought censure upon him. Muhammad and a small group of followers left their home town of Mecca for Medina, where they organized a Muslim COMMUNITY. Muslims today regard Muhammad as the Perfect Man, the archetype of humanity, and they attempt to follow the example of his life. It is also widely held that Muhammad will serve as an advocate for them on JUDGMENT Day when they meet God.

MULTICULTURALISM   The belief that society should celebrate and support the racial and ethnic backgrounds of all its members, including their languages, CUSTOMS, and IDEALS.

Multiculturalism raises many questions for ethicists about what is fair and just in a world of many cultures. It arose in response to what was perceived by many to be the failure of society in general, and the education system in particular, to cater adequately to increasingly diverse needs. In the United States, for example, although more than 25 percent of all school children are from minority backgrounds, school curriculum is often still focused almost exclusively on the English language and white American history and culture. Many people believe that by effectively ignoring the contributions and achievements of minority cultures, this focus has a detrimental effect on the motivation and self-esteem of minority students. Further-more, it is argued that the failure of the school system to teach an inclusive curriculum rein-forces racist and discriminatory stereotypes among children from nonminority backgrounds (*see* RACISM; DISCRIMINATION). Finally, support-ers of multiculturalism argue that there are many positive benefits to a vibrant climate of diverse beliefs where ideas can combine and cross fertil-ize, stimulating innovation and creativity.

Opponents of multiculturalism see the pol-icy as divisive and counterproductive. They believe that multiculturalism has the effect of reinforcing minority cultures, thereby "ghet-toizing" minorities into uncooperative cultural enclaves. Furthermore, many also believe that immigrants in particular have an OBLIGATION to assimilate successfully into the dominant culture of their adopted country, especially because this is supposed to make it easier for them to be pro-ductive, cooperative members of society. *See also* IMMIGRATION.

MURDER   To kill another human being intentionally.

Murder is arguably the most serious and irreversible HARM that one human being can inflict on another, and as a result, it is techni-cally prohibited in all known societies. Despite this, there are a remarkable number of exemp-tions to the PROHIBITION, and this makes the issue a surprisingly complex one for ethicists.

Least controversially, self-defense is widely seen as an acceptable justification for killing another human being. Similarly, killing an enemy in wartime is also widely seen as permissible, although this attitude is slowly changing (*see* PACIFISM). More controversially, many people believe that killing criminals is a PERMISSIBLE ACT, particularly those criminals who are themselves guilty of murder (*see* CAPITAL PUNISHMENT; *LEX TALIONIS*). Others believe that killing is justifiable to end suffering, as in SUICIDE or EUTHANASIA.

Finally, many societies have historically permitted INFANTICIDE (the killing of young children), par-ticularly where the child is severely disabled or the parents cannot afford to care for it.

Other problems arise for ethicists when defining what is actually a human being for the purposes of the prohibition. For example, peo-ple disagree about whether a FETUS is a human being and, therefore, whether it is possible to describe ABORTION as a form of murder. Simi-larly, many disagree on whether individuals who are suffering from BRAIN DEATH or from an apparently irreversible coma can any longer be said to be human beings, and therefore they further disagree on whether turning off their life support is a form of murder.

MYSTICISM   The belief that knowledge can be acquired through a spiritual access to the divine.

Mystics believe that through spiritual con-templation or through ecstasies, select people can achieve moral knowledge that is not acces-sible by sense perception, reason, or ordinary thought. Mysticism is usually associated with a religious tradition—there are elements of mysti-cism in BUDDHIST ETHICS, CHRISTIAN ETHICS, HINDU ETHICS, ISLAMIC ETHICS, and JEWISH ETHICS.

Some thinkers hold that mystical experi-ences are gifts from GOD and are not subject to the control of the mystic. Others hold that mys-tical experiences can be achieved through a spe-cial discipline including prayer, fasting, and meditation. Most mystics claim that the knowl-edge achieved in a mystical experience cannot be communicated fully in language. To com-municate mystical experiences, thinkers often rely on stories and metaphor. In this way they attempt to suggest the TRUTH that is revealed (*see* REVELATION) in their mystical experiences, although they do not claim to be able fully to describe it.

NARCISSISM Excessive preoccupation with or LOVE of oneself.

The term *narcissism* comes from the myth of Narcissus. Narcissus was a handsome young man who fell in love with his own image as he saw it reflected in a pool of water. Narcissus would admire himself for hours. One day Narcissus saw his reflection in a pool of water that was near to a precipice. As he bent to kiss his own reflection, he fell into the pool and drowned. Narcissism, thus, denotes self-love or SELF-INTEREST beyond what is healthy and leads to self-destructive behaviors.

Narcissism bears on MORALITY because narcissistic individuals are often unable to relate in a respectful way to other people or to the environment. Narcissism is characterized by extreme SELFISHNESS. Because narcissistic people are completely absorbed in self, they cannot treat others as ends in themselves or as people with projects and needs that may have comparative value to their own.

NATIONALISM Pride in one's own nation, often manifested as a chauvinistic belief in that nation's inherent superiority.

Although national pride is not in and of itself a bad thing, experience tells us that nationalistic sentiments often lead to intolerance, RACISM, and MILITARISM arguably because, by emphasizing the achievements and culture of our nation, we may implicitly denigrate others. For example, the refrain "land of the free, and home of the brave" may be interpreted by some to imply that other countries are both less free and less brave, although there is no evidence for this one way or another. Furthermore, if one is convinced of the superiority of one's own nation, it seems logical that other countries should also benefit from these advantages—by military conquest if necessary.

The intolerance that nationalism can create is evidenced most clearly in the FASCISM of German and Italian politicians during World War II. This nationalism provided the JUSTIFICATION for expansionist military campaigns, as well as the genocide of minority groups (*see* HOLOCAUST).

When assessing nationalism, it is important not to fall into the trap of ETHNOCENTRISM. Before we criticize as a threat nationalist sentiments expressed by foreign leaders and crowds, it pays to acknowledge that fervent nationalism is also common in *our own* country, as evidenced by the average political convention or campaign speech. If we perceive the nationalist sentiments of others to be a threat to us, then it is highly likely that others will see our nationalism as a threat to them.

NATURAL LAW Sometimes called the law of nature, the rules that are equally binding on all humans by virtue of their nature as human beings.

The idea of a natural law can be traced back at least as far as ancient Greek philosophy. The stoics (*see* STOICISM) believed that there were universal laws of action (*see* ACT) that affected all human beings and were inherent to the world itself. In CHRISTIAN ETHICS, natural law is used to explain how each of GOD's rational creatures can know his will without depending on REVELATION.

Thomas AQUINAS was one of the most famous natural-law philosophers. The key concept is that the law is something that stands apart from human beings as a part of the natural order of the universe, and MORALITY is a matter of following the law. In contemporary moral thought, those who appeal to natural law usually do not invoke a religious dimension; instead, they argue that there are certain conditions, such as FREEDOM, that are necessary in order for human beings to live well. Later theories, like earlier versions of natural-law theory, hold that the natural law is universal and binding on all people, irrespective of differing desires or preferences.

NATURAL RIGHTS   A subcategory of HUMAN RIGHTS, thought to be fundamental because they are based on NATURAL LAW.

If one accepts that central moral principles (*see* PRINCIPLE) can be justified by reference to natural processes, then it may also follow that these principles imply the existence of a set of fundamental RIGHTS. For example, as human beings are obviously endowed with the abilities of reason and autonomy, one might conclude that people, therefore, have a right to exercise these endowments freely. Hence, a natural-law view of MORALITY seems to imply rights such as a right to freedom of conscience and speech as well as a right to freedom from arbitrary arrest and torture.

Historically, the idea of natural rights was developed by various proponents of LIBERALISM from the seventeenth century onward, who tended to emphasize concepts such as INDIVIDUALISM, private PROPERTY, and EQUALITY. This focus, however, has been at the expense of a number of concepts central to non-Western views of morality, such as environmental stewardship and COMMUNITY. As a result, the idea of natural rights has fallen into disfavor, and many now see it as unnecessarily ethnocentric (*see* ETHNOCENTRISM). Instead, many now believe that natural rights are a fiction, neither more nor less fundamental than any other human right, such as the right to adequate health care and a decent education.

NATURALISTIC ETHICS   Ethical theories that hold that moral VALUES arise from natural facts about the world and human nature.

Moral positions that derive value from some natural property in the world or in human beings are described as naturalistic. In naturalistic ethics, the fact that something *is* the case implies that it *ought* to be the case (*see* IS/OUGHT DISTINCTION). There are a variety of types of naturalistic ethics. One rather rudimentary type is SOCIAL DARWINISM, which holds that the principle of the survival of the fittest should apply to human as well as to nonhuman communities.

Other naturalistic ETHICS base moral worth on standards such as sickness and health. Friedrich NIETZSCHE is often described as a naturalist philosopher in this sense. Nietzsche looked to instances of sickness and health, strength and weakness, and narrowness or creativity to describe what was morally worthy and what was decadent.

Finally, naturalistic ethics deny supernatural explanations for ethical value. They maintain that ethics, like other natural phenomenon, can be investigated and understood empirically (*see* EMPIRICAL KNOWLEDGE).

NATURALISTIC FALLACY   The PRACTICE of identifying an ethical concept (*see* ETHICS) with a natural one.

The naturalistic fallacy was described by G. E. MOORE in his work *Principia Ethica* (1903). Moore argues that it is unsound to equate the natural with the GOOD. For example, consider the argument: "It is morally acceptable to kill animals for food because other mammals kill for food and people are mammals." The PRINCIPLE of the naturalistic fallacy contends that it is WRONG to equate the natural ACT of animals killing for food with a morally acceptable act. While killing animals may or may not be morally acceptable, it requires JUSTIFICATION beyond the fact that other animals, or even our ancestors, have done so. Moore also accused

UTILITARIANISM of committing the naturalistic fallacy by equating pleasure or happiness with the good, but this accusation is controversial.

It should be noted that although the term *naturalistic fallacy* is widely used in informal logic, there are those who hold that natural properties are good (*see* NATURALISTIC ETHICS) and would, therefore, not consider the naturalistic fallacy to be a FALLACY at all. *See also* FACT/VALUE DISTINCTION.

NAZISM A German social and political movement in the twentieth century that was based upon authoritarianism, RACISM, NATIONALISM, and MILITARISM.

That National Socialist party, from which the word *Nazism* was coined, gained ascendancy after Germany's defeat in World War I. Nazism is most closely associated with Adolf Hitler, the German leader who attempted to subjugate all nations and races to Nazi rule. The Nazis advocated the systematic oppression or elimination of the "racially impure."

The Nazis held that DEMOCRACY and LIBERALISM were weak and ineffectual forms of government, for they gave AUTHORITY to those who did not understand it. Accordingly, Hitler established a dictatorship with himself as *Fuhrer,* or leader. Nazism's most notorious tenet is its blatant racism. The so-called Aryan races of northern Europe were said to be intellectually, culturally, and physically superior to all others. Hitler embarked upon an aggressive campaign to rid the world of the weak, particularly the Jewish people, whom he viewed as a genetically inferior race bent on taking over Europe.

Along with Nazism's racism went its strident nationalism. To the Nazis, Germany was the locus of Aryan racial superiority and, hence, had both the destiny and the responsibility to appropriate or destroy what inferior races possessed. Last, Nazism was a militaristic movement. Not only was Germany famous for its hostile and ruthless attacks on other nations, but those within the Nazi party were prone to inflict violence on one another. The final appeal of the Nazis was always to fear and POWER.

Most contemporary ethical discussions of Nazism concern neo-Nazism, a loose collection of factions and parties sympathetic to Hitler's principles. Contemporary debate concerns what sort of protection the law, especially free-speech laws such as the First Amendment (*see* BILL OF RIGHTS), allows for race or hate speech. According to many critics, the original Nazi party was able to gain power precisely because the opponents of Nazism did not act swiftly and aggressively enough. Neo-Nazi movements thus challenge the balance between freedom of speech and the FREEDOM and DIGNITY of those groups targeted by neo-Nazi IDEOLOGY.

NEGATIVE/POSITIVE OBLIGATIONS The distinction between the duty not to do something (negative OBLIGATION), and the duty to perform an action (positive OBLIGATION).

Obligations may require us not to ACT in certain ways or to act in certain ways. Obligations that require us not to act are termed *negative.* These may include obligations like "Do not murder," or "Do no unneccesary harm." Notice that neither of these obligations directs people to any positive action. "Do no unnecessary harm" does not direct us to be helpful, only not to be harmful. Negative obligations are particularly characteristic of minimalist ETHICS (*see* MAXIMAL VS. MINIMAL ETHICS).

Obligations that direct us to perform certain actions are termed *positive.* These obligations may include actively caring (*see* CARE) for children or family members, telling the TRUTH, or aiding those in need. Positive obligations are characteristic of maximalist ethics.

NEGLIGENCE Careless or inadvertent behavior that causes HARM or damage where that harm or damage could have been avoided by a reasonable person taking reasonable precautions.

Negligence is a problem for many ethicists because a person who causes harm through negligence seems to lack an INTENTION to commit the harm—the so-called guilty mind (*see* MENS REA) that is important to many ethical systems. Negligence is not necessarily the same as pure accident, however, because it is possible to argue that a negligent person does in fact make a decision that could potentially have put others at risk, even if the exact nature of the risk isn't necessarily clear.

Ethicists sometimes distinguish between advertent negligence, also known as recklessness, and inadvertent negligence, or simply negligence. Recklessness, in this case, occurs when someone is aware that his or her actions could result in harm but chooses to take that risk regardless. For example, a worker digging a hole might go off to lunch without covering the hole, assuming that the chance of someone falling in is small. Here, the worker is knowingly putting the public at risk, even though he or she was not purposely trying to injure others. In these cases, few have a problem with holding such a person accountable.

Inadvertent negligence, on the other hand, refers to any incident where damage or harm is caused accidentally, although a reasonable person in the same circumstances would have foreseen the possibility of harm and taken appropriate steps to avoid it. For example, a worker who displays warning signs but no barrier around a hole he or she is digging might be found negligent if someone who was blind fell into the hole. In this case, the worker has not allowed for the possibility that a person with poor sight might walk by, although one might argue that any reasonable person should be aware of such a possibility.

With inadvertent negligence, it seems that the primary determinant of blameworthiness is whether someone, through his or her actions, can be said to have assumed a responsibility for the safety of others. In these cases, many argue that ignorance is no excuse because we expect people who undertake potentially hazardous tasks to assume some responsibility for ensuring that their behavior is both safe and responsible.

NEW TESTAMENT *See* BIBLE.

NIETZSCHE, FRIEDRICH (1884–1990) German philosopher and philologist who was the most influential nineteenth-century critic of MORALITY and religion.

Nietzsche was influenced by the ancient Greek and Roman civilizations, which celebrated aristocratic VALUES. He was critical of modern Western civilization because he believed that it placed more value on slavish or slavelike characteristics (*see* SLAVERY) than on POWER and strength. Thus, he called for a "transvaluation of values." This call required a critical reappraisal of the values we currently hold. Nietzsche attacked Judaism (*see* JEWISH ETHICS) and Christianity (*see* CHRISTIAN ETHICS) for upholding HUMILITY, poverty, and kindness as IDEALS. He believed that these characteristics were really a disguised form of resentment adopted by people who did not believe they were strong enough to ACT as they truly wished to act. Rather than value any type of meekness, Nietzsche celebrated PRIDE, strength, creativity, talent, and EXCELLENCE. By proposing a transvaluation of values, Nietzsche challenged readers to value what they would truly value if they had no fear of other people. He set out to turn values upside down, so to speak, maintaining that strength is better than weakness, health better than sickness, wealth better than poverty, and beauty better than ugliness.

Nietzsche's ideal is of the healthy human being, in both body and mind, who has the COURAGE to say "yes" to life and to act according to his or her own WILL. Nietzsche believed that most people look for someone else to follow, and he dubbed the masses as "the herd." Nietzsche criticized the herd for being lazy and timid, for conforming to the opinions of others instead of expressing their own ideas, and for being resentful. By contrast, Nietzsche praised artists who had the courage to be original and who set their own styles instead of copying the work of others. He characterized his ideal in the image of the Overman (*Übermensch*), who rises above the weaknesses of the modern character and gives a singular, original style to his life. Nietzsche's interpretation of our motives (*see* MOTIVE) for moral action is central to his critique of modern moral thought. Nietzsche believed that human beings have a tendency to withdraw from or avoid the challenges in life and then to rationalize their behavior or to disguise their faults by trying to make vices (*see* VICE) appear virtuous. For example, people who do not have the courage or ambition to accomplish things themselves may preach the virtues of meekness and poverty, or they may become resentful of those who are accomplished and criticize them. Such reasoning often takes the form of "sour grapes": "I could have done that, but I didn't want to," or "It isn't right to be interested in or pursue fame or glory for oneself."

Healthy individuals, in Nietzsche's view, do not follow the opinions of others but go their own way doing what they will. They are not concerned for the approval of others. Healthy people are not overly concerned with pleasure or comfort, although they do not shun them. They are prepared to SACRIFICE and suffer for their ideals when necessary, but sacrifice and suffering are not valued in and of themselves, as they are in many moral philosophies. Moreover, healthy individuals are not concerned for the consequences of their actions but rather concentrate on the quality of their acts: whether or not they are living up to their own standards of moral excellence. In this sense Nietzsche espouses a type of MORAL PERFECTIONISM, although the "virtues" that comprise his ideal are far different from those of most VIRTUE ETHICS.

Nietzsche's ideas have had an impact on a number of fields of study in the twentieth century, including art, literature, politics, religion, and psychology. Sigmund FREUD, for example,

acknowledges his indebtedness to Nietzsche's analysis of human motivation. Nietzsche's belief that we redirect our anger at ourselves when we fear to express it to others who are stronger than we are influenced Freud's understanding of the concept of guilt and SHAME.

NIHILISM   The belief that nothing holds any VALUE.

Nihilism is the attitude that there exists no ground for moral TRUTH and that all VALUES are illusory. Nihilists have no positive belief set and hold that life has no meaning or purpose. Nihilists often view the conditions around them to be so flawed that it would be better to destroy them than to have them exist in their present state, even though they have no positive or constructive course of action to offer. Thus, nihilists are often viewed as dangerous because they will tear down what is valuable to others without offering anything to replace those values. Nihilists evinced either a lack of regard for anything destroyed or the belief that anything that could withstand destructive forces would emerge stronger and, therefore, better. Friedrich NIETZSCHE, in whose philosophy nihilism plays an important role, argued that nihilism was characteristic of the cultural crisis he observed in the late nineteenth century.

Historically, nihilism is often associated with a philosophical movement in Russia during the nineteenth century. In this sense nihilism is associated with materialism, or the belief that anything that cannot be proven to exist by science does not in fact exist. It was also associated with the belief that society necessarily breeds hypocrisy and a separation of human beings from their true natures. This use of nihilism was popularized in Ivan Turgenev's novel *Fathers and Sons*. The character Ivan in Fyodor Dostoyevsky's *The Brothers Karamazov* is another famous nihilist character of that era.

Nihilism is sometimes incorrectly used to indicate that someone does not hold a particular religious belief. In some cases, it has been used interchangeably with ATHEISM. This use is misleading and fails to capture the real cynicism and despair of nihilism. It is possible to be an atheist but to, nonetheless, have a deep sense of moral value. Nihilism is not the lack of belief in a particular set of moral values but the denial that any moral value exists at all. Nihilism is also sometimes confused with RELATIVISM, or the belief that each person makes or chooses his own values. By contrast, the nihilist holds that any values we enjoy are only so enjoyed if we are able to forget the underlying meaninglessness of our existence.

NIRVANA According to Buddhism, the extinction of all distortions in the mind that keep humans from seeing reality as it truly is; Ultimate Reality.

Nirvana is not GOD, in part because it is entirely devoid of qualities or characteristics, including such anthropomorphic or humanlike qualities as PERSONHOOD. For most Buddhists, nirvana is the opposite of SAMSARA, the "Wheel of Becoming," that is, ordinary human existence, dominated as it is by suffering in all its inescapable forms: birth, illness, rejection, confusion, loss, and death (*see* DEATH AND DYING).

For other Buddhists, nirvana and samsara represent one and the same reality; the only difference lies in perspective or perception. The person caught in samsara sees things as having substantive reality (*see* MAYA) and is attached to them; therefore, he or she experiences confusion and suffering. The one freed from samsara is ultimately devoid of self-being and is attached to nothing; therefore, he or she is free from suffering and confusion. It should be noted that Buddhism distinguishes between pain and suffering. Pain is inherent in the human condition by right of our physical body. Suffering is a psychological condition we bring ourselves because of faulty thinking, attitudes, and perspectives.

The PSYCHOSPIRITUAL DISCIPLINE of Buddhism, which always includes a high standard of MORALITY, leads to the elimination of the mental distortions and barriers that cause human suffering and bondage, thereby giving rise to experiencing or living in the state of nirvana.

For some Buddhists, nirvana occurs only after death, when the fully realized one leaves forever the samsaric cycle and becomes one with the Ultimate—in Buddhism commonly characterized as Void or Emptiness, indicating that it is without limitation. For other Buddhists, nirvana can be realized while alive and even maintained through subsequent lifetimes, as one voluntarily assumes rebirth in the samsaric cycle in order to help suffering beings find release. The latter is known as a *bodhisattva*. *See also* BUDDHIST ETHICS; EIGHTFOLD PATH; FOUR NOBLE TRUTHS; KARUNA; PRAJNA.

NONMALEFICENCE The principle that persons should do no HARM.

Nonmaleficence is often considered to be one of the first principles of ETHICS, as well as a basic moral duty (*see* OBLIGATION). In MEDICAL ETHICS, for example, the principle "First of all, do not harm" is derived from the HIPPOCRATIC OATH, a set of rules drawn up by the ancient Greek physician HIPPOCRATES. It is also stated as a first principle in the moral philosophy of Thomas AQUINAS.

The principle of nonmaleficence can be distinguished from the principle of BENEFICENCE, which bids persons to do good, because it is possible to not harm others even when not doing them any positive good (*see* MAXIMAL VS. MINIMAL ETHICS).

The principle of nonmaleficence tells us that we should not harm anyone either physically or mentally. Emotional distress as a result of teasing or ridiculing, for example, counts as an instance of harm. People may also be harmed by being restricted in their actions or by being denied opportunities. A number of moral RULES appear to be derived from the nonmaleficence principle. The rule "Do not kill" tells us to avoid a specific kind of harm, as does the rule "Do not steal" or the rule "Do not discriminate," by denying others' rights or opportunities.

The nonmaleficence principle is usually interpreted to mean that people should not harm one another intentionally (*see* INTENTION), allowing that people may not be responsible for causing accidental harm. By being careless, however, people may put others at risk of injury, and this may also be considered a violation of the principle of nonmaleficence. A person who drives recklessly, for instance, endangers the lives of other people even if there is no intention of doing harm.

Of course, people cannot always avoid harming one another, if only accidentally, so there is a question about when or under what conditions harm is justified. In fact, people deliberately harm others in a number of ways, for example, in war, in self-defense, and in competitive activities such as sports and business. These types of harm, even though deliberate, are often thought to be justified. In a theory like UTILITARIANISM, harm is thought to be justified by a greater GOOD or benefit. The harm caused by an act may then be regarded as a SACRIFICE that is needed to bring about a greater good. In other theories, such as Thomism, harm may be justified if it is an unintended side effect of a good that is intended (*see* DOUBLE EFFECT). In cases of self-defense, a person would be justified in harming another if the harm were secondary to the primary purpose of defending oneself. In this view, one might justifiably kill in self-defense, but it should never be one's intention to kill. Rather, one should strive to use the minimal necessary force to defend oneself. Shooting an intruder might be justified if one believed one's life to be in danger. But shooting an intruder if there was another way of subduing the intruder or shooting the intruder in the back as he or she flees the house would not be justified.

The principle of nonmaleficence is often interpreted to mean that we should not do harm to others, thinking that it is morally permitted to harm oneself; that is, people sometimes think that substance abuse is morally permitted because no one else is being harmed. Suicide is often justified on the same grounds. Traditionally, however, the nonmaleficence principle has been thought to apply universally to everyone, including oneself. In this view, deliberately harming oneself is just as wrong as harming another. Indeed, it is because one's own life and welfare are important that self-defense can be justified. *See also* JAIN ETHICS.

NONVIOLENCE   The principle that one should never resort to VIOLENCE under any circumstance and that LOVE and COMPASSION are necessary for achieving positive social change.

The principle of nonviolence has been present in various philosophies throughout the centuries, including early Christianity, as well as various Indian philosophies, most notably Jainism *see* JAIN ETHICS, where the principle is known as *ahimsa* (literally "nonhurt"). Today, however, the most well-known figures in nonviolence are twentieth century HUMAN RIGHTS activists, including U.S. CIVIL RIGHTS leader Martin Luther KING, Jr., Tibetan spiritual leader the Dalai Lama, and most notably Indian independence leader Mohandas Karamchand GANDHI.

Nonviolence is fundamentally based in the principle that all human life is sacred and should be respected and in a belief that violence and hatred can only lead to more violence and hatred. True practitioners of nonviolence completely forswear all violence against others, even in self-defense, preferring instead to reflect compassion and love back at their tormentors. They believe that although violence can force people to change their behavior in the short term, in the long term only compassion and love can truly transform an opponent into a convert and friend.

It is important to note that nonviolence does not imply passivity. In fact, nonviolence arguably *requires* a personal response to injustice and OPPRESSION. Nonviolent action usually involves both attempts at moral persuasion, as well as various forms of CIVIL DISOBEDIENCE, including boycotts, labor strikes, demonstrations, and noncooperation with AUTHORITY. *See also* PACIFISM.

NORM   The accepted standard of behavior in a particular group or society.

A norm refers to a behavior or attitude that we have come to expect in a given society. As a general rule, norms are not written laws or expectations but rather are understood on the basis of social interaction. For example, it is not a law that one must eat with silverware, and not all food requires silverware, but it is a social norm to use silverware, particularly when eating with others. Norms reflect what has come to be appropriate behavior in society.

Ethical norms (*see* ETHICS) refer to those ethical practices (*see* PRACTICE) and beliefs (*see* FAITH) that are predominant in a society. Most societies will contain a variety of norms, and not all norms will be upheld by all members of a society. Although there may be some overlap between them, ethical norms are understood to be less binding than moral norms (*see* MORALS). Additionally, ethical norms are more likely than moral laws to change over time. For example, to commit a murder is to violate more than an ethical norm against killing, but to transgress a moral and legal injunction not to kill. However,

abstinence from sexual relationships before marriage, once a widely held social norm in many cultures and in some cultures a moral law, is now less widely held.

NORMATIVE RIGHTS   *See* RIGHTS.

NORMATIVE ETHICS   The branch of ETHICS that attempts to determine what actions (*see* ACT) are RIGHT, how we can have knowledge of right actions, and what motivates us to act morally (*see* MORALS).

Normative ethics seeks to establish what we ought to do, why we ought to do it, and how we can know what we ought to do. Normative ethical positions may be either consequentialist (*see* CONSEQUENTIALISM) or deontological (*see* DEONTOLOGY). Consequentialists claim that ethical norms (*see* NORM) should be established based on actions that produce the most desirable outcomes. Deontologists, on the other hand, claim that ethical norms should be established based on the MOTIVE or CHARACTER of an ethical action, or on the VIRTUE of the moral RULE that governs the action.

Normative claims in ethics are evaluative: they detail what we ought to do. Normative claims are sometimes contrasted to descriptive claims, which describe how people behave. *See also* IS/OUGHT DISTINCTION.

O

OBEDIENCE   The ACT of following a RULE or command from an AUTHORITY. This authority may be understood to be either secular (*see* SECULAR ETHICS) or divine.

Obedience to rules or authorities is often thought to be morally justified (*see* JUSTIFICATION), even required. However, the moral significance of obedience varies from context to context, particularly with respect to secular authority. The obedience of a soldier to a captain, for instance, may be moral or immoral, depending on circumstances. If the captain orders the soldier to murder civilians as an act of revenge, we may judge that the soldier is morally justified in disobeying the command. Generally speaking, the point of having rules or authorities is to bring about obedience, structure, order, or conformity. If a rule of driving states that we should stop for stop signs, then we are expected to obey in order to fulfill our obligations as a motorist and to prevent the harm that the rule is designed to prevent. Problems arise concerning the justification of rules and whether or when rules have exceptions.

OBJECTIVISM   The ethical position that moral truths (*see* TRUTH) and responsibilities (*see* RESPONSIBILITY) have reality and standing independent of human subjectivity (*see* SUBJECTIVISM) or opinion.

Objectivist ETHICS holds that there are existing moral obligations (*see* OBLIGATION) and that these obligations apply to all persons. Thus, objectivists are opposed to relativists (*see* RELATIVISM), who claim that MORALITY is dependent on cultural context or personal opinion, and to

skeptics (*see* SKEPTICISM), who argue that we have no way to know moral truths if they exist.

A central problem in objectivism is demonstrating that moral truths are in fact objective.

OBJECTIVITY   The position that TRUTH is independent from the observer.

The concept of objectivity suggests that there are truths that exist independent of human beings and their passions (*see* PASSIONS AND EMOTIONS), desires (*see* DESIRE), wishes, or beliefs (*see* FAITH). Truth is, thus, held to be separate from any individual's opinion of the truth. An individual's beliefs might match up to the objective truth, in which case the belief would be correct, or it might deviate from the objective truth and, thus, be incorrect or false.

Philosophers disagree as to whether there is objective truth or whether truth is completely dependent on human interpretation. Even among those who agree that objective truth exists, there is disagreement as to whether human faculties can access objective truth or whether our perceptions are always distorted by our senses.

In common language, objectivity is often used to describe a position that is fair (*see* FAIRNESS) or disinterested. An objective view of the situation, in this sense, would be one in which the viewer is not importing his or her own preferences or beliefs. Science often puts forward claims to objectivity in this sense; this notion, too, is controversial. Those who contest an objective standpoint hold that we are never able to offer a truly objective opinion or achieve real objectivity because all of our interpretations of facts and situations are colored by our past experiences, our VALUES, and the very means by which we process information and form beliefs (*see* FACT/VALUE DISTINCTION).

OBLIGATION A duty or an ACT that a person is bound to do, or something people owe to themselves or others.

The words *obligation* and *duty* are usually used interchangeably. They are sometimes differentiated when the word *duty* is used to mean a type of action people are required to perform because of their position or station in life; for example, teachers may have a duty to tell the truth, at least as they understand it, to their students. By contrast, the word *obligation* is reserved for reference to particular acts that are required because they fall within a class of acts regarded as duties. Thus, one may be said to have an obligation not to lie on a particular occasion because of a general duty that binds us not to lie. However, a particular type of act required by duty may be an exception to the RULES and, hence, may not be an obligation. In these senses of the words, then, people are sometimes not obliged to do their duty.

In deontological ethics (*see* DEONTOLOGY), acts are classified as being obligatory or required, prohibited (*see* PROHIBITION) or forbidden, and permitted or not prohibited. An obligatory act, morally speaking, is an act people must do. A prohibited act is one they must not do. A permitted act (*see* PERMISSIBLE ACT) is one that a person may or may not choose to do. All obligatory acts are permitted, but not all permitted acts are obligatory. All obligatory acts are RIGHT, but not all right acts are obligatory. Purchasing a box of popcorn at the movies may be permitted, but it is not obligatory. Choosing to save that money for charity is a right act, but is also not obligatory. Buying a movie ticket to see the movie is both right and obligatory; that is, to sneak in the movie would be stealing, which is prohibited. Some acts that are right also have a special MERIT because they are "above and beyond" the call of duty (*see* SUPEREROGATION).

Risking one's life to save another person is not only right but is also heroic.

Moral judgments (*see* JUDGMENT) or arguments are usually about what is or is not an obligation or a duty or about what is or is not permitted, morally speaking. If someone says that you have an obligation to attend a wedding because the groom attended your wedding, you might argue in return that it would be a nice thing to do to attend the wedding but that you do not have an obligation to do so. You may not think that the groom's presence at your wedding is a good enough reason for attending his, or you may have a good reason for not attending. People are often said to have obligations because CUSTOMS, like that of exchanging favors, so dictate or because such an action is traditional. Thus, in everyday conversation *obligation* often means what is expected or "the done thing." Such reasoning refers to customs or ETIQUETTE. With the exception of relativists (*see* RELATIVISM), philosophers usually try to discover universal rules or principles (*see* PRINCIPLE) that apply more broadly to all cultures, societies, or groups in order to differentiate between custom and moral obligation.

OBSCENITY An exhibition or representation of a human being or of human VALUES without regard to a basic sense of human DIGNITY.

Obscenity refers to acts (*see* ACT) or images that put the human body on display in such a way as to devalue its worth. It is a difficult concept to define, as behaviors or images that some people find degrading are not viewed as degrading by other members of the same society. Obscenity usually concerns sexual representation but may also have GREED, GLUTTONY, or VIOLENCE as its subject.

The problem of determining a legal definition of *obscenity* that protects public sensibilities without infringing on FREEDOM of expression or artistic creativity has been a major challenge to Western legislative bodies in the twentieth century. The landmark U.S. Supreme Court case of

Miller v. California (1973) attempted to resolve some of this difficulty by giving communities (*see* COMMUNITY) greater control over determining what was obscene based on local standards, particularly in the case of material that might be considered pornographic (*see* PORNOGRAPHY).

The Supreme Court articulated the following standard for obscenity, sometimes called "The Miller Test:" (1) whether the average person, applying contemporary community standards, would find that the work, taken as a whole, appealed to the prurient interest; (2) whether the work depicts sexual conduct in a patently offensive way, as defined by the state LAW; and (3) whether the work, taken as a whole, lacks serious literary, artistic, political, or scientific value. This definition is far from absolute (*see* ABSOLUTES), as there is still debate, even within small communities, about what is patently offensive or who, if anyone, can be held to be the average person. However, it was the INTENTION of the Court to allow just such debates to occur and allow the issue of obscenity to be addressed at the local, rather than the national, level.

OFFENSIVE BEHAVIOR Actions (*see* ACT), including speech, that transgress social norms (*see* NORM) in such a way as to cause distaste, upset, or mild HARM but which generally fall short of OBSCENITY, VIOLENCE, or profanity.

Offensive behaviors range from mildly offputting to severely disturbing. When offenses are considered mild, they are addressed through social means, such as informal censure or disapproval. For example, parents may find their teenager's clothes offensive, particularly if they contain graphic images or language. While the parent may be upset or embarrassed by such clothing and may even attempt to forbid its wear, teenage wardrobe choices are not generally considered to be a deeply harmful issue. However, people who choose to expose their genitalia spontaneously in public places are considered not only to be offensive but also indecent. Thus, such

actions are on occasion not only for social disapproval but also for legal restriction.

The line between offensive behavior, which may be upsetting but must be tolerated (*see* TOLERANCE) in a free (*see* FREEDOM) society, and obscene or profane behavior is often difficult to define and is not necessarily constant among different people or in different social situations. Although we may believe it is impolite or even immoral (*see* IMMORALITY) to act offensively, such actions are often not, and often should not be, illegal. The United States Constitution, for example, does not guarantee us a RIGHT not to be offended, although the Supreme Court has determined that we have a right not to encounter obscene or profane material in public places or over public airways or to endure profane or abusive verbal assaults.

OPPRESSION The systematic domination of one social or political group by another group or groups.

All forms of oppression involve an inequality in POWER. Oppression occurs when one or more groups deny another group access to certain social, financial, or political goods. The oppression may be direct and violent (*see* VIOLENCE), as in a military dictatorship, or indirect, as in subtle but prejudicial (*see* PREJUDICE) racial attitudes (*see* RACISM). In most cases the oppressors believe (*see* FAITH) that the oppressed group is in some way inferior or undeserving of certain RIGHTS or privileges.

The most common forms of oppression are based on race, gender, age, nationality, religion, economic status, sexual preference, physical and mental ability, and physical appearance. One example of racial oppression is the treatment of African Americans in parts of the United States during the first half of the twentieth century. African Americans were considered second-class citizens and were denied many rights, such as voting and owning certain kinds of PROPERTY to which whites had access. An example of gender oppression, men in the

United States have traditionally received as much as 50 percent higher wages than women for comparable work.

There is some debate as to what constitutes oppression as opposed to behavior that may be prejudiced, rude, unsociable, or unfortunate (*see* MORAL LUCK). For example, if handicapped people are unable to enter public buildings, this may be seen as a type of oppression. However, would we say that the exclusion of handicapped people from certain types of elective activities because of their disabilities constitutes oppression? For example, should allowances be made so that handicapped athletes can compete in mainstream professional sporting leagues?

In cases of widespread, systematic oppression, we are left with the difficult task of determining who is responsible (*see* RESPONSIBILITY). For example, in the oppression of Native American, who is morally culpable? Some would argue that present generations cannot be held responsible for the oppression of past generations. Others argue that a society built by taking unfair advantage of the labor or goods of others must compensate those groups. For example, Americans may be obliged to return some or all of their land and wealth to Native Americans. Those who support AFFIRMATIVE ACTION contend that special consideration is due to those members of groups that have been oppressed until they gain equal (*see* EQUALITY) opportunity to obtain social goods.

ORGAN DONATION   The PRACTICE of consenting to have an organ or organs removed for transplant (*see* ORGAN TRANSPLANTS) into another person in need of that organ or organs.

It is possible to remove organs from one person and implant them into another for the purpose of replacing a defective organ in the recipient. Examples include blood, bone marrow, kidneys, the liver, parts of the eye, and heart. Blood, bone marrow, and kidneys can be donated while the donor is still living. The liver, parts of the eye, or the heart are donated only after the donor is declared dead or brain dead (*see* BRAIN DEATH).

Currently the donor must give permission prior to the removal of any organ or prior to their death for an organ to be harvested. If no information is available about the deceased's wishes, then family members may make that decision for them. Because more people exist who are in need of organ transplants than there are people who donate the needed organs, there is controversy surrounding the harvesting of organs. Many believe that it is too invasive to a corpse to remove organs without consent. Others feel that the COMMON GOOD outweighs the PRIVACY of the deceased and believe that unless someone has expressly forbidden the harvesting of organs after death, consent should be assumed.

ORGAN TRANSPLANTS   The removal of a functioning body part from one person or animal and its surgical placement in another person.

There are times when one or more of a person's organs will fail. The person will die unless replacement organs can be found. The discovery of immune suppressing drugs has allowed for the successful transplantation of organs from a person or animal into another person. Examples include the heart, lungs, kidneys, bone narrow, and liver. Although the patient will usually have to continue extensive medical care after a transplant, her or his life expectancy and quality of life will greatly improve.

Issues that currently surround organ transplants include the cost of the procedure, the relatively low availability of donor organs, and the determination of who is to receive these operations. The medical community has established criteria to place patients with greater medical need at the top of donor lists. With the high cost of the procedure, there is controversy surrounding a patient's ability to pay and whether patients who can afford the operation should have more ready access to organs than those who cannot. Some have suggested that the rationing of organs to the wealthy is already occurring. *See also* ORGAN DONATION.

ORTHODOXY   Adherence to an established doctrine, particularly a religious doctrine.

Conventions that are firmly established are called orthodox. An unorthodox belief (*see* FAITH) is one that is not widely held or is in opposition to convention. Orthodox refers to conformity to an established CODE, particularly a religious one. For example, Orthodox Jews adhere strictly to the TORAH and TALMUD and apply these principles to modern life.

OUTING   Revealing to the public a person's HOMOSEXUALITY.

Homosexuality is the sexual preference for persons of the same sex. Traditionally there has been widespread DISCRIMINATION and even VIOLENCE against homosexuals. Homosexuals have been refused housing and entrance into the military and are forbidden to marry legally. Homosexuals were one group targeted by Nazis (*see* NAZISM) during the HOLOCAUST. In some countries and in some states in the United States, homosexual activity is considered illegal. For these reasons, many have opted to keep their sexual preference hidden.

When a person chooses to announce his or her homosexuality publicly to relatives, friends, or the COMMUNITY at large, this is called coming out. Activist groups support events such as a National Coming Out Day to offer support for homosexuals who wish to make their LIFESTYLES known.

On occasion people who wish to keep the sexual preferences private (*see* PRIVACY) have been forcibly "outed," or announced publicly to be homosexual, by others. An outing may happen as a result of a detractor who hopes to HARM an individual by announcing that person's sexual preferences. On the other hand, outings are sometimes performed by homosexual activists who believe that it is important to the acceptance of homosexuality for the public to be aware of prominent homosexual public figures, regardless of whether those figures wish to be known as homosexual. Such activists justify (*see* JUSTIFICATION) this invasion of privacy by arguing that the public has a RIGHT to know and that any embarrassment caused to public figures is unimportant compared to the social GOOD that results from a wider acknowledgment of homosexual practices (*see* PRACTICE).

P

PACIFISM   *See* NONVIOLENCE.

PAIN   *See* HEDONISM.

PAIN MANAGEMENT   The control of
pain through any means including, but not limited to, medication, exercise, physical therapy,
meditation, or forms of alternative care such as
spinal adjustments or acupuncture. Pain management most often refers to relief of long-term
pain conditions such as arthritis or cancer rather
than the relief of episodic pain.

There are two main areas of ethical discussion with respect to pain management: the
abuse of pain-management techniques and the
adequate control of long-term pain. The abuse
of pain-management techniques can include the
use of addictive pain killers for their mood-
enhancing qualities and the use of pain killers to
excel beyond the limits of pain in athletics.
Mood enhancement is an unwanted side effect
of the most powerful pain-relieving medica-
tions—narcotics. Although many narcotics have
initially been marketed as nonaddictive, experience after general use has rarely proven this
true. Some athletes are given narcotics for relief
of truly painful conditions, but because sports
require continued physical activity, the risk of
addiction either because of continued pain,
mood enhancement, or performance enhancement is very high. For this reason, there are
physicians who refuse to prescribe narcotics to
any athlete who continues to practice or compete in a sport.

Adequate management of chronic pain is a
complicated issues: it concerns people with
chronic and or terminal illness. In chronic illness,

pain management does little to effect the course
of a disease but affects the quality of LIFE greatly.
Therefore, a balance must be found between
pain relief, side effects, convenience, and cost.
For example, morphine is an excellent pain
reliever and can be given by mouth, for a low
price, but it is very addictive. It affects a person's
ability to work and interact and can cause damage after years of use. Management of pain associated with terminal illness, by definition, does
not carry the risk of long-term side effects, and
long-term costs are less of an issue than with
chronic pain. The real issue is the use of pain control to improve the quality of an individual's life.
It is controversial among physicians whether
addiction to pain medication should be an issue
for chronically ill patients. To return to the earlier example, morphine may be a better pain-
management choice for the terminally ill person
because it offers excellent pain relief, is inexpensive, and enhances mood, and its interruption of
the ability to perform a job is often not an issue.

PASCAL'S WAGER   The position that in
the absence of absolute (*see* ABSOLUTES) knowledge of GOD, it is better to have FAITH than not
to believe.

Blaise Pascal was a seventeenth-century
French philosopher, mathematician, inventor,
and physicist. In Pascal's writing *Pensées* (1670)
he raised a number of skeptical arguments *see*
SKEPTICISM) concerning the nature of God. Pascal argued that it was impossible to demonstrate
God's existence definitively. Pascal then
expressed the possible positive and negative
outcomes of believing in God without proof.
Pascal posited that if there were a God, then

only GOOD could come of believing in God, but deep HARM, even eternal PUNISHMENT, could result from not believing in God. If there were no God, he further reasoned, good could still come of belief in a benevolent (*see* BENEVOLENCE) God. Furthermore, he could conceive no harm in this belief that outweighed the possible harms of not believing in God if there were a God. Therefore, the "best bet" for eternal HAPPINESS was to believe in God whether there was a God or not.

Pascal's wager has been often criticized but is usually not regarded in the proper context of the overall task of the *Pensées*. Viewed in isolation, Pascal's wager seems like a calculating, even shallow interpretation of the motivations for religious belief. However, the wager is best understood within the larger project of Pascal's work, which seeks to illustrate to readers that religious certainty comes through inspiration rather than reason.

PASSIONS AND EMOTIONS   States or dispositions of feeling.

Although some philosophers distinguish between passions and emotions by arguing that the former are more intense varieties of the latter, most contemporary philosophers view the terms as roughly synonymous. Examples of passions or emotions include fear, grief, embarrassment, remorse, joy, and lust. Passions and emotions are powerful motivators (*see* MOTIVE) for human behavior, and philosophers seek to explain the role of passions in the moral life, particularly as they relate to REASON and action (*see* ACT). Ethicists (*see* ETHICS) ask the question, for instance, of whether reason or the passions tell us what is RIGHT and WRONG and whether our reason or passion is dominant in governing moral action.

It is difficult to determine the relationship between emotions and passions and VALUE or goodness (*see* GOOD) until we can clearly delineate what emotions and passions are. One tradition argues that an emotion is simply a conscious feeling that we observe within ourselves. Another tradition sees emotion as a motivation to do something that we see as either desirable (*see* DESIRE) or undesirable. A further tradition claims that an emotion is neither a conscious feeling nor a motivation to act but a physiological change such as an increased heartbeat or an adrenalin rush. Although some philosophers have called for a comprehensive theory that would unite these various elements, no such theory has emerged. Still, the relationship between passion and reason remains a key point in ethical theory.

The ancient world was nearly unanimous in its belief that a good life was possible only when the emotions were held in check by reason. PLATO compares reason to a charioteer who must keep tight reins on the horse of the passions. ARISTOTLE agreed with Plato, although Aristotle was perhaps more tolerant toward emotion, arguing that the good life involved having emotions in the right degree in the right way. EPICTETUS, a great stoic teacher (*see* STOICISM), argued that a good life is a virtuous life and that a virtuous life is a life in which we have trained our passions so that they do not force us to want what we have no control over. Within the Christian tradition, AUGUSTINE believed that SIN consisted in a conflict of loves or desires. A good Christian did not allow his or her emotions to carry the soul away from the LOVE of GOD (*see* CHRISTIAN ETHICS).

David HUME was the first to challenge the traditional view of emotions. He argued that reason was a slave of the passions, that is, that reason could not motivate us to do what is right. Our passions told us what was good and naturally desired it; reason could only act as a guide to the passions. This view was challenged by Immanuel KANT, who believed that reason was utterly opposed to the emotions and was the sole source of moral knowledge as well as of moral motivation. Many contemporary ethicists adhere to one of these positions or attempt to occupy a middle ground.

PATERNALISM   Any ACT of BENEFICENCE or omission by a person or group that limits the AUTONOMY of another person or group for the purpose of helping them.

Many ethical systems require people both to respect the autonomy of others, and to try and promote the best interests of others whenever possible. Sometimes, however, these goals conflict. For example, most people would agree that suicide is rarely, if ever, someone's best option. If we were to respect individual autonomy fully, however, we would be bound not to interfere. Many ethicists, therefore, have sought to create guidelines for deciding when, if at all, we should interfere with the autonomy of another.

In the debate, many ethicists have seen a need to distinguish between two forms of paternalism. The first, "weak" or "soft" paternalism (or, sometimes, antipaternalism), originated in the works of John Stuart MILL (although he never used the term himself) and holds that intervention is only permissible in cases where individual behavior is nonvoluntary or severely restricted or where the COMPETENCY of an individual is unclear. For example, intervention would be permitted when someone, apparently under the influence of noxious fumes, is about to jump off a building. In this case, the person is clearly not competent to make such a decision and can legitimately be restrained from jumping until he or she is no longer affected. However, if later discussions reveal that the person is rational and determined, the person should be allowed to commit suicide should he or she still desires to do so. In general, weak paternalists have no objection to paternalism when the individual concerned is not considered fully competent, such as in the case of children or the mentally ill (see INSANITY).

The second form of paternalism is known as "hard" or "strong" paternalism and holds that there are instances where one may act paternalistically toward a fully competent and rational adult. In this case, the circumstances under which paternalism may be justified remain restricted. For example, a hard paternalist might argue that paternalism is justified where the benefits to the individual significantly outweigh the costs of paternalism, that the paternalistic action does not put the individual at risk, and that paternalism should only be used as a last resort. For example, a hard paternalist might permit a doctor to treat a patient who refuses a blood transfusion, because the cost of that refusal (death) far outweighs the benefits of a transfusion. Additionally, a hard paternalist might argue that paternalism is acceptable where individual choices are irrational or based on misinformation, even though the person is otherwise a competent adult. For example, a hard paternalist is likely to support a LAW that requires motorcycle riders to wear helmets not only because such a law is likely to be a relatively minor inconvenience to the rider but also because individual riders are likely to underestimate the risks of not doing so.

There are a wide number of possible behaviors that may constitute paternalism, from coercive INTERVENTION, such as the deprogramming of cult members to the simple withholding of information, such as a doctor refusing to inform a patient about her or his disease "for their own good" (see INFORMED CONSENT). In such circumstances, one must be careful not to assume that one's own preferences are necessarily those of others—just because we have certain preferences does not mean that others ought to share those preferences. It is therefore imperative that, before we act paternalistically toward others, we first ensure that our own behavior is both impartial (see IMPARTIALITY) and motivated by an understanding of the reasons behind the personal choices others make (see EMPATHY).

PEACE STUDIES   Academic discipline concerned with peace and CONFLICT RESOLUTION.

Peace studies is a growing field. There are presently more than 200 universities in the

United States where students can explore the nature of peace and the causes of conflict. Peace studies programs are usually multidisciplinary and so combine the approaches and expertise of a variety of fields including philosophy, political science, sociology, psychology, economics, and agricultural sciences. Peace studies programs address causes of war and VIOLENCE, means of supporting HUMAN RIGHTS, conflict resolution in multinational situations, and in some cases domestic violence. *See also* NONVIOLENCE.

PERFECT/IMPERFECT DUTIES   A distinction that marks the difference between an OBLIGATION that allows leeway in determining how to achieve it and one that does not.

In the philosophy of Immanuel KANT, perfect duties are those duties that do not admit to various courses of action. For example, the duty to tell the truth does not admit of exception. We are not allowed to tell the truth sometimes, or to some people, or only part of the truth, or even to remain silent if silence creates a false impression. Our duty is to tell the truth at all times.

By contrast, imperfect duties may be achieved in more than one way. For example, the duty not to lie is imperfect as it admits of the possibility of saying nothing. The duty to help others is also imperfect because it does not specify whom to help, or how often, or the degree of sacrifice that is demanded on one's own part. While the duty assumed by some monks, for example, to own nothing is termed *perfect,* the duty to give to charity is termed *imperfect.*

PERFECTIONISM   *See* MORAL PERFECTIONISM.

PERMISSIBLE ACT   An ACT that is condoned by an ethical CODE.

Acts are considered permissible when they are allowed or permitted by an ethical code. Acts are prohibited (*see* PROHIBITION) when they are disallowed by an ethical code. For example, UTILITARIANISM holds that all those acts that cause the greatest good for the greatest number are permissible, while those acts that cause more harm than good are prohibited.

PERSONAL ETHICS   One's individual standard of moral behavior.

The concept of personal ETHICS refers to a person's ethical beliefs (*see* FAITH). These beliefs form a CODE that guides individual action (*see* ACT). People may be said to have strong personal ethics, meaning that they have a strict code of ethics and that they adhere to it. Conversely, they may be said to have weak personal ethics or to lack personal ethics, meaning that they do not have a strong CONSCIENCE or that they always act only in their own best interest. When *personal ethics* is used in this sense as a kind of evaluative judgment, it appeals to an ethical NORM, which acknowledges the importance of respect for others in ethical decision making such as is found in DEONTOLOGY, UTILITARIANISM, or COMMUNITARIANISM. Strictly speaking, however, EGOISM is also a form of personal ethics, although it does not necessarily involve regard for others.

Personal ethics is sometimes contrasted with PROFESSIONAL ETHICS or institutional ethics. This contrast indicates points where one's personal code is at odds with the code of one's business, school, government, church, or profession. For example, one's personal ethics might be maximalist, meaning that one should bring about the best possible outcome in all situations. However, one's professional obligations might be minimalist, meaning that one should avoid harm and wrongdoing. Imagine that you work for the Environmental Protection Agency and become aware of a situation that you believe to be hazardous but one that falls short of the government's defined point of action. Your personal ethics may drive you to make this information public, whereas it might be consistent with your professional duties to address the situation through different channels (*see* MAXIMAL VS. MINIMAL ETHICS).

Relativists (*see* RELATIVISM) reduce all ethics to personal ethics, holding that there is no ethical standard above and beyond the standard people choose for themselves. By contrast, objectivists (*see* OBJECTIVISM) hold that there is an independent moral standard and that we should strive to emulate that standard in our personal ethics.

PERSONHOOD

The state of being human; having legal or moral RIGHTS and duties (*see* OBLIGATION).

The concept of *personhood* is often cited as a minimum standard for receiving moral consideration; that is to say, we hold that people deserve moral consideration simply by virtue of being human beings. There are certain minimum standards of treatment guaranteed to all people in a society because they are human, in acknowledgment of their personhood. Some moral theories, such as that of Immanuel KANT, hold that people should never be treated as means to an end (*see* ENDS/MEANS); their personhood means that they should always be treated as inherently valuable, as an end in themselves.

There is some controversy as to what characteristics must be present to establish personhood. Some moral thinkers hold that personhood begins at the moment of human conception; therefore, they conclude, from the moment of conception a person is present who deserves moral and legal protection. This belief motivates the pro-life position in the debate over ABORTION. Others argue that personhood is achieved only by actually existing human beings and not by potential human beings or fetuses (*see* FETUS). This belief motivates the pro-choice position in the abortion debate.

There are other controversies surrounding personhood as well. Children, for example, deserve moral protection but do not have the same moral obligations as do adults. Similarly, the mentally incompetent deserve full moral consideration but do not incur the responsibilities of moral personhood. Finally, there are those who argue that the notion of personhood as a basis for MORAL AGENCY is too limiting because it leaves out animals and the environment as viable parts of a moral community. *See also* ANIMAL RIGHTS; ENVIRONMENTAL ETHICS.

PHILANTHROPY

The voluntary redistribution of private wealth for public GOOD.

The PRACTICE of philanthropy involves the gift of privately amassed wealth to nonprofit organizations, educational foundations, or other charitable activities by individuals or corporations. Philanthropy is a type of CHARITY, but it is usually characterized by large donations to establish or support ongoing endeavors to contribute to the quality of public life. Some of the best known philanthropic organizations are the Carnegie Foundation, Ford Foundation, MacArthur Foundation, and Rockefeller Foundation in the United States and the Nuffield Foundation in England, the Volkswagenwerk Foundation in Germany, and the Toyota Foundation in Japan.

PHYSICIAN-PATIENT RELATIONSHIP

A privileged relationship, first described in the HIPPOCRATIC OATH, that assigns special RIGHTS and responsibilities (*see* RESPONSIBILITY) to physicians and patients.

The relationship between patient and physician has been considered inviolate. It is an agreement between the two parties that the patient will be completely honest (*see* HONESTY) and that the physician will hold that honesty in confidence (*see* CONFIDENTIALITY), seeking only to work for the patient's GOOD. It is the groundwork by which physicians must operate because without honesty the physician is unable to gather the medical history required to diagnose accurately and treat or prevent illness. This honesty is rewarded when the physician does not divulge these facts without the patient's consent. It fosters a feeling of mutual purpose that allows physician and patient to work together toward a common goal. *See also* MEDICAL ETHICS; STANDARDS OF CARE.

PIAGET, JEAN (1896–1980) Swiss psychologist famous for his study of the development of REASON in children.

Piaget is best known for his study of the psychological development of children. He noticed in testing the intelligence of children that children often gave the same or similar wrong answers at different ages. Through a careful study of these results, Piaget put forth a theory concerning how reasoning develops and suggested that there are significant differences in our ability to reason at different ages, which are not attributable to intelligence alone. Piaget then began to study the differences in how children think and solve problems at different stages in their development.

In terms of ETHICS, Piaget's work was the basis for work in the areas of MORAL DEVELOPMENT and MORAL PSYCHOLOGY.

PLAGIARISM The ACT of presenting another person's words or ideas as one's own.

Plagiarism occurs when someone uses the work of another person without obtaining that person's permission or without giving that person proper credit. Plagiarism is an attempt by someone to pass off copied work as original work. The most blatant form of plagiarism is to copy directly from another source without properly citing that source. For example, if someone copies information for a report directly from an encyclopedia without publisher's permission, that constitutes plagiarism. Plagiarism is not limited to direct quotations: it is also plagiarism when a person "rewords" someone else's original ideas, whether those ideas occur in print or were expressed in a discussion. Instances of plagiarism are considered a form of theft or stealing. They are immoral (*see* IMMORALITY) in the same way that taking someone else's property or money without their permission is immoral.

PLATO (427–347 B.C.) An ancient Greek philosopher who was a student of SOCRATES and a teacher of ARISTOTLE.

Plato is one of the most influential figures in the history of philosophy. He wrote dialogues, in the form of conversations, in which Socrates appears as the main character, setting forth both his own and Plato's opinions.

Many of Plato's dialogues are dedicated to the discussion of ethical ideas (*see* ETHICS). He examines TEMPERANCE in *Charmides,* piety in *Euthyphro,* and LOVE in *The Symposium.* In *The Republic,* after a long investigation, he defines the idea of JUSTICE as the harmony of the soul in accordance with REASON. Comparing the soul to the state, he argues that a just soul, like a just state, has all of its parts ordered according to their proper functions, where reason rules over the passions (*see* PASSION AND EMOTION) as wise (*see* WISDOM) kings rule over the state. One of Plato's doctrines is that VIRTUE comprises both knowledge and action (*see* ACT) and that error is the result of ignorance. The ultimate goal of ethics, leading a good life, requires knowledge of goodness and virtue. Plato's ethics aims at the achievement of the GOOD and moral perfection (*see* MORAL PERFECTIONISM).

Plato is known for his IDEALISM: the theory that ideas have a reality of their own or that they exist and have a mode of being that is independent of the physical or sensible world. Indeed, in Plato's view, the things we observe in our sense experience are what they are or have certain kinds of being because they possess the characteristics or forms expressed by the ideas. This is often called Plato's doctrine of forms. Triangles, for example, are triangles because they have the form of triangularity, which we understand in the definition of that idea. Triangles in the physical world are said to be "copies" of ideas or forms, and even "poor copies" at that, for nothing in the actual world is as perfect as its ideal form. No triangle is a perfect triangle; we know this because we know what a perfect triangle would be like based upon the definition of triangularity.

Plato's ethics is also idealistic, in the sense that ideas such as justice and virtue express the kinds of perfection people seek. To be clear about such ideas, by philosophic examination, is to understand the goals of human life. One needs to understand the idea of justice, Plato reasons, in order to know what it means to be just or to aim at and achieve justice in one's life. Confusion about such ideas leads to error. The highest and most noble of all ideas, he points out in *The Republic*, is the idea of the good. Ultimately, everything that is good is good because it "participates in" or has the characteristic of goodness expressed by this idea. To aim at being just or virtuous is, ultimately, to aim at being good, the goal of the moral life.

The existence of ideas does not depend on our thinking about them or on how we define them. Plato held that ideas have a reality of their own, independent of our minds or souls. In Plato's view, we discover ideas and the truths (*see* TRUTH) about them; we do not invent or create them. Indeed, ideas, like justice and triangularity, are universal and eternal. Their true definitions are the same everywhere and for all time. Thus, Plato is an objectivist (*see* OBJECTIVISM) in holding that truth is not dependent on personal opinions but on the very nature of objective reality.

PLEASURE PRINCIPLE

The tendency for people to strive to achieve immediate pleasure and avoid or seek relief from immediate pain.

The pleasure principle is understood to be a strong motivating (*see* MOTIVE) factor in most moral theories. Human beings seem to be naturally drawn toward what they find pleasurable and naturally averse to what they find painful. However, the proper motivating role of pleasure in moral theories is debated. Some theories, such as EGOISM, HEDONISM, and UTILITARIANISM, have sought to incorporate our DESIRE for pleasure into MORALITY. Utilitarians argue, for example, that morality consists in maximizing pleasure while minimizing suffering. In each of these theories, pleasures and pains can be understood to be based in physical pleasures and pains but also to include "higher" pleasures such as education or art. The pleasure principle is geared toward immediate over delayed gratification, thus the importance of MORAL EDUCATION even in theories that assign pleasure a central role in morality.

Other theories acknowledge that human beings are drawn toward the pleasurable but teach that this does not mean that the pleasurable is moral or that humans *should* be motivated by it. Deontological ethics (*see* DEONTOLOGY) holds that actions (*see* ACT) are moral in so far as they follow valid moral RULES and may dictate that we avoid or forgo pleasures or that we endure some amount of suffering or pain. Again, because such theories recognize that the attraction of pleasure and the revulsion from pain are strong impulses, moral education is a process of teaching human beings to impose a new "moral" set of VALUES over their natural inclinations.

PLURALISM

Tolerance of different and often incompatible views.

Pluralism is the belief that there is more than one view of the truth. Pluralists hold that there are multiple true positions, even when those positions contradict one another. In ETHICS, pluralism is the belief that there is more than one moral truth or more than one idea of the GOOD, but it does not hold that all positions are equally true or equally good.

Pluralists do not demand that all views of the good be reconcilable into a single, systematic theory. Pluralism is, thus, opposed to absolutism (*see* ABSOLUTES), which holds that there are coherent, universal truths. On the other hand, pluralists do not believe that any and all views are true. In this sense, they are opposed to relativists (*see* RELATIVISM), who hold that any view of the truth is equal to any other. For example, a pluralist may hold that there is more than one correct view concerning when a war is just, but that nonetheless murder for profit is always wrong.

POLITICAL CORRECTNESS Suppressing the expression of certain attitudes and the use of certain terms in the belief that they are too offensive or controversial; often used in the abbreviated form *PC*.

For the most part, political correctness is a response to a growing acknowledgment that ideas can contain implicit meanings that may have the effect of offending or marginalizing certain groups in society. In most cases, political correctness simply involves substituting potentially offensive terminology with inoffensive terminology. For example, using the word *man* to refer to the human race as a whole may undervalue the contribution of women to society. Therefore, we now generally prefer to use less controversial terms such as *humans* or *people*. In other cases, ideas can become so loaded with negative connotations that we may deem it necessary to avoid the term altogether. For example, the term *Negro* has become so confused by racism that we now prefer to substitute the term *African American* or its equivalent.

Political correctness becomes a problem when it takes the form of a hypersensitivity to the possibility of offending another person. When taken to extremes, political correctness can seriously interfere with one's ability to express an idea clearly and succinctly. For example, because some feminists see the word *female* as derogatory, it now common to use *women* instead, even in cases where the usage is both grammatically incorrect and confusing. Hence, *women athletes* may be used even when one intends to include young girls.

Political correctness is particularly dangerous when it has the effect of censoring new ideas because of their association with more controversial ones (*see* CENSORSHIP). For example, because the science of eugenics was used by Nazis to justify the Holocaust, it is now difficult to discuss openly new technologies that enable us to screen unborn children for genetic defects. In these cases, because a new idea cannot be easily conveyed in a short period of time, people will often have formed an opinion about it before it has been given a genuine hearing and may even refuse to consider it based on an initial emotional reaction.

POLITICAL LIBERTY *See* FREEDOM.

PORNOGRAPHY Sexually explicit images or literature intended primarily for the purpose of inducing sexual arousal in the viewer or reader.

The moral status of pornography has been the subject of significant disagreement during the twentieth century, and indeed the exact definition of what constitutes pornography is itself a matter of considerable debate. For the most part, however, the term *pornography* is intended to refer exclusively to images or literature depicting nudity and consensual sex and excludes images or literature depicting extreme OBSCENITY, such as sexual images of TORTURE, RAPE, or children. Additionally, the term *pornography* is not intended to include images and literature of artistic, educational, scientific, or cultural significance.

According to moral conservatives (*see* CONSERVATISM), pornography is objectionable because it depicts sexuality as if it were completely divorced from what they see as its essential surrounding context of LOVE, COMMITMENT, and procreation. As a result, they argue, it is not illogical to assume that pornography also has the effect of denigrating these VALUES in the wider community, thereby undermining traditional family arrangements and encouraging promiscuity.

Civil libertarians (*see* LIBERTARIANISM), on the other hand, see the MORALITY of pornography as a matter for individual CONSCIENCE. According to this view, those who wish to restrict pornography are trying to impose their own morality on others and, in the process, to advocate a violation of the First Amendment right to free speech (*see* BILL OF RIGHTS). If the right to freedom of speech cannot protect unpopular or controversial forms of expression such as pornography, they argue, it becomes useless, because popular and noncontroversial forms of expression are unlikely to need protection.

In recent years some of the most influential debates on pornography have occurred between feminist thinkers who are far from united on the issue. On the one hand, scholars such as Catharine MacKinnon and Andrea Dworkin argue passionately that pornography is inherently degrading to women because it treats them as sex objects who exist for the pleasure of men. According to these feminists, pornography is a form of rape because in viewing the pornographic image, the male viewer seizes and possesses *all* women in his mind and, thereafter, carries that perception of ownership into his daily life. In fact, according to this account it is virtually impossible in a male-dominated society for a woman to be seen as anything other than a sexual object, regardless of whether she is in a pornographic video, in bed with her husband, or walking along a street on the way to work.

Pro-pornography feminists such as Nadine Strossen and Betty Dodson, on the other hand, see the view that women cannot be sexual without being oppressed by men as demeaning and paternalistic (*see* PATERNALISM). This view, they argue, appears to define female sexuality exclusively by its effect on men through the implication that women have no choice in how they define and express their sexuality. Indeed, feminists who advocate the censorship of pornography imply that women themselves have no desire to read and view pornography or to eroticize the naked human body, although this is demonstrably not the case. Finally, because censorship was historically used to deny women access to information about important issues such as CONTRACEPTION and to reinforce "good

girl" stereotypes, pro-pornography feminists argue that censoring pornography can only serve to reverse women's hard-won gains.

POVERTY   A standard of living that falls below the minimum necessary to participate effectively in one's community.

The debate concerning income inequality and poverty is complex and difficult to summarize. For starters, there is much debate about the extent to which we have a RESPONSIBILITY to help anyone at all. Of course, most would agree that some support is necessary, particularly in cases where people cannot afford basic necessities such as food, clothing, and shelter—a condition known as absolute poverty. More controversial, however, is the debate about what should be done with those who, while not starving, cannot afford to participate in regular society, a condition known as relative poverty. Some argue that society owes nothing to these people, as there are always opportunities for one to better oneself. Others argue that this position ignores the very real difficulties faced by those who have virtually nothing. For example, an inability to afford new clothes can make it difficult to present oneself properly for a job interview, and the inability to afford a telephone can make it difficult to access emergency services. Furthermore, even if one has access to these things, without sufficient education one may not have the knowledge necessary to take advantage of the opportunities that do exist.

Opinions also differ on the extent to which a modern society should tolerate severe income inequalities and an underclass of the severely disadvantaged. According to some, it is inevitable in a capitalist society that some people will be rich and others poor (*see* CAPITALISM). By this account, people are poor either because they have not made an effort to succeed or because they have skills irrelevant to the marketplace. Opponents, on the other hand, argue that poverty in a capitalist society is a combination of bad luck, either in the market or in the circumstances of one's birth and economic EXPLOITATION. In all likelihood, however, poverty exists because of a combination of all these factors. Unfortunately, it is difficult, if not impossible, for an objective observer to determine which factor has been the most influential in any individual case. One's position on the subject of assistance to the poor is therefore likely to be based on whether one believes that it is better to help the poor, knowing that some assistance will go to the undeserving, or whether this is simply a price that must be paid in order to get help to those who truly need it.

Overall, most debates on poverty assume that assistance to the poor is a gesture of GENEROSITY from the rich. In this case, the assumption is that the poor should really be thankful if they get anything at all. Others, however, argue that EGALITARIANISM demands a more equal distribution of wealth. At the very least, they argue, even if we accept that income inequalities provide incentive for people to succeed, surely incentive need not cost the hundreds of thousands, or even millions, of dollars a year made annually by a few economic elites. *See also* COLONIALISM.

POWER   The ability to achieve a goal or DESIRE.

Power refers to the ability of a person or of a society to realize its goals. Power may be exercised physically, as when one person overpowers another person. Physical power may also be exercised in a positive manner, as when one person assists another person in moving a heavy object. Ethical issues (*see* ETHICS) surrounding physical power concern when, if ever, it is appropriate to HARM someone and how to protect the weaker members of society from the stronger if the stronger desire to exercise their power in attempt to deny the liberty (*see* FREEDOM) of others.

Power can also refer to influence or economic force. Many moral discussions of power concern who has the power to distribute the goods in a society and whether those goods are distributed equally (*see* EQUALITY). For example, for many years political power was wielded almost exclusively by men. Some moral thinkers argue that a society is not just (*see* JUSTICE) unless each person has the possibility to share equally in the power base of a society.

Power in a society may also refer to the ability of that society to make and enforce rules that govern the behavior of its citizens. Ethical problems in political philosophy are concerned with who has the AUTHORITY to make such RULES and now those rules can be enforced.

PRACTICAL ETHICS   *See* APPLIED ETHICS.

PRACTICE   The usual or accepted way of doing something.

A practice is a habit (*see* HABITS) or custom (*see* CUSTOMS). It is a cultural NORM. For example, it may be our practice to greet people we meet with a handshake. Moral practices are the ethical norms that are developed in a community or culture.

Practice also means to develop skill through repeated, systematic exercise, as to practice a sport or a musical instrument. This sense of practice is important for VIRTUE ETHICS, which associates moral VIRTUE with our ability to practice and develop virtues in our daily lives. For example, we may practice self-restraint when angry or self-control when faced with temptation.

PRAGMATISM   The position that the meaning or TRUTH of a belief (*see* FAITH) is determined by the outcome of adhering to that belief.

Pragmatism is a theory of truth, which argues that ideas are true if they operate effectively in the world. Pragmatism is most closely associated with the U.S. philosophers Charles Sanders Peirce and William James. James's views on pragmatism are particularly important for ethics as he held that all beliefs, even a belief in GOD, are true insofar as they "work" in the world. While working in the world is a complicated matter, the essential point is that if a belief in God made for a better life and society, then such a belief would be true. PASCAL'S WAGER is also frequently cited as an example of a pragmatic religious principle.

In ordinary ethical language, *pragmatism* also means that what works is true. The guiding notion is that the idea of truth must be closely related to the idea of success. An ethical principle that always led to a negative consequence would not be valuable (*see* VALUE) to a pragmatist. A pragmatist is in this sense more interested in consequences than in moral RULES.

PRAJNA   One of the two highest realizations of Buddhism; WISDOM.

Wisdom represents the fullest development of the first step in the EIGHTFOLD PATH, "Right Views." It indicates an understanding founded on insight into the working of reality—phenomenal and ultimate. Phenomenally, in terms of what appears (*see* MAYA), reality is seen by Buddhists to be marked by three characteristics: (1) perpetual change, (2) unsatisfactoriness (*see* FOUR NOBLE TRUTHS), and (3) absence of self or EGO (in the sense of a permanent, self-sufficient entity). Ultimately, reality is seen by Buddhists to be empty, that is, without "own-being" or without a self-subsistent nature. Buddhists content that everything that is is what it is by right of relationship to what it is not. Therefore, everything gains its appearance of reality and is defined as something distinct, by right of relationship or interdependency. Nothing exists in and of itself, apart from conditions of support. Everything is contingent, thus empty of self-sufficiency.

The highest wisdom of Buddhism sees the phenomenal, or material, world and the noumenal, or spiritual, world as one integrated world, that is, nondual (*see* GOD); the realm of time and space, the empirical world, and the Ultimate are mysteriously nondifferent. Donald

S. Lopez, Jr., in *The Heart Sutra Explained*, translates an important Buddhist text that puts the matter succinctly: "Form is emptiness; emptiness is form. Emptiness is not other than form; form is not other than emptiness."

The Buddhist view of emptiness should be distinguished from NIHILISM, a view that life is ultimately meaningless. The Buddhist view of emptiness is integrally connected to the second of the two highest Buddhist virtues, KARUNA, or "compassion." Buddhists understand wisdom to be so thoroughly informed and infused by compassion that without compassion so-called wisdom is not in fact wisdom. *See also* BUDDHIST ETHICS; DHARMA.

PREDESTINATION   The belief (*see* FAITH) that people are preselected before birth for salvation or damnation.

The doctrine of predestination holds that one's fate is determined by GOD before birth. This means that a person is destined for either heaven or hell, irrespective of GOOD deeds done during this life. Predestination plays an important role in Calvinist CHRISTIAN ETHICS.

PREJUDICE   A preconceived JUDGMENT.

A prejudice is a belief or opinion that a person holds without sufficient grounds. Prejudices are biases (*see* BIAS) on which other opinions or positions are formulated. A person can be prejudiced for or against an idea or another person, but in either case the position is held without enough knowledge or information.

We usually think of prejudices as attitudes that are harmful (*see* HARM) to others. Often, prejudices engender anger or hostility toward another group of people. For example, racial prejudice indicates a bias against others based on their race alone without any corresponding facts. People who hold prejudices usually believe that their own group is superior to other groups. Prejudice often leads to DISCRIMINATION, the denial of one group's equal access to social goods based on a single characteristic such as race, gender, or religion. Prejudice is distinct from discrimination in that prejudices are attitudes, while discrimination refers to actions (*see* ACT) that arise from prejudices.

Prejudice appears to be learned and is documented only in individuals above the age of three. *See also* CIVIL RIGHTS; RACISM; WOMEN'S RIGHTS.

PRESCRIPTIVE VS. DESCRIPTIVE ETHICS Prescriptive ETHICS is the view that ethical language is equivalent to giving ethical commands; descriptive ethics holds that the meaning of ethical terms does not involve such commands.

Prescriptivism is associated with the moral philosophy of the twentieth-century English philosopher R. M. Hare. Hare held that moral views were essentially the giving of moral commands. Moral disputes occur when different moral commands are given, and MORAL CONFLICT occurs when two or more moral commands are given, not all of which can be followed. Prescriptive ethics consists of moral commands that hold for all people in similar situations; For example, the command "Do not lie" means that all people in a similar situation are morally bound not to lie, but it does not mean that no persons should never lie.

Prescriptive ethics may be contrasted with descriptive ethics. Descriptivism holds that evaluative terms such as *good* do not imply a command but are rather simply descriptions of natural states.

PRICHARD, H. A. *See* INTUITIONISM.

PRIDE Pleasure in one's own attributes or accomplishments.

Pride has both a negative and a positive connotation. In its negative sense, pride is one of the CARDINAL SINS. This type of pride is excessive LOVE or interest in oneself (*see* SELF-INTEREST). Thomas AQUINAS considered it the most deadly SIN of all. Pride causes people to esteem themselves well above their fellow human beings and to remove themselves from OBEDIENCE to any higher AUTHORITY. It is often expressed as contempt for others.

In its more positive sense, pride is a healthy CARE and interest in those things that one is or has accomplished. We may take pride in a job well done, for example, or pride in our appearance. Pride in this context is a sign of self-respect: it indicates that we regard ourselves and our efforts as valuable and worthwhile.

PRIMA FACIE DUTY An OBLIGATION for which there is an appropriate or reasonable ground (*see* REASONABLENESS).

A duty may be said to be prima facie when there are evident reasons for performing it. For example, we may have a moral prima facie duty not to lie based on the moral rule (*see* RULES), "Do not lie." Prima facie duties do not admit of exception; they are duties simply because MORALITY dictates a certain course of action (*see* ACT). This type of duty is contrasted with an "all things considered" duty, which one is obligated to perform only if the good reasons for carrying out the duty override the reasons for not carrying it out. For example, a consequentialist (*see* CONSEQUENTIALISM) might argue that there is no prima facie duty not to lie but that rather truth-telling is a type of "all things considered" duty to be performed when the benefits outweigh the harms.

PRINCIPLE A fundamental RULE, LAW, or doctrine, from which other rules or judgments (*see* JUDGMENT) are derived.

In ETHICS, principles are basic moral beliefs on which judgments about actions (*see* ACT) or the CHARACTER of persons are founded. A principle of many religious ethical systems is the GOLDEN RULE: "Do unto others as you would have them do unto you." Many secular ethical systems (*see* SECULAR ETHICS) operate on a principle of EQUALITY, which holds that all people should be treated in the same manner. Principles of JUSTICE may be grounded in equality but may also hold that people who are different in significant ways deserve different consideration, the goal being that all persons are treated fairly (*see* FAIRNESS). Another frequently cited moral principle is "Do no HARM" (*see* NONMALEFICENCE), and on the basis of it, we may judge in a particular case that it is WRONG for one person to harm another.

Principles are general, even universal, beliefs in that they are supposed to apply to everyone. They are like other rules in this respect, but, logically speaking, principles come first, before other rules, in the sense that rules are derived from principles but principles are not derived from rules. Thus, we often cite rules to justify (*see* JUSTIFICATION) particular judgments and then cite principles to justify those rules. A person may make the judgment, for example, that copying another person's exam is wrong and then give as a reason the rule, "Cheating is wrong." If then asked why cheating is wrong, the person who made the judgment might reply, "Because cheating shows disregard for the person who actually did the work, and regard for people is morally GOOD." When it comes to citing principles, we have arrived at our ultimate reasons, or our most fundamental moral beliefs.

Principles are sometimes thought to be absolute (*see* ABSOLUTES), or without exception, whereas less fundamental, lower-level rules may have exceptions. Whether or not principles have exceptions, however, depends on the kinds of principles they are. If there is more than one principle at issue, it then seems possible for principles to conflict with one another and have exceptions. Positive principles that bid us to perform acts of certain kinds are likely to conflict because doing one kind of thing often precludes doing another. Telling the truth, for example, may conflict with the principle "Do no harm" because telling the truth can sometimes hurt others. A system with only one principle, such as

UTILITARIANISM, is likely to avoid this difficulty, simply because there is no other principle with which its guiding principle can conflict.

Ethical systems or theories often differ in the principles they profess. Egoistic systems (*see* EGOISM), for example, are based on the idea that SELF-INTEREST is the basis of all moral judgment. These systems differ from altruistic (*see* ALTRUISM) or benevolent (*see* BENEVOLENCE) systems, which maintain that people either are or ought to be motivated (*see* MOTIVE) by LOVE for others. Theories that hold that, ultimately, acts should be judged by consequences (*see* CONSEQUENTIALISM) are different from theories that hold that acts should be judged by intentions (*see* INTENTION) or motives. On the other hand, some people believe in the same principles but order them differently. Nearly everyone believes in freedom, for instance, and also that people should not be harmed, but some think we should risk harm in the name of freedom, and others want to restrict freedom to prevent harm. Some codes (*see* CODE), such as the "code of the streets," tend to rank LOYALTY above JUSTICE, and others, such as the legal system, tend to give priority to justice over loyalty.

Some psychological theories of MORAL DEVELOPMENT claim that people do not reach moral maturity until they make their moral judgments on the basis of principle, instead of the basis of social convention or self-interest. People frequently judge acts by social rules, but because social rules are not always good, or if good, sometimes have exceptions, the rules appear to need justification by moral principles, or principles are needed to justify exceptions.

Whether and how moral principles can be justified has been a matter of philosophic examination and debate. Some philosophers have argued that first principles cannot be justified because they are first principles and cannot be derived from any higher or more fundamental belief. But even if principles cannot be proven, they can be discussed by explaining why they are principles.

Substantive ethical theories try to uncover the first principles of ethics and also explain why they are foundational principles. German philosopher Immanuel KANT, for example, held that justice is the first principle on which all moral rules and judgments are founded because this principle is demanded by REASON. Thomas AQUINAS, a medieval theologian, claimed that the first principles of ethics are "do good" and "avoid evil" because people, by nature, are inclined to seek what they perceive as good and avoid what they perceive as evil.

PRISONER'S DILEMMA   A paradox invented in the mathematical study of human interaction called game theory.

In game theory, human encounters are broken down into strategies, with each person trying to succeed as well as he or she can. Sometimes a person can only do well when another does poorly. This is a "game of conflict." The Prisoner's Dilemma involves a CONFLICT OF INTEREST and is noted in ETHICS because it shows that what is GOOD for a group is not always what is best for each member of the group.

In the prisoner's dilemma two prisoners, Prisoner A and Prisoner B, are held separately for a joint offense and are offered the same deal by the police. The deal, designed to get both prisoners to confess, offers each the opportunity to confess or to remain silent. If neither prisoner confesses, the prosecutor will find a lesser charge and each prisoner will serve two years. If Prisoner A confesses while Prisoner B remains silent, Prisoner A goes free while Prisoner B receives ten years in prison. Conversely, if Prisoner B confesses while Prisoner A does not, Prisoner B is released and Prisoner A serves ten years in prison. If both confess, both will be convicted and each will serve six years.

If the prisoners are able to trust one another not to confess, they will each go free after only two years. However, if one prisoner confesses in order to receive the least possible sentence, one or both prisoners will be jailed. While it may

seem best from each prisoner's own point of view to confess, if *both* prisoners do so, they will each serve the maximum possible jail time. The DILEMMA is whether to remain silent and risk a harsher punishment if the other confesses or to speak first and ensure a shorter jail term. Cooperation by the prisoners will yield the best result for them, but to achieve this result they must be able to trust the other not to ACT.

Other ethical issues may be understood on the prisoner's-dilemma model. For example, conservation efforts depend on the cooperation of all parties. There is a temptation not to conserve a scarce resource out of fear that others will not conserve. If others do not conserve, not only has the person who cooperates with the conservation effort suffered, but no ultimate good has been done. If everyone acts in their short-term individual interests and takes from a scarce resource because they are afraid others will not conserve, the resource is depleted. Thus, we must decide if and how to cooperate without absolute assurance that others will follow suit—the essence of the prisoner's dilemma.

PRIVACY   The concept of a sphere in which the public has no right to interfere and for which there is no public authority.

A private sphere implies a domain of thought, preference, and action in which the public has no right to intrude or attempt to control. This domain is normally thought to include personal taste, certain kinds of personal information, and family and home matters. People cannot be scrutinized in these areas without good cause, such as evidence that the mistreatment of a family member is occurring. Although the U.S. constitution does not specifically guarantee a right to privacy, the BILL OF RIGHTS has been interpreted by the Supreme Court to give rise to a private sphere in which neither the government nor private individuals has a right to interfere with the activities of consenting adults.

Invasions of privacy are considered indicative of a lack of regard for the DIGNITY of another person and are usually considered immoral (*see* IMMORALITY) when they occur for any reason other than a legitimate fear that HARM is occurring. This qualification is controversial, however, as it is no simple matter to establish what counts as actionable harm. Furthermore, libertarians (*see* LIBERTARIANISM) argue that adults have the right to harm themselves in private as long as they are not harming others. Issues of privacy within family groups are also complicated especially with regard to young adults who are reaching the age of consent but still live in their parents' home. *See also* PRIVATE AND PUBLIC MORALITY.

PRIVATE AND PUBLIC MORALITY
The distinction between personal and civic ethical requirements.

The distinction between private and public MORALITY marks the distinction between the sphere in which the government or community has no AUTHORITY (private) and the sphere that is governed by common agreement or public authority (public). Private morality refers to those moral positions and beliefs (*see* FAITH) that have to do with personal choice. Religion, for example, is considered a matter of private morality in the United States and is not legislated by the state, although its private practice is protected by the state. Public morality concerning actions (*see* ACT) that bear upon civil society. One's duties (*see* OBLIGATION) to the public WELFARE of others falls under public morality, for example, the moral duty to respect the property of others. Some duties may be both public and private. Telling the truth in court, for instance, reflects a private duty not to lie as well as a public duty to tell the truth under oath.

PRO-CHOICE   *See* ABORTION.

PROFESSIONAL ETHICS   Codes of conduct (*see* CODE) established by professionals to govern ethical behavior within that profession.

Professional ETHICS address the intersection between business, the professions, and moral behavior. Nearly all professionals have their own ethical codes that determine the standards of ethical behavior and evaluation within that profession. For example, in the medical profession the HIPPOCRATIC OATH serves as a basis for professional ethics. In the engineering profession, ethical conduct is described in the code of the National Society of Professional Engineers, as well as detailed in professional codes adopted by special branches of engineering, such as electrical, civil, and mechanical engineers.

Issues commonly addressed within professional ethics codes are appropriate professional-client relationships, conflicts of interest (*see* CONFLICT OF INTEREST), INFORMED CONSENT, acting with competence (*see* COMPETENCY), CONFIDENTIALITY, AFFIRMATIVE ACTION and equal opportunity, and corporate social RESPONSIBILITY. *See also* JOURNALISM ETHICS; MEDICAL ETHICS; PHYSICIAN-PATIENT RELATIONSHIP.

PROHIBITION   A rule (*see* RULES) or injunction against a certain activity.

A prohibition is a rule or command to refrain from something. For example, people under seventeen years of age are prohibited from seeing R-rated movies without a parent. People without a driver's license are prohibited from driving. While a person may still decide to engage in a prohibited activity, there is usually a social or legal sanction if that person is caught.

The term *Prohibition* also refers to the period in U.S. history from 1920 to 1933, during which the Eighteenth Amendment prohibited the manufacture, sale, or transportation of alcoholic beverages. The Eighteenth Amendment was repealed in 1933 by the Twenty-First Amendment.

PROJECTIVISM   The view that we project qualities on the world that are in fact in our own minds and then take them to be objective qualities (*see* OBJECTIVISM) in the world.

Projectivism describes a situation by which human beings "project" what they perceive onto objects in the outside world. For example, we may see a wagon and think of it as red. We project the color red, which we perceive, onto the wagon. If we had different faculties of perception, we might experience the wagon in a completely different way.

In ETHICS, projectivism describes the view that the moral worth or VALUE of something is a projection of our attitude toward it. We tend to project a positive moral value toward those things that we find pleasurable or useful. Toward those things we tend to fear, we project a taboo or negative moral worth.

PRO-LIFE   *See* ABORTION.

PROMISCUITY   *See* SEXUAL ETHICS.

PROMISE   To give one's word that one will do something.

A promise is a pledge that one will follow through with an activity. A promise may be a pledge to complete a task or show up for a meeting. Alternatively, it may be an agreement not to do something, such as a promise not to give away a SECRET. Keeping promises is considered a sign of good character and consistency in ETHICS. However, promises can give rise to MORAL CONFLICT when they give rise to tension with other duties, such as HONESTY, LOYALTY, or OBEDIENCE. For example, you may promise a sibling to keep information in confidence but then be put in a position where you have to lie to do so, causing conflict between your OBLIGATION to your sibling and your obligation to tell the truth.

PROPERTY   Something that one owns.

Property is a feature of society that allows people to have as their own certain possessions. To have a possession as one's own means that one has the right to use that property and has some degree of control over it. It is not always the case, however, that one has total control over one's property. For example, if you own a house, then it is your property. You can decide who to invite in and who to exclude. If someone forces his or her way into your house, that is a legal offense. If that person takes anything from your house without your permission, that is a further offense. On the other hand, you cannot do anything you wish with your house. There are RULES and ordinances governing what can be done with your property. These may include rules governing the appearance of the property or what types of activities can go on within the property.

Some philosophers have believed that the right to own property is a natural right. For example, John LOCKE holds that we have a right to those things in which we invested our labor. Others, such as Karl MARX, have argued that property is immorally (*see* IMMORALITY) divisive in a society and is at the root of social injustices.

PRUDENCE   Sound judgment in practical affairs.

Prudence is one of the four CARDINAL VIRTUES. In general, prudence is that capacity that allows us to assess a situation and determine what is GOOD and what is bad and, moreover, how to achieve what is good and avoid what is bad. Prudence, then, is a kind of practical WISDOM that aids the other virtues, such as JUSTICE and MERCY.

ARISTOTLE described prudence as the ability to apply correct reasoning to HABITS and practices (*see* PRACTICE). Prudence helps us to discern the GOLDEN MEAN in an action (*see* ACT), separating bravery from foolhardiness and temperance from deprivation.

PSYCHOSPIRITUAL DISCIPLINE   A program of self-cultivation based on observance of moral precepts, development of specific attitudes and perspectives, and exploration of one's own mind.

MYSTICISM in religion often includes a discipline or practice that is designed to facilitate personal transformation—that is, transcendence. Transcendence refers to the process of moving through and beyond whatever constitutes a block or limitation in one's life. The human mind must create and project (*see* PROJECTIVISM) boundaries on objective and subjective reality to gain a sense of order in both the outer and inner world. These boundaries are essential to human life, both personal and social. Without them, INSANITY and chaos would reign. However, sometimes these boundaries are needlessly placed, misplaced, or no longer needed as people mature. If unneeded boundaries remain in place and are not transcended, removed, or dissolved, personal growth comes to an end.

Personal transformation can only occur where there is absolute HONESTY, where INTEGRITY and genuinely harmonious interpersonal relations are highly valued. Rigorous adherence to moral principles and practices is essential to this end. Therefore, MORALITY is foundational in a psychospiritual discipline. Although the specifics of the ethical system may vary, the quality of the moral life expected in all psychospiritual disciplines is consistently high.

Although differences occur in the various psychospiritual disciplines, they tend to agree on the development of specific perspectives and attitudes. Many of these bear on morality while others extend beyond it—at least as morality is typically understood. These perspectives and attitudes include FAITH, LOVE, and SELFLESSNESS, among others. Ultimate Reality—distinguished from (or not reducible to) ordinary reality—is always presumed (*see* GOD). It is perfect alignment or accord with this Reality, by means of transcendence, that constitutes the objective of the psychospiritual disciplines.

Finally, psychospiritual disciplines invariably include a program of contemplation or meditation, a method of exploring one's own consciousness. Both morality and the development of specific perspectives and attitudes entail considerable self-understanding and introspection.

Meditation carries this inwardness still further. Essentially, meditation is a process of nonjudgmental watching, without attachment, of whatever arises in consciousness. It presumes a degree of inner calmness and enhances this over time so that it becomes a steady tranquility. Because it increases one's powers of attention and awareness, meditation becomes the means of gaining insight into the nature of self and reality that is not otherwise attainable.

The effects of observing a psychospiritual discipline—commonly over a period of many years and under the direction of a teacher, guru, sage, adept, or spiritual master—include relaxed self-confidence, ability to trust, absence of fear and worry, clarity and perception, sense or harmony and connection, and recognition of reality as interdependent and nondual. *See also* BUDDHIST ETHICS; CHRISTIAN ETHICS; CONFUCIAN ETHICS; HINDU ETHICS; ISLAMIC ETHICS; JAIN ETHICS; JEWISH ETHICS; TAOIST ETHICS.

PUBLIC HEALTH That area of health-care research, prevention, treatment, and policy that is related to the health of a large population or group.

Public health involves the health of large populations that have similar characteristics. Ethical issues in public health often focus on racial and ethnic minorities, pregnant women and newborns, alcoholics, substances abusers, the elderly, and the mentally ill. Ethical issues in public health also arise regarding the practice of each of the health-care professions, environmental health, the study of health-care policies, and programs and practices funded or controlled by the government, enacted through legislation or under the jurisdiction of the courts.

The study of disease epidemics, or epidemiology, is an important area of public health. Ethical issues in epidemiology include the justification for health-care practices that are routinely used to prevent or limit the spread of diseases. For example, as a matter of public health, should children be required by law to be immunized against childhood diseases such as polio, diphtheria, and measles, which have been the cause of thousands of deaths in the past? Other moral issues concern how to handle quarantines and education and prevention of diseases such as AIDS.

There are two types of ethical issues involved in environmental health. The first considers the extent to which the government should be able to prevent individuals and businesses from releasing substances into the environment that create health risks to others. Issues such as the amount of governmental regulation appropriate for controlling the release of toxic substances into the sewage system or the prevention of smokers from smoking in public places because of the dangers of secondary smoke inhalation to nonsmokers are examples of the first type of ethical concern in environmental health.

A second kind of issue in environmental health considers whether the government should add substances to the environment that effectively prevent or reduce illness. For example, some objected that the addition of chlorine and fluoride to water violated individual liberty.

Public-health studies on large populations can help predict the types of health-care problems that may be prevalent in certain segments of the population. The rural poor, homeless, mentally ill, mentally retarded, and substance abusers often have no source of health care other than government-provided care. This situation raises ethical issues concerning the extent of the public's duty (*see* OBLIGATION) toward the socially disadvantaged and the medically fragile. For example, we must consider the extent of our moral duty toward less-advantaged members of society in terms of the treatment and prevention of serious illness.

PUNISHMENT
A penalty imposed upon an individual as a consequence of wrongdoing.

Punishment involves the intentional infliction of unpleasantness on another human being and is, thereby, a violation of the central tenet of most moral systems: do no HARM. This being the case, punishment is an issue that demands significant moral JUSTIFICATION. Although punishment can be invoked in many instances, such as by a parent against a child, most ethical debates concern the use of punishment as a response to CRIME.

Historically, punishment was justified according to the principle of *LEX TALIONIS*, that is, "an eye for an eye," although we now accept that this has serious limitations. For example, how can it be applied to white collar crime? Others have argued that punishment is simply a criminal's "just desert." Known as retributivists (*see* RETRIBUTION), these commentators often argue that punishment is necessary as a form of collective repudiation of crime or simply because it would be unfair for victims of crime to suffer while criminals do not.

This retributivist position has been criticized by utilitarians (*see* UTILITARIANISM), who believe that punishment can only be justified when it promotes a greater good, such as the reduction of crime. The three common utilitarian justifications for punishment are therefore concerned with the ways in which punishing criminals may be beneficial to society. First, punishment can act as a DETERRENCE to crime, either specifically where an individual offender is discouraged from reoffending or generally where potential offenders are deterred because they see what might happen to them if they are caught. Second, punishment is supposed to have a reformative or rehabilitative effect, although the evidence now suggests that this is not the case with most common methods of punishment, particularly incarceration. Finally, punishment in the form of incarceration or execution (*see* CAPITAL PUNISHMENT) can reduce crime by keeping potential offenders out of society.

The amount of punishment appropriate to a crime is also an issue of concern for ethicists. Most importantly, we generally believe that punishment should have some relationship to the severity of the crime; in this belief, minor crimes are subject to minor penalties, and major ones to major penalties. In addition, many now believe that there is a limit to the sort of punishment that should be imposed on a criminal, regardless of the crime committed, a principle echoed in the U.S. Constitution, which prohibits "cruel and unusual punishment."

Problems, however, arise for ethicists when applying all these principles to real life. For example, to what extent should various excuses, such as insanity, be accepted as mitigating factors when deciding on appropriate punishment? Similarly, with increasing evidence that individuals from abusive or disadvantaged backgrounds have a much higher likelihood of committing crime, to what extent should the social and genetic background of a criminal affect our response to their crime?

Furthermore, it is easy to assume that punishments are too lenient or even pleasant, but evidence suggests that common punishments are far more unpleasant than the average person realizes. Prisons, for example, not only involve confinement away from friends and family and the loss of career and social opportunities but also a significant threat of violence and abuse, including the widespread RAPE of both women and men. Therefore, before responding to crime based on an initial gut reaction, it is extremely important to have a good understanding of all circumstances relevant to both the punishment and the crime. *See also* JUSTICE.

PURITANISM Strictness and austerity, usually linked with strong religious FAITH.

Puritanism is so-called after the Puritans, a group of Protestant reformers within the Church of England. The Puritans wanted to purify the church of all Catholic influences and placed a heavy reliance on personal devotion to GOD and strict doctrine. Many immigrated in the 1600s to the United States, where they established a community in New England. Puritans were characterized by their devoutness to God, the simplicity of their tastes, and their strict moral conduct. Puritans believe that human beings are inherently sinful (*see* SIN) and that only by strict prayer and discipline can one remain godly.

PURPOSE *See* TELEOLOGY.

Q

QUR'AN   The Qur'an, or Koran, is the sacred scripture of Islam (*see* ISLAMIC ETHICS).

The word *qur'an* means "the reading." In the Muslim FAITH the Qur'an is believed to be the actual words of GOD as revealed (*see* REVELATION) to MUHAMMAD between 610 and 632. The Qur'an is believed to validate similar teachings received earlier by Jews (*see* JEWISH ETHICS) and Christians (*see* CHRISTIAN ETHICS). The Qur'an contains 114 suras, or chapters, and with the exception of the opening sura the chapters are arranged by length, with the longest appearing earlier in the text. The standard version of the Qur'an was adopted during the reign of the caliph Uthman (644–656).

The main teachings of the Qur'an concern the wonder and glory of God, his mercifulness (*see* MERCY) and absolute (*see* ABSOLUTES) truthfulness (*see* TRUTH). The faithful are called to believe absolutely in God and his goodness, to evince gratitude, and to seek signs of divine goodness in everyday life. All people are subject to a final JUDGMENT or Judgment Day when God will determine whether they have followed the path of God's guidance and will thus be rewarded or have failed to follow God's guidance and will thus be punished.

The Qur'an also reveals commandments regarding MARRIAGE, DIVORCE, PROPERTY, cleanliness, and war.

R

RACISM   PREJUDICE directed at people based on their ethnic origin.

Racism refers to attitudes and behaviors that deny the DIGNITY and RIGHTS of individuals and groups based on race. Perhaps the most noted example of racism in the twentieth century has been the actions of the Nazis in Germany (*see* NAZISM; HOLOCAUST). Under the leadership of Adolf Hitler, the Nazi party embarked upon an agenda of "racial purity," which included a horrendous campaign to imprison, exile, or murder Jews in order to eliminate them from Germany and German culture. South African apartheid, under which a small white minority ruled the black majority in South Africa, is another example of a racist government. The treatment of African Americans in the United States (*see* JIM CROW LAWS) is also an example of institutionalized racism. African Americans were denied voting and other civil rights in some parts of the United States through the 1960s. Programs such as AFFIRMATIVE ACTION and laws (*see* LAW) governing equal opportunity in hiring are an attempt to offset racism and establish legal and social EQUALITY.

Although societies can take steps to stop institutionalized or socially sanctioned racism, it is far more difficult to address a culture's racial attitudes. Racism usually takes a less overt, but still damaging, form. Racist attitudes are expressed in stereotyping certain groups as more or less industrious, more or less intelligent, more or less virtuous, and more or less passionate. Assessing people as more or less suitable as friends, coworkers, or mates based on race is also indicative of racist attitudes.

Most ethical theories hold racism to be morally abhorrent because it assigns VALUE to people based on an external, nonmoral characteristic such as skin color rather than on that person's character or actions (*see* ACT). Some relativist theories (*see* RELATIVISM), however, acknowledge that within certain cultures institutionalized racism such as that found in CASTE systems exists and is considered moral from within that culture.

RAPE   Forced sexual intercourse upon an unwilling participant (*see* SEXUAL ETHICS).

There are two types of rape: forcible rape on an unconsenting partner using VIOLENCE or the threat of violence, and STATUTORY RAPE, which is any sexual intercourse with a person under a certain age. Engaging in sexual activity with a person of any age who is unable to give consent, either because of mental deficiency or because the person is unconscious, is sometimes considered statutory rape.

Forcible rape is usually defined as sexual intercourse with a woman against her will using violence, the threat of violence, intimidation, or fraud. The commission of rape by fraud occurs when a person pretends that what will take place is not sexual intercourse, or when a person pretends to be someone other than he is (for example, the victim's husband). It is now generally believed that rape is not the result of sexual desire, but rather the desire to exercise power over the victim. There is a higher acquittal rate in rape than in other crimes because there are usually not any witnesses other than the accused and the victim. Thus, even when sexual intercourse is established, it can be difficult to prove that the victim did not consent and that the accused was aware of this. Victims may also be reluctant to report incidents of rape fearing that they will not be believed or that their own behavior will be "put on trial."

That forced sexual activity or sexual activity with unconsenting minors is WRONG is generally acknowledged. There are a number of controversial instances in which people disagree as to whether a rape has occurred. "Date rape" has become an important issue in the last twenty years and refers to situations in which parties who are known to each other and most often are on a date together have a sexual experience that one party later states was without consent. This may be because the person consented to some sexual contact but was then forced into intercourse or because the person had used drugs or alcohol in such a way as to interfere with the ability to give consent. While RESPONSIBILITY and accountability are very difficult to establish in these cases, it is generally held to be best morally and legally to refrain from sexual intercourse if there is any question about the ability of the partner to give consent. A second controversy surrounding this issue is the question of spousal rape. Because sexual relations are traditionally considered a part of the marriage contract, it was once common to consider sexual intercourse a "right" of marriage. Therefore, it was not possible for a wife to be raped by her husband, even if sex occurred without her consent. More recent thinking recognizes unconsenting sexual intercourse between married persons to be thought of properly as rape. Finally, because the act of rape has been traditionally defined as forced vaginal intercourse, men have not been considered potential victims of rape although there are laws against sodomy. Currently, however, the notion of rape has been broadened to include other forms of sexual conduct, and men are, under certain circumstances, considered to have experienced rape.

RATIONALITY   The capacity to ACT in coherent ways, which can be described as working toward a goal.

Rationality is the ability to speak and act in ways that make sense. We say people are rational when they are able to make plans that are in their own best interest and to devise strategies that seem likely to achieve those plans. We say people are irrational when there seems to be no consistency to their behavior or when their behavior is sporadic and unpredictable. In another sense, irrational behavior may also be perfectly understandable but yet not based in REASON. Prejudice, for example, is comprehendible to us even if we do not share a person's prejudicial views. However, we might describe a person as irrational if that person always acted on prejudice without regard to the facts.

In daily life, rationality is usually praised, while irrational behavior is condemned. In moral theory (*see* MORALS), however, there is active debate as to whether the proper motives for MORALITY are rational or irrational. Thinkers such as PLATO, ARISTOTLE, and Immanuel KANT assign an important role to rationality in ethical thought (*see* ETHICS). On the other hand, egoists (*see* EGOISM), intuitionists (*see* INTUITIONISM), and those who subscribe to theories of MORAL SENTIMENT often claim that morality has an irrational or prerational basis. This means that morality is motivated by emotions, passions (*see* PASSIONS AND EMOTIONS), intuitions, or sentiments that are not governed by reason.

RAWLS, JOHN (1921–)   Harvard philosopher noted for his conceptualization of rule utilitarianism (*see* UTILITARIANISM) as well as a new theory of JUSTICE.

In the 1950s, Rawls helped to define *rule utilitarianism*. This version of utilitarianism claims that society's pleasure is not maximized when we make exceptions to certain RULES, even when the exceptions lead to a short-term GOOD. For example, one criticism of classical utilitarianism is that it allows for unjust actions, such as creating scapegoats. If a town is facing a riot, utilitarian theory might allow for a suspected criminal to be punished even though that person's guilt or innocence has not been legally established, especially if that person's punishment would restore order and stability to the community. Rule utilitarians, however, argue that the greatest good for the greatest number is not achieved by defying the legal system in this case. They argue that the fear that will be created if every person believes that he or she may be denied due process will outweigh the good done by calming the riot. This amendment to utilitarianism satisfies many critics who felt that traditional utilitarianism led to many actions that we would normally consider unjust, such as the punishment of a person before a proper trial.

Rawls's second major contribution to ETHICS came in 1971 with the publication of his book *A Theory of Justice*. We need regulations, he held, to help us to live peacefully together; we need rules—principles (*see* PRINCIPLE) of justice—to decide to whom the basic goods produced in a society, such as income, wealth, opportunity, and freedom, should be distributed. The best way to establish social principles, Rawls argued, was to decide what principles free and equal people would select. Thus, he conceived of the *veil of ignorance,* an imaginary position from which people could choose the rules that would govern them but would do so without knowledge of their own race, gender, age, social status, or other "prejudicial" factors (*see* PREJUDICE). Rawls believed that under these conditions they would want an equal distribution of all the basic goods of society so that they would have an equal chance at securing these goods.

Rawls acknowledges that sometimes equality does not work to everyone's benefit; therefore, the people who decide on principles of justice would permit inequality whenever inequality best helps the people who are disadvantaged (*see* AFFIRMATIVE ACTION). However, Rawls insisted that freedom and opportunity must be equal. As a result of his inquiry, he proposes that free and equal people, ignorant of their own place in society, would accept two principles of justice: (1) everyone is to have equal freedom; and (2) other basic goods, such as income and wealth, should be equally distributed unless an unequal distribution helps the worst-off members of society. Because these rules would be selected under ideal conditions, Rawls claims that we should accept them as principles of justice.

REASON The faculty, or ability, to create a logical chain of inference.

Reason is our ability to think rationally (*see* REASONABLENESS). To use reason is to move from one idea to another according to the principles of LOGIC. We call people reasonable when they ACT in such a way that we can infer the logical sequence that motivates their actions. We call an explanation reasonable when we can follow the order of events giving to support it.

ARISTOTLE discussed two types of reasoning: inductive reasoning and deductive reasoning. Deductive reasoning is that reasoning that allows us to move from general principles to particular events. For example, if we believe that lying is wrong and that X is a lie, then we should be able to deduce that X is wrong. Inductive reasoning is that reasoning that allows us to move from particular events to general principles. For example, we may observe that if we break confidences, then people tend to stop telling us secrets. From those experiences we might form the conclusion that if you tell a secret, people are less likely to trust you. Of course this will not always be the case, but our reason allows us to form an inductive guideline for action.

Immanuel KANT discussed two types of philosophical reason that are important for knowledge and ETHICS. Pure reason gives us a priori (*see* A POSTERIORI) principles, or principles that can be known through reason alone without experience. Practical reason yields a posteriori principles that concern how we should act.

In ethics, the term *reason* is often used in contrast to other foundations of knowledge, such as FAITH, belief, INTUITION, PREJUDICE, or sense perception.

REASONABLENESS   Attitudes or behaviors in accordance with REASON.

Reasonableness indicates a willingness or commitment to adopt reason as a motivation (*see* MOTIVE) for action (*see* ACT) or belief (*see* FAITH). We say people are reasonable when they give good reasons for their actions or when they accept sound reasoning from others as explanation. We say people are unreasonable when they refuse to give or accept such reasons. For example, we often say that people who act out of prejudice are unreasonable; by this we do not mean that we cannot fathom their actions but that their reasons for acting do not appear to be sound. People may be considered to be generally unreasonable, meaning that they are difficult to talk to or work with on almost any point. So too, people may be quite reasonable in ordinary circumstances but appear unreasonable on certain topics. You might have neighbors, for instance, who are cooperative and friendly in every way but consistently refuse to control their dogs because it is "too much trouble." If after you have pointed out the trouble and distress it causes others and the fact that such behavior violates a local ordinance the neighbors still refuse to attempt to control their pets, we would call this behavior unreasonable.

RECIPROCITY   Giving back, in turn, something equivalent to what one has received.

Reciprocity means that people give to others in the manner that they receive from others. For example, if you are invited over to someone's home for dinner, you may reciprocated by extending them an invitation to your home. Exchanging favors is also a form of reciprocity. On the other hand, people sometimes reciprocate harms as well as benefits. In this sense, reciprocal behavior takes on shades of REVENGE. The more common usage, however, is to denote an exchange of altruistic behaviors (*see* ALTRUISM). Ethical theories (*see* ETHICS) based on cooperation argue that the reciprocal behavior is more ethical and more successful than MORALITY based on SELF-INTEREST alone.

REGULATIVE IDEAL   *See* IDEALS.

REHABILITATION   The restoration of a former state of GOOD health, reputation, or status in society.

Rehabilitation aims to reestablish someone to health or social well-being. After an illness or injury, for example, there is often a period of rehabilitation as people strive to achieve or even surpass their former state of health. In moral terms, rehabilitation usually refers to the reinstatement of a transgressor into a social or civil society. For example, the goal of the modern prison system purports to be at least in part rehabilitative. The idea is that time served in prison should also serve to best equip an inmate to return to a productive life as a law-abiding citizen. Unfortunately, in practice, the modern prison system does not evince a strong rehabilitative function, although it is certainly the case that the individual offenders may be rehabilitated and return to constructive lives.

RELATIVISM   The theory that there are no absolute standards and that all TRUTH is relative to a person or culture.

Ethical relativism is the variety of relativism concerned with the moral standards of RIGHT and WRONG. According to ethical relativists, no universal NORM of goodness or rightness exists. What seems right to a person or group is right; there is no higher court of appeal.

The majority of Western philosophers have opposed relativist theories. The first and most influential group of relativists were the ancient Greek SOPHISTS, who were famous targets for the biting criticisms of SOCRATES and PLATO. Following Plato, the tradition has argued that the nature of goodness is independent of what any particular person believes. The theory of ethical universals, as such antirelativist theories are called, was championed in the modern era by Immanuel KANT. According to Kant, the moral LAW is given by REASON and is both independent of experience and universally binding. In this view, every rational creature without exception is bound to obey the moral dictates of reason.

Recent decades have seen a renewed interest and reevaluation of relativism through the works of such philosophers as J. L. Mackie and Richard Rorty. Most moral philosophers now distinguish between two types of relativism: cultural relativism and individual relativism. Individual relativism is the doctrine that states that what is right depends on the view of a specific individual. According to this view, if a man believes that extramarital affairs are morally permissible but his wife does not, then extramarital affairs are right for him but wrong for her. Cultural relativists more moderately claim that there are binding moral norms, but that they are relative to specific cultures. Thus, one culture may have prohibitions against the use of slaves, whereas another culture does not. In this view, slavery is right for the one culture but wrong for the other.

The problem with all types of relativist theories is that they seem unable to account for how strongly people feel about certain immoral acts (*see* IMMORALITY). For instance, if a Nazi soldier believes that torturing Jews is morally permissible, can we only say that such behavior is right for him but that it is not right for us? Many ethicists object and say that we must be able to make the stronger claim that his action is wrong, regardless of what the soldier may believe.

RELIGION AND MORALITY   The relationship between ethical norms (*see* NORM) and religious FAITH.

Most of the discussion about religion and MORALITY centers on the question of whether religion is necessary for morality. If morality requires religion, then we seem unable to account for the fact that some moral people are not religious. If morality does not require religion, then this seems to call into question the absolute (*see* ABSOLUTES) nature of religion and the relationship of the GOOD to the divine.

Modern Western ETHICS has held religion and morality to be distinct. For example, Immanuel KANT argues that the moral law is authoritative independent of religious teaching. Religion need not be inconsistent with morality, however, and in fact may help people to obey (*see* OBEDIENCE) the moral law. Philosophers also cite the variety of religious and moral life that exists today as further evidence of the independence of religion and morality. Not only do people within the same religious tradition sometimes hold very different moral beliefs, but many nonreligious people are extremely moral. In light of such considerations, it seems difficult to maintain the thesis that morality requires religion. Although some thinkers counter along Calvinist lines that even nonreligious persons are in fact believers whose knowledge is distorted by SIN, this view is not generally accepted.

If religion and morality are in fact distinct, in what relationship do they stand to one another? In PLATO's *Euthyphro*, SOCRATES poses a famous DILEMMA: either the gods LOVE what is holy because it is holy, or it is holy because the gods love it; that is, either morality is binding independently of the divine WILL, or the divine will causes morality to be binding. The difficulty is that if we accept the second option—that the holy is holy because the gods love it—then were the gods to command a horrific morality such as cruelty to children, that morality would be good by virtue of being loved by GOD. However, if we accept the first option—that the gods love what is holy because it is holy—then we are acknowledging a moral entity that supersedes the gods and is recognized by them.

Moral philosophers of the major theistic faiths, Judaism (*see* JEWISH ETHICS), Christianity (*see* CHRISTIAN ETHICS), and Islam (*see* ISLAMIC ETHICS), often argue that the dilemma posed in the *Euthyphro* is too exclusive; that is, it assumes that God and morality can be understood independently of one another. While Christians, for instance, certainly appeal to God as the JUSTIFICATION for what they do, it would be a confusion to think that God could suddenly command an EVIL morality; the Christian concept of God is of a God who is good and cannot do evil. This conception departs from the polytheistic culture in which Plato was writing. However, other philosophers object that if God can do anything, then it is logically possible for God to do evil; hence, the problem of the relationship of morality and religion remains problematic for these thinkers.

RESPONSIBILITY   Those acts (*see* ACT) for which one is accountable.

A responsibility is something that one is bound to do either through PROMISE or OBLIGATION or because of one's role in a group or community. If a responsibility is shirked, there is normally some type of social, financial, or legal penalty. In ETHICS, responsibility may indicate a duty to the moral law, as in DEONTOLOGY, or it may refer to a duty toward another human being, as in our responsibility to our families or our responsibility not to cause undue harm to others.

The question of whether we have minimum or maximum responsibilities toward others is a complex one in moral theory. Those who subscribe to a minimalist view of responsibility would argue that we have the responsibility not to harm or interfere with others. For example, we have the responsibility not to lie. Those who subscribe to a maximalist view of responsibility would argue that we have to go beyond a PRINCIPLE of not harming others and that we actually have the responsibility to help others. In the maximalist view we might have the responsibility, for example, to give money to charity rather than to spend it on private entertainment

because we have the responsibility to relieve suffering whenever possible (*see* MAXIMAL VS. MINIMAL ETHICS).

RETRIBUTION   To give or receive reward or PUNISHMENT.

Retribution is compensation for an ACT. In the positive sense, retribution may be payment for a service, or it may be an HONOR or reward for a GOOD deed. In every day language, retribution usually has a negative connotation and implies punishment or REVENGE for wrongdoing. In the religious sense, retribution implies the reward or punishment that is received after death.

RETRIBUTIVE JUSTICE   *See* PUNISHMENT.

REVELATION   Disclosure of TRUTH, often taken to be divine in nature.

A revelation is enlightening or surprising knowledge. In common language, we may take any surprising fact to be a revelation. We might say, for example, "It was a revelation to me that you could cook so well." In moral thought, revelation more particularly refers to a communication of divine truth. In this sense, revelation is often opposed to REASON. Revealed truths are immediately and directly given to a chosen person or to a person who practices (*see* PRACTICE) certain spiritual, physical, and emotional disciplines (*see* MYSTICISM); they are not accessible to everyone at will. On the other hand, truths achieved by reason are supposed to be attainable by any person exercising proper reasoning. Thus, moral teaching based on revelation tend to cluster moral AUTHORITY around an elite or specially chosen group, while moral teachings based on reason are meant to be accessible to all persons.

REVENGE   Retaliation in order to gain satisfaction or punish (*see* PUNISHMENT).

Revenge is a passion (*see* PASSIONS AND EMOTIONS) that arises from real or imagined WRONG.

It is the DESIRE to strike out and hurt someone who has injured us in some way. For example, people may desire to gain revenge on someone who harms a member of their family. People often feel that what they desire is a just revenge—"an eye for an eye," so to speak. In this case the desire is to inflict an equal harm as was originally believed to be committed. Other times revenge is a passion that seeks to inflict even further punishment on the offender. For instance, we sometimes read about people who have killed the new partners of former boyfriends, girlfriends, husbands, or wives out of JEALOUSY and revenge.

Revenge has held varying positions in different moral theories. Some moral theories seem to demand revenge as a part of a CODE OF HONOR or LOYALTY. Others prize FORGIVENESS and CHARITY, seeing revenge as a SIN. In legal terms, revenge is not a socially acceptable MOTIVE for punishment or retaliation.

REVERSE DISCRIMINATION   *See* AFFIRMATIVE ACTION.

RIGHT   To be correct, as one is right if one gives the correct answer to a question.

An ACT is said to be right, in the most general sense, if it is not WRONG, or if morally speaking it is permitted or allowed (*see* PERMISSIBLE ACT). However, in action, there may be more than one right thing to do in the sense that any one of two or more alternatives may be permitted, just as, at any given time, many acts would be wrong. If there were not a conflicting duty or OBLIGATION, it would be right, on any occasion, to eat or sleep or take a walk, for none of these acts is morally wrong. Duties and obligations limit what action or choice is right at a particular time. On a given occasion, one might, for example, have a duty to help a particular person who is suffering, in which case it would be cruel to eat one's dinner calmly while the other person suffered.

Some ethicists (*see* ETHICS) have spoken of "the right thing to do," as if, on any particular occasion, there were one and only one right thing a person could do. This position stems from the belief that people should always do their best and that anything less than their best would be wrong. Thus, the right culminates in the one best act a person can perform. Such ethical theories are said to be optimific or maximific (*see* MAXIMAL VS. MINIMAL ETHICS) because they require people to do the best, or the most GOOD, that they can do.

The idea of an act's rightness should be distinguished from someone's RIGHTS, although these concepts are related. If an act is right, in the sense of being morally permitted, then a person has a right to do it if he or she has the ability and opportunity to perform that act. But it doesn't follow from this necessarily that the person has a right in the sense that other people have a duty or obligation to help that person to perform the act or even that they must refrain from interfering. Walking on the sidewalk is generally a right thing to do because it is not prohibited (*see* PROHIBITION), morally speaking, but it does not necessarily follow from this that other people must provide sidewalks for us to walk on, or even that they must move out of our way, or that we "have a right" to sidewalks. The expression *having a right* is often meant to imply that others have a corresponding duty to enable us or at least not to interfere with our actions. If we have a right to life, then others have a duty not to kill us, and if we have a right to education, then we suppose that someone ought to provide it. The notion of moral rightness and rights are related in the sense that one cannot have a moral right to do what is morally wrong.

How we can determine what is morally right or morally wrong is perhaps the most fundamental question of ethical theory. Moral philosophy is an attempt to discover the characteristics of right acts: what about them makes them right or how we can know whether and when acts are right. For example, some theories hold that acts are right because of their consequences (*see* CONSEQUENTIALISM), and others argue that acts are right because they obey or conform to moral rules (*see* DEONTOLOGY).

RIGHT CONDUCT   *See* BUDDHIST ETHICS.

RIGHT LIVELIHOOD   *See* BUDDHIST ETHICS.

RIGHT LIVING   *See* BUDDHIST ETHICS.

RIGHT TO DIE   The RIGHT to refuse medical treatment and hasten one's own death (*see* DEATH AND DYING).

To prolong life in the face of disease is a basic tenet of medicine. Recently, however, doctors, lawyers, and laypeople have debated the ETHICS of this goal. It is argued that our struggle to delay death has become unnatural and that we should be able to meet our deaths in the manner of our own choosing. The case of Karen Ann Quinlan in 1975 was an initial test case. She was a young woman in a coma, and her parents Joseph and Julia Quinlan fought against her doctors to allow the life-support machines to be turned off. Their work on behalf of their daughter has led to the gradual ethical and legal acceptance of the right of family members to discontinue life support and/or artificial feeding for patients in a permanent vegetative state.

Karen Quinlan was an extreme case and more clear-cut in retrospect than other cases. An elderly patient who refuses medical treatment while competent is usually allowed that right. However, patients who have not made their wishes clear before losing the ability to make decisions concerning aggressive care create distinct problems for MEDICAL ETHICS. Technology exists to keep bodies alive long after the ability to cure is passed. A person with Parkinson's disease may be trapped in a body that does not move under its own will. Arthritis may painfully cripple men and women long before a natural death. Proponents of the right

to die believe that people have the right to refuse medical treatment, outside help, and even food and water if they are not able to feed themselves. More-aggressive proponents believe that assisted SUICIDE is just an extension of the right to die, but this is much more controversial. All sides believe that the mental health of the patient must not be in a question at the time the decision is made.

RIGHT TO LIFE   The position that human LIFE begins at conception and deserves constitutional protection from that movement on. Those who hold a RIGHT to life position are opposed to ABORTION, arguing that it is the intentional killing of a human being. *See also* FETUS.

RIGHTS   Benefits or freedom (*see* FREEDOM) that each member of a group or class is thought to be morally entitled to.

The concept of rights emerged in seventeenth- and eighteenth-century LIBERALISM and was particularly significant in the rhetoric of the French and American revolutions. Rights are inherently individualistic (*see* INDIVIDUALISM), in that they apply exclusively to individuals and not groups; they are also egalitarian (*see* EGALITARIANISM) in that everyone within the designated group is entitled to them, regardless of any other personal characteristic they may have.

All rights impose a subsequent duty on others to respect or even promote those rights. In ethics, a distinction is sometimes made between rights that impose on others a duty to refrain from certain behaviors, known as negative rights, and rights that impose upon others an OBLIGATION to act in a certain way, known as positive rights. For example, the right to freedom of speech implies that we must not stop others from speaking and is, therefore, a negative right. The right to universal health care, on the other hand, is a positive right because it seems to impose upon some people an obligation to pay for the health care of those who cannot afford it.

According to some, only a specific group of negative freedoms known as NATURAL RIGHTS can legitimately be described as rights at all. These rights, including the right to LIFE, liberty, and private PROPERTY, are supposed to be both unchangeable and inalienable; that is, they exist automatically and cannot be taken away. This idea has been criticized most colorfully by Jeremy BENTHAM as "nonsense upon stilts." According to Bentham, rights only exist when supported by the force of LAW and are, therefore, simply an artificial mechanism used to mandate respect for universal and socially desirable principles. In addition, it can be argued that because even fundamental rights, such as the right to life, appear to be subject to exceptions, such as for capital punishment or euthanasia, it is difficult to see how any single principle can truly be described as universal and unalterable. *See also* ANIMAL RIGHTS; BILL OF RIGHTS; CHILDREN'S RIGHTS; CIVIL RIGHTS; DISABILITY RIGHTS; EQUAL RIGHTS AMENDMENT; GAY RIGHTS; HUMAN RIGHTS; WAIVING OF RIGHTS; WOMEN'S RIGHTS.

ROBERT'S RULES OF ORDER The most commonly used system of parliamentary procedure in North America.

To facilitate ethical decision making in groups, RULES for governing who can speak and on what topic at groups meetings have evolved. The purpose of these rules is not to restrict FREEDOM but to create an equal and fair opportunity for all the members of a group to contribute to the group or to conduct business there.

Robert's Rules of Order is the most common of such rules. The rules, first published in 1876, are quite lengthy and specific, consuming more than 300 pages. Many groups use a simplified version of these rules, adopting only the major principles.

Robert's Rules of Order are intended to help people work effectively in a group. They govern the agenda and the process for putting matters on the agenda. They establish the principle of a majority vote and mandate that all members in a group have equal RIGHTS, equal privileges, and equal obligations (*see* OBLIGATION). This means that although there is majority rule, the rights of minorities are also protected. All decisions deserve full discussion, and all members of the group must understand the discussion and questions during the meeting, including understanding the effects and consequences of those decisions.

ROUSSEAU, JEAN-JACQUES (1712–1778) Swiss-born social, ethical, and political philosopher associated with Romanticism.

In 1755 Rousseau published a treatise entitled *A Discourse upon the Origin and Foundation of the Inequality Among Mankind,* usually referred to as the Second Discourse. In this writing Rousseau described a state of nature that was free, innocent, healthy, and happy. In the state of nature, people had a natural sympathy for one another, which bonded them together. This view of the state of nature is radically different from that proposed by Thomas HOBBES, who argues that the savagery of nature is what gives rise to the SOCIAL CONTRACT. In Rousseau's view the social contract was not a vehicle of JUSTICE and order, as Hobbes argued, but rather an imposition of POWER on the poor by the rich. Rousseau followed the Second Discourse in 1762 with a treatise entitled *The Social Contract* in which he defended his vision of a just society in which all members participated equally in lawmaking. In his writings on education, Rousseau emphasizes the importance of physical health, feelings, sense experience, and a reunification of human beings with nature over REASON and the intellect.

RULE UTILITARIANISM *See* UTILITARIANISM.

RULES Regulations for RIGHT conduct or behavior.

Rules are laws (*see* LAW) or guidelines given by an AUTHORITY and meant to guide right action (*see* ACT). That authority may be external, such as a parent, government, or religious order, or the authority may be internal, such as the rules dictated by REASON or conscience. Rules are mean to regulate action and, thus, create a stable, functional, or efficient environment; for example, a parent may have a rule that all homework has to be done before the television is turned on for entertainment, or states have rules that govern which side of the road you can drive on and at what speed.

Moral rules (*see* MORALS) are rules that govern ethical behavior (*see* ETHICS). Deontologists (*see* DEONTOLOGY) hold that moral rules should MOTIVATE all ethical behavior and that these rules are absolute (*see* ABSOLUTES) and universal. For example, the rule "Do not lie" should apply to all people at all times. For a deontologist, moral rules have objective value. In contrast, a consequentialist (*see* CONSEQUENTIALISM) adheres to the principle that moral rules are established by outcomes of actions. UTILITARIANISM holds, for example, to the moral rule, or maxim, of creating the greatest happiness and causing the least suffering in each situation.

S

SACRIFICE The surrender of something valued for the sake of an ideal, belief or goal.

The concept of sacrifice, which stems from a word meaning "to make holy," has a rich and varied history. In the ancient world, the killing of people or animals was sometimes viewed as a way of currying divine favor or of expressing gratitude to the gods. In one biblical story, Abraham was commanded to kill his son Isaac as a sacrifice to the Lord. At the last moment, Abraham was commanded to free Isaac and an animal sacrifice was made instead. The concept of a sacrifice is crucial to the Christian doctrine, which views the crucifixion of JESUS as a sacrifice performed for the sake of the world's salvation.

Besides its religious meanings, sacrifice also has an important place in secular MORALITY. Parents may sacrifice their own needs, for example, in order to benefit their children. Self-sacrifice of this kind is usually seen as a VIRTUE. The sacrifice of others for the sake of one's own interest is, in contrast, considered immoral (*see* IMMORALITY). The moral worth of sacrifice is therefore dependent on who or what is being sacrificed and for what reason.

Some thinkers have argued that ethical systems that place a high VALUE on sacrifice are in fact based on weakness. Friedrich NIETZSCHE, for example, argued that self-sacrifice, especially the Christian version, was a pseudo-virtue that weak people created in order to make themselves feel effective against stronger people. Related to this idea is the contemporary concept of a *martyr syndrome,* which describes someone who consistently suffers hardships for the sake of feeling important or gaining attention. Most ethicists admit that self-sacrifice may sometimes be motivated by selfish desires but believe that genuine and morally worthy self-sacrifice is also possible.

SAMSARA Hindu and Buddhist characterization of the cosmic process and human predicament, described as the wheel of perpetual becoming because it entails endless reincarnation; driven by the law of cause and effect (*see* KARMA).

Hinduism and Buddhism share a common worldview and understanding of the fundamental problem that humans have in this world. The Indian view of nature and history is cyclical, which means that the cosmic process is understood as one of ceaseless becoming or change. In Hinduism, three major gods represent and execute the cyclical, repetitive process: Brahma creates, Vishnu preserves, and Shiva destroys. Buddhism denies or ignores the gods and simply affirms the process in terms of cosmic law (*see* DHARMA): arising, remaining, ceasing.

The human predicament is one of entrapment in this ongoing process. Death (*see* DEATH AND DYING) does not end the process because, from the Indian perspective, death is not an end but a transition to another round of existence. As long as the Hindu is ignorant of his or her essential identity with Brahman, the Ultimate, rebirth continues. As long as the Buddhist is ignorant of his or her true nature and, thus, plagued by avarice and hatred, rebirth continues.

According to Hinduism and Buddhism, the phenomenal world, the world of time and space, is illusory (*see* MAYA), unreal, or at best relatively real. As long as one buys into appearances—that is, attaches to the outer and the obvious—one remains imprisoned in the chain of existence following existence. Indian philosophic-religious systems consider the uncritical valuation of the apparent world to be supreme naïveté, resulting in perpetual becoming through rebirth following rebirth.

For the Hindu, the samsaric cycle ends with MOKSHA, liberation; for the Buddhist, it ends with NIRVANA, enlightenment. In all cases, the process ends only by taking up a PSYCHOSPIRITUAL DISCIPLINE that invariably entails a demanding morality. *See also* BUDDHIST ETHICS; HINDU ETHICS.

SANCTIONS In ETHICS, the things that motivate us to ACT morally (*see* MORALITY).

When assessing any moral CODE, it seems fundamental to ask why we should obey it and not some other code. In other words, what force exists to legitimate the code? In ethics, the forces that support our decisions to act morally are known as sanctions. Sanctions may involve incentives for doing RIGHT and disincentives for doing WRONG. For example, the sanctions of a particular moral code may include both the possibility of an afterlife of pain and suffering if we do EVIL and the possibility of an afterlife of pleasure if we do GOOD. Sanctions may come from an internal source, such as our own CONSCIENCE and instinct; an external source, such as the JUDGMENT of our peers; or both.

SARTRE, JEAN-PAUL (1905–1980) A French atheistic existentialist (*see* ATHEISM; EXISTENTIALISM) known both for his literary works and his philosophy. His novels and plays include *Nausea* and *No Exit,* and his best known philosophic works are *Being and Nothingness* and *Existentialism Is a Humanism.* He was also the lifelong companion of Simone de BEAUVOIR, the feminist philosopher.

In his philosophy, Sartre argues that existing individuals are not predetermined to ACT in any way by external forces or even by their own natures, but instead are free to choose the kinds of people they will be. He speaks of FREEDOM of choice, however, not so much as a gift but rather as a burden because people must bear full RESPONSIBILITY for all the choices they make. They cannot blame others, whether that be their parents or society, and they cannot even blame the conditions in which they find themselves. Nothing *makes* them do what they do; it is always their free choice. Moreover, there is nothing to guide them in their choice; no principles (*see* PRINCIPLE) or RULES can guarantee that any choice is RIGHT. People must simply make their choices and accept the consequences, even though the consequences may be unpredictable.

Sartre recognized that this type of freedom is frightening and that it causes anxiety. People try to deny their freedom and responsibility by citing circumstances that are "out of their control." To be free, Sartre tells us in *Being and Nothingness,* is to be nothing or "no thing" in the sense that people are not things that have fixed natures. If they had fixed natures, they would be determined by their natures, but people are not so determined because they are free. At the same time, people are afraid of being nothing or nobody and want to be somebody or something that is fixed and solid, such as a physical object. So they tend to think of themselves as a specific kind of being such as a doctor or lawyer, an intellectual or an athlete. They then try to explain their behavior to themselves and others accordingly, as if their behaviors were determined by the ideas they have of themselves. "I cannot do the dishes; I'm a man," someone might claim, as if being a man prevented doing certain household tasks. "I cannot see you because I have to work" or "I am too busy" are other common examples. Sartre's point is that one can but that one chooses not to.

Thinking of oneself in a certain role or occupation is like play-acting. Sartre calls it SELF-DECEPTION or bad FAITH, for in order to escape from freedom, people pretend to be something they are not. Being self-conscious, they see themselves mirrored in the eyes of others; this is the power of "the look." When others look at us, we may feel on the spot, wondering what they see or think. To make them see us in a favorable light, we then pretend to be what we would like them to see. We try to convince them and even ourselves that our pretension is true. People may claim, for example, that they are homosexual by nature, but Sartre argues that nobody simply is or is not a homosexual; everyone is free to choose or not choose to engage in homosexual acts. Such self-deception causes ALIENATION or PREJUDICE because people are separated from one another by the images they have of themselves.

Sartre denies that rules or reasons can determine what is morally correct. Rules contradict one another and are too general and vague to tell us what is right or wrong in particular cases. Therefore, he concludes, we must simply choose to make something a value for ourselves. His theory is decisionalist in this respect, for he believes that activities take on VALUE because we choose them and become engaged in them. We do not choose them because they are first known to have VALUE.

SCIENCE, ETHICS OF The branch of APPLIED ETHICS that deals with the moral implications of scientific methods and research. The ethics of science considers questions such as how to conduct research, how to use research results, how to define scientific progress, and last but not least how to behave as GOOD scientists. This last point concerns standards such as: scientists may not manipulate data, should deduce their results transparently, should use intersubjective and comprehensible experiments that deliver in repeatable results, should follow rules of fair play with colleagues, should work precisely and reliably, and should obey a critical distance to their field of research.

The moral VALUE of technology has been the focus of attention within the ETHICS of science in recent years; because of major twentieth-century developments in physics and biology,

weapons of almost unimaginable destructiveness are now possible. The need for a modern ethics of science is marked by the development of atomic weapons. The atomic bombing of Hiroshima at the close of World War II encouraged discussion on the meaning of scientific progress and forced researchers to consider their own RESPONSIBILITY for the possible outcomes and possible applications of their work. Interestingly, a similar problem existed in the early 1920s in relation to the cruelty of the gas weapons used in World War I; the debate was soon abandoned.

But in such a complex scientific and technical world, we must ask whether the single researcher is the appropriate subject of responsibility. After analyzing the scientific system more thoroughly with all its mechanisms, forces, and benefits for researchers and research communities, the ethics of science became oriented to the problem of influence and henceforth the responsibility of the individual. No single person makes decisions on important questions: defining objects of research, research directions, research methods, and application of the research results. Therefore, the appeal to ethical conduct of the members of a research organization or community seems to be misguided.

The debates in the scientific community on the ethics of science have resulted, at minimum, in an increased awareness of the problems inside the scientific community. In some cases, scientists publicized research results too early, leading to problems while society debated the implications of findings that were not yet final—and in some cases were ultimately dismissed. This has been especially true of the fields of GENETIC ENGINEERING and artificial intelligence.

Institutional solutions that combine ethical expertise and scientific knowledge have been established in the form of ethics committees that consider and evaluate research programs in medicine, genetic engineering, and biotechnology. In some other cases moratoria have been proposed, that prohibit the application of results in a specific field of research until a consensual decision can be made. Such moratoria give time to consider new knowledge of opportunities and disadvantages of new technologies—in effect, a voluntary self-censorship of science in the name of responsibility.

Another important problem of the ethics of science considers questions of what instruments, experiments, and methods are ethically allowed in research. This is one aspect of the debate on ethical standards for animal experiments (see ANIMAL RIGHTS) and those using human embryos. Further important questions consider norms for experiments with uninformed people, experiments with mentally ill or handicapped people, and experiments on people who are forced to take part (see INFORMED CONSENT).

Disputes considering the involvement of people in experiments have their roots in the 1940s. At that time prisoners of war, inmates of concentration camps, and mentally ill people were used in medical experiments. Even in the U.S. uninformed citizens, soldiers, and prisoners were used in experiments to investigate the impact of ionizing radiation on human bodies.

The ethics of science also questions whether there ought to be any limits to research questions. Genetic research, computer-aided intelligence research, and inquiries into the brain and personality all have the potential to compromise the essential DIGNITY of the human being. Already, prenatal genetic testing forces parents to face increasingly difficult questions concerning abortion and health care, for example.

Another issue in the ethics of science concerns determining which scientific projects should receive the limited amount of public funding available. For instance, new developments in submarine technology now allow for exploration into the very deepest regions of the ocean. Although the information gleaned from such exploration would be welcomed by the scientific community, the results are not likely to affect a great number of people. A cure for cancer, on the other hand, would positively affect many people. Some would argue that the second kind of research should have priority over the first because every dollar spent on deep-sea exploration is a dollar that could be used to help save someone's life.

SECRET   Knowledge that is kept hidden.

A secret is something one knows but does not reveal or promises not to reveal (see PROMISE). Secrets differ widely in their nature. For example, if you are planning a party for a friend's birthday, you may wish to keep it a secret in order to make it a surprise. Secrets can also involve private information, such as something personal that a friend confides to you that he or she does not wish others to know. If the information does not imply that your friend is risking HARM, then it is normally considered moral (see MORALITY) to keep this confidence and not betray the secret. On the other hand, a person who is committing adultery may try to keep that a secret in a way which is harmful or unfair to a spouse.

Sometimes people are asked or pressured to keep secrets in a way that is immoral (see IMMORALITY). For example, a company has a right to ask its employees to keep secret new developments but not if those developments are risking the health and safety of the employees or the community (see WHISTLE-BLOWING). Adults may ask children to keep secrets when there are instances of emotional or physical abuse occurring at home and threaten harm if such secrets are revealed. Such demands are immoral; workers and children are not bound to keep these types of secrets.

Deciding when to keep a secret and when to reveal it can be the cause of a moral DILEMMA. Usually, a secret should only be revealed when there is the threat of harm to someone who may be affected by it. When in doubt, it can be helpful to find someone in whom you can confide and seek another opinion on whether a secret is dangerous and should be shared or whether the confidence should be protected.

SECULAR ETHICS Systems of conduct and MORALITY that do not arise from religious views.

Secular ETHICS refers to ethical positions that are independent from religion. Secular ethics holds that RIGHT and WRONG are determined without reference to a divine WILL or law. For example, UTILITARIANISM, which holds that those actions (*see* ACT) are right that create the greatest good for the greatest number, is an example of a secular ethics. Secular ethics may VALUE the same characteristics and actions as do religious ethics, but they differ in their JUSTIFICATION for those VALUES. For example, both a secular and religious ethic may hold that it is wrong to murder; the religious ethic, however, may justify this by appeal to the Ten Commandments, whereas secular ethics might appeal to the dignity of all human persons independent of divine creation.

SEGREGATION The discriminatory division (*see* DISCRIMINATION) of the members of a society.

The term *segregation* is usually associated with the separation of members of a society based on race, but it may be based on gender, religion, or any other quality. In a segregated society goods, services, public spaces, and daily interactions are regulated so that members of segregated groups are either kept separate or do not meet as equals (*see* EQUALITY) in society.

Segregation is the opposite of integration. In an integrated society opportunities, goods, and services are available without consideration to any group membership. All people are free to take part in social activities, including securing employment and housing, participating in commerce, and voting.

It is rare to find a society in which there is no segregation. Segregation is called de facto when there are no laws that mandate separation, but the social climate is such that people keep their private lives separate. Segregation is called de jure when there are laws that enforce the separation of groups.

SELF-CONTROL The ability to control one's impulses, PASSIONS AND EMOTIONS.

Nearly all ethical theories hold that moral behavior involves some type of training, whether based on REASON, INTUITION, sentiment, or REVELATION. Self-control is the capacity to restrain certain desires (*see* DESIRE) or inclinations so as to act within the bounds of MORALITY. For example, people who have quick tempers may have to exercise self-control so as not to show disrespect to others or pick fights. Self-control differs from TEMPERANCE in that self-control implies that a person experiences passions that are out of balance with the moral life but can learn to discipline them. Temperance implies that one has trained one's character to not experience excessive desires.

SELF-DECEPTION To play a role, however unconscious, in misunderstanding a situation.

Self-deception involves believing what is not true (*see* TRUTH) or refusing to acknowledge what is true, based on one's motives (*see* MOTIVE) or desires (*see* DESIRE). Self-deception is not simply mistakenness about what is the case but rather a misunderstanding of something that would be obvious to someone who was not motivated to misunderstand it. For example, we may deceive ourselves about the role a loved one plays in wrongdoing when it is obvious to others. In ETHICS, we may practice self-deception when we rationalize ethical behavior that we suspect, under closer self-scrutiny, would be in conflict with our stated VALUES.

Self-deception is a complicated concept for philosophers because it implies that one both knows something and is able to conceal from oneself what is known. However, when we consider the strong influence of passions (*see* PASSIONS AND EMOTIONS), desires, and fears, we can understand how people might cover up what they know with the stronger motivation to believe what they want or need to be true. In almost all moral theories, moral action demands that we actively root out self-deception and ACT with as complete a self-understanding as we can achieve.

SELF-EVIDENT   The characteristic of being obviously true (*see* TRUTH).

For something to be self-evident means that it should be true automatically for anyone who sees it. No inference or further argument is held to be necessary. For example, when the Declaration of Independence states "We hold these truths to be self-evident . . . ," this means that they are not considered to need any further justification because anyone should be able to recognize their validity.

Self-evidence is a controversial ethical notion because different ethical propositions may be self-evident to different people. For example, it may be self-evident to one person that all people should receive equal amounts of social goods, but to another it may be self-evident that all persons should receive the social goods they require, whether or not that is equal to the needs of another.

SELF-INTEREST   The concern for one's own well-being.

Self-interest refers to looking out for one's self and regarding what is in one's own best interest. To be self-interested is to consider what is to one's own advantage in a given situation. For example, if you want to keep your money, it is not in your best interest to leave your wallet or purse lying open in a public place unattended. To ACT self-interestedly means prudent attention to what will bring the best outcome for yourself; it does not necessarily mean to act to the exclusion of other people's interest. For example, it may be in your self-interest to compromise during an argument if your greater interest is served by group consensus. When people conceive of

their own interests as always more important than other people's interests, we say they are excessively self-interested or selfish (*see* SELFISHNESS).

SELFISHNESS   To be concerned only with oneself.

Selfishness is the state of excessive SELF-INTEREST. Selfish people are those who care only for their own interests or well-being without thought to the needs of others. Selfish people always pursue their own advantage, failing to include others even when it would not disadvantage them to do so. Selfishness is related to GREED and to a lack of GENEROSITY.

SELFLESSNESS   The state of being unselfish.

Those who are selfless have little or no concern for themselves, reserving instead all of their concern for others. Selflessness is connected to GENEROSITY. If people do not care for themselves but also do not care for others, then we do not say they are selfless. Selflessness is often associated with a MORAL SAINT or person who makes great SACRIFICE so that other people may have what they need. Although maximalist moralities (*see* MAXIMAL VS. MINIMAL ETHICS) encourage the pursuit of selflessness, it is more common for a morality to encourage a balance of generosity and SELF-INTEREST with selflessness being considered a type of heroic VIRTUE.

SELF-LOVE   *See* NARCISSISM.

SELF-REALIZATION   Actualizing one's potential as a person.

The terms *actuality* and *potentiality* were used by the ancient philosopher ARISTOTLE, who explained all changes as the actualization of potentiality. An acorn can become an oak tree, he reasoned, because an acorn has the potential to reach maturity in the form of an oak. People, according to Aristotle, also have the potentiality to become mature people by using their talents or developing their abilities. The *telos*, or goal, of the moral life (*see* TELEOLOGY) is the actualization of human potentialities by doing the kinds of things that are appropriate to human life. He spoke of the self-actualized person as being magnanimous, as having a big soul, and as having a life filled with goodness. Such a person is literally at the top of his or her form, doing well at all the kinds of things he or she is capable of doing.

The ideal of MORAL DEVELOPMENT is expressed in a number of recent psychological theories, such as those of Carl Rogers and Abraham Maslow. Rogers speaks of a self-image, or ideal self, that expresses the goals of an individual, and Maslow lists a number of characteristics that he believes a self-actualized person will have, including self-acceptance, independence, and sociability. The idea of self-realization also finds expression in everyday moral discourse (*see* DISCOURSE ETHICS), as people often admire and praise human achievement in the arts or in sports, for example, and are often critical of individuals who fail to use their talents. "Be all that you can be" has been used as a slogan to advertise organizations that are supposed to help people develop their abilities, and people who do not develop them are sometimes referred to as "vegetables" or "couch potatoes" to indicate that the life they are living is not fully human in the moral or philosophic sense.

SELF-RIGHTEOUSNESS A negative term suggesting a narrow-minded moral attitude.

Self-righteousness describes a deep conviction or belief (*see* FAITH) in one's own high moral standing, especially in comparison with other people. Whereas to be righteous is to be morally RIGHT or to obey the moral law, to be self-righteous is to be excessively prideful about one's moral beliefs. Self-righteous people are held to lack WISDOM and do not display the virtues of LOVE or CHARITY. People who condemn the actions of others without considering their situation are often called self-righteous.

SEXISM Unwarranted DISCRIMINATION based on a person's gender.

Sexism occurs when a person's gender is used to deny equal opportunities or benefits in housing, employment, education, public accommodation, and public office. For example, if a man and a woman perform the same task but a man receives higher pay or better benefits, this is considered sexism. Sexist attitudes are those attitudes that stereotype what type of work a person is capable of or qualities a person must have, based on gender. The idea that women belong in the home or that men make better business executives than women is considered sexist.

Not all sexual discrimination is considered unethical or illegal. For example, small employers and individuals seeking personal care or live-in care in their homes, gender-specific schools, summer camps, and youth groups, as well as health, accident, auto, and life insurance underwriters are among those providers of goods and services who lawfully may discriminate on the basis of gender, consistent with their own personal preference or with statistical data. *See also* WOMEN'S RIGHTS.

SEXUAL ABUSE Unethical sexual contact, especially that which is nonconsensual or otherwise coerced.

Sexual abuse is not always recognized as a moral WRONG by those who engage in it or by their victims. Any sexual contact between adults and children, however, is usually considered to be sexual abuse. There is an ethical presumption that children lack the capacity to give INFORMED CONSENT to the sexual contact. Even if a child consents, the consent is not considered to be valid or to be given freely. The consent is invalid because the child is incompetent to make autonomous (*see* AUTONOMY) choices that balance the harms (*see* HARM) and benefits of sexual activity. The consent also is not given freely because there is presumed to be an imbalance of AUTHORITY, dependency, and trust between adults and children. Adults presumably have greater physical strength, psychological control, and social authority than children. Therefore, relationships between children and adults generally empower adults to compel OBEDIENCE and compliance by children. Also, children typically are physically and psychologically dependent upon adults and trust adults to protect them from harm. This imbalance in authority, dependency, and trust makes children more susceptible than adults to being compelled to engage in sexual activity. That element of compulsion makes the sexual relationship a form of abuse.

Analogous discrepancies exist between the POWER and authority of teachers and students, physicians and patients, counselors and clients, clergy and parishioners, employers and employees, jailers and prisoners, and so on. Sexual contact among people in such relationships is generally regarded as likely to be abusive. There are inherent power discrepancies between such people, making it questionable whether sexual contact between them is chosen freely (see FREEDOM). The relationship is inherently one of such great dependency on the part of the employee, client, student, patient, and so on that fraud, deception, and undue influence may prevent genuine consent. For these reasons most codes of PROFESSIONAL ETHICS prohibit sexual contact within these types of relationships.

Sexual abuse should be distinguished from SEXUAL HARASSMENT and other forms of sexual exploitation, even though sexual harassment sometimes precedes abuse and sexual exploitation sometimes also includes elements of sexual abuse. See also RAPE.

SEXUAL ETHICS   The part of moral theory that address sexuality and intimate relationships, including matters of ADULTERY, consent, DESIRE, HONESTY, MARRIAGE, PRIVACY, and RESPONSIBILITY.

In some moral codes (see CODE), sexual relations are only permitted between two people who are married. Other moral theories permit sexual relationships between adult persons who are not married, but condone only monogamous relationships or those where each person has one and only one sexual partner. When a person has multiple or frequently changed sexual partners, that person is sometimes labeled as promiscuous, which carries a negative connotation. The view that sex should occur only within marriage also has implications for the types of sexual relationships that can be viewed as moral. For example, homosexual relationships (see HOMOSEXUALITY) could not be considered moral according to this view because homosexuals are not allowed to marry (see GAY RIGHTS).

In the past, it was common for ethical thinking to focus more on the context of the relationship than on its quality. As long as sexual intercourse took place only inside of marriage, there was less attention paid to whether it was consensual or mutually satisfying. Currently, it is more common for the focus of sexual ETHICS to be on the character of the relationship. Although views are divided as to whether sexual relations should be confined to marriage or to a single partner, most people agree that sexual relationships should occur between mutually consenting adults and that the activities should be agreed upon and pleasurable to all parties.

While there is no generally agreed upon sexual ethic, just as there is no generally agreed upon religious or political ethics, there are some common themes in most writings on sexual MORALITY. Marie M. Fortune's book *Love Does No Harm: Sexual Ethics for the Rest of Us* (1985) offers the following five guidelines based upon the principle of doing the least HARM. These guidelines are meant to preserve the integrity of sexual experiences, while allowing a wide berth of privacy and free choice (see FREEDOM).

First, sexual relationships should take place among peers. That means that when you are ready to choose a sexual partner some people, specifically those people who hold positions of AUTHORITY in your life, are off-limits as sexual partners. Most codes of PROFESSIONAL ETHICS specifically denounce professionals from engaging in sexual relationships with clients, teachers with students, clergy with parishioners, etc.

Second, partners should both consent to a sexual relationship. This means that both people should have the chance to say "yes" or "no" to sexual activity. People who are too young, uninformed, or emotionally unready or who are intoxicated or asleep cannot give consent to sexual activity (see RAPE; SEXUAL ABUSE; STATUTORY RAPE). People who feel threatened for their jobs, livelihood, or safety also cannot give true consent (see SEXUAL HARASSMENT).

Third, sexual morality involves taking responsibility for protecting oneself and one's partner against sexually transmitted diseases (see AIDS) and unwanted pregnancy. Fourth, sexual ethics concerns the sharing of pleasure. Partners should be aware of and concerned for both their own needs and the needs of the other. Finally, sexual morality requires TRUSTWORTHINESS. Sexual partners should be faithful to their promises (see PROMISE) and commitments (see COMMITMENT) to one another.

Sexual ethics requires a certain amount of sexual maturity. There is no definite age at which people reach such maturity. For purposes of both physical and emotional health, however, it is important to take the time to get to know oneself and develop a sexual morality that is in keeping with one's needs, character, and larger moral outlook.

SEXUAL HARASSMENT Sexual intimidation at school, in the workplace, or in other places of public accommodation.

Sexual harassment generally involves unwelcome verbal or other behavior of a sexual nature short of physical contact. It can include lewd verbal or written comments about genitalia, sexual orientation, or behavior; sexually suggestive gestures, and photographs and other media. Sexual harassment can, but need not, include demands for sexual favors, the promise of rewards for sexual conduct, or threats of penalties for refusing sexual advances. Sexual harassment is a civil offense and is illegal in the workplace, in educational settings, and in other places of public accommodation, such as government facilities.

The term *sexual harassment* came into wide use in the 1980s when the issue of sexual intimidation in the workplace was legally addressed in the 1986 Supreme Court case of *Meritor Savings Bank v. Vinson*. In this case a female bank teller charged that she was subjected to "a hostile working environment" because of her gender, and the Court found in her favor ruling that employers must guard against such an environment in the workplace. Employees must not be subjected to unwelcome sexual advances (physical or verbal), requests for sexual favors, or any situation in which submission to sex is in any way a condition of employment or evaluation of performance. If an employee's performance is inhibited by unwanted sexual contact, sexual harassment is occurring. *See also* SEXUAL ABUSE.

SHADOW Rejected features of one's total nature that are relegated to the unconscious because they are considered negative, undesirable, or immoral (see IMMORALITY). According to the analytic psychology of Carl G. Jung, every human being, regardless of culture or religion, holds within the unconscious everything that is unliked and unwanted about one's total self. These denied and rejected aspects constitute the shadow. The shadow consists of everything that one not only wants to keep others from recognizing but also does not want to acknowledge to oneself. Among other things, the shadow may contain thoughts, fantasies, desires, and urges that are considered immoral.

Consisting as it does of the "unlovely" qualities of human nature, the content of the shadow is repressed and forced into the unconscious.

There, it occasionally gathers energy and manifests itself through dreams or nightmares, errors in self-expression (saying or writing what one does not intend), emotional outbursts, and impulsive, apparently uncontrollable behavior.

Jungian psychologists agree that repressed features of one's nature are inevitably projected (*see* PROJECTIVISM) onto others. This means that others appear to take on the negative qualities which in fact lie in oneself.

SHAME   The feeling that others may rightly disdain you.

Shame is a powerful feeling that results when we feel we have transgressed a social or moral norm held by people whom we admire and who wish to admire us. For example, we may feel shame if we are caught lying to our parents. Shame is a deeper or more humiliating feeling than GUILT, which is the uncomfortable feeling that one has done something WRONG and is deserving of PUNISHMENT. Shame can be a strong, though not necessarily positive, moral motivator (*see* MOTIVE), as when people rebuke an action by saying, "You should be ashamed of yourself for X." What they are really saying is not only that X is wrong but that you bring contempt on yourself by participating in X. The act of invoking shame is itself a moral question and should be approached with moral care. For example, while there may be good cause to say, "You should be ashamed of yourself for stealing from your parents," there may not be good cause to say, "You should be ashamed of yourself for crying."

SHARI'A   Literally, "path," "way"; the legal system of Islam.

Islam holds that religion is not simply one aspect among many aspects of life but rather that it is a total way of life. For example, instead of upholding a strict separation of church and state, as is the ideal in the United States, Islam calls for religion to govern all dimensions of life. In fact, Islam sees itself as fully and truly Islam only when it governs society in addition to managing matters of FAITH, PRACTICE, and MORALITY. Shari'a is the comprehensive legal system that seeks to address all dimensions of Muslim life.

Shari'a is founded on four sources ranked in order of decreasing AUTHORITY: QUR'AN, HADITH, analogy, consensus. For instance, if a moral question is not addressed in the Qur'an, Muslims turn for guidance to MUHAMMAD's words and actions as found in Hadith. If the moral question pertains to something modern, like genetic engineering, it is highly improbable that either the Qur'an or Hadith will speak to the issue. In this case, a Muslim can turn to a third source: learned scholars. These scholars of Islam will investigate the first two sources to determine if there is anything to be found there that is analogous to genetic engineering. If this fails, these same authorities will draw from their comprehensive understanding of the letter and spirit of Islam in order to reach a consensus among themselves on the proper course of action for Muslims. The final source finds its authentication in one of Muhammad's sayings recorded in Hadith. N.J. Coulson, in *A History is Islamic Law,* reports Muhammad as having said: "My people will never agree in an error." The nature of this final source of Shari'a is such that no issue could arise on which it would be impossible for an official and authoritative decision to be reached.

As is true in all cases, religious or secular, it remains for the individual to decide whether or not, and to what extent, the pronouncements of the legal, religious, or moral authorities will be heeded. *See also* ISLAMIC ETHICS.

SHEMA   Literally, "hear"; the first word of Deuteronomy 6:4: "Hear, O Israel, the Lord is our God, the Lord is One."

Shema names the entire verse and has come to be regarded as the central confession of FAITH in Judaism, the affirmation of monotheism. The Shema plays an important role in formal worship and is typically recited several times a day by devout Jews. Ideally, such recitation is a reminder of the Jew's obligation to obey divine commandments, that is, to fulfill both liturgical and moral requirements.

SHI'A   Smaller of the two major divisions of Islam, making up approximately 10 percent of the world Muslim population; they are distributed mainly in Iran and Iraq but are found in smaller numbers in many parts of the Muslim world.

The Shi'a and the SUNNI split in the early years of Islam over the question of the rightful succession to MUHAMMAD. Shi'ites believed that the Prophet's successor should be someone from his family. This office fell first to 'Ali, Muhammad's cousin, who was in turn succeeded by his sons and then by their sons. The successors are known as imams and are the final AUTHORITY in Shi'a Islam for determining matters of FAITH, PRACTICE, and MORALITY. The imam of the largest branch of the Shi'a is believed to be in hiding and is represented by a small core of ayatollahs. The imam of another significant branch is known as the Aga Khan, a title that passes to each succeeding spiritual and temporal leader of the community.

From the outside, differences between Shi'a and Sunni Islam appear minimal, pertaining more to matters of politics and governance than belief or ritual. In Muslim countries where both groups reside, however, tensions can mount at times and be centered in perceived differences. In a county where Muslims are a minority, such as the United States, Sunnis and Shi'ites tend to affirm what they hold in common, which is unquestionably most of what constitutes their respective faiths. *See also* ISLAMIC ETHICS.

SIN   Violation of a religious precept.

The biblical sense of sin is "missing the mark," that is, failing to achieve what is desirable from the perspective of VIRTUE or going astray. Sins of omission as well as commission are recognized: "Anyone who knows the right thing to do and fails to do it, commits sin" (James 4:17). In the Christian tradition, sin is believed to be universal: "All have sinned and fall short of the glory of GOD" (Romans 3:23).

The universality of sin has led some to argue that it is inborn, that humankind is victimized by "original sin." Although there is no explicit biblical passage to this effect, there are some that can be so construed. Others deny an inherited tendency in either direction, toward sin or holiness, thus allowing humans to opt, in freedom, for or against a godly life.

Roman Catholic thought distinguishes between mortal sins and venial sins, the former leading to eternal damnation and the latter, while serious, carrying less-ultimate consequences. The seven deadly sins are character traits that give rise to objective sin: PRIDE, covetousness, LUST, anger, GLUTTONY, ENVY, and sloth.

The Christian philosophical theologian Paul Tillich offers a particularly broad, nonsectarian analysis of sin. Sin is ALIENATION, estrangement, separation. Every ACT or attitude of sin gives rise to division: within the sinner (guilt, remorse), between the sinner and the person sinned against, and between the sinner and God. Tillich understands estrangement to result from three human conditions or states: unbelief; HUBRIS, or "pride"; and concupiscence, or strong desire. Unbelief represents a total turning away from God, a denial of his existence or relevance. Hubris makes humans the measure of all things, elevating humankind to the realm of the divine. It confuses limited truth and goodness with ultimate truth and goodness. Hubris refuses to acknowledge one's actual condition or state; it denies such personal realities as confusion, error, ignorance, insecurity, or loneliness. Concupiscence names the acquisitive spirit, the limitless thirst to draw all of reality into one's self, and is most dramatically seen in rampant sensualism and CONSUMERISM.

In contrast to Christianity, Judaism does not accept the notion of original sin. The Jewish faith holds that people are not born either good or bad Rather, they are born with both good and bad inclinations, and the free moral will to choose. Sin occurs when people choose to follow their bad inclinations.

The notion of sin and the forgiveness of sin is given little attention in most Eastern religions. Rather, there is a focus on DHARMA, KARMA, and the notion that wrong actions produce punishment while right actions produce rewards. Salvation is not dependent on forgiveness of sin, but rather concerns doing greater good than evil in order to evolve to a higher state through reincarnation. *See also* CHRISTIAN ETHICS; JESUS; JEWISH ETHICS, LOVE.

SITUATION ETHICS   The view that moral decisions must be grounded in specific situations rather than in universal LAW.

Situation ethics is most closely associated with Joseph Fletcher's book *Situation Ethics: The New Morality*. Fletcher argued in the 1960s that ETHICS is, and has been, predominately rule-bound (*see* RULES) or legalistic. Situation ethics is an attempt to respond to the reality of moral LIFE, which often necessitates modifying, making exceptions to, or even throwing out certain rules. For instance, lying can sometimes be viewed as morally justified if it prevents great harm.

The focus of situation ethics is LOVE, usually interpreted as in CHRISTIAN ETHICS. Fletcher appealed to the work of theologians Paul Tillich and Rudolf Bultmann to demonstrate that both JESUS and Paul preached an ethic of love rather than law. According to Fletcher's view, only love is sufficiently adaptable to ACT as a guide through complicated moral problems. Because love may, in extreme situations, lead us to commit immoral acts (*see* IMMORALITY) such as adultery or theft, critics of situation ethics have claimed that situation ethics reduced MORALITY to subjective inclination.

SKEPTICISM   Systematic doubt of all knowledge claims and justifications (*see* JUSTIFICATION).

Skepticism refers to the denial that there can be justified knowledge. Skepticism may be either partial or whole. People who are wholly skeptical deny that there can be any valid knowledge. We cannot know for a fact what is true; the most we can do is ACT *as if* we know what is true (even this must be done with great caution). Partial skeptics are those who believe that we can only have knowledge in certain areas, but that in other areas we cannot have certain knowledge. For example, a person may have confidence in the scientific method but be skeptical that we can have any knowledge about metaphysical or supernatural things.

With respect to ETHICS, radical or total skepticism holds that we can have no moral justification or moral knowledge with respect to either the source of moral LAW or the rightness of moral action. Partial skepticism holds that we can have some types of moral understanding but that other types of knowledge either do not exist or are unattainable. Skepticism about moral knowledge does not imply, however, that skeptics do not hold moral action as necessary or binding; for example, they may hold that we have a moral duty to act even when we cannot justify these actions or when these actions carry with them a degree of uncertainty.

SLAVERY   The condition in which one human being is owned as property by another human being.

Slavery, by any account, is a fundamental violation of HUMAN RIGHTS; yet despite this it has been widespread for most of human history. It was tolerated and even promoted, for example, by many ardent supporters of all major religions, including Buddhism, Christianity, and Islam. It was even widely accepted by many prominent Enlightenment thinkers who otherwise thoroughly believed that human beings had an inalienable RIGHT to "LIFE, liberty (*see*

FREEDOM), and the pursuit of HAPPINESS" (*see* LIBERALISM). Of those who signed the American Declaration of Independence, it is a matter of record that the phrase "all men are created equal" was not intended to include slaves—after all, many of the signatories were slave owners themselves.

The forms that slavery has taken have undergone a considerable transformation over time. In Ancient Rome, Greece, and Israel, slaves retained some personal RIGHTS, and may even have been of the same racial group as their masters. In these times, conditions existed for setting slaves free, and intentional mistreatment of slaves was subject to PUNISHMENT, although this was not always enforced. Since the 1500s, however, slavery has become much more closely associated with RACISM in European cultures. Where previously slaves had been taken from "barbarian" tribes as the spoils of war or pressed into servitude because of bankruptcy, slavery soon came to be associated with individuals of African and native North American decent. With the impact of the Enlightenment and its emphasis on individual rights, however, it became necessary for supporters of slavery to argue that the races most commonly pressed into slavery were inferior and less than human. As a result, it became possible to justify allowing a slave master to treat slaves in whatever way he or she felt appropriate. Slaves could be worked to death, beaten, killed, sexually abused, and generally subjected to treatment that would horrify us if perpetrated even against animals today.

Even today, slavery exists in a number of forms around the world. It can take the form of indentured servitude or debt bondage where someone is effectively forced into servitude to pay off debts. For example, it was not uncommon historically for an employer to pay for the transport of migrants to a new land on the assumption that the migrant would then have to work to pay for the costs of transportation. Later, these migrants would find that their employer made sure their debt could never be paid off because of interest and ongoing living expenses. In some countries, it remains acceptable for children to be purchased from their families to be used as cheap labor or to be forced into prostitution. Similarly, young girls in some countries may be "married" to husbands for the payment of a fee and thereafter used for sex or forced labor entirely at the husband's whim.

Overall, the institution of slavery provides ample evidence, if any is needed, that human beings are capable of affirming the most lofty moral principles and simultaneously supporting utterly inhuman behavior. The institution of slavery serves as a warning to us that MORALS alone are insufficient without EMPATHY for our fellow human beings. Clearly, when we truly see others as human beings worthy of our respect, it becomes harder to justify servitude under any circumstances. The founders of the American state may not themselves have been forced to confront the contradictions inherent in their beliefs, but later generations would find it increasingly difficult to ignore them.

SLIPPERY SLOPE ARGUMENT   The argument that an action (*see* ACT) which is not wrong in and of itself may nonetheless be morally objectionable because of its likelihood to lead to WRONG action.

The slippery slope argument gets its name by analogy. We are asked to imagine a slippery slope upon which, if we take one step, we may quickly find ourselves sliding uncontrollably and dangerously. Slippery slope arguments are held to be like this in that one seemingly innocent step can lead to unwanted conclusions. For example, some people argue the legalization of marijuana should be opposed not because marijuana is in and of itself more dangerous than drugs that are legal but rather because of its perceived association with such addictive drugs as heroin or cocaine. On this argument, legalizing marijuana is the first step on the slippery slope of condoning, if not legalizing, the use of "hard drugs." Slippery slope arguments are generally opposed by libertarians (*see* LIBERTAR-IANISM) and others who argue that if an action is not wrong in and of itself, or if an action harms only a consenting adult agent, then we should not prohibit it, regardless of its possible ramifications.

SMITH, ADAM (1723–1790)   Scottish economist and philosopher famous for his analysis of free economic markets.

Adam Smith is best remembered for his 1776 book, *An Inquiry into the Nature and Causes of the Wealth of Nations,* in which he addresses free market economies and argues that, when properly regulated, they are the most efficient economic system. Smith also argues that such economies best emulate nature.

Smith was also a well-respected moral philosopher. In 1759 he published *The Theory of Moral Sentiments* in which he investigated the nature of VIRTUE as well as the psychological mechanisms by which we recognize virtue and VICE. Smith's moral philosophy had much in common with that of David HUME, particularly in its reliance on MORAL SENTIMENT.

SOCIAL ACTIVISM   A commitment to vigorous political action (*see* ACT) as the only effective response to social evils (*see* EVIL)

Social activists typically reject theory or discussion as solutions to abiding problems such as animal abuse, homelessness, racism, sexism, and militarism. At the heart of social activism is the view that change is desirable and that change can only be brought about when people become personally involved in the problems they wish to solve.

Social activism may be direct or indirect. Direct activists identify a problem and attempt to solve it by immediate actions. For example, activists who are concerned about homeless people may organize and set up shelters. Social

activists may even break the LAW in acts of CIVIL DISOBEDIENCE, as when underground activists helped draft resisters escape the United States in the 1960s and 1970s. Indirect activists, on the other hand, attempt to bring about change by raising the awareness of the public or the relevant authorities. They may stage marches, demonstrations, or rallies in order to draw attention to an issue that they feel has been neglected or ignored. For example, proponents of gay rights may hold a vigil in front of the White House in the hopes of attracting the attention of governmental officials, the media, and the public.

SOCIAL CONTRACT   The theory that a morally legitimate government depends on the consent of the governed.

Some societies are democratically organized (*see* DEMOCRACY); others are ruled by dictators. Likewise, some societies are heavily regulated by government; others, less regulated. Furthermore, a society can be designed to promote EQUALITY or to permit great inequalities. Social CONTRACT theory represents an attempt to determine which among the many alternative forms of government, if any, are morally proper. The key idea is that, given the power a government has over lives and liberty, a government is morally legitimate only if it is acceptable to the governed.

One way to address questions about proper forms of government is to ask people whether they accept their government. But consent is tricky. People can be conditioned to accept immoral circumstances as normal. The consent of a biased or a socially conditioned person is not true moral consent. To be morally justified, a government must be the sort that unbiased people would accept.

Social contract theory is an attempt to determine the basic form of government people would endorse if their consent were free and unbiased. Social contract theorists think that they can eliminate BIAS by defining a state of nature, a place where people are living without government or dominating social structures. The kind of government, if any, that such free and equal people would select would be a government supported by genuine consent.

Social contract theorists such as Thomas HOBBES, John LOCKE, and Jean-Jacques ROUSSEAU defined what it would be like for people to live in a state of nature and then attempted to determine what form of government people in the state of nature would accept. Each theorist arrived at a different conclusion about what the state of nature would be like. Locke believed that people would get on fairly well in the state of nature but would need a government for protection, to provide a basic legal system, and to provide for basic social systems, such as roads and money. People would consent to a very basic government, one that has limited powers (see POWER) and does for people only what they cannot do for themselves. Hobbes held a dramatically different view, for he believed that people are basically selfish and that without a strong and dictatorial government they would always be in or near a state of war.

The conclusions drawn by Locke and Hobbes about the state of nature might themselves be biased by their own circumstances. Modern contract theorists, such as John RAWLS, have developed a more abstract concept of the state of nature, which Rawls calls the "original position." Rawls's original position is occupied by hypothetical people or imaginary people, like players in a game rather than actual people, who are defined in a way that is meant to eradicate bias. For example, to eliminate racial bias, Rawls's imaginary people are defined as not knowing their own racial identity. Rawls then reasoned about what basic social structures such unbiased people would accept. He believes that unbiased people would want to protect, as much as possible, the well-being of the least well-off members of society. See also CIVIL RIGHTS; ENLIGHTENMENT ETHICS; HUMAN RIGHTS.

SOCIAL DARWINISM   Social philosophy advocating the survival of the most socially fit.

A social philosophy is a theory of society that states the principles (see PRINCIPLE) upon which a society should run. Social Darwinism took the scientific hypotheses of Charles Darwin concerning EVOLUTION and applied them to ethical and political thought. The result is the view that the "survival of the fittest" was not only a principle of nature but a guiding principle of ETHICS. Thus, social Darwinists hold that it is in a society's best interest for its strongest members to flourish, owing no debt to its weaker members.

SOCIAL JUSTICE   A PRINCIPLE of community organization based on EQUALITY and FAIRNESS.

The term *social justice* means many different things to different people, just as it is difficult to find agreement on the way in which equality and fairness can be realistically applied to the real world. In recent times, however, the term has become most closely associated with modern LIBERALISM. According to liberals, social justice can only be achieved through respect for individual AUTONOMY and CONSCIENCE and through a commitment to assist those who have been most disadvantaged by DISCRIMINATION and EXPLOITATION.

Another conception of social justice is provided by twentieth-century philosopher John RAWLS, who argued that a just society is one organized on the basis of principles that would be mutually agreed upon by individuals unaware of any personal details about themselves, such as sex, race, religion and class. This view of justice is a version of SOCIAL CONTRACT theory, which holds that a just society is one based on the mutual agreement of all parties involved. In this view, all individuals in a society, acting independently of each other, agree ("contract") to accept the AUTHORITY of the state in exchange for being provided with certain services, such as protection and education.

According to this theory, a government (and therefore society) is only just while it retains the consent and support of those governed by it.

SOCIALISM   A social and political system in which the most important forms of economic production are owned by the state or by collective groups of people. In contrast to a communist system (*see* COMMUNISM), a socialist system may involve less state ownership and less state involvement in citizens' lives.

In a socialist system, the state controls education, health care, transportation, and production of major goods such as automobiles and utilities. Some political theorists believe that a socialistic system avoids the EXPLOITATION found in CAPITALISM, in which many basic services, such as health care, may be most adequately provided only to those who can afford it. Basic services tend to be more equally provided in a socialistic country. Some believe that socialism is the only way to ensure DEMOCRACY because it limits economic POWER and political privilege. In capitalism, the rich and those who control industry often have greater influence on the government than do ordinary citizens.

Others believe that a socialistic system is highly inefficient because economic decisions made by a central government cannot fully comprehend which goods should be produced and how they should be distributed. In capitalism, such decisions are decentralized or made in the marketplace by individual producers and consumers. With high taxation to pay for government services, a socialist system deprives people of the ability to make their own spending decisions. Another fear is that central management of the economy takes democratic power away from the people and gives too much power to government. Nevertheless, government activity that is widely accepted in capitalistic countries, such as Social Security and the graduated income tax, would have been considered socialistic before the Great Depression of the 1930s.

SOCIOBIOLOGY   The theory that all social behavior has a biological basis.

Sociobiology is most closely associated with the work of Edward O. Wilson. His book *Sociobiology: the New Synthesis* (1975) introduced the term *sociobiology* and the idea that human society could be understood in terms of genetics and EVOLUTION. Certain characteristics advantageous to a society are genetically selected and passed on through evolution. In a sense, sociobiologists take Charles Darwin's theory of individual selection and apply it to societies, arguing that there are traits such as altruism that are beneficial to groups and that are perpetuated genetically. Opponents of sociobiology argue that there is too much emphasis on inheritance of social characteristics and not enough emphasis on the environment or on MORAL EDUCATION in acquiring moral characteristics.

SOCRATES (469–399 B.C.)   An ancient Greek philosopher often looked upon as a model of philosophic life.

Socrates did not leave a written account of his philosophy, but he did carry on conversations on philosophic topics, especially ETHICS. Much of what is known about Socrates is contained in the dialogues of his student PLATO. In the dialogues, Socrates appears as the main character and expresses both his own and Plato's ideas. The early dialogues of Plato, *Apology, Crito,* and *Phaedo,* are sources for learning about Socrates' life and ideas. These writings contain an account of Socrates' trial for impiety and corrupting the youth of Athens, including his defense against these charges. In his defense, Socrates describes himself as a "gadfly" who irritates others by questioning their beliefs and as a "midwife" who helps them bring forth ideas. He claimed that he was not able to teach but could only help others discover what they already knew. He differed from others, he said, in knowing that whatever wisdom he had came from knowing that he did not know, whereas others claimed wisdom in areas where they did not have knowledge. Thus, Socrates claimed to be wise through his ignorance. Such paradoxical sayings are examples of Socratic irony.

Socrates has stood as a MORAL EXEMPLAR for many thinkers throughout history. He is famous for many of his sayings, such as "The unexamined life is not worth living," and for his courageous pursuit of TRUTH and VIRTUE. He is also known for his dedication to a LIFE of REASON and his rigorous method of examining ideas called the Socratic method.

SOCRATIC METHOD   A method of searching for truth through questioning made famous by PLATO's portrayal of SOCRATES in the Platonic dialogues.

The Socratic method, or process of *elenchus,* refers to Socrates' cross-examination of his contemporaries in order to determine whether or not they had the knowledge they claimed to have. Socrates himself claimed that whatever wisdom he possessed resided in his knowledge of his own ignorance. Using the Socratic method, he questioned poets, politicians, and craftsmen in Athens in order to determine whether or not they were true experts in their fields. In each case, the method yields no satisfactory answers, leading Socrates to conclude that people do not in fact have the wisdom they believe themselves to have and are better off if they continue a process of questioning.

SOPHISTRY   Knowingly using false REASON for advantage.

The Sophists were a professional group of teachers in early Greece characterized by teaching success in politics. The Sophists did impart knowledge but were better known for teaching argumentation and rhetoric. SOCRATES objected to the teachings of the Sophists because they were directed at profit rather than true knowledge. The Sophists sought to teach young men how to persuade others rather than to seek the

TRUTH. In order to do this, the Sophists would try to confuse, misdirect, or shout down their opponents or, alternatively, overwhelm them with clever speech. Thus, sophistry has become synonymous with putting forth views that may appear to be logical or wise but are in fact simply meant to persuade without regard for the truth. It is the disregard of truth and the attempt at intellectual "bullying" that gives sophistry an unethical connotation.

SOVEREIGN   A person who has the highest AUTHORITY in a given place.

A sovereign is a ruler with supreme authority. In politics a king and a queen are called sovereigns because they are the highest or last authority in the land. On the other hand, in a DEMOCRACY the people are considered to be sovereign because the final authority in the society is held to rest with them. In ETHICS, thinkers such as Immanuel KANT and the Enlightenment thinkers (*see* ENLIGHTENMENT ETHICS) speak of the individual as acting as sovereign in ethical LIFE. This is a call for individuals, through reason, to be self-governing or to have control of their passions (*see* PASSIONS AND EMOTIONS) and desires (*see* DESIRE).

SPINOZA,   BARUCH   BENEDICT (1632–1677)   Dutch philosopher heralded as one of the most important thinkers of the seventeenth century.

Spinoza's ethical thought is rationalist (*see* RATIONALITY). In his work he tried to show how a person who was guided by REASON would ACT. He believed that all virtuous actions guided by the understanding could be attributed to two types of strength of character: tenacity and nobility. These characteristics occur in balance with a sense of practical self-advantage. Spinoza's moral philosophy is explained in his work *The Ethics,* published posthumously in 1677.

SPORTS ETHICS   A field of APPLIED ETHICS in which questions about the MORALITY of acts in sports or questions about activities related to sports are examined.

The literature on sports ETHICS has grown considerably in recent decades, as has the literature in other fields of applied ethics. Traditionally, sports have occupied a rather important place in the literature on ethics not as a subject of investigation but as a model for moral JUDGMENT and reasoning (*see* REASON). PLATO, himself a wrestler, discussed examples from sports in his dialogues, and the Stoics (*see* STOICISM) frequently used examples from sports to illustrate the principles of their philosophy. In contemporary ethics, the RULES of morality have been compared to the rules of sports or of games to illustrate different kinds of rules and distinguish their applications. Thus, for example, rules that define moves within a game have been distinguished from rules that regulate such moves, and these, in turn, have been distinguished from rules that govern tactics or strategies for playing. There are rules that define what it means to strike out in baseball, for example, or what it means to make a touchdown in football. These are different from rules that regulate the play, specifying penalties for violations. In ethics, there appear to be similar rules, such as those that define what it means to make a promise and those that determine whether or not promises ought to be kept. Sports have been also been cited in philosophical and moral literature to illustrate the VALUE of EXCELLENCE in performance, as one of the ways in which individuals may attain SELF-REALIZATION. They have also been used to demonstrate the meaning of JUSTICE OR FAIRNESS, as in the idea of SPORTSMANSHIP or playing by the rules. The idea of teamwork is often used as a model of cooperative performance.

Other moral questions arise over issues of justice or fairness in the management or administration of sports. DISCRIMINATION against women or minorities is one of these issues, as women are not normally allowed to participate in games against men and because the same financial support is not available for woman's sports as for men's sports.

Some people argue that the amount of money commanded by professional athletes has become an ethical issue. In collegiate athletics, there are strict rules governing the ethics of recruiting athletes, as well as the types of attention and "compensation" college athletes may receive. Schools also have an ethical obligation to truly educate the athletes they recruit and not just exploit their athletic abilities during the time of their collegiate eligibility. On the other hand, athletes are also criticized because they may receive special treatment by schools and are given more and better scholarships than academically gifted students. School administrations often provide equipment and travel expenses for athletes, for example, while denying the same for the band that accompanies them to sporting events. Scandals in sports are often reported in the newspapers when teams or players cheat by using drugs, for example, or by engaging in unfair recruiting practices, or by allowing ineligible players to participate in games.

The conduct of, or the participation in, some sports has been challenged on the ground that those sports are immoral (*see* IMMORALITY). Bullfighting and cockfighting, for example, are sometimes said to be immoral and in many places are illegal because of the level of violence involved and because the aim or intention of the sport is to cause harm or death. Boxing has also been questioned for the same reason because the purpose of the sport is to cause harm to an opponent.

Other sports, such as football, may cause injury, even death, but such injury is accidental, one might argue, and not the purpose of the game. Within a game like football, players may be said to be ethical if they play by the rules and do not intend to injure their opponents, but they would normally be thought to be unethical if they violated the rules or tried to cause injury. Rules committees frequently change the rules of games, sometimes for moral reasons, when, for example, they try to make a game safer for the participants by requiring them to wear protective clothing or by ruling out various kinds of violent acts.

SPORTSMANSHIP   Virtuous conduct before, during, and after competition including, but not limited to, adherence to the RULES of sport.

The refinement of skill through competition is held by many to be a basic part of human nature. We can trace this competition from ancient times to modern through the tradition of the Olympic games. The worldwide emergence of individual and team sports showcases human beings pitted again the clock, the scorekeeper, themselves, and opponents. Sportsmanship, however, entails going above and beyond the basic requirements of excelling at competition and following the rules. It includes the athlete's behavior before and after the game.

Sportsmanship necessitates the exhibition of total commitment to a cause or the team, without regard for self or personal recognition, with respect for the opponent, and with no desire to embarrass them either by defeating them mercilessly or in giving less than your best when the score is out of hand. Sportsmanship is humility in victory and graciousness in defeat. Good sportsmanship is displayed when opponents acknowledge each other with respect—for instance, when two tennis players meet at center court and shake hands, or when two football coaches meet at midfield for one to congratulate the other. The tip of a hat in acknowledgment of someone else's achievement is good sportsmanship, as is the hunter giving the quarry a fair chance.

It is interesting and at times disturbing to observe some of the celebrating and staged theatrics of the modern-day professional athlete. Poor sportsmanship displayed in the form of taunting, baiting, and uninhibited demonstrations of self do not endear them to those who were taught to play hard but clean, and these demonstrations also set a poor example for young athletes and fans.

The idea of sportsmanship can be extended into the arenas of workplace, school, church, or any situation where there is person-to-person interaction under predetermined conditions. The word *sportsmanship* conjures up a wide variety of images, from the chivalrous knight to the good-natured athlete to the conscientious business competitor. Good sportsmanship is a display of an attitude that expresses itself both in the way people play the game and live their lives. When you treat others as you yourself would like to be treated, you are exhibiting the best VIRTUES of sportsmanship and are showing respect not only for your opponent but also for yourself. *See also* SPORTS ETHICS.

STANDARDS OF CARE   The general medical practices (*see* PRACTICE) considered to meet the norms of medical professionalism in a given region.

To provide an understanding of general medical practices in a given region, the term *standards of care* has been used, implying a level of care that is expected to be given in an area. It is not uniform across the world. Medical care changes as medical science advances, but not all advances are put into practice immediately or put into practice at the same time in all places. Time, clinical experience, and further research often delay the general acceptance of new treatments and procedures. Much of the more-advanced care available requires sophisticated technology that is not available in all areas and therefore is not considered the standard of care for that locale. Standards of care are required to be able to determine MALPRACTICE in a given region because medical care changes with availability. For example, a physician in a remote South American village that does not have reliable electricity is not expected to diagnose a subtle bone fracture with X-ray, but a physician practicing in the metropolitan United States would be expected to start with an X-ray and move on to a bone scan, MRI, or other more-advanced imaging techniques if the diagnosis is elusive.

STATE OF NATURE   *See* SOCIAL CONTRACT.

STATUTORY RAPE   Unlawful sexual intercourse with someone under the age of consent. The age of consent may vary from age 14 to 18 but is usually defined as between ages 16 and 18.

Statutory rape refers to sexual intercourse between an adult and an individual under the age of consent, even if that intercourse is consensual. There are several gradations of statutory rape. If an individual who is over eighteen has sexual relations with an individual who is under the age of consent but there is less than a three-year difference between their ages, misdemeanor statutory rape occurs. If there is more than a three-year difference, it is considered felony statutory rape. If the minor is under the age of fourteen, and the age of consent is over fourteen, sexual relations are considered child molestation. It is the responsibility of the older person to know the age of the younger person in a sexual relationship. The courts do not accept ignorance of age as an excuse for statutory rape. Both men and women can be convicted of statutory rape if their sexual partner is under the age of consent.

STEBBING, SUSAN L. (1885–1943) English logician and philosopher.

Susan Stebbing is most famous for her book *A Modern Introduction to Logic,* a perceptive discussion of different theories of logic and the metaphysical problems related to them. She also wrote many books and articles on what is now called "critical thinking," the practice of identifying and evaluating various techniques of argumentation.

Stebbing's importance for ETHICS lies in her view of knowledge and RATIONALITY. Throughout her career she maintained a commitment to cool and careful reasoning, which she believed was necessary to guard against both SELF-DECEPTION and the deception of others. By appealing to emotions and weakness, unscrupulous people are able to persuade themselves and others to believe and do irrational things. Only a commitment to TRUTH and clarity can protect us. Further, Stebbing's books display a commitment to intellectual HONESTY. In her view, we must face the facts of our world squarely—even if they cause us pain and unpleasantness.

STEWARDSHIP   MORAL RESPONSIBILITY for the management of one's LIFE, the RIGHTS of others, and the environment.

The concept of stewardship is related to that of a steward, someone appointed to oversee a property or service. In ETHICS, stewardship stresses RESPONSIBILITY rather than rights; that is, we are not free to do as we please but are obligated to ACT for the GOOD of others and for the environment as well. The notion of stewardship is crucial to CHRISTIAN ETHICS, for instance, where human beings are conceived of as servants who owe their existence and livelihood to GOD and are directed to be good stewards of themselves and the earth.

STOICISM   An ancient school of philosophy that teaches that people can obtain peace of mind, or HAPPINESS, by becoming indifferent to external circumstances.

Stoicism is derived from the teachings of the Greek philosopher Zeno (336–264 B.C.) who founded the Stoic school, the *Stoa Poikile* or Painted Porch, named after the place in Athens where stoicism was taught. The philosophy later became popular in Rome and was advocated by such famous Romans as Cicero, Seneca, and Marcus Aurelius. They believed in a LIFE of VIRTUE, consisting of self-discipline and dedication to duty (*see* OBLIGATION) and in service to the state. Stoicism has also had a very strong influence throughout history in the writings of Christian theologians, for example, and in the ethical theories of modern philosophers such as Baruch Benedict SPINOZA and Immanuel KANT.

The Stoics emphasized the importance of living according to nature or according to NATURAL LAW, which is the LAW by which GOD governs the universe. We as individuals cannot change this law, but we can choose to live in accordance with it, or we can spend our lives fighting against it. The rational course, according to stoicism, is to accept what we cannot change and, hence, learn to be happy with our lot in life. This means that we must learn to control what we can control—our PASSIONS AND EMOTIONS—and to accept what we cannot control—what happens outside us—as fate or as God's will. *See also* EPICTETUS.

SUBJECTIVISM   The view that the source of ethical beliefs is grounded in our individual situations rather than in an objective reality (*see* OBJECTIVISM).

Subjective views are real, but their source is located in the habits, character, will, and environment of a specific individual. Thus, they may or may not be shared by others. Objective views, on the other hand, are verifiable by appeal to an external source and should be the same for all persons.

The debate between subjectivists and objectivists in ethics rests on the final source of moral AUTHORITY. If MORALITY is subjective, then final moral authority rests in individuals and their perspectives. This view gives rise to RELATIVISM. Subjectivism also raises questions with respect to how to interpret and evaluate ethical statements. If, on the other hand, moral authority is objective, then moral laws that apply to groups of people or even to all people exist. Objectivists, however, are left with the problem of explaining the source of this objective moral authority as well as how we are able to apprehend this source without coloring it with our own individual interpretations. The subjectivism/objectivism split is perhaps the deepest and oldest division in moral theory. It has been a constant theme in SKEPTICISM since the early Greek thinkers.

SUBSTANCE ABUSE   Excessive use of products that have a mood- or mind-altering effect.

Controlled substances such as tobacco and alcohol products and illegal chemicals called street drugs have mood- or mind-altering properties with a potential for abuse. Some substances can impair judgment and coordination (alcohol, cocaine, marijuana); have psychotropic effects and cause hallucinations (LSD, psilocybin mushrooms); and evoke feelings of acute perception and sensory arousal (cocaine), euphoria (heroin, peyote), tranquility (marijuana), disassociation from reality (cocaine, PCP/angel dust), relaxation (tobacco products, prescribed sedatives and tranquilizers), or sleepiness (alcohol, prescription hypnotics).

Substance abuse should be distinguished from the separate moral and legal issue of the illegal use of a controlled substance. A person who occasionally smokes marijuana, for instance, is breaking the law but is not necessarily abusing that substance. Likewise, a person who smokes or drinks while under the legal age is not by that fact alone abusing a substance, although that person is breaking a law, which is a separate moral problem.

Substance abuse should also be distinguished from dependence upon a chemical substance when that substance is needed for normal function. Understood in this way, dependence is not abuse. For example, diabetics are insulin-dependent, and asthmatics are bronchodilator-dependent. When dependency becomes addiction and use exceeds what is needed for normal function, then continued use of the dependent substance is medically and morally questionable. Addiction is different from dependence in that it is marked by increased craving for more-frequent and larger doses of the substance, and the increasing harmful side effects of escalated usage are not outweighed by the beneficial effects of the substance.

Any substance can diminish the capacity of the person using it to make autonomous choices (*see* AUTONOMY). For example, a common side effect of painkillers is grogginess. The person using the drug makes a reasoned decision to trade off some capacity for alertness and choice for freedom from pain. Most people do not find this choice morally problematic when it is necessary for anticipated recovery from temporary illness or to ease the pain of dying (*see* DEATH AND DYING).

However, when the time spent without the capacity for autonomy is extended, as in the case of the abuse of street drugs, or when the substance creates grave health risks, as in the case of nicotine products, then serious moral issues arise. To the extent that substance abuse causes incurable fatal disease or erodes the capacity for autonomy, it is a form of self-inflicted moral harm. Consider the example of the abuse of tobacco products: in addition to the harm caused to oneself, people who abuse such products also have duties to both their families and others who become ill due to secondhand smoke and to society, which ultimately provides the resources for treatment and research of cancer, emphysema, and heart disease.

Unfortunately, the impaired abuser who lacks the capacity to act autonomously often risks causing harm to others. Such chemical substances as alcohol, cocaine, and PCP, which profoundly impair JUDGMENT and which free users from inhibitions, also pose risks to nonusers who may become victims of automobile accidents caused by, or of VIOLENCE committed by, substance abusers. In many people's minds it is this risk to third parties rather than PATERNALISM toward substance abusers that justifies legal sanctions against some forms of substance use and justifies the criminalization of nonprescription use of certain controlled substances.

SUBSTITUTED JUDGMENT The replacement of one JUDGMENT with another.

Substitutive judgment is best illustrated by means of an example. Ramirez and Ho are

professors who are conducting a search for a new faculty member. After a lengthy interview process, they select Smith as their candidate. The dean in charge of the school vetoes their decision and selects Brown. The dean's decision can be seen as a substituted judgment, in that her judgment regarding the best person for the job replaced the judgment of the search committee. The question then arises of when, if ever, it is morally proper for a person or persons to overrule the judgment of another.

The notion of substituted judgment is crucial in political theory. In the English political system, for example, citizens vote for a local representative who will then speak for them in Parliament. According to democratic theory (*see* DEMOCRACY), the politician's judgment on political issues in some sense stands for or represents the opinions of the voters and in this sense can be seen as a kind of substituted judgment.

In MEDICAL ETHICS, substituted judgment means that one person makes a medical decision for another person who is unable to make such a decision—for example, due to unconsciousness—on the grounds of what the substitute judge believes the incapacitated person would decide.

SUICIDE The intentional taking of one's own LIFE.

Suicide is usually defined as the deliberate ending of one's own life. This definition is controversial, however, as there are a variety of reasons people end their lives. The term *suicide* is usually reserved for those persons who take their own life to end pain or suffering or to avoid SHAME. When people end their lives or sacrifice themselves for a religious cause, we may call this martyrdom and accord it a different type of moral consideration.

There are heated debates as to whether suicide is ever morally justifiable. For example, some people argue that people who are terminally ill and in great pain with no hope of recovery are entitled to choose to end their lives and even deserve the help of a medical professional to do so (*see* EUTHANASIA). Libertarians (*see* LIBERTARIANISM) argue that people have the right to do with their own persons as they wish, including the RIGHT TO DIE.

Opposed to this argument are those who hold that suicide violates one's obligation to oneself, to other persons, or to GOD and is thus immoral (*see* IMMORALITY).

SUMMARY RULES   *See* ROBERT'S RULES OF ORDER.

SUNNI   Larger of the two major divisions of Islam.

Sunni makes up approximately 85 percent of the world Muslim population, distributed in nearly all parts of the world. In the early years of Islam, Sunni and SHI'A split over the question or rightful succession to MUHAMMAD. Some Muslims, those who came to be known as Sunnis, believed that Muhammad's successor should be the person most qualified to lead, without any arbitrary restriction, such as filial lineage.

The word *Sunni* is derived from *sunna,* meaning PRACTICE or custom (*see* CUSTOMS). Thus, Sunnis are those who follow the practice or custom established by the Prophet. Though the name might seem to indicate that Sunni Muslims give higher regard to Muhammad than Shi'ites, both communities extend utmost respect and allegiance to him.

While there are identifiable difference between Sunni Muslims and Shi'ite Muslims, these differences are minimal in light of all they hold in common. *See also* ISLAMIC ETHICS.

SUPEREROGATION   Actions regarded as "above and beyond" the call of duty, (*see* OBLIGATION), such as those performed by heroes or saints.

Supererogatory acts (*see* ACT) are neither duties nor morally WRONG; they have a special merit, even higher than duty. They may sometimes be referred to as acts of CHARITY.

If supererogatory acts are possible, then it must be possible to do more GOOD than duty requires. Thus, we often think of duty as a minimum requirement for acceptable behavior. In the requirements for a class in school, for example, the teacher may list things a student must do to pass the course, but a good student may do more than is required. In such a case, his or her acts may be supererogatory, and students are sometimes given prizes for such exceptional performance. Some ethicists have held that such acts must also require a special SACRIFICE in order to be supererogatory or that they must be characterized by ALTRUISM.

Not everyone, however, agrees that there are such things as supererogatory acts. Utilitarians (*see* UTILITARIANISM), for example, have maintained that everyone is always morally required to do his or her best, and if this is so, then it would be impossible to do more than is required. When attacking the Roman Catholic doctrine of indulgences—the idea that salvation can be earned by performing good deeds—leaders of the Protestant Reformation criticized the church's acceptance of the doctrine of supererogation. Holding that people are saved by GOD's grace alone and not by good works, they argued that a person could not do more than is required to earn salvation because, in their view, salvation could not be earned through any action. *See also* CHRISTIAN ETHICS; MAXIMAL VS. MINIMAL ETHICS.

SURROGATE MOTHERHOOD   An arrangement whereby a woman bears the genetic child of another individual or couple, agreeing to hand that child over to the individual or couple after the child's birth.

Surrogacy has only recently arisen as an issue for ethicists because it is only through medical technologies, such as IN VITRO FERTILIZATION, that surrogate motherhood has become possible. Some ethicists see surrogacy as problematic because it undermines the traditional biological process of parenthood and is therefore unnatural or even a "CRIME against nature" (*see* NATURAL LAW). Such people, however, rarely object to other "unnatural" medical procedures, such as artificial life support, and may therefore be guilty of inconsistency (*see* DOUBLE STANDARD).

More problematically, others object to a surrogacy because it seems to devalue the role of birth mother and elevate the role of genetic parent. Implicitly, this seems to reduce the importance of the birth mother to simply that of "incubator" and is therefore fundamentally at odds with most traditional conceptions of motherhood. Furthermore, it has been argued that such a conceptualization also undermines the importance of women generally by treating female reproductive capacity as a commodity, only incidentally related to the woman herself. Additionally, while surrogate mothers are usually poor, those who buy their services are generally rich, and this, some critics claim, is evidence that surrogacy is exploitative (*see* EXPLOITATION) and possibly even akin to SLAVERY. Finally, surrogacy may contribute to a perception of children as property who may be bought and sold at the whim of parents that are too self-centered to adopt genetically unrelated children.

Supporters of surrogacy tend to argue that women have a RIGHT to use, or to contract others to use, their bodies as they wish. Furthermore, they may assert that the role of birth mother, is, in fact, relatively insignificant when compared to a family's genetic relationship, coupled with a lifetime of CARE and LOVE. Finally, supporters are likely to argue that a surrogate mother is no different from any other human being who uses his or her physical labor or mental skills to earn a living. *See also* BIOETHICS.

SYLLOGISM   *See* LOGIC.

TABOO A deeply ingrained social PROHIBITION.

A taboo is a forbidden action or a restriction against a forbidden action. The notion of a taboo is that an action is WRONG because it offends a sacred or mystical entity and that there are usually religious or supernatural SANCTIONS against breaking a taboo. Taboos may concern the preparation and eating of certain foods, visiting sacred sites, or engaging in sexual activities with partners (such as family members) considered to be off-limits. Taboos differ from other social prohibitions in that they are a part of a society's deepest social training; for example, both incest and public drunkenness are forbidden in society, but most people feel a deep revulsion against incest, while public drunkenness is considered unlawful, unwise, or embarrassing.

TALMUD Literally, "learning, lesson, teaching"; an extensive commentary on the Hebrew BIBLE, or Torah; sometimes called the second or Oral Torah, in contrast with the Bible, the first or Written Torah (the Oral Torah has long been available in written form; an English translation comprises thirty-two volumes).

Two compilations exist, the Palestinian Talmud (also called the Jerusalem Talmud), edited around 450 B.C., and the Babylonian Talmud, completed a century or so later. Only the Bible exceeds the Talmud in AUTHORITY for Jews.

In the Talmud, one finds the GOLDEN RULE of Hillel, one of the most respected rabbis of biblical times: "What is hateful to you, do not do to your neighbor; this is the whole of the Torah, the rest is commentary, go and learn it." *See also* JEWISH ETHICS.

TAO "Path, road, way"; the Way that governs the cosmos and all in it; central PRINCIPLE of Taoism (pronounced "dow" and increasingly spelled *Dao*).

Lao-tzu, reputed author of the *Tao-te Ching,* "The Book of the Way and Its Power," was the first to attribute metaphysical, or transcendent, significance to the word *tao,* a significance now primary in Taoism. Michael LaFargue, in *The Tao of the Tao Te Ching* (p. 84), translates Chapter 25 of the *Tao-te Ching* to read: "There was a chaotic something, yet lacking nothing, born before Heaven and Earth. Alone. Still. Standing alone, unchanging. Revolving, endlessly. It can be thought of as Mother of the World. I do not know its name, one can call it 'Tao.' One can call it 'The Great One.'" The Tao is invisible, inaudible, formless, eternal, nondual, nonexistent in itself though existent in manifestation. Not only do all thing emanate from the Tao but they also return to it.

The Tao in itself is unabated mystery, so much so that concepts and words cannot reach it. The intellectually elusive nature of the Tao is affirmed in the opening lines of the *Tao-te Ching,* as translated by LaFargue (p. 94): "The Tao that can be told is not the invariant Tao; the names that can be named are not the invariant Name."

The Tao is not GOD, although it is the Ultimate Reality for Taoists. *See also* TAOIST ETHICS; TE.

TAOIST ETHICS Ethical principles (*see* PRINCIPLE), perspectives, attitudes, and conduct based on the TAO as set forth in the Chinese classic *Tao-te Ching* and in the later development of Taoism as a philosophy and religion.

Tao, "path, way," is the Ultimate Reality in Taoism and is most fully manifest in humans in the form of TE, moral purity and the tacit AUTHORITY that invariably attends it. Broadly speaking, Taoist ethics is grounded in the natural order of things; it is an ETHICS of nonexertion, tranquility, humility, and one that avoids drawing attention to itself.

Robert G. Henricks, in *Lao-Tzu: Te-Tao Ching*, translates a Taoist ranking of moral VALUES as set forth in the *Tao-te Ching* (38:7–10): "When the Way is lost, only then do we have VIRTUE; when virtue is lost, only then do we have humanity [humaneness]; when humanity [humaneness] is lost, only then do we have righteousness; when righteousness is lost, only then do we have propriety." Taoism asserts that the true person of Tao is not even conscious of living morally because the principles of MORALITY have become his or her total nature and constitute the only way he or she can live. When one becomes conscious of oneself as one who lives a moral LIFE, one has thereby ceased to be moral in the fullest sense of the term. The *Tao-te Ching* (38:1–2), as translated by Henricks, declares: "The highest virtue is not virtuous; therefore it truly has virtue. The lower virtue never loses sight of its virtue; therefore it has not true virtue." Taoism holds that the highest morality is possible only in one who not only is without self-preference but is without consciousness of self as distinctive from others. In giving, the Taoist makes no valuational distinction between the one giving and the one receiving.

A Taoist ideal is that of *we-wei*, "inaction," or more properly "natural action," action in accord with the Tao (*see* BHAGAVAD GITA). The *Tao-te Ching* (38:3), in Henrick's translation, avers: "The highest virtue takes no action, yet it has no reason for acting this way." Henry Wei, in *The Guiding Light of Lao Tzu*, renders the *Tao-te Ching* (3:4) as: "Practice non-interference and there will never be any misrule." Far from advocating inaction, Taoism proposes a form of action that is less intent on imposing the will of

the actor on a situation than in drawing out what is GOOD, that is, of the nature of Te, in the situation itself. The focus is not so much on the actor as on the action and not so much on the action as on the context within which the action occurs. Taoist action, rather than being self-centered or self-assertive, is other-centered and nonassertive.

The *Tao-te Ching* uses water as a metaphor for several ethical values, especially humility and beneficence. According to John C. H. Wu's translation in *Tao-te Ching* (8:1): "The highest form of goodness is like water. Water knows how to benefit all things without striving with them. It stays in places loathed by all men. Therefore, it comes near the Tao." Taoist morality, along with commitment to the welfare of others, disclaims any hint of ostentation.

TE   "VIRTUE, POWER"; the energy of the TAO; the qualities of the Tao that each thing in the cosmos uniquely manifests (pronounced "duh" and increasingly written *De*).

The central text of Taoism is the *Tao-te Ching*, commonly translated, "The Book of the Way and its Power." Te denotes both virtue or moral, as well as the persuasive power that inevitably accompanies the virtuous, moral life that is lived in conformity with the Tao. Thus, a more complete translation of *Tao-te Ching* would be "The Book of the Way and Its Moral Power."

The intimate connection between Te and Tao is set forth in Chapter 51 of the *Tao-te Ching*, as translated by Michael LaFargue in *The Tao of the Tao Te Ching:* "Tao produces them, Te rears them, makes them grow, nurses them, settles them, heals them, sustains them, protects them. Produces but does not possess; works but does not rely on this; presides but doesn't rule. This is the mysterious Te." *See also* TAOIST ETHICS.

TELEOLOGY   A doctrine that explains why an ACT is RIGHT or WRONG, according to its end or purpose.

In teleological ethics, actions are viewed as means to ends (*see* ENDS/MEANS) or as ways of reaching objectives. Actions are judged accordingly as they achieve or fail to achieve the ends of goals they are intended to achieve. For example, a good navigator will know which way or which means will take a ship to its destination. A good builder will know what to do or which actions ought to be performed to build a house. People who lack such knowledge are likely to choose the wrong means or to perform acts that are wrong.

Teleologists usually try to determine what the ultimate ends of human action are, regarding them as ultimate goods, to clarify the goals or purposes of human life. Money, for instance is a good, but according to ARISTOTLE, it is good only as a means to other goods. Money is not good as an end or good in itself. Ultimate ends are often called intrinsic goods, or goods that are desired for their own sakes, to distinguish them from instrumental goods, which are desired or chosen as a means to something else. A person who plays the viola, for example, just because that person likes to play and not as a means to something else regards playing as an intrinsic good. A person who plays the viola in order to make money and does not particularly enjoy the music itself regards playing as a means to an end, an instrumental good. Some things may also be good as both a means and an end. If a person plays the viola because she loves to play and is also able to make a living through music, then music may be both a means and an end. Knowledge is another example of something that is often desirable both for its own sake and as a means of achieving other things.

Aristotle thought that HAPPINESS is the ultimate *telos,* or end of human action, because it is not desired for the sake of anything else, but everything else is desired because of it. However, Aristotle also believed that other goods, such as knowledge, were components of the happy life and hence desirable as ends in and of themselves. Hedonists (*see* HEDONISM), such as EPICURUS, also speak of happiness as the ultimate

human good, but they define happiness as a life of pleasure, whereas Aristotle speaks of happiness as SELF-REALIZATION.

Teleology is often contrasted with DEONTOLOGY. Deontologists believe that acts are right or wrong in and of themselves, regardless of their ends of consequences—or at least not simply because of their ends or consequences. For example, lying and cheating, they would argue, are wrong things to do even if by lying or cheating one might achieve good ends. While teleologists are concerned with the character of the ends sought, they judge right and wrong in light of the end an action serves.

TEMPERANCE   A moral VIRTUE involving moderation in all desires (*see* DESIRE).

Temperance is the virtue of not having excessive desires with respect to physical pleasure and pain. A person who desires neither too much nor too little of something—such as wine, sweets, or TV viewing—is considered temperate. Temperance is considered to be different from SELF-CONTROL in that self-control implies the managing of excessive desires, while temperance implies that those desires do not occur. Temperance leads to the GOLDEN MEAN and is considered one of the CARDINAL VIRTUES.

TEMPTATION   The enticement to do something unethical or immoral (*see* IMMORALITY).

A temptation is something that draws us to perform an ACT that we believe to be WRONG or unwise. For example, we may be tempted to break a diet by eating our favorite dessert; in this case, the temptation is probably not immoral, but it may be unwise. A temptation may also be something that leads to more serious transgressions or SIN; for example, lust may give rise to the temptation to commit adultery.

TEN COMMANDMENTS   Central religious and moral CODE of Judaism, carrying virtually identical AUTHORITY in Christianity; also known as the Decalogue, literally, "ten words."

The Ten Commandments are found in Exodus 20 and Deuteronomy 5 in the BIBLE and in HALAKAH, the comprehensive Jewish system of LAW.

The Ten Commandments, condensed from Exodus 20, consist of the following directives:

1. You shall have no other gods before me.
2. You shall not make for yourself an idol.
3. You shall not make wrongful use of the name of the Lord your GOD.
4. Remember the Sabbath day, and keep it holy.
5. HONOR your father and your mother.
6. You shall not MURDER.
7. You shall not commit ADULTERY.
8. You shall not steal.
9. You shall not bear false witness against your neighbor.
10. You shall not covet.

See also CHRISTIAN ETHICS; JEWISH ETHICS; LYING.

TEN PRECEPTS   *See* BUDDHIST ETHICS.

TEST-TUBE BABIES   *See* IN VITRO FERTILIZATION.

TOLERANCE   Peaceful coexistence with others holding different basic beliefs (*see* FAITH) and VALUES.

To be tolerant means to be able to get along with and accept others who do not believe as you do. For example, in the United States, the principle of religious freedom means that we agree to tolerate and to respect differing religious views. Tolerance may also apply to differing standards of sexual ethics and different political beliefs. Tolerance of a variety of moral and political viewpoints is held to be the cornerstone of a free and democratic society (*see* DEMOCRACY).

Tolerance is controversial in that many feel it is difficult to draw the line between being tolerant of divergent views and accepting views that our MORALITY demands we ACT against. In the debate over abortion, for instance, pro-life activists argue that they cannot tolerate abortion's legality as simply a different political, moral, or religious belief because to their way of thinking that it endangers human life.

TORAH   The collection of writings that make up the first five books of the BIBLE.

The Torah is considered to be a unified work and tells the story of the creation of the world up through and including the death of Moses. The Torah includes a group of laws (*see* LAW) and commandments given to the people of Israel that govern their special relationship with GOD. *See also* CHRISTIAN ETHICS; JEWISH ETHICS; TEN COMMANDMENTS.

TORT   A private or civil WRONG not covered by the LAW of CONTRACT that causes demonstrable damage.

Tort law provides a legal remedy in instances where an individual or company wrongfully suffers some form of financial, material, or physical damage that is the fault of another individual or company (the tortfeasor).

Many torts, such as assault, battery, DEFAMATION, and reckless NEGLIGENCE, are also crimes (*see* CRIME) under the criminal code. In tort law, however, unlike criminal law, cases do not need to be proven "beyond reasonable doubt" but simply "on the balance of probabilities." For this reason, it occasionally occurs that individuals found not guilty of a crime may still be found liable in tort law for the same actions.

The primary purpose of tort law is to return the injured party, in so much as is possible, to a state substantially similar to the one that they enjoyed before suffering the tort. No court can turn back the clock, however, and therefore the most common remedy that a court will award is monetary compensation, known as damages. The total compensation awarded is based on an estimation of the victim's total loss, including such things as loss of income (over an entire lifetime if necessary), pain and suffering, and the cost of fixing the damage. Additionally, in cases where the court deems the tort to be particularly objectionable, additional costs, known as punitive or exemplary damages, may be awarded against the tortfeasor as a form of additional PUNISHMENT.

TORTURE   The infliction of agonizing pain in increasing intensity.

Torture is the deliberate infliction of pain and terror on an individual. Historically, torture has been carried out as PUNISHMENT or for the purposes of interrogation. Torture may also be the expression of sheer cruelty without purpose. In fact, many argue that because torture is a very ineffective way to get any sort of accurate information from a subject, torture is always and only cruel and cannot be claimed to serve any other purpose. Torture victims are almost always forced to view or examine the instruments of torture before they are used. Torture is meant to create the illusion in the victim that the torturer has absolute POWER and must be obeyed in all demands. It is almost universally denounced as a HUMAN RIGHTS violation. Groups such as Amnesty International are dedicated to exposing and ending instances of political torture.

TRADITION   *See* CUSTOMS.

TRAGEDY   A drama or situation in which a person is faced with extreme misfortune.

In ancient Greece, a tragedy was a play in which a hero's single character flaw led to his downfall. More loosely, a tragedy can be any situation in which a person is overwhelmed by especially horrific and arbitrary circumstances. In the novel *Sophie's Choice* (1979) by William Styron, for instance, a mother is tragically forced by a concentration-camp guard to choose which of her two children she will sacrifice.

The concept of tragedy has a rich history in ETHICS. Ancient moral philosophy focused on the VALUE of tragic plays. ARISTOTLE thought that they were emotionally useful to the audience, whereas PLATO thought that they overplayed the importance of luck in the moral life. Debate in the nineteenth century revolved around the question of whether life itself was tragic. Others in the twentieth century have asked whether we are even able to understand moral tragedy.

TRANSCENDENTALISM   The belief (*see* FAITH) in things that transcend, or are beyond, sense experience.

Transcendental entities are held to be beyond space and time and not encountered in sense experience. In Platonic philosophy (*see* PLATO), for example, the Forms are transcendent types that exist independently of any particular instance of that thing. Some people argue that GOD is transcendent, although others argue that God can be perceived through sense experience and thus that God is not transcendent.

Transcendentalism is often associated with the nineteenth-century movement centered around the Transcendental Club led by Ralph Waldo Emerson and included Henry David Thoreau. This group was heavily influenced by German IDEALISM and romanticism, and MYSTICISM. They advocated self-reliance and voluntary, simple communal life.

TRANSVALUATION OF VALUES   The reevaluation and reordering of commonly held VALUES.

The transvaluation of values is a phrase derived from the philosophy of Friedrich NIETZSCHE. It refers to the part of Nietzsche's philosophy that examines the things we currently hold to have positive or negative moral worth. Nietzsche argued that we should ascribe VALUE to things in terms of their value to a healthy human life, not based on their supposed value for reaching an afterlife or other moral reward. Nietzsche subscribed to a NATURALISTIC ETHICS that held that the things that produce stronger, more vital, more creative human beings are preferable to those things that engender meekness, weakness, or resentment. These ideas are expressed in Nietzsche's writings *Beyond Good and Evil, Genealogy of Morals,* and *The Antichrist.*

TRUSTWORTHINESS   The quality of being deserving of the faith of others.

Trustworthiness is a VIRTUE that is related to HONESTY. To be trustworthy means that others can have confidence in your INTEGRITY. We consider a person to be trustworthy when that person tells the truth, keeps confidences, and is fair in his or her dealings. For example, a friend who always keeps his or her promises would be trustworthy. A person who charges you too much for an item when you do not know its worth is untrustworthy.

TRUTH   The state of affairs expressed by correct beliefs or opinions; reality, or a correct description of reality; fact.

In logic, propositions are sentences, statements, opinions, or beliefs that are, by definition, either true or false. They are true if they correctly describe a state of affairs and false if they do not. If someone says, "It is raining outside," and it *is* raining outside, then that person's statement is true. True statements are, therefore, sometimes said to *correspond* to reality, or the way things really are. The truth of scientific opinion, in turn, is supposed to be subject to testing by observation and experimentation. Such testing is referred to as empirical verification, or verification by sense experience.

Some philosophers, however, have questioned whether it is even possible to compare beliefs with reality, or ideas in our minds with things outside our minds, to see if they correspond. For this reason, they have rejected the correspondence theory of truth. Instead, they have held that we can only compare ideas with other ideas to see if our ideas *cohere* (*see* COHERENCE). According to a coherence theory of truth, beliefs are said to be true if they cohere with other beliefs and not because they correspond with external reality. Indeed, in idealist theories such as PLATO's, reality is determined by ideas: whatever is real must be rational (*see* RATIONALITY), and whatever is irrational must be false.

Even if one supposes that scientific statements describe the external world, there is a serious question about whether ethical statements do. Is the statement "X is good" true because it correctly describes X, as the statement "X is brown" is true because X really is brown? Another way to ask this question is to ask whether there is a property of goodness, as there is a color or property of brownness, such that things in nature either have or do not have this property. If so, we might further ask if the property of goodness can be discovered by observation or experiment. Many people would be inclined to say "No" on the ground that moral statements do not express facts in the same way that scientific or empirical statements do. It seems possible to give a complete description of an object, observing that it is hard, round, or green, without ever mentioning whether it is good or bad. Indeed, if we were asked to look for its goodness, we would probably not know what to look for. One might argue, as G. E. MOORE did, that good is a *nonnatural* property, but that does not seem to be very informative. One might hold instead, as the emotivists did (*see* EMOTIVISM), that there is no such property. In Moore's view, moral statements are either true or false, but according to the emotivists, moral statements are neither true nor false.

Another, more traditional, philosophic view is that truth in ETHICS is different from truth in science (*see* SCIENCE, ETHICS OF). Whereas scientific truth has been said to consist of the correspondence of ideas to nature, ethical truth has been said to consist of the correspondence of nature or of actions to ideas. The point is that ideals, goals, or perfections do not exist in nature but in our minds, and we judge nature by our ideas of what it should be. Our ideas, in turn, are said to be true not because they describe things in nature but because they are rational or coherent. This difference between ethical truth and scientific truth is supposed to be indicated by the fact that moral statements are *prescriptive,* whereas scientific statements are *descriptive.* In MORALITY we prescribe the way the world should be, according to our ideas; we do not describe the way it is (*see* IS/OUGHT DISTINCTION).

In opposition to all theories of moral truth, moral skeptics (*see* SKEPTICISM) hold that there is no such thing as moral truth or that, if there is, it cannot be known. Emotivists, we have noted, take the stronger of these positions, maintaining that moral statements are neither true nor false. In everyday conversations, skeptical attitudes are frequently expressed when, for example, people ask the question "How can anyone really know that X is true?" This question is usually used in a rhetorical way, not as a request for information but as a way of implying that no one can answer it because no one can know the answer or because there is no truth to be known. In support of moral skepticism, moral controversies or differences of opinion are often cited to demonstrate that no one really knows that answers to moral questions or that there are no answers at all.

Questions about truth also arise in morality because people are ordinarily expected to tell the truth or at least not to lie (*see* LYING). In traditional ethical theories, truth is regarded as a fundamental VALUE, and knowledge, or the discovery of truth, is often said to be one of the goals of the moral life. The idea of moral fault, in turn, has sometimes been defined as wandering away from the truth. The moral dictum "Tell the truth," however, is usually interpreted to mean "Tell the truth as you see it," for persons do not always know what the truth really is. The fundamental requirement seems to be that we should not deceive, or try to deceive, others or even ourselves, as expressed in the maxim "Do not lie." The rule "Do not lie" is different from the rule "Tell the truth," because among other things, the former rule but not the latter is easily observed by saying nothing at all (*see* MAXIMAL VS. MINIMAL ETHICS). The rule "Do not lie" may also be said to be a perfect duty (*see* OBLIGATION) because it is quite clear about what it requires, whereas the rule "Tell the truth" is imperfect because it does not specify where, when, to whom, or under what conditions truths should be told. It is always possible to obey the former rule, but it is not possible to tell each and every truth (*see* PERFECT/IMPERFECT DUTIES).

TYRANNY   *See* OPPRESSION.

TZEDAKA   In Judaism justice, righteousness.

Tzedaka is the moral standard GOD expects of his people according to the COVENANT, the agreement between God and the Hebrews according to which he will be their God if they will be his people. The prophets of the Hebrew BIBLE set forth a standard of MORALITY as SOCIAL JUSTICE unsurpassed in world literature. Isaiah (56:1) is representative of this standard: "Thus says the Lord: Keep JUSTICE, and do righteousness." The fulfillment of ceremonial duty without tzedaka is unacceptable. Virtually with one voice, the prophets insist that the Jews uphold the high standard of tzedaka or suffer persecution and exile. *See also* JEWISH ETHICS.

UPANISHADS The verses that comprise the conclusion of the Vedas, the main Hindu Scriptures.

The Vedas scriptures come from the period 1500–700 B.C., the Vedic period when the Aryan people migrated into the Indus valley, and are composed of four main parts. The *Rig-Veda,* or verses of WISDOM, is a book of prayers and hymns. The *Yajur-Veda* describes the proper forms of sacrifices (*see* SACRIFICE). The *Sama-Veda* is a book of chants. The *Athar-Veda* is a book of magic and philosophical speculation. The *Vedanta* is a school of Hindu philosophy dedicated to protecting the literal TRUTH of the Upanishads. *See also* HINDU ETHICS.

UTILITARIANISM An ethical theory that holds that an ACT is RIGHT or WRONG according to the utility or VALUE of its consequences.

Utilitarianism is a consequentialist ethical theory (*see* CONSEQUENTIALISM). According to utilitarianism, an act that produces more GOOD than HARM has greater utility than an act that produces more harm than good. Utilitarians usually speak of the comparative utility of alternative acts according to the balance of good or pleasure over harm; those actions that generate the greatest good for the greatest number are said to be the most ethical.

The utilitarian PRINCIPLE is often referred to as the greatest HAPPINESS principle, although the principle has been formulated differently by different thinkers. It was given this name in the nineteenth century when utilitarianism was founded by Jeremy BENTHAM, James Mill, and later expounded on by John Stuart MILL. The early utilitarians believed that people ought to produce as much happiness as they can. These authors were social reformers, sometimes referred to as radicals in their day, who wanted to improve the lives of the socially marginalized.

Utilitarianism grows out of HEDONISM, which measures happiness in terms of pleasure and pain. Early utilitarians held that people should try to produce as much pleasure and avoid as much pain as possible, not only for themselves but for everyone. Classical utilitarianism differs from hedonism in its ALTRUISM or BENEFICENCE and nonegoism (*see* EGOISM). It maintains that people should be concerned about the interest or welfare of others, as well as their own: "Everyone counts as one and nobody as more than one." Other versions of utilitarianism simply hold that one should maximize pleasure and minimize pain in each action, but that one does not have a strong obligation to produce as much pleasure as is possible. (*See* MAXIMAL VS. MINIMAL ETHICS).

Some utilitarians are not hedonists. For instance, at the beginning of this century, G. E. MOORE, himself a utilitarian, argued against the hedonists, maintaining that *good* cannot be defined by *pleasure.* Moore developed a form of utilitarianism called ideal utilitarianism, according to which goodness cannot be inferred from pleasure but can be discovered only through intuition (*see* INTUITIONISM). Moore was also an objective utilitarian who held that the rightness or wrongness of acts is determined by actual consequences and not simply by consequences that are intended or anticipated. He held that it is our duty to produce the best possible consequences, even though we cannot always predict what the consequences of our acts will be.

Utilitarianism has been criticized on just these grounds: that the consequences of acts cannot be predicted accurately and, hence, that the rightness or wrongness of acts cannot be known. It is also claimed that because quantities of pleasure and pain or of good and evil cannot be measured and compared, the theory cannot be applied. But utilitarians have responded that the theory is no worse off in this respect than any other scientific or empirical theory, for we must simply try to learn from the past, make predictions accordingly, and we must correct our hypothesis if they turn out to be wrong. There may not be units of pleasure and pain or of good and evil, but greater and lesser quantities of goods and can be estimated and the preferences of individuals can be ranked.

Utilitarians have also been criticized by deontologists (*see* DEONTOLOGY), who claim that obligations are determined by moral RULES and not by consequences or at least not by consequences alone. These critics actually view utilitarianism as an immoral theory, using good ends to justify evil means (*see* TELEOLOGY); that is, acts that are justified according to the utilitarian principle or according to consequences may be unjustified according to moral rules such as "Do not lie." A person who followed the utilitarian principle would not repay a debt, for example, as required by moral rules, if that person could find something better to do with the money or could produce better consequences by using it elsewhere. The utilitarian principle might even justify the execution of an innocent person if it would produce greater good than any other alternative or "the greatest happiness for the greatest number." Even John Stuart Mill struggled with this question of JUSTICE versus utility.

One attempted answer to this type of criticism has been the development of rule utilitarianism, a kind of synthesis of utilitarianism and deontology. According to rule utilitarianism, the utilitarian principle is properly used to determine the kinds of rules we should have so that we can apply these rules in judging particular acts. For example, rule utilitarians would argue that we cannot execute an innocent person even if in the short term this would seem to create more happiness in society because to establish the rule of executing innocent people in order to calm public unrest would cause more harm than good. In this way, rule utilitarianism seems to meet the criticisms of deontologists who claim that utilitarianism ignores moral rules. However, rule utilitarianism does not speak to the will or attitude with which an action must be done, and in this way it still differs from deontology.

By contrast, act utilitarians believe that every act should be judged by the utilitarian principle only, according to consequences, independently of other moral rules. J. J. C. Smart, a contemporary act utilitarian, has argued that moral rules are superfluous. If acting according to a moral rule produces the greatest utility, then the rule adds nothing to the principle; if acting according to a moral rule does not produce the greatest utility, the rule is then opposed to the principle of utility and should be abandoned.

UTOPIA   An ideal society.
Utopia is taken from the Greek words meaning "not-place" or nowhere. Utopias are imaginary societies that are meant to illustrate the author's vision of what the best society would be like. *The Republic* of PLATO, for example, represents Plato's vision of the ideally just society.

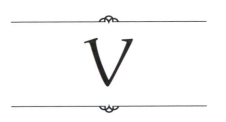

V

VALUE To recognize the worth of something.

To value something is to hold it dear and to seek to preserve or enhance it. We may value some things because of their instrumental worth. For example, people may value cars not only because they are costly but also because with the car they can go where they want at their convenience or can seek employment outside the distance that could be reasonably walked each day. The car, thus, has instrumental value as a tool that helps to improve the owner's life.

We may also value something because of its sentimental worth. A childhood toy, for instance, may no longer hold any monetary value; we may no longer play with that toy or derive enjoyment from its use. If the toy reminds us of fond childhood memories, however, or was a favorite companion during childhood, then we may feel it has sentimental value.

Some things are valuable because of their intrinsic worth. Paintings may be valuable because of their beauty; music may be valued for its harmony or expressiveness. When something is valued for its inherent goodness or DIGNITY, we say that it is morally valuable. For example, we value people simply because they are human beings. Although we may like or love some people more than others, we show all people a certain regard because we value them as persons. *See also* EXTRINSIC VALUE; FACT/VALUE DISTINCTION; INTRINSIC VALUE.

VALUE JUDGMENT A pronouncement about a state of affairs that includes a moral evaluation.

A value JUDGMENT is a statement that includes a moral assessment. Value judgments may be open or concealed. Open value judgments express a person's MORAL: "It is wrong to receive charity" is an open value judgment on those who accept charity. Value judgments may also be concealed in statements that sound like facts: "People on welfare don't want to work or else they would get jobs" may sound like a fact or argument, but it is also a value judgment, a claim that there is something morally wrong with people on welfare and that they are lazy. Concealed value judgments are misleading: they mask a moral position that should first be considered and then adopted or rejected on its own merits.

VALUES Those ideals that a person holds dear and finds morally compelling.

One's values combine to form moral direction or moral principles (*see* PRINCIPLE). People who have strong moral principles are often said to have a strong set of values, while people who have weak moral principles are said to have weak values. To have FAMILY VALUES, for instance, means that a person's moral life is guided by considerations of family and the types of actions that are best for families. The concern for family matters will outweigh other actions that might be to that person's short-term advantage. Such a person will also try to build communities that are considered to be best for families. On the other hand, people whose values center around money may gear all of their actions toward acquiring wealth. Such a person will desire that rules and principles are such that there is as little obstacle as possible to acquiring, protecting, and keeping wealth.

VALUES CLARIFICATION Exercises composed of games and strategies that are aimed at helping people to articulate their ideals or VALUES.

The idea of values clarification arises from the work of Lawrence KOHLBERG in the area of MORAL DEVELOPMENT. Values clarification is a theoretical or intellectual approach aimed at moral ideas and reasoning (*see* REASON) and the process by which individuals reach moral decisions. Values-clarification exercises are led by people who are supposed to guide the process without expressing their moral views or attempting to influence any particular outcome. Typical exercises ask those participating to imagine that they must select a small group of people to survive or represent the human race and then provide a list of these people and their characteristics from which to choose. Then participants might be asked to choose from the list of names those people who will either be given a fallout shelter in case of nuclear war or go on a space expedition to another planet.

Values clarification exercises can be helpful in developing moral-reasoning skills and in encouraging people to think for themselves rather than to follow RULES given by an AUTHORITY figure. On the other hand, some people object to the "neutral" way in which the values-clarification process takes place. They argue that it is wrong to be morally neutral in discussing issues such as which people should live and which people should die or the allocation of precious social resources. Some also object to values clarification on the basis that it teaches students that ethical decision making is relative to each person and not derived from an objective source (*see* OBJECTIVISM; SUBJECTIVISM).

VEGETARIANISM The practice of abstaining from the eating of the meat of animals.

Vegetarians are people who, for moral reasons, chode not to eat the meat of animals. They argue that people can survive healthily without eating meat and, therefore, have an OBLIGATION not to cause HARM or suffering to animals to survive. Some people, however, practice vegetarianism for other reasons, for example, because they feel healthier when they avoid meat. Some vegetarians extend their belief by refraining from the use of any animal products, such as leather goods or chemicals and products that contain animal ingredients or that have been tested on animals. A special class of vegetarians, called vegans, refrain from using any products derived from animals, including products such as milk and eggs taken from live animals. *See also* ANIMAL RIGHTS; JAIN ETHICS.

VEIL OF IGNORANCE *See* RAWLS, JOHN.

VICE A characteristic or habit (*see* HABITS) that leads to immoral behavior (*see* IMMORALITY).

A vice may be an immoral action, such as lying, or it may be the cause of an immoral action, as when the love of money motivates theft. Vice is often opposed to VIRTUE. For instance, generosity is a virtue, greed a vice. The excessive love of something, which is in and of itself not bad, can also be a vice. Thus, people sometimes name an activity such as smoking, drinking, shopping, or eating sweets as their vice. When a person is consumed by vice, we say they have a vicious nature.

VIOLENCE Resort to unlawful force to achieve one's ends.

In moral terms, violence is an ACT that exceeds lawful force. For example, a child may be forced to study without that force being considered violent. However, we call it violence if children are beaten if they do not study or bring home good grades, even if it is in their best interest to study. Violent actions are also those that cause emotional, mental, or physical HARM to someone without regard to that person's best interest. For example, a surgical technique may cause physical harm, but if it is performed with consent and to achieve a better long-term result for a patient, we do not consider this harm violent.

Some types of actions are within the LAW and are consensual but are nonetheless controversial and are sometimes called violent. For example, sports such as boxing, rugby, or football are within the limits of the law but are predicated at least in part on physically harming other participants (*see* SPORTSMANSHIP; SPORTS ETHICS). Representations of violence on television and in movies are also ethically controversial. Many people feel that even though no actual violence is occurring, viewing simulated violence as entertainment can make people indifferent to real violence in society. *See also* MORAL EDUCATION.

VIRTUE   An inherently valuable moral quality or disposition.

A virtue is a quality that is held to be morally valuable or worthy in a given moral tradition. For example, in a moral tradition that prizes survival as the ultimate moral goal, strength would be considered a virtue. In moral traditions that are based on following moral law, wisdom is considered a moral virtue. There are specific virtues that have been widely recognized as valuable to the moral LIFE, and these are often referred to as the CARDINAL VIRTUES of CHARITY, COURAGE, FAITH, JUSTICE, LOVE, TEMPERANCE, and WISDOM.

Moral theories that hold that the cultivation of virtue is the foundation of ethical life are called VIRTUE ETHICS.

VIRTUE ETHICS   Ethical theories that focus on VIRTUE, as opposed to rules or consequences, as the core of the moral LIFE.

The term *virtue ethics* refers to those moral theories that hold that MORALITY is a matter of cultivating inner traits, or virtues, that cannot be expressed in terms of moral rules, goals, or consequences. The virtuous person is able to perceive what is GOOD and just and wants to ACT on those perceptions. Virtue ethics focuses on the inner state of a person. Virtuous people have something inherently good and admirable in their characters,

so much so that their actions are RIGHT because they come from such a character and not because they are in accord with a rule. Such people are looked upon as MORAL EXEMPLARS. MORAL EDUCATION is a matter of learning to shape one's own character with such exemplars as guides.

There are different forms of virtue ethics, but most trace their origins to either PLATO or ARISTOTLE. For Plato, virtue ethics concerned the quality of a person's inner state, and he prized health, beauty, harmony, and a strength of the soul as the virtues that we should emulate. Aristotle put more emphasis on the ability to form a character that could make just decisions. Both conceptions of virtue ethics recognized the CARDINAL VIRTUES of TEMPERANCE, JUSTICE, COURAGE, and WISDOM. In the Middle Ages, Christian moral philosophers (*see* CHRISTIAN ETHICS) added the virtues of HOPE, CHARITY, and FAITH to the cardinal virtues.

Virtue ethics is distinct from other ethical theories in which virtue plays a role: in virtue ethics, the emphasis rests on the character of the agent and not on the agent's ability to follow rules or to realize an ethical goal. In virtue ethics, there is little or no emphasis on judging other people's actions and great emphasis on cultivating the virtues in oneself. There are many ethical theories that include virtue as an important ethical concept, but they hold that morality is first and foremost a matter of either following moral rules or of achieving the right types of consequences in action. While these theories may recognize the importance or even necessity of virtue for the moral life, virtue tends to play a supporting role to something more fundamental, such as moral law or *telos* (*see* TELEOLOGY). For example, in UTILITARIANISM morality is determined by achieving the greatest good for the greatest number. While people may be encouraged to be virtuous, or while the willingness to act in such a way as to produce the greatest good may be considered virtuous, it is also possible to be moral without cultivating the cardinal virtues.

VIRTUES   *See* CARDINAL VIRTUES; VIRTUE ETHICS.

VIVISECTION   The dissection (or, informally, the exposure to any kind of harm) of live animals for the purpose of furthering scientific knowledge.

The use of live animals for scientific research sometimes involves exposing them to harmful substances to test their reactions. Sometimes, such as in cosmetic testing, research animals may be deliberately injured in an attempt to anticipate how a human might react to the misuse of a product. Other times, animals are used to test how well drugs work or to develop new surgical procedures and devices. When the animal has served its research purpose, it is "humanely" killed, or euthanized.

A traditional argument in favor of vivisection is based on the belief (*see* FAITH) that animals do not have "rational souls," or are not capable of REASON. According to this reasoning, animals do not have rights (*see* ANIMAL RIGHTS), and humans have no specific moral OBLIGATION to refrain from harming them if there is a specific benefit to human beings. Vivisectionists justify experimentation on live animals because it helps humans to avoid diseases, debilitation, and dysfunction. On this account, the only possible moral limit on vivisection would be the minimization of the animal's pain.

The central argument against vivisection is that the ability to reason is an inadequate moral criterion for ethical consideration. Infants and profoundly retarded individuals may lack the ability to reason, but clearly it is immoral (*see* IMMORALITY) to consider them candidates for vivisection. Another argument against vivisection opposes the vivisectionists's claim that the scope of MORALITY extends only to members of our own species. *See also* SCIENCE, ETHICS OF.

W

WAIVING OF RIGHTS   The voluntary renunciation of a moral or legal FREEDOM.

The concept of the waiving of RIGHTS is complex, and moreso given the complexity of the notion of rights. There are at least four distinct kinds of rights: claim rights, liberty rights, POWER rights, and immunity rights. People are said to have a claim right to a certain GOOD, such as acquirement of wealth, when other people have a duty (*see* OBLIGATION) not to interfere with their obtainment of that good. People are said to have a liberty right when they are not bound either to partake or refrain from partaking in a certain good. People have power rights when they are legally or morally justified in partaking of a certain good, and immunity rights when they are free from the power rights of other people.

Waiving of rights is most commonly spoken of in connection with legal rights. For example, the *Miranda* rule guarantees that people who are arrested in the United States have the right to an attorney, among other things, if they so choose. The police are obligated by law to inform suspected criminals of these rights. Whether guilty or innocent, people under arrest have the right to be informed of their *Miranda* rights as well as the right to legal protection against self-incrimination. Police are under an obligation not to mislead suspected criminals about their legal rights, and the courts have a duty to interfere with the procurement of legal representation by the suspected criminals and to provide such representation if the suspected criminal cannot.

To waive one's rights means that one fully understands them and chooses not to exercise them. If under arrest, for example, to waive the right to a lawyer means that a person agrees to speak about the situation to the police and understands that all that is said may be introduced into court, even if the testimony is damaging. Sometimes police or other authorities may suggest that a person waive his or her rights by suggesting that if he or she has done nothing wrong, there is nothing to fear from an investigation and no need for a lawyer. The implication is that if a suspect exercises his or her rights, the action is suggestive of guilt. Although this tactic may be useful to the police, it is unprofessional or immoral (*see* IMMORALITY) if suspects feel pressured not to exercise their rights to full representation.

Miranda rule is an example of a guarantee of a type of rights that we may choose to waive. Other more-basic rights, such as the constitutional guarantee of life, liberty, and the pursuit of happiness, may not be waived in a legal sense. Although one might chose privately not to exercise these rights, one cannot legally waive the right to liberty and sell oneself into slavery, for example. Currently, moral debate centers around the question of whether individuals have a right to die, thus in effect legally waiving their right to life. Currently, this right is only legally recognized in very carefully articulated medical circumstances.

WAR   *See* JUST-WAR THEORY.

WAR CRIMES   Violations of internationally accepted standards of conduct during or leading up to war (*see* JUST-WAR THEORY).

War crimes (*see* CRIME) may involve a violation of INTERNATIONAL LAW, or they may simply be offenses against human decency. Although war necessarily leads to both pain and suffering, inhumane acts or decisions that are not justified by any overriding military necessity are generally considered morally unacceptable.

Our modern view of war crime is most strongly influenced by the trials of prominent Nazis at Nuremberg, Germany, following World War II. At the Nuremberg trials, three categories of offense were distinguished: crimes against peace (initiating a war of aggression), conventional war crimes (the mistreatment of prisoners or civilians, the use of prohibited weapons, etc.), and crimes against humanity (broad-based mistreatment of a civilian population, including enslavement and GENOCIDE). Although controversial at the time, the Nuremberg tribunal also established that defendants could not escape conviction for war crime simply because they were following orders.

Although international tribunals may theoretically be convened to try prominent war criminals, most war criminals are tried by either the victorious powers following a conflict or the courts of the country where the violator is resident. War crimes, however, are rarely prosecuted, and penalties, for the most part, are relatively light. In one prominent example, although more than 100 unarmed civilians were massacred by U.S. forces in a single incident at My Lai during the Vietnam conflict, only one junior officer was later convicted of the crime, and he served only a short time in prison as a result—this despite findings that the U.S. Army had officially sanctioned the targeting of unarmed civilians and that My Lai was not an isolated incident.

WELFARE   In the United States, the term applied to public assistance, or social programs of financial relief offered to those falling below an established income per year.

Welfare programs offer assistance to those who are without work and unable to provide for themselves and their families. Welfare programs are intended to be temporary subsidies to give people time and opportunity to regain employment. Most welfare recipients fall into the Aid to Families with Dependent Children category, indicating the growing proportion of single-parent families. Statistically, the remaining parent is usually the mother who often finds herself unable to both care for the children and earn a viable income.

Although the typical family stays on welfare for less than three years, an image of the welfare recipient as unfairly benefiting from the system has arisen, causing ethical and political disagreement concerning the JUSTICE and VALUE of the welfare system. In fact, there are generations of families for whom welfare is a way of LIFE, but this is the exception rather than the rule. Nonetheless, many citizens feel it is wrong when their tax dollars are spent to support people who in their view should be working.

Welfare programs are undergoing significant reform. Among the changes are the shift to "work-fare" programs, which are structured so that if the adult provider does not secure employment within a given period of time, then that person must accept a job designated by the state.

WHISTLE-BLOWING   Reporting conduct by an employer that is illegal or is in contradiction to the health and welfare of the community.

Within PROFESSIONAL ETHICS the term *whistle-blowing* describes the situation where an employee or employees must report the activities on the part of their employer to the appropriate regulating or governmental agency or to the press. Such activities might include, but are not limited to, fraud, threat to the environment, misuse of resources, substandard products, or any other practices that endanger public health or safety.

Employees normally attempt to resolve concerns within a company and with an immediate supervisor. If this proves impossible and an employee decides to blow the whistle to put a stop to a company's activities, the following steps apply. First, the employee should document the problem and verify all documentation. Second, the employee should inform an immediate supervisor. If the concern cannot be resolved at this level, the employee should pursue the matter up the managerial line until there are no further options within the company. It is prudent to be aware of what support is available for whistle-blowers within the company and how they have been treated in the past. If there is any retaliation or change in attitude toward the employee as a result of pursuing these concerns, these events should be documented including dates if possible. It may be advisable to contact a lawyer. If the matter is still unresolved, a whistle-blower may choose to go outside the company. In this case it is necessary to determine the appropriate agency to whom to report the problem: professional association, public-interest group, regulatory agency, or law-enforcement agency for example. When blowing the whistle, concerns must be voiced professionally. Only facts that can be verified should be reported, and they should not be exaggerated for effect. It is important for the whistle-blower to decide how important it is to remain anonymous. Throughout the procedure, all events should be documented as carefully as is possible.

WICKEDNESS   Maliciousness; the character of one who is morally corrupt.

Crucial to the concept of wickedness is the notion of consistent and characteristic wrongdoing. A GOOD person always or almost always does good; a person of lesser VIRTUE is more prone to doing WRONG; a wicked person repeatedly does EVIL.

WILL   The human faculty responsible for CHOICE, decision, and voluntary actions (*see* ACT).

The will is held to be that part of us that initiates action: to will an action is to want to do that action. The will is held to be a complex part of the human being and is important to our understanding of ethical agency and of reward and PUNISHMENT. The crucial debate is the extent to which we have free will (*see* FREEDOM) versus the extent to which our will is determined by other factors. To have free will is to be able to make original choices for which we are responsible. Most accounts of MORAL RESPONSIBILITY assume that we have free will and that, to the extent that our will is determined, we are still morally responsible for cultivating a moral character capable of free moral choice. Immanuel KANT, for example, focuses on the moral importance of willing the RIGHT thing as opposed to the consequences of the actions we perform.

If, on the other hand, our will is predetermined by the nature of our environment, then many argue we are less responsible or not responsible at all for what we will. This line of reasoning is often taken when arguing that a person should not be held responsible morally or legally for an action that is generally considered immoral (*see* IMMORALITY) or unlawful. For example, suppose that a person commits a murder. If that murder is regarded as an act committed of free will, even if there were circumstances that could explain why someone would wish to commit a murder, then we hold the murderer morally responsible for the action. However, if an argument could be made that the murderer was not responsible for the actions because of his or her environment, then we might hold the perpetrator less responsible for the action or even acquit that person of any wrongdoing.

WISDOM   Knowledge or understanding that combines reflection and prudence.

Wisdom is a VIRTUE that arises from the integration of reflection about the nature of life, and specifically ethical life, with sound practical judgments (*see* JUDGMENT). *Sophia,* or reflective wisdom, is aimed at understanding the nature of reality and goodness. *Phronesis,* or practical wisdom, is aimed at forming a reasonable vision of the good life and deciding what to do in particular circumstances.

We say people are wise when they are able to evaluate complicated situations and arrive at a solution that is both just and takes into account the particular nature and character of the people involved in the situation. We say that people are unwise when they are rash or unreflective or when they blindly follow rules without considering the nature of a given situation.

WOMEN'S LIBERATION   *See* WOMEN'S RIGHTS.

WOMEN'S MOVEMENT   The campaign to win women RIGHTS equal to those enjoyed by men.

The modern women's movement began during the eighteenth and nineteenth centuries in response to the increasingly apparent contradiction between the Enlightenment claim that "all *men* are created equal" and the obvious disadvantages faced by women in society. Among the earliest campaigners for women's rights was Mary Wollstonecraft, who published *A Vindication of the Rights of Women* in 1792, in response to the clear male BIAS in the works of French revolutionary philosophers such as Jean-Jacques ROUSSEAU. Although her work was neglected at the time, the principles she discussed were to gather force into the next century until it became impossible for society to ignore the protests of WOMEN'S RIGHTS advocates.

By the mid-nineteenth century, a number of prominent writers and campaigners had emerged to champion the rights of women. These were mostly women who had become empowered through their involvement in various political campaigns that relied heavily on women participants, including the antislavery (*see* SLAVERY) movement in the United States and the temperance movement to ban alcohol in the United States and Great Britain. At this time, the campaign for women's rights evolved into the suffrage movement, which focused primarily on winning for women the rights to vote, to own property, and to access higher education. It was also during this period that influential philosopher John Stuart MILL loaned his weight to the cause with his publication of *The Subjection of Women*. Eventually, in the period between the two world wars, women's rights campaigners in most Western countries won women the right to vote.

In the years that followed the success of the suffrage movement, the women's movement entered a brief hiatus as gains were consolidated, in part because it was felt that EQUALITY for women would follow naturally from the right to vote, but by the 1960s it became apparent that this was not the case. In fact, in a significant number of areas, including equal access to employment and wages, women's opportunities had arguably suffered. As a result, a number of women activists emerged to challenge the apparent contradiction between the legal equality that women had achieved in a number of areas and the continuing domination by men in employment and positions of AUTHORITY. In the United States, this campaign came to be popularly known as the Women's Liberation Movement, and it eventually won a number of important concessions for women, including passage of laws (*see* LAW) outlawing sex DISCRIMINATION and mandating wage equality. A campaign to amend the U.S. Constitution to guarantee equality of the sexes, however, was unsuccessful (*see* EQUAL RIGHTS AMENDMENT).

Although women today have effectively achieved legal equality with men, women continue to suffer a number of disadvantages that are not so easy to fix with legislation. As a result, the women's movement has begun to emphasize social and cultural impediments to true sexual equality. Unlike the women's movement of the past, however, this leaves few concrete goals and no obvious targets. Unlike legal discrimination, subtle discrimination is hard to identify and even harder to combat. In some instances, given the lack of any other obvious culprit, some extreme feminists have begun to criticize men in general ("the patriarchy") for the disadvantages that remain. It is most likely, however, that the subtle biases that continue to disadvantage women are perpetuated equally by both men and women. Any solution to residual sexual inequality must involve far more complex and potentially far more controversial solutions than those that have worked for women in the past. *See also* FEMINIST ETHICS.

WOMEN'S RIGHTS Those RIGHTS that are thought to apply exclusively or predominantly to women and girls.

A number of modern ethicists have seen a need to separately identify those rights that they perceive to be of particular importance to women because of a growing acknowledgment that traditional applications of rights have tended to exclude, at least in part, the needs and experiences of women. It is more difficult to say, however, whether the problems with rights result from a failure to apply the idea of rights to women's experience sufficiently or whether, in fact, the problems stem from a BIAS in the idea of rights itself. Although there is much disagreement on the nature and extent of women's rights, the idea typically encompasses such things as the right to FREEDOM from sex DISCRIMINATION, the right to equal treatment with men (*see* EQUALITY), the right to control one's own reproductive health (including access to ABORTION), and the right to freedom from sexual VIOLENCE.

Arguably, women's rights are simply a subset of HUMAN RIGHTS. A right to freedom from RAPE, for example, could be described as an application of the right of all human beings to be free from cruel and inhuman treatment, such as torture. Similarly, if women have a right to adequate reproductive health care, this right is arguably derived from the right of all human beings to good health. In these cases, it is argued, where governments and societies have

insufficiently addressed issues of importance to women, this can be corrected through more aggressive enforcement of human rights and through initiatives designed to ensure that the needs of women are not ignored.

Some commentators have argued that traditional conceptions of human rights are themselves flawed. Most specifically, they claim that LIBERALISM, from which the concept of rights emerged, has a male bias because of its emphasis on the "public" sphere, which was historically an almost exclusively male realm. This emphasis, it is argued, is most evident in liberalism's defense of "private" behavior (traditionally including treatment of women and the organization of the family) as a matter for individual CONSCIENCE. According to some, this concept has been detrimental to women because it provides an excuse for failing to address the many ways in which women are disadvantaged in the private sphere. For example, women, on average, remain responsible for a majority of "private" housework, despite the fact that the right to autonomy has liberated women to enter the "public" workforce. It could therefore be argued that any modern account of human rights is insufficient unless it is also able to take into account the many subtle and overt disadvantages faced by women in modern society. *See also* FEMINIST ETHICS; WOMEN'S MOVEMENT.

WORK Effort or labor expended in the creation of a tangible or intangible good.

To work is to invest time, talents, physical strength, ideas, or some combination of these into making some good, providing some service, or creating an environment or condition. When you prepare for a test you are working. When you take care of a yard or house you are working. When you train yourself to enter a profession you are working.

Societies have differed in the ways in which they have valued work. Work may be rewarded by money, by esteem, or by appreciation. Some work, although it is very important, goes unrewarded and unnoticed. Some societies, for example, have focused only on work that draws a wage. Many ethical thinkers feel that SOCIAL JUSTICE depends on having ample opportunity for constructive work as well as on fair compensation for that work.

WRONG   A transgression or action against a LAW, rule (*see* RULES), or PRINCIPLE.

To do something that is wrong means to deviate from a rule or principle. For example, if a class is not allowed to compare answers on their homework assignments, then it is wrong to do so. If a person holds that it is right to be honest but then tells a lie to get out of trouble, then telling the lie is wrong.

To wrong someone is to transgress a social or moral principle with respect to that person. Suppose Steven is jealous because a girl he really likes prefers John, another boy in his class. If Steven starts rumors about John to make him seem less attractive, then Steven wrongs John. His intentions are to lower John in the eyes of someone else, hoping that he, Steven, will then look better.

What is considered to be right or wrong is defined by the moral principles that are operative in a certain environment. In deontological ethics (*see* DEONTOLOGY) the same actions are held to be right and wrong for all people. For relativists (*see* RELATIVISM), right and wrong may be determined by personal or societal belief.

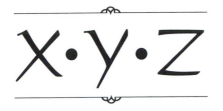

YAHWEH   In the Jewish FAITH, the proper name of the GOD of Israel.

Yahweh expresses both the name and the essence of God. The name *Yahweh* suggests not only being and becoming but moreover a personal forceful REVELATION in and through nature in response to the need of the Jewish people.

YOGA   Hindu discipline for achieving true self-understanding.

Yoga is a set of practices (*see* PRACTICE) by which the self can come to be freed of its connections with the material world and gain insight into its true nature. Through the practice of moral restraint and spiritual and physical exercise, practitioners of yoga are able to achieve a state of meditation in which complete self-understanding is possible. *See also* HINDU ETHICS.

ZEN   Literally, "meditation"; a form of Japanese Buddhism with distinctive methods of meditation leading to NIRVANA, final realization.

Zen is a comprehensive PSYCHOSPIRITUAL DISCIPLINE that includes traditional Buddhist ways of meditating and also the koan, a seemingly intellectual puzzle or problem that cannot be resolved by means of the rational mind. A koan is designed to thoroughly frustrate the thinking mind so that a larger, more inclusive and nonjudgmental consciousness will spring naturally into operation. Examples of common koans include: "What is the sound on one hand clapping?" "Who were you before your mother and father were?" and "The iron cow sits on top of a 100-foot flagpole giving birth to a calf." The resolution of koans such as these constitutes a profound release, or liberation, from the usual confusions and constraints of the mind.

The solving of koans, supported by the full regimen of Zen training, leads to satori experiences, brief glimpses into the true nature of reality. Among those who persevere, practice continues for months and years until these brief glimpses become permanent realization.

A mental state that the Zen practitioner attempts to maintain both in formal meditation and in ordinary awareness is that of attending to whatever arises in the mind or in the environment without preference, JUDGMENT, resistance, or projectivism. The objective is to be present totally with what is. This is the main perspective that informs the common linking of Zen with motorcycle maintenance, archery, tennis, and business.

MORALITY is prerequisite to Zen practice and becomes the natural way of living for the accomplished practitioner. This morality rises far above conventional expectations when lived by the most advanced Zen Buddhists. For example, Hakuin, one of the most notable figures in Japanese Buddhism, was once accused by a neighbor girl of getting her pregnant. Her parents were furious and insisted that Hakuin raise the child. Without defense or indignation, Hakuin agreed. About a year later, so the account goes, the neighbor girl told her parents that the real father was a young man in the village. Her parents were deeply embarrassed. They went to Hakuin hoping he would give the child back. He agreed, without recrimination or annoyance. *See also* BUDDHIST ETHICS.

ZIONISM   The term used to identify efforts to return Jews to their ancient homeland, Israel; the longing to establish a Jewish nation-state.

The term *Zionism* was coined toward the end of the 19th century. Leon Pinsker and Theodor Herzl called for the establishment of an independent homeland for Jews who were dispersed throughout the world. Neither insisted that Palestine be that homeland. Brazil, among other places, was considered for a time.

Twentieth-century Zionism emerged from the rampant antisemitism of nineteenth-century Europe, climaxing in Hitler's attempt to eradicate the Jews in the HOLOCAUST. Following World Wars I and II, Jewish immigration to Palestine greatly increased. The rising influx of foreigners, especially in light of their educational backgrounds and financial power, caused alarm among the Muslim and Christian Arabs of Palestine, whose ancestry in the land reaches back for centuries.

No one clearly confronted the harsh reality of the competing claims of Palestinians and Zionists to a single, limited amount of land considered holy by both. Then, in 1947, the United Nations voted to partition Palestine into Arab and Jewish states, a position roundly rejected by all Arab nations. In retaliation, an Arab army invaded Israel hoping to reclaim the land granted to Israel. Israel defeated the invaders, and to date there appears to be no permanent resolution to the antagonistic claims of Palestinians and Zionists.

Not all Jews agree on a definition of *Zionism*. Some understand Zionism to be a religious or cultural ideal and are opposed to it as a political objective. Some Orthodox rabbis, for example, see the establishment of Israel as a forbidden attempt to bring about the Messianic age. Reform Jews who believe Judaism is purely a religious FAITH also object to political Zionism.

Political Zionism raises crucial moral issues and is also controversial outside Judaism. Many non-Jews are opposed to it for moral reasons. Among these are people who hold great appreciation for Judaism as a religion and culture and have deep feeling for the Jews as a people. Their opposition to political Zionism stems from the effect it has had on Muslim and Christian Palestinians who, because of Zionism, have suffered displacement from their homes and land, restriction of personal and political freedom, and death. The irrational actions of radical Zionists and Palestinians have served only to aggravate the situation and thereby to postpone a solution.

Hope for resolution of this difficult problem rests in the sane leadership of both sides, who will be required to take actions that will be seen as hostile by the extremists of their respective communities and supporters. These actions, if they are to initiate peace and reconciliation, will need to be informed by such moral principles as JUSTICE and FAIRNESS.

SELECTED BIBLIOGRAPHY

Acton, H. B. *Kant's Moral Philosophy*. London: Macmillan, 1970.

Addams, Jane. "Child Labor Legislation: A Requisite for Industrial Efficiency." *Annals of the American Academy of Political and Social Science*. Vol. XXV. Philadelphia, 1905.

Addams, Jane. *A New Conscience and An Ancient Evil*. New York: Macmillan, 1912.

Addams, Jane. "Why Women Should Vote" (pamphlet). New York: National American Women's Suffrage Association, 1912.

Armstrong, Karen. *A History of God*. New York: Alfred A. Knopf, 1993.

Beauvoir, Simone de. *The Ethics of Ambiguity*. Translated by Bernard Frechtman. New York: Citadel Press, 1970.

Beauvoir, Simone de. *The Second Sex*. Translated by H. M. Parshley. New York: Vintage, 1974.

Bedau, Hugo Adam. *Making Mortal Choices: Three Exercises in Moral Casuistry*. New York and Oxford: Oxford University Press, 1997.

Beecher, Catherine Esther. *An Appeal to the People on Behalf of their Rights as Authorized Interpreters of the Bible*. New York: Harper & Bros., 1860.

Beecher, Catherine Esther. *The Elements of Mental and Moral Philosophy Founded Upon Experience, Reason, and the Bible*. Hartford, Conn.: 1831.

Beecher, Catherine Esther. *An Essay on Slavery and Abolitionism with Reference to the Duty of American Females*. Philadelphia: Henry Perkins, 1837.

Berlin, Isaiah. *Karl Marx: His Life and Environment*. 4th ed. New York: Oxford University Press, 1978.

Berlin, Isaiah. *Two Concepts of Liberty*. Oxford: Claredon Press, 1958.

Blofeld, John, trans. *The Zen Teaching of Huang Po*. New York: Grove Press, 1959.

Borg, Marcus J. *Jesus: A New Vision*. San Francisco: Harper, 1987.

Bowden, John. *Who's Who in Theology: From the First Century to the Present*. New York: Crossroad, 1992.

Bowring, Richard. *Murasaki Shikibu: Her Diary and Poetic Memoirs, a Translation and Study*. Princeton, N.J.: Princeton University Press, 1982.

Bulger, Ruth Ellen, Elizabeth Meyer Bobby, and Harvey V. Fineberg, ed. *Society's Choices: Social and Ethical Decision Making in Biomedicine*. Washington, D.C.: National Academy Press, 1995.

Campbell, Alastair V. *Medical Ethics*. 2d ed. New York: Oxford University Press, 1997.

Card, Claudia. *Feminist Ethics*. Lawrence: University of Kansas Press, 1991.

Carson R. *Silent Spring*. Boston: Houghton Mifflin, 1987.

Cavell, M. *The Psychoanalytic Mind: From Freud to Philosophy*. Cambridge: Harvard University Press, 1993.

Cecil, Andrew R. *Equality, Tolerance, and Loyalty, Virtues Serving the Common Purpose of Democracy*. Austin: University of Texas Press, 1990.

Cleary, Thomas. *The Essential Tao*. San Francisco: Harper, 1991.

Conway, Daniel. *Nietzsche and the Political.* London: Routledge, 1997.

Conway, Daniel. *Nietzsche's Dangerous Game: Philosophy in the Twilight of the Idols.* London and New York: Cambridge University Press, 1997.

Coppleston, Frederick. *A History of Philosophy: Volume II Augustine to Scotus.* Westminster, Mo.: The Newman Bookshop, 1950.

Coulson, John. *Logic for Lunatics: A Fabulous Primer.* London and New York: Sheed and Ward, 1960.

Coulson, N. J. *A History of Islamic Law.* Edinburgh: University Press, 1964.

D'Arcy, M. C. *The Mind and Heart of Love.* New York: Henry Holt, 1847.

Dasgupta, Surama. *Development of Moral Philosophy in India.* New York: Frederick Ungar Publishing Co., 1961.

Dodd, C. H. *The Founder of Christianity.* New York: Macmillan, 1970.

Edwards, Mark. *Printing Propaganda and Martin Luther.* Berkeley: University of California Press, 1994.

Fisher, Roger. *Getting to Yes.* New York: Penguin Books, 1991.

Fletcher, George P. *Loyalty: An Essay on the Morality of Relationships.* New York: Oxford University Press, 1993.

Fortune, Marie M. *Love Does No Harm: Sexual Ethics for the Rest of Us.* New York: Continuum, 1985.

Fromm, Eric. *The Art of Loving.* New York: Harper & Row, 1956.

Gandhi, Mahatma. *The Quintessence of Ghandi in His Own Words.* Compiled by Shakti Batra. New Delhi, India: Deepak Kupur for Madhu Muskan, 1984.

Geach, Peter. *Logic and Ethics.* Boston: Kluwer, 1991.

Gewirtz, Jacob L. *Moral Development: An Introduction.* Boston: Allyn & Bacon, 1995.

Gilligan, Carol. *In a Different Voice: Psychological Theory and Women's Development.* Cambridge: Harvard University Press, 1982.

Goergen, Donald. *The Mission and Ministry of Jesus.* Wilmington: Michael Glazier, 1986.

Gold, Gerald. *Gandhi: A Pictorial Biography.* New York: Newmarket Press, 1983.

Gough, J. W. *The Social Contract.* Oxford: Clarendon Press, 1957.

Gowans, Christopher W. *Innocence Lost: An Examination of Inescapable Moral Wrongdoing.* New York and Oxford: Oxford University Press, 1994.

Gowans, Christopher W., ed. *Moral Dilemmas.* New York and Oxford: Oxford University Press, 1987.

Gutmann, Amy. *Liberal Equality.* Cambridge: Cambridge University Press, 1980.

Habermas, J. *Justification and Application: Remarks on Discourse Ethics.* Cambridge: MIT Press, 1993.

Hans, Jonas. *The Imperative of Responsibility.* Chicago: University of Chicago Press, 1984.

Henricks, Robert G. *Lao-Tzu: Te-Tao Ching.* New York: Ballantine Books, 1989.

Herrigel, Eugen. *The Method of Zen.* New York: Vintage Books, 1974.

Hick, John. *An Interpretation of Religion.* New Haven, Conn.: Yale University Press, 1989.

Hildegard of Bingen. *Secrets of God.* S. Flanagan, ed. & trans. Boston: Shambhala, 1996.

Hoagland, Sarah. *Lesbian Ethics: Toward New Value.* Palo Alto, Calif.: Institute of Lesbian Studies, 1989.

Hoff, Benjamin. *The Tao of Pooh.* New York: Viking/Penguin, 1983.

Holmes, Robert L., ed. *Nonviolence in Theory and Practice.* Belmont, Calif.: Wadsworth, 1990.

Houlgate, Stephen. *Freedom, Truth and History: An Introduction to Hegel's Philosophy.* London and New York: Routledge, 1991.

Howell, Joseph H., and William F. Sale, ed. *Life Choices: A Hastings Center Introduction to Bioethics.* Washington, D.C.: Hastings Center Studies in Ethics, 1995.

Hunt, Arnold D., et al. *Ethics of World Religions*. rev. ed. San Diego, Calif.: Greenhaven Press, 1991.

Jaini, Padmanabh S. *The Jaina Path of Perfection*. Berkeley, Calif.: University of California Press, 1979.

Kittay, Eva, and Diana Meyers, eds. *Women and Moral Theory*. Totowa, N.J.: Rowman & Littlefield, 1987.

Kohlberg, Lawrence. "Resolving Moral Conflicts within the Just Community." In *Moral Dilemmas: Philosophical and Psychological Issues in the Development of Moral Reasoning*, edited by Carol Gibb Harding, 71–97. Chicago: Precedent Publ., 1985.

Kytle, Calvin. *Gandhi: Soldier of Nonviolence*. rev. ed. New York: Seven Locks Press, 1982.

LaFargue, Michael. *The Tao of the Tao Te Ching*. Albany, N.Y.: State University of New York Press, 1992.

Lamprecht, Sterling Power. *The Moral and Political Philosophy of John Locke*. New York: Russell, 1962.

Levine, Stephen. *A Gradual Awakening*. New York: Doubleday, 1979.

Lindberg, Carter. *Beyond Charity: Reformation Initiatives for the Poor*. Minneapolis: Augsburg Fortress, 1993.

Livingston, Donald W., and Marie Martin, eds. *Hume as Philosopher of Society, Politics, and History*. Rochester: University of Rochester Press, 1991.

Lloyd, Genevieve. *The Man of Reason: "Male" and "Female" in Western Philosophy*. Minneapolis: University of Minnesota Press, 1984.

Lopez, Donald S., Jr. *The Heart Sutra Explained*. Albany, N.Y.: State University of New York Press, 1988.

Luddy, Ailbe J. *The Case of Peter Abelard*. Westminster, Md.: The Newman Bookshop, 1947.

Lukes, Steven. *Moral Conflict and Politics*. Oxford: Clarendon Press, 1991.

MacDonald, Scott. *Being and Goodness: The Concept of the Good in Metaphysics and Philosophical Theology*. Ithaca, N.Y.: Cornell University Press, 1991.

MacKinnon, Catharine. *Only Words*. Cambridge: Harvard University Press, 1993.

Mill, John Stuart. *On Liberty*. London: Watts, 1948.

Moncrieff, C. F. trans. *The Letters of Abelard and Heloïse*. London: Guy Chapman, 1925.

Moore, Charles A. ed. *The Indian Mind: Essentials of Indian Philosophy and Culture*. Honolulu: University of Hawaii Press, 1967.

Nagel, Thomas. "The Fragmentation of Value." In *Moral Dilemmas,* edited by Christopher Gowans, 174–87. New York and Oxford: Oxford University Press, 1987.

Newman, Barbara. *Sister of Wisdom: St. Hildegaard's Theology of the Feminine*. Berkeley: University of California Press, 1989. (originally Aldershot: Scholar, 1987).

Nicholson, Reynold A. *Studies in Islamic Mysticism*. Cambridge: Cambridge University Press, 1921.

Niebuhr, Reinhold. *The Nature and Destiny of Man*. New York: Charles Scribner's Sons, 1955.

Nikhilananda, Swami. *Hinduism: Its Meaning for the Liberation of the Spirit*. New York: Harper & Brothers, 1958.

Noddings, Nel. *Caring: A Feminine Approach to Ethics and Moral Education*. Berkeley, Calif.: University of California Press, 1984.

Norton, D. *The Cambridge Companion to Hume*. Cambridge and New York: Cambridge University Press, 1993.

Nozick, Robert. *Anarchy, State, and Utopia*. New York: Basic Books, 1974.

Nygren, Anders. *Agape and Eros*. London: SPCK, 1953.

Pattison, George. *Kierkegaard: The Aesthetic and the Religious*. London: Macmillan, 1992.

Payne, Robert. *The Life and Death of Mahatma Gandhi*. New York: Dutton, 1969.

Pearson, Carol S. *Awakening the Heroes Within.* San Francisco: Harper, 1991.

Pelikan, Jaroslav and Lehman, Helmut T. eds. *Luther's Works.* Philadelphia: Muhlenberg Press, 1957.

Pippin, Robert B. *Hegel's Idealism: The Satisfactions of Self-Consciousness.* New York: Cambridge University Press, 1989.

Pippin, Robert B. *Idealism as Modernism: Hegelian Variations.* Cambridge: Cambridge University Press, 1997.

Radhakrishnan, S. *Eastern Religions and Western Thought.* 2d ed. London: Oxford University Press, 1939.

Rawls, John. *A Theory of Justice.* Cambridge: Harvard University Press, 1971.

Raz, Joseph, ed. *Practical Reasoning.* Oxford: Oxford University Press, 1978.

Rescher, N. *Ethical Idealism.* Berkeley: University of California Press, 1987.

Scarry, Elaine. *The Body in Pain: The Making and Unmaking of the World.* New York: Oxford University Press, 1985.

Searle, John R. "Prima Facie Obligations." In *Practical Reasoning,* edited by Joseph Raz, 81–90. Oxford: Oxford University Press, 1978.

Sharp, Gene. *The Politics of Nonviolent Action.* Boston: Porter Sargent, 1973.

Singer, Peter. *In Defence of Animals.* Oxford: Basil Blackwell, 1985.

Slote, Michael A. *Goods and Virtues.* Oxford: Clarendon Press; New York: Oxford University Press, 1983.

Sloyan, Gerald S. *Jesus in Focus: A Life in Its Setting.* Mystic, Conn.: Twenty-third Publications, 1983.

Solla Price, D. J. de. *Little Science, Big Science.* New York: Columbia University Press, 1963.

Spellman, W. M. *John Locke.* New York: St. Martin's Press, 1997.

Statman, Daniel, ed. *Moral Luck.* Albany, N.Y.: State University of New York Press, 1993.

Strossen, Nadine. *Defending Pornography: Free Speech, Sex, and the Fight for Women's Rights.* New York: Doubleday, 1996.

Suzuki, D. T. *What is Zen?* New York: Perennial Library, 1972.

Swinburne, Richard. *Responsibility and Atonement.* New York: Oxford, 1989.

Tawney, R. H. *Equality.* 4th ed. London: Allen & Unwin, 1971.

Taylor, Richard. *Freedom, Anarchy, and the Law: An Introduction to Political Philosophy.* Englewood Cliffs, N.J., Prentice-Hall, 1973.

Ten, C. L. *Crime, Guilt, and Punishment: A Philosophical Introduction.* Oxford: Oxford University Press, 1987.

Terkel, Susan Neiburg. *People Power.* New York: Lodestar, 1996.

Tillich, Paul. *Systematic Theology.* Vol. I, Chicago: University of Chicago Press, 1951.

Tillich, Paul. *Systematic Theology.* Vol. II, Chicago: University of Chicago Press, 1957.

Tobias, Michael. *Life Force: The World of Jainism.* Berkeley, Calif.: Asian Humanities Press, 1991.

Unterman, A. *Jews: Their Religious Beliefs and Practices.* Boston: Routledge & Kegan Paul, 1981.

Vaughan, Frances. *The Inward Arc: Healing and Wholeness in Psychotherapy and Spirituality.* Boston: Shambhala, 1986.

Waithe, Mary Ellen, ed. *A History of Women Philosophers.* Boston: Kluwer Academic Publishers, 1991.

Walzer, Michael. *Spheres of Justice: A Defense of Pluralism and Equality.* New York: Basic Books, 1983.

Watt, William. *Companion to the Qur'an.* Rockport: OneWorld Publications, 1995.

Watts, Alan W. *The Spirit of Zen.* New York: Grove Press, 1958.

Wei, Henry. *The Guiding Light of Lao Tzu.* Wheaton, Ill.: Theosophical Publishing House, 1982.

Weiss, Raymond L., and Charles E. Butterworth. *Ethical Writings of Maimonides.* New York: New York University Press, 1975.

Wilber, Ken. *No Boundary: Eastern and Western Approaches to Personal Growth.* Boston: Shambhala, 1981.

Williams, Bernard. "Consequentialism and Integrity." In *Consequentialism and Its Critics,* edited by Samuel Scheffler, 20–50. Oxford: Oxford University Press, 1988.

Williams, Bernard. "Ethical Consistency." In *Practical Reasoning,* edited by Joseph Raz, 91–109. Oxford University Press, 1978.

Williams, Bernard. *Moral Luck.* New York: Cambridge University Press, 1981.

Wollstonecraft, Mary. *A Vindication of the Rights of Woman.* London: Dent, 1965.

Wu, John C. H. *Tao Te Ching.* Boston: Shambhala, 1990.

Zolondek, L., trans. *Book XX of al-Ghazālī's Ihya' Ulum al-Din.* Leiden: E. J. Brill, 1963.

INDEX

Page numbers in **boldface** indicate main entries.